AFRICAN ECONOMIC HISTORY

Ralph Austen

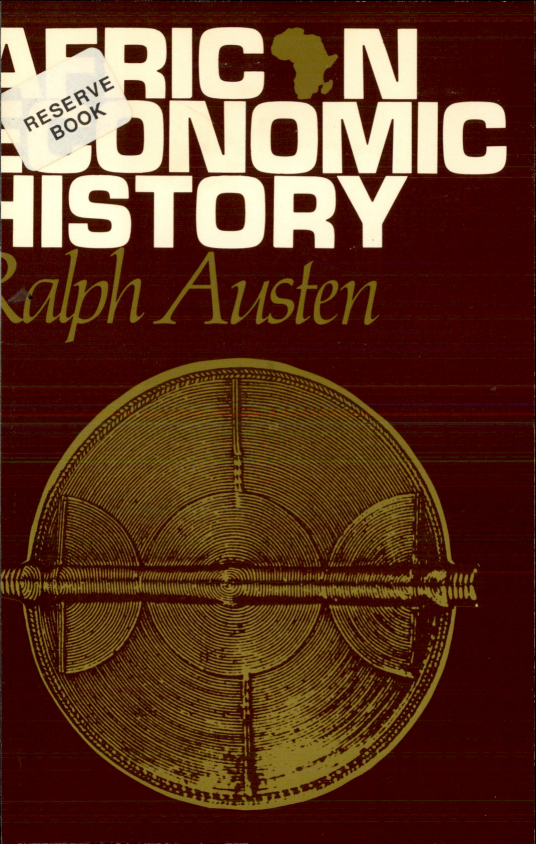

African Economic History

African Economic History

Internal Development and External Dependency

Ralph A. Austen

Professor of African History
University of Chicago

James Currey
LONDON

Heinemann
PORTSMOUTH NH

James Currey Ltd
54b Thornhill Square, Islington
London N1 1BE

Heinemann Educational Books Inc.
70 Court Street, Portsmouth
New Hampshire 03801

British Library Cataloguing in Publication Data

Austen, Ralph A.
  African economic history: internal development & external dependency
  1. Africa——Economic conditions
  I. Title
  330.96   HC800

  ISBN 0-85255-008-1
  ISBN 0-85255-009-X Pbk

Library of Congress Cataloguing in Publication Data

Austen, Ralph A.
  African economic history.
  Includes bibliographies and index.
  1. Africa, Sub-Saharan——Economic conditions.   2. Africa, Sub-Saharan——
Commerce——History.   3. Africa, Sub-Saharan——Foreign economic relations.
  4. Africa, Sub-Saharan——Dependency on foreign countries——History.
  I. Title.
  HC800.A97   1987   330.967   86-25639

  ISBN 0-435-08017-2

Typeset in 10/11 pt Palatino by Colset Private Limited, Singapore
Printed in the United States of America

rsh 716803

88/11/10 13

Contents

List of Figures, Maps and Tables

Acknowledgements

This book has taken far longer to complete than can be justified by the final results. Moreover, in those many years of reading, writing, discussion and rewriting I have accumulated more debts to colleagues, family, librarians, and publishers than I can possibly bring myself to remember, let alone recognize publicly (other than in my, perhaps too many, notes and bibliographical entries). With due regard for those who should be mentioned here but are not, let me just note a few of these obligations. First of all, to Wes Johnson of UC Santa Barbara for initially getting me into this project well over a decade ago. To my colleagues in the University of Chicago Workshop in Economic History (especially the late and much-missed Arcadius Kahan) who will themselves probably not want to accept responsibility for the form which their teachings of the dismal science have taken here. To my colleagues and students in the core course of the MA Program in Social Sciences, who will recognize their ideas and my lectures in much of what follows. To the other students in my courses in African economic history, who suffered through preliminary versions of this book and especially Chuck Schaefer, who introduced my original typescript to the civilizing influence of the university computer system. To the attendants and advisors at the various clusters of that computer system, who put up with my repeated ineptness in taking over from Chuck, and especially to Sam Wilson for helping me with graphs and maps. To the efficient and helpful staffs of two truly great libraries, the Africana collection at Northwestern University and the Regenstein at Chicago. And finally to those at the other home which I so often abandoned for Regenstein: Ernie, Jake, and Ben; they may not have realized it at the time but without their particular and loving combination of patience and impatience I would probably still be in my cramped little study trying to put the finishing touches on this manuscript.

Ralph A. Austen
University of Chicago

Introduction

This book is about two overlapping topics: the growth of production and exchange systems within Africa and their relationship to more developed economies outside the continent. The announcement of such an agenda is less likely to inform readers of what to expect than to prompt further questions. Most will wonder what substantive material will be covered, since Africa remains an obscure and confusing region for otherwise educated audiences outside the continent and even within it. Those initiated into the still-young but very contentious literature on African economic history will want to know the present author's position among the competing theoretical/methodological perspectives.

The short answer to all these queries is that the work attempts to be as broadly comprehensive and eclectically synthetic as possible. Nevertheless, there has been some selection of focus and commitment to interpretation which requires a more lengthy preliminary explanation.

The scope and organization is not, I hope, very controversial. The book covers the entire portion of the African continent south of (and partially including) the Sahara Desert, although some regions not easily incorporated into general patterns (particularly the Nilotic Sudan and the adjoining Horn of Africa) receive little attention. Chronologically, the account ranges from the beginnings of food-source domestication to the post-colonial regimes of the contemporary era. In the initial and most autonomous phase of economic development, Africa will be dealt with on a continent-wide basis; the subsequent era of pre-colonial contact with external economies will be examined though comparative studies of major regions; the chapters on the impetus, effect, and aftermath of European colonialism use a continental-topical approach. Although this form of presentation was derived from the perceived logic of the issues addressed here, it is similar to that used in other recent general works on Africa.[1]

So much for 'Africa' and 'history' at least in their narrowest sense. It is not so easy to define the other key items in the title of this book: 'economic', 'development' and 'dependency'. Let me begin with a simple statement of what I mean by the more obviously controversial of these terms. 'Development' is here understood as a sustained strengthening of productive capacities and market integration in opposition to both 'underdevelopment' – the decline of these elements in the economy – or 'growth without development' – a simple expansion of the exploitation of existing resources through existing means. 'Dependency' is defined as a relationship between two economic partners in which the more advanced technology and organization on one side pre-empts – whether purposefully or not – the development opportunities of the other.

My aim in pursuing these concepts is to avoid as much as possible the ideologically charged debates with which they – and the more elusive notion of the economy itself – are surrounded. However, it would be naive or disingenuous

1

to claim an 'objective' position above the battle. The analytic perspective used here must, therefore, be delineated in relation to the more overtly partisan schools of interpretation already arrayed upon the field. These may be divided into two major camps: one committed to a market (or liberal, classical/neo-classical, rational choice) perspective,[2] the other committed to structural (subdivided into substantivist,[3] Marxist,[4] and dependency theory)[5] perspectives.

In analysing Africa the proponents of each of these approaches assume sharply divergent models of economic actors and their motives. For the market theorists, the actor is an individual or 'firm' negotiating with various factors in the material and social environment to maximize returns on effort or minimize risks to security. Structural analysis focuses upon collective entities: either (for substantivists) a harmonizing social order determining the rules of economic behaviour or (for Marxists and *dependistas*) a hierarchical system in which dominant and subordinate classes and/or world regions struggle over economic control. For understanding the internal development and external relations of the African economy, there are three more specific issues of historical analysis on which the position and achievements of these perspectives have to be considered: the explanation of change; the distinction between distributive and productive sectors of the economy; and the linkage of empirical data to theoretical concepts.

At the most abstract level, market theory is ahistorical and unconcerned with change while structuralists are all devoted to examining stages of development leading from the past to the present. In the practice of African economic history, however, scholars committed to the market model have produced most of the work analysing specific changes. This paradox does not validate one of these perspectives over the other, but rather demonstrates the difficulty of using any exclusively.

The strength of the market approach in explaining change lies precisely in its assumption that any enduring economic situation represents an equilibrium between the various elements of which it is made up. Such a system does not itself generate change since it is rational in its own terms. But, because any given historical situation is seen not as a structure with an inherent logic of its own but rather as the fortuitous intersection of its various components, there is no assumption of any systematic resistance to change. Historians working within this perspective can thus look for moments of change in the economy and explain them very simply as responses to alterations in important elements of the previous equilibrium as, for example, demographic/environmental shifts, access to new markets, or the introduction of new transportation and production technologies.

The limitations of the market approach become evident when economic changes are predicted from some positive alteration in the opportunity horizon, but do not take place. In a number of very critical cases market analysis can explain the apparent conservatism of Africans in the face of potential increases in material gain by calculating the accompanying costs of the necessary changes and treating the observed economic behaviour as a rational strategy of risk aversion.[6] But the form taken by these insurances against risk (and, it often turns out, some of the forms of risk-taking) are not adequately explained by the market model nor, in cases where the risk itself is social rather than material, is the source of danger.

The structural approaches to economic history assume that the social forms taken by economic organization and economic conflict provide the essential basis of understanding change. Each version of this approach which is relevant to African history has defined a set of structures through which change is manifested:

the substantivists stress institutions of exchange; the Marxists modes of production; and dependency theorists the world system. However, all these models of large-scale development encounter difficulties when utilized to explain specific instances of African transformation. The substantivists treat change as exogenous to Africa and quite openly focus on explaining the ability of Africans to resist the encroachments of the market, despite plentiful evidence of spontaneous African 'market' behaviour.[7] Marxists argue, from the model of European capitalism, that all modes of production are altered by the growing contradictions between their constituent dominant and subordinate classes; but it has been difficult to identify this kind of conflict as the basis for change in African economies.[8] Finally, dependency theory seizes directly upon metropolitan European capitalist growth as the force behind the 'underdevelopment' of African economic structures, an argument which fails to account for the variety of internal development patterns discovered by historians of all persuasions working closely with African data.[9]

Structuralist perspectives thus appear more valuable for explaining the conditions and particularly the limitations of change in the African economy rather than its causes. It is essential to any historical analysis to recognize that historical developments do take place within some kind of institutional-social setting, a dimension of the past which tends to be downplayed by the market model of universal economic rationality.[10] Such structures are not the absolute barriers to internal development which substantivists and *dependistas* often postulate, nor are they the dialectically driven engines of change proposed by Marxists. Nevertheless, without taking structural perspectives into account, we cannot understand the context within which Africans have responded to opportunities for economic development, nor the consequences of such events for further changes.

A second issue, one which has divided Marxist students of African economic history from both market theorists and substantivist or dependency-theory structuralists, is the question of defining the economy in terms of distribution or production. Market models of analysis are, as the name suggests, focused upon distribution: the real or fictive instrument of change is a market which sends price signals as to the costs and benefits of various efforts according to which the actor allocates available resources (including the 'factors of production' such as land, labour, and capital). Substantivist theory argues that different forms of social organization are characterized by different forms of exchange: the autonomous, price-setting market is unique to modern capitalism; societies organized around households allocate goods according to social rules of distribution; and intermediate 'archaic' societies allow political authorities to appropriate and redistribute the main portion of circulating wealth. Dependency theory argues that the main instrument by which the capitalist 'core' of the world system controls the dependent 'periphery' is the market, although the goal of such domination is to prevent the periphery from developing production systems competitive with those of the core.

A major contribution of Marxist scholars to African economic history has been their insistence that various economic systems be defined in terms of relationships in the productive sector. This perspective has encouraged a far more thorough investigation of the economic meaning of social institutions than was possible by merely considering exchange relations. Marxism also brings into focus the role of technology, a vital issue for understanding all aspects of the African economy, but one given little attention by other theoretically oriented economic anthropologists or historians.[11] Moreover if we consider social structures as a critical conditioning factor, rather than a motor, of economic change, a better case can be made for the coherence of institutions and behavioural patterns tied directly to maintaining material survival rather than to the distribution of discretionary goods.

Once having said all this, it is important not to fall into the common Marxist vice of 'production fetishism'. In many instances of economic development physical survival is not at stake and the issues economic historians need to look at may involve the acquisition of material goods for purposes of controlling discretely social, political or cultural relationships. Further, technology is as important in the distributive dimensions of the economy – via transportation and communication – as it is for production. Marxists have attempted to resolve these issues by distinguishing between total 'social formations' and their determinate 'base' in modes of production. Unfortunately, for African cases the attempt to define indigenous modes of production has led only into an endless and dimly lit corridor of debates among Marxists themselves.[12] Many of the categories established, such as 'tributary' and 'slave' modes, seem in any case to deal more with distribution than production.

Finally, for Africanist Marxists, as for Marx himself, the privileged analytical position granted to production is often based less on analytic grounds than on moral or even racist ones.[13] 'Merchant capital' and its variants are viewed as inherently parasitic upon 'the sons of the soil' and not contributive to long-run economic development. While the economic history of Africa will be shown to display numerous cases where integration into wide markets has failed to promote, or has even arrested in some respects, transformations of production, no assumption is made that these problems arise either from 'imperfections' in an idealized market or the domination of market over production interests. Instead, a central theme of this book will be the problem of linkages[14] between various systems of production in which the market is a necessary but sometimes problematic element.

All history makes some claim to empiricism, to the use of primary evidence for the recreation of the past *'wie es eigentlich gewesen'* ('as it had really been').[15] All economic study contains major elements of abstraction; we are interested here not in unique events and heroic individuals but patterns of continuity and change which account for the experience and behaviour of large groups of ordinary people. The problem of reconciling empirical accuracy with theoretical coherence affects all schools of economic historiography which have focused upon Africa, although in very diverse forms.

Market theory reduces all historical action to an admittedly artificial model of rational choice among negotiable alternatives. In its most extreme form (seldom practised by Africanists) this perspective can turn into a mathematical exercise which has no relationship to the empirically perceived world.[16] Even when used more moderately, the market approach often loses sight of the critical distinction between an individual and a firm in the Western context and the figures who are assigned these roles in various African historical and cultural contexts. The trade-off (as market theorists would put it) for this particular form of abstraction is a high degree of analytic rigour which often provides the best, or at least an indispensable, explanation for historical developments.

Structuralists impose their own concepts of exchange categories, class relations, or centre–periphery system upon the mundane or obscure data of the African past. Here again it is easy to move to a level of abstraction that parts company with empiricism generally and the study of history in particular, as some 'structuralist Marxists' have consciously attempted to do.[17] Even more-restrained versions of structural approaches, specifically derived from the study of non-Western societies, tend to reify their concepts in forms which have little value for the analysis of empirical data. But the patterns perceived by structuralists do address differences between historical situations, and in some manner must be employed to make sense of the wide range of economic institutions which the historian encounters – and which often encountered one another – in the African past.

In order to utilize the insights of theoretical work on African economic history but avoid its pitfalls, the chapters which follow will refer to various perspectives when introducing issues to which they are relevant but eschew as much as possible the special language of the perspectives when actually pursuing these issues. Some terms and concepts, such as the market, dependency, and class, will be employed, but in general, the practice here will be to follow, in more catholic fashion, the motto of an anonymous colleague, 'Whenever I see the words "mode of production" I release the safety catch on my eraser.' The purpose at hand is to understand specific problems in African economic history rather than to test or develop propositions of universal significance.[18]

A book which thus steers its way between the major interpretive trends of its subject matter runs the risk of having no shape of its own. The shape which this work is attempting to project may perhaps best be defined by turning from a critique of theory to a very abstract statement of the central substantive argument. African economic history is considered here as a doubly paradoxical process: development linked to risk; and dependency linked to marginality. Thus the chapters which follow will demonstrate a continuous expansion of African productive capacities and market integration from the earliest emergence of domesticated food production through modern mechanization and electronic communication. However, each stage of this development is closely and consciously involved with very major risks: first to subsistence, a key motivation inhibiting the earliest production changes and a constant threat arising from more recent ones; and secondly to autonomy, threatened by close economic relations with more technologically advanced external societies. Dependency upon these trans-Saharan and overseas partners represents the realization of one of these risks as Africa has become steadily more integrated into the world economy. However, as that economy itself has grown since the Middle Ages, the role of Africa within it has successively diminished: from a vital source of precious metals for Europe and Asia, to a supplier of servile labour for the New World, to the exporter of a more varied array of primary goods for a world market that has many alternative sources of tropical commodities.

There is an ultimate paradox in using such internally contradictory themes to hold together a theoretically eclectic book on an already diffuse topic. The proof of this methodological pudding will have to come in the reading of the substantive chapters, although the issues raised here will be reiterated, with a somewhat more contemporary application, in the final sections of the work. Even then, the adherents of more positive theory as well as readers looking for direct guidance in the solving of Africa's immediate and very pressing economic problems will no doubt be frustrated. I hope that they will nevertheless find some insights worthy of their consideration. For others with a less specifically committed approach to African economic history, this book may at least illuminate some of the most critical issues of the subject and help to integrate it into their own conceptions of African studies and comparative economic history.

Notes

1. E.g., Curtin, Feierman, Thompson and Vansina (1978).
2. Among the major representatives are Curtin (1975); Hopkins (1973); Schneider (1974).
3. The principal spokesmen for this perspective are Polanyi, Arensberg and Pearson (1957); Polanyi (1966); Dalton (1968, 1969); Bohannan and Bohannan (1968).
4. Statements of Marxist historiography on Africa include Bernstein and Depelchin (1978–9); Crummey and Stewart (1981); and Freund (1984). For an introduction to the more developed (mainly French) Marxist anthropological literature see Seddon (1978).
5. The most prominent works of Africanist dependency theory are Amin (1974); Rodney (1972); and Wallerstein (1976) but these derive from the Latin Americanist studies of Frank (1967) and Dos Santos (1970).
6. McCloskey (1976).
7. Polanyi (1964, 1966). For a critique see Johnson (1966).
8. Law (1978); see also Chapter 1, below.
9. For a synthesis of both leftist and liberal critiques of dependency theory, see Cooper (1981) pp. 8–12.
10. An attempt to integrate neo-classical and institutional analysis has been made by the prominent economic historian, Douglas C. North (1981); but see also Field (1981).
11. Austen and Headrick (1983).
12. Foster-Carter (1978); Law (1978). The editors' introduction in Crummey and Stewart (1981) does little to overcome these difficulties. For an attempt to retain the concept of modes of production in modified form, see Freund (1984) pp. 35–8.
13. Marx himself set the tone for this form of analysis in his *Class Struggles in France*; the fullest development of the argument for Africa is Kay (1975).
14. I am using this concept in the form presented by Hirschmann (1958), especially pp. 100–17. It can also be argued that the Marxist notion of 'luxury production', see Sraffa (1960), as with many other positions of dependency theorists in the 1960s and after, can be found in the best of the liberal developmentalist literature of a decade or more earlier. (For a discussion, see Hopkins (1976).)
15. The phrase is from Ranke (1824).
16. For a rare Africanist example, see Ryan (1975).
17. Hindess and Hirst, (1975) p. 351, for example, 'reject the notion of history as a coherent and worthwhile object of study.' For a critique of structuralist Marxism by a Marxist historian who has strongly influenced the approach used here, see Thompson (1978).
18. For a fuller historiographic development of this position, see Austen (1981).

Bibliography

Amin, Samir (1974), *Accumulation on a World Scale* (2 vols, New York: Monthly Review Press)

Austen, Ralph A. (1981), 'Capitalism, class, and African colonial agriculture: the mating of Marxism and empiricism (review article)', *Journal of Economic History*, vol. 41, pp. 657–63

Austen, Ralph A. and Daniel Headrick (1983), 'The role of technology in the African past', *African Studies Review*, vol. 26, nos. 3/4, pp. 163–84

Bernstein, Henry and Jacques M. Depelchin (1978–9), 'The object of African history: a materialist perspective', *History in Africa*, vol. 5, pp. 1–19; vol. 6, pp. 17–43

Bohannan, Paul and Laura Bohannan (1968), *Tiv Economy* (Evanston: Northwestern University Press)

Cooper, Frederick (1981), 'Africa and the world economy', *African Studies Review,* vol. 24, nos. 2/3, pp. 1–86

Crummey, Donald and Charles C. Stewart (eds) (1981), *Modes of Production in Africa* (Beverly Hills: Sage)

Curtin, Philip D. (1975), *Economic Change in Precolonial Africa: Senegambia in the Era of the Slave Trade* (Madison: University of Wisconsin Press)

Curtin, Philip, Steven Feierman, Leonard Thompson, and Jan Vansina (1978), *African History* (Boston/London: Little, Brown/Longman)

Dalton, George (ed.) (1968), *Primitive, Archaic, and Modern Economies: The Essays of Karl Polanyi* (Garden City, NY: Anchor)

Dalton, George (1969), 'Theoretical issues in economic anthropology', *Current Anthropology,* vol. 10, no. 1, pp. 63–102

Dos Santos, Theotonio (1970), 'The structure of dependence', *American Economic Review,* vol. 60, no. 2, pp. 231–6

Field, Alexander (1981), 'The problem with neo-classical institutional economics: a critique with special reference to the North-Thomas model of pre-1500 Europe', *Explorations in Economic History,* vol. 18, pp. 174–98

Foster-Carter, Aidan (1978), 'The modes of production controversy', *New Left Review,* 107, pp. 47–78

Frank, André Gunder (1967), *Capitalism and Underdevelopment in Latin America* (New York: Monthly Review Press)

Freund, Bill (1984), *The Making of Contemporary Africa. The Development of African Society since 1800* (Bloomington/London: Indiana University Press/Macmillan)

Hindess, Barry and Paul Q. Hirst (1975), *Precapitalist Modes of Production* (London: Routledge, Kegan Paul)

Hirschmann, Albert O. (1958), *The Strategy of Economic Development* (New Haven: Yale University Press)

Hopkins, A.G. (1973), *An Economic History of West Africa* (London/New York: Longman/Columbia University Press)

Hopkins, A.G. (1976), 'Clio-antics: a horoscope for African economic history', in Christopher Fyfe (ed.), *African Studies since 1945: A Tribute to Basil Davidson* (London: Longman), pp. 31–48

Johnson, Marion (1966), 'The ounce in eighteenth-century West African trade', *Journal of African History,* vol. 7, no. 2, pp. 197–214

Kay, Geoffrey (1975), *Development and Underdevelopment* (London: Macmillan)

Law, Robin (1978), 'In search of a Marxist perspective on pre-colonial tropical Africa', *Journal of African History,* vol. 19, no. 3, pp. 441–52

McCloskey, Donald N. (1976), 'English open fields as behavior towards risk', *Research in Economic History,* vol. 1, pp. 124–70

Marx, Karl (1964), *The Class Struggles in France* (New York: International Publishers)

North, Douglas C. (1981), *Structure and Change in Economic History* (New York: Norton)

Polanyi, Karl (1964), 'Sortings and "ounce trade" in the West African slave trade', *Journal of African History,* vol. 5, no. 3, pp. 381–93

Polanyi, Karl (1966), *Dahomey and the Slave Trade: An Analysis of an Archaic Economy* (Seattle: University of Washington Press)

Polanyi, Karl, Conrad M. Arensberg and Harry W. Pearson (1957), *Trade and Market in the Early Empires* (Glencoe, NY: Free Press)

Ranke, Leopold von (1824), *Geschichten der Romanischen und Germanischen Völker von 1494 bis 1514*

Rodney, Walter (1972), *How Europe Underdeveloped Africa* (London/Washington, DC: Bogle L'Ouverture/Howard University Press)

Ryan, T.C.I. (1975), 'The economics of human sacrifice', *African Economic History Review,* vol. 2, no. 2, pp. 1–9

Schneider, Harold K. (1974), *Economic Man: The Economics of Anthropology* (New York: Free Press)

Seddon, David (ed.) (1978), *Relations of Production: Marxist Approaches to Economic Anthropology* (London: Cass)

Sraffa, Piero (1960), *Production of Commodities by Means of Commodities* (Cambridge: Cambridge University Press)

Thompson, Edward P. (1978), *The Poverty of Theory and Other Essays* (New York: Monthly Review Press)

Wallerstein, Immanuel (1976), 'The three stages of African involvement in the world-economy', in Peter C.W. Gutkind and Immanuel Wallerstein (eds), *The Political Economy of Contemporary Africa* (Beverly Hills: Sage), pp. 30–57

1

The Dynamics of Subsistence
African Domestic Economies in Historical Perspective

Every study of historical development must have a base point, a past situation treated as 'given' from which changes begin. The point chosen for this purpose here is the shift from foraging to domesticated food production, which was closely linked to the beginnings of African metallurgy and the emergence of major exchange systems within the continent. It is this form of development which will be referred to as the African domestic economy, in contrast to the contact economies arising around the commercial frontiers connecting pre-colonial Africa with the outside world, and the colonial and post-colonial economies resulting from European occupation of African territory.

Most historical studies of the African economy begin at a point closer to the present, usually dating from the beginnings of international trade. While such an approach is frequently berated as ethnocentric, if not colonialist and racist, it pervades the work of even liberal and radical revisionist historians. The problem is less one of ideology than of technology: the inadequacy of the research tools of archival and field-work social science for comprehending economic transformation in a remote and non-literate African past.

The result of such obstacles has been the survival of an economic equivalent to the 'ethnographic present', that fictional situation of stasis by which anthropologists used to seal off their contemplations of pre-colonial African societies from the disorderly notion of indigenous history. Economic scholars speak of an African 'domestic economy' (or 'lineage mode of production' or 'domain') which is essentially devoted to subsistence rather than market exchange, and reproduction of its existing forms rather than investment in more efficient production. Africa thus remains an anti-image of the dynamic West which retains the monopoly on history earlier assigned to it by Hegel.[1]

As indicated in the Introduction, the data presented here will not suggest a total reversal of this comparison. It is essential in understanding African economic development to recognize the limitations of indigenous change as compared to the West, particularly in the area of technology. But the African domestic economy still has its own history of origin, diffusion, organization, and market integration. However, to examine this process it is necessary to make something of a leap of faith into a realm of research uncontrolled by most of those concerned with economic development: the academic compartment officially designated as 'prehistory' and ruled by archaeologists, along with biologists and physical anthropologists. It is these scholars who have looked intensively at the problems of change in the early African economic past. There are serious problems in subjecting the data of prehistoric research to historical economic analysis; many of the 'models' by which the more adventurous specialists have attempted to move in this direction are themselves derived from the very contemporary analogues whose origins they are in turn expected to explain. Nonetheless, it is only by using whatever means are available to contemplate the historical dimensions of these remote developments that we can understand the dynamics of the Africans' adaptation to their own environment and ultimately the meaning of their responses to external contact and penetration.

From foraging to domesticated food sources: the beginnings

The base point of the present work will be the hunting-and-gathering economies which dominated sub-Saharan Africa up to approximately the second millennium BC. It is, of course, also possible to treat foraging systems historically and particularly to trace the economic rationality behind their adoption and development of gradually more efficient tool and weapon kits. However such an effort would require still more elaborate excursions into the unfamiliar problems of skeletal, artefact, and site analysis, radio-carbon and other forms of dating, and even questions of human biological evolution. The pursuit of these issues in Africa is of immense concern for world prehistory, but for later African development the evolution of foraging systems is not significant enough to warrant the effort it would take to present it properly here. The question we must focus on, therefore, is how the historical economies based on plant cultivation and animal husbandry emerged from the later stages of foraging.[2]

From the perspective of both Westerners and the vast majority of African peoples, the underlying logic of the transition from foraging to domestication seems so self-evident as not to require any explanation. Foraging represents savagery, man still in a state of nature; domestication represents civilization, the movement from nature to culture. History appears to provide support for such a view by its evidence that stabilized food production has been a necessity for the establishment of complex societies which subsequently absorbed, exterminated or relegated to marginal landscapes those groups which had not made such advances by themselves.

In a very broad sense this evolutionary pattern is as true for Africa as anywhere else in the world. At the level of specific historical change, however, it is misleading both as a characterization of the actual circumstances under which such transformations first took place and as an indicator of their meanings for later processes of development.

The shift from foraging to domestication in sub-Saharan Africa probably owes something to the stimulus of nearby Mediterranean societies which entered this stage earlier, but their influence appears to have been severely limited. First, the specific technology of wheat and barley in these temperate regions is not transferable to the African tropics where different rainfall and soil conditions prevail. Secondly, plant domestication took hold in Africa during a period – from the second millennium BC to the end of the early first millennium AD – when the desiccation of the Sahara had severely inhibited contact with the Mediterranean, rendering impossible any diffusion of larger cultural systems which might make domestication a social attraction or necessity. The beginnings of domestication in sub-Saharan Africa are thus connected less with the movement towards a higher form of human organization than with the degeneration of what appears to have been a very satisfactory set of foraging systems. The questions which have to be asked thus concern not how methods of controlling food supplies were 'discovered' but rather why they needed to be taken up at all.

The notion that major changes in the African economy can be traced to a situation of equilibrium for which we have very little documentary evidence ought to be treated with suspicion as the possible creation of market-economic fantasy rather than historical research. However Marxists of various sorts have been particularly convinced that African foraging economies were internally stable, even referring to them as 'the original affluent society' or as models of egalitarianism. Such claims are at best exaggerated and in part wrong; there is clearly a higher status for male hunters than for the more productive female gatherers in known African foraging groups. But the important point is that resulting tensions which may have existed cannot in themselves explain the transition to another form of food production, particularly agriculture, in which, as Marxists have more insightfully noted, women are quite obviously exploited.[3]

What is it exactly that we do know about late foraging economies in Africa? The archaeological record provides us with basic information about the distribution in time and space of populations engaged in terrestrial hunting and gathering or fishing. For analysis of the former, and far more common type, analytic models have been projected into the past from the few surviving African peoples who depend upon wild food sources, especially the San/Bushmen of the Kalahari Desert.[4] Despite similarities in technology and the scale of social units, it is not clear to what extent these 'refuge' communities accurately represent the situation that existed when hunting and gathering still dominated the continent. However, since modern foragers are reduced to inhabiting relatively unfavourable regions, it can be assumed that they are not better off than their more free-roaming predecessors. It is thus significant that their diets compare favourably, in both caloric intake and protein content, with those of other Africans. None of these peoples come close to exhausting the resources in their constricted environments and the amount of labour required to maintain subsistence allows extensive opportunities for leisure.

Archaeology alone tells us of another, somewhat more dynamic foraging economy which developed over wide areas of Africa between the Equator and the Mediterranean from the ninth to the third millennia BC around then abundant inland lakes and rivers. This 'aquatic civilization' was able to support larger, more stably settled populations than hunting and gathering.[5] It thus appears as a logical step between foraging and domestication. However there is nothing in the internal logic of such an economy which demands transformation. All that can be said of fishing systems is that they are more susceptible than other foraging systems to exogenous pressures for change. These pressures can come from a variety of sources but in the African case two factors were important: external contacts and environmental desiccation.

External contact explains the transition to domesticated food production only in one major African case, that of the lower Nile Valley, whose closeness in physical distance and ecological conditions to the Middle East renders it unrepresentative of the rest of the continent. In Egypt the experience of settled fishing peoples with local plants and animals provided a 'pre-adaptive' basis for quickly taking up already developed domesticates from western Asia at around 5000 BC.[6] Elsewhere in comparably dense aquatic settlements of what J.E.G. Sutton has called 'Middle

Africa' such changes did not take place for several millennia.[7] The necessary condition was a crisis of population pressure upon undomesticated resources.

No such pressure was felt by hunting-and-gathering foragers because their way of life contains built-in population checks: low body weight limiting female fertility during much of the year; long lactation periods with accompanying sexual abstinence because of the unsuitability of foraging foods for infants; frequent walking to daily and seasonal food sources, which discourages birth intervals producing more than one non-ambulant child at a time. Infanticide was probably an accepted last resort for checking excessive births.[8] It is thus not surprising that hunting-and-gathering populations could maintain themselves for so many millennia in the sub-equatorial portions of Africa.

The aquatic foragers farther to the north, on the other hand, had made themselves vulnerable to climatic changes that, in a series of waves from the fifth to the second millennium BC, shrunk the lakes and rivers which had allowed this culture to spread so widely. In the Sahara and possibly in portions of Ethiopia this desiccation led directly to the adoption of domesticated cattle as a major food source. Farther south the eventual results were the domestication of local cereals – mainly millet and sorghum – and the development of an entire new agricultural life style. The complexity and importance of this process require somewhat lengthier examination.

Probably the earliest occurrence of the domestication of sub-Saharan African food plants took place in Ethiopia between the fourth and sixth millennia BC but it is unlikely that this event had much impact on the rest of the continent.[9] Little is known, in any case, of the circumstances surrounding this transformation within Ethiopia, due to lack of archaeological research.

Domesticated food production did diffuse out of Ethiopia in the form of pastoral peoples who occupied what is now Kenya and northern Tanzania during the first millennium BC. Historians have puzzled a good deal over whether these 'stone bowl peoples' also cultivated plants.[10] From an economic perspective, the significant message of their cultural records is that domesticated cereals, while probably known and even present to a limited extent, were not important to subsistence. Whatever pressures may have initiated population movements from Ethiopia, they were resolved by the availability of rich, open pasture lands in the adjacent regions of East Africa. Thus pastoralism sufficed as the staple of the newcomers while indigenous local populations continued to live from foraging. Agriculture, as a major element in the East African economy, would await the spread through the region of Bantu-speaking peoples linked to West Africa.

West Africa (specifically, the area from present-day Mauritania to the Niger Bend) functioned as a major source of early continent-wide economic change because it was subjected to a mixture of less easily relieved demographic and climatic pressures. The earliest archeological evidence of agriculture in this region points to the domestication of indigenous grains: millet at Tichett in south-central Mauritania about 1000 BC and rice in the central Niger River Valley about a millennium later.[11] The better-studied and more representative Tichett site shows a clear progression from aquatic foraging to cultivation as the local climate became drier.

The Niger settlements are newer and contain indications of cattle-keeping preceding agriculture. This is typical of Saharan populations, which had begun to combine fishing with pastoralism during the early phases of desiccation. With increasing dryness during the second millennium BC these groups were forced to move south into the present cattle zone of the West African sahel. Unlike East Africa, pastoralists here encountered larger remnants of formerly aquatic populations already shifting to agriculture. The pressures generated by the inter-relationship of these groups were exacerbated by generally poorer local pastures and the restriction of pastoral movement southward, where the Guinea forest tse-tse flies threatened the health of large livestock.[12]

Within the West African forest it is also impossible to cultivate millet or related sorghum plants. Rice can be, and is now, grown in part of this region but only after considerable adaptation from its savanna river-bed sources. Domestication of food sources in the forest thus centred around two other indigenous plants, the oil palm and the yam.[13] The dating of this process is difficult because artefacts (particularly wooden digging tools) do not survive as well in the humid forest as in the drier savanna and desert while the yam – the more critical of the local domesticates – leaves no kernels which can be traced in any kind of archaeological record. Palm, which is found in early sites, remains today largely a 'protected' rather than a fully cultivated crop and thus tells us little about domestication.

It is possible that domestication took place in the West African forest entirely independently of the environmental and population factors operating farther to the north. However the location of the known early sites of forest crops at the savanna edge and the inclusion among them of cereal crops suggests an influence from drier regions and the broader patterns of economic change operating there. Development under stress thus seems to provide the model that best characterizes the earliest major shift to domesticated food production in sub-Saharan Africa and, as will be seen below in this and the next chapter, provides both a direct explanation and a paradigm of comparison for further transformations in the rest of the continent.

Domesticated food production and metallurgy: diffusion and intensification

For all its uncertainties, the explanation of the earliest food production in sub-Saharan Africa remains relatively simple: it concerns a single dimension of techno-logical change in a fairly stable population, largely cut off from the outside world. Later transformations in regions outside of West Africa are far more complicated because shifts in agriculture are now associated with the introduction of iron-working, the continent-wide spread of Bantu-speaking peoples, and the adapta-tion of new food crops from outside Africa.

In dealing with these changes it is difficult to distinguish economic history – here defined as the organization of production and exchange – from culture history; the general process of change in technology, language, social organization, and ideas. Obviously the two are not really separable but for present purposes the many problems of culture history will be dealt with summarily while stress is placed on the relevance of these changes to the economy.

What the cultural record tells us fairly clearly is that within a large part of Africa domesticated agriculture was introduced rather rapidly by iron-using peoples who were probably Bantu-speakers. Whether ironworking was invented independently in Africa or, and by what routes, entered the sub-Saharan regions from outside need not concern us here.[14] The significant factors are the rapid transition from the neo-lithic to the iron age, without an intervening bronze age, and the forms of metal-lurgy which developed.

Domestic African ironworking is characterized by sophisticated smelting processes combined with much simpler techniques for forging metal into finished goods. African smelters used charcoal fuel and large furnaces whose heating capacities were increased by the use of tuyères (blowpipes) to introduce air under pressure. The resulting intermediate metal 'bloom' contained very high levels of carbon, leading some scholars to refer to it as steel. However, in the subsequent forging stage, which turned the spongy and polluted bloom into usable metal, most of the carbon content was lost, leaving what was essentially a high-quality wrought iron. Early Asian and European blacksmiths who worked, as Africans did, without the aid of power-driven furnaces, usually produced steel in the forging process by very elaborate methods of quenching, annealing, and cementing (the major exception is crucible or 'damascene' (Damascus) steel formed in furnaces by a process so difficult to emulate that its products became a highly valued export throughout the ancient and medieval world).[15]

There is some evidence that African artisans were capable of using cementing techniques, but little indication that they did so regularly to produce steel implements. The apparent incentive for early Asian and European steelmaking was the need to replace previously available weapons made of bronze.[16] Bronze blades are sharper and more elastic than those made of iron in its ordinary form. For Africans, on the other hand, iron replaced not bronze but stone and wood and the characteristic products were not knives and swords but axes, spearheads and arrowheads, adzes, and hoes. Although there is nothing 'backward' about this initial form of African metallurgy (in fact, indigenous iron was superior to imported European varieties up until modern times), the absence of a domestic steel industry would contribute to later African dependence upon foreign sources for sword blades and gun barrels.

A general pattern of 'Bantu migrations' has been established by scholars on the basis of the linguistic homogeneity of most of Equatorial, East, and Southern Africa. More specific models of the spread of these languages depend upon comparative lexicographical analysis, the dating of 'iron age' settlements throughout the region, and their classification according to ceramic types. The details of these models have, with the progress of research, become more, rather than less, controversial.[17] What remains generally accepted is that Bantu culture originated in West Africa subsequent to the development of agriculture (i.e. before the first millennium BC) and that its most rapid spread southward across East Africa is also associated with iron. Finally it appears clear that Asian crops, which entered East Africa during the first millennium AD, came too late to have had any influence on the basic diffusion of Bantu-speaking peoples or their culture.

Given the association of agriculture, iron, and large-scale population movements, what are the economic factors connecting them? Since West African iron-age cultivators remained relatively stable during this period (it is nowhere contended that the earliest Bantu-speakers represent a significant proportion of the West African population) there is no very obvious answer to this question.

Iron apparently made no dramatic impact upon early African agriculture. Iron hoe blades are not radically more efficient than wooden implements in the generally shallow systems of African soil preparation. There is also evidence that because of high production and transport costs they spread relatively slowly until becoming more easily available through expanded trade networks.[18] In the archaeological record and in African ideologies, iron is less closely associated with production and reproduction than with destruction and authority. Weapons and the regalia of rulers are the most prominent creations of metallurgy. Smithing is often surrounded with a status separating its practitioners from food production: in the Western Sudanic zone of West Africa and parts of Ethiopia metalworkers belong to 'impure' castes; in West-Central Africa they are associated with kingship and violence; in much of East Africa and the Sahara they are descendants of sub-jugated ethnic groups (often former foragers) and very widely they are the special dependents of political authorities.[19]

None of these beliefs inhibit the adaptation of metallurgy to agriculture nor do they contradict other beliefs associating smiths with cultivating tools, which are certainly their principal products in modern times. The pre-eminence given to violence, however, suggests that the initial economic impact of metal may have been felt most strongly in hunting and in clearing forest areas, thus encouraging the exploration and settlement of new zones. The production of charcoal also places great strain on tree resources, thus raising still further the cost of iron or else, in relatively uninhabited regions, encouraging further migration. The cost effect partially explains the specialized patterns of production and exchange of iron in West Africa; the avoidance of high costs accounts for the rapidity of migration in Bantu Africa.[20]

Another distinction between much of Bantu Africa and West Africa is the combination in the former area of cattle husbandry and agriculture within the same populations. As already noted in the discussion of pastoral migrations into West and East Africa, the difference here can be traced to ecology: there are no consistent boundaries in East Africa between grazing and cultivating zones so that early pastoralists met no obstacles to their own dispersion and later emerging Bantu cultivators could adopt cattle while settling apart from the pastoralists. In relatively recent South African history, the continually expanded demands for new pasture land by such mixed domesticators culminated, during the early nineteenth century, in a massive and violent population shift known as the Zulu *mfecane* (see Chapter 7). Similar patterns on a smaller scale may explain the earlier movement of Bantu populations through East Africa into the southern sub-continent.[21]

Chronologically, the last set of innovations in African systems of food production came with the introduction of new Asian and American crops that supplemented the indigenous staples of millet, sorghum, yam, and rice.[22] Before discussing these importations, it should be noted that the traffic of diffusion was not all one-way. African-derived sorghums, known as durra, became a major South Asian food crop in the first millennium BC; after 1500 African yams displaced indigenous varieties in much of the tropical New World, while the banana reached the Americas from Asia by way of Africa.

The Asian contributions to African food-crops consist of bananas, both sweet varieties and the dry, starchy plantain, and new varieties of cocoyam (taro) and rice. Of these the plantain-banana is the most important, since it became the main staple of several highland areas in East and East-Central Africa, which could thus support the strains of dense populations and the heavy demands made on forests by metallurgy. The precise date and entry point for this Asian crop complex is difficult to establish, although it probably took place about the first century AD via the Mozambique–Madagascar channel, thus coming after the basic patterns of the Bantu iron-age economy had been established.[23]

As a result of the opening of trans-Atlantic navigation in the fifteenth century, manioc (cassava) and maize (American corn) were gradually introduced into western and eastern Africa. Manioc spread throughout the continent as a drought-resistant, high-caloric but very low-protein starch source. Maize was taken up over a similarly wide area, proving particularly adaptable to savanna–forest borderlands and river basins. Before colonial times it seldom became a dominant crop nor even as important a diet supplement as manioc, but it enjoyed a particular advantage in zones of long-distance trade as its grains could easily be dried and used as portable food for caravan porters, and the crews and cargoes of slaving ships.[24]

The mature domestic economy: organization of production

The previous discussion of technological innovations in the domestic African economy has essentially followed a market model of analysis. Changes in the methods or locale of food production were explained as responses to alterations in the balance between populations and the physical environment. What this explanation lacks is a sensitivity to the social context within which such changes took place; an abstract African 'economic man' has been substituted for real historical actors. Unfortunately archaeological records, which are our only direct link to this stage of African development, tell us little about anything beyond ecology and technology.

In the absence of contemporary accounts we are forced into the paradoxical position of using information gathered from field observations of recent African rural societies – the ominous 'ethnographic present' – to explain the distant past. At one level, the assumption that these modern peoples represent a long-surviving way of life is justified: archaeology does indicate that African production techniques did not change radically once major domesticated animals and food crops had been introduced although, as the previous section has shown, this process of invention and diffusion went on until relatively recent times. The ethnographic record also gives us some idea of African social responses to change although in more limited or different form than the major food-production innovations.

The message in all of this evidence is that African economies were organized mainly to conserve existing sources of subsistence rather than to exploit opportunities for increased profit. Such an attitude is normal in any situation where most productive effort is dedicated to the necessities of life, and risks can result in starvation rather than mere declines in discretionary income. The problem is somewhat more complicated in the African case, however, because it would be inaccurate to argue either that most peoples lived at the margin of their available resources or that they resisted historical opportunities for change. The caution of economic behaviour derives rather from the association of past changes with threatening ecological pressures and – as will be seen – the linking of later opportunities for profit with external social conflicts. The resulting strategies and institutions thus express a conservative dynamic: an adaptation to change which is neither avoidance nor direct embrace.

In the immediate strategies of African food production this dynamic takes the form of extensive pastoralism and swidden agriculture. The common denominator of both these systems is the use of large land areas at relatively low levels of yield for each unit of input. For pastoralists, this means maintaining large herds, scattered among a variety of pastures. Swidden, or shifting, agriculture is a more significant sector of the African domestic economy and requires further description.[25]

Swidden farmers all employ a variety of fields on a rotating basis. The many different swidden systems found in Africa are usually classified according to the length of time a given plot is allowed to lie fallow before it can be cultivated again. At the extreme, in certain forest areas, this may amount to twenty-five years, or ten years in less-favoured open zones. More commonly, however, the periods of fallow range from one to eight years with a resultingly narrow geographical range over which 'shifting' actually takes place. At the other end of the scale there are areas in Africa where permanent or annually planted crops offer a continual food supply from the same piece of land, such as among 'wet rice' planters of West African river valleys and the plantain-banana growers of volcanic soil and/or high rainfall regions of East Africa. However, most African rice is grown on 'dry' fields rather than in standing water, requiring the same five-year fallow typical of root or cereal crops. Banana trees likewise have shorter yield periods outside the few most favoured zones; only in the latter can they serve as a dominant staple.

Compared with food-production systems in more developed parts of the world, African pastoralism and farming do not provide very efficient outputs. African cattle are generally fairly thin, produce little milk, and often overgraze their pastures. In swidden agriculture, the crop outputs per planted hectare are not impressive. Moreover the two forms of food production are seldom integrated: even when the same farmer owns cattle and fields, the manure of the former is usually not available to fertilize the latter. Preparation for planting is almost always done manually with sticks and hoes rather than with animal-driven ploughs, and animals are seldom used to transport farming goods.

Such apparent defects cannot be written off as ignorance or laziness, as many colonial agronomists learned to their grief. The African environment presents serious obstacles to continuous, intensive productivity and many of the inherited as well as the innovative practices of indigenous husbandmen are designed to minimize the risks presented by these conditions.

Pastoralists are thus threatened by drought, flood, disease and the theft of animals. A large and scattered herd is the best insurance against complete loss from any of these disasters even if individual animals are thus less well-nourished.[26] When, through extremes of drought or prosperity, the general ratio of livestock to environmental resources has become untenable, African pastoralists have shown themselves willing to strike out into new regions. The history of the continent is therefore continually marked by major pastoral migrations – not only the massive movement of Bantu-speakers to the south in the first millennium AD but also the spread of the Fulani and Berbers across the West African sahel and Sahara from the early second millennium and the movement of Nilotic peoples north and south in eastern Africa since about 1600.[27]

Agriculturalists are faced by extreme concentrations of seasonal rain and sunshine which tend to leach nutrients out of soil which has been cleared for planting. These effects may be exacerbated by casual manuring or by ploughing which exposes more of the topsoil than is necessary to cover seeds. Mature plants are also subject to attacks from the rich variety of parasites which abound in the tropics. Insurance here is provided by natural restoration of fertility through fallow and a scattering of plots within cultivated areas. By the same logic African farmers readily adopted new crops from Asia and the Western hemisphere because these could be added to the existing repertoire, offering another form of diversification and thus protection against risk. Only in the case of the Asian plantain-banana, and that mainly in the single region west and north of Lake Victoria in East Central

Africa, did technological change of this kind allow a major alteration in social patterns. Otherwise, as among pastoral migrants, new ventures were undertaken with the aim of preserving existing conditions of life.

The general failure of Africans to integrate cattle into agriculture can again be explained by ecological as well as demographic factors. In the major cultivation zones of the West and Central Sudanic savanna of West Africa, cattle are regularly brought into agricultural areas during the dry season in order to feed on the stubble of harvested crops and to provide manure deposits. However, their retention there during the rest of the year, when cultivation actually takes place, would involve major disease risks to the animals. Moreover the deeper ploughing which would be possible with animal traction exposes thin local topsoils to even more leaching than is already the case. Finally, the maintenance of cattle in even healthy farm areas throughout the year entails costs in human labour and feed grain which are only justified when the resulting increases in agricultural products can be exchanged profitably for other goods.[28] In much of the domestic African economy, no such market opportunities existed because of low population densities, barriers to transport between existing populations, and difficulties in protecting stored food surpluses against weather and vermin threats.

The organization of African food production thus appears to conform to a degree of market rationality by maintaining a general balance between human effort and available resources. However such an analysis can mislead us into assuming that the domestic African economy had everywhere achieved optimal levels of production within its environmental constraints. It can in fact be demonstrated that higher yields were possible in much of the African food sector without real ecological risk.[29] Plough cultivation, for instance, was quite viable under the soil conditions and mixed farming and pastoral conditions which characterized much of the parts of Central and Southern Africa inhabited by Bantu-speakers, although this technique was not in fact adopted until the colonial period (see Chapter 7). Moreover, as will be seen later in this chapter, opportunities for exchange of surpluses existed in a number of African situations even without the stimulus of extra-continental contacts. Finally ecological calculations provide only a range, rather than a precise equation, for the level of productivity which will be found in any particular African society.

To understand the basis for various kinds of African food economies we must go beyond the technical organization of production itself to the context of social institutions and even ideologies within which this work takes place. It is particularly deceptive to speak of African food-producing units as 'firms' in a market-economic sense since in this type of economy there are no distinctions between the organizations which produce goods, those which consume them, and those which define the general socio-political order.

Marxist anthropologists have cast valuable light upon the relationships between production and broader social organization through their attempts to define various sectors of the African domestic economy as 'modes of production'. However, the resulting schematizations are not very useful in explaining the transitions between different types of production systems, as already seen, and they also assume an unrealistic degree of correspondence between economic and social forms within any one system. Thus it is striking to note the absence of deep kinship structures among the surviving forager societies of Africa and their almost universal presence as a fundamental organizing principle among domesticated food producers. However, outside Africa foragers have developed deep kinship systems and we have no way of knowing the social organization of the majority of African foraging economies, which did not survive into historical times. Among the many and well-known pastoral and agricultural peoples of Africa, kinship and related residential age, and cult organizations present a richness of variation which cannot possibly be reduced to any 'base' of production needs.[30]

Still the multiple roles played by social units in African societies concentrated on food production have a tendency (although even at this level there are important exceptions) to keep output below the maximum allowable by physical conditions. In market terms we can define these relationships as insurances against the loss of labour and provisions necessary for survival. They may even offer negotiable resources for the concentration of labour, as in the cases of wealthy men who purchase additional wives or the services of male age groups to harvest cereal crops. But as perceived within the society these institutions take on the additional load of defining an individual's entire identity and are thus more forcefully applied than considerations of material utility alone would dictate. The basic resources of these societies – land, cattle, and labour – are not allocated by individual entrepreneurs or markets but rather by authorities (often collective ones) who are at least as concerned with the repercussions of their decisions on kinship, status, and political relations as they are with productivity.

Marxist students of the African domestic economy have perhaps performed their greatest service by focusing upon the role of women, at once the key factor of production and reproduction, of market exchange, and personal ties. Through such analysis it is possible to see the complex rules of marriage as a medium through which male elders maintain a kind of class domination over apparently egalitarian food-production systems. Simultaneously the need to maintain these rules imposes its own logic upon the division of labour. The accumulation of cattle, because it is a masculine prerogative and provides the currency for kin and marriage ties, is given precedence far beyond its nutritional return or, in some cases, the bearing capacity of the environment. The tools and tasks of cultivation are defined by sexual characteristics unrelated to efficiency. Technological innovations, particularly those linking cattle and cultivation, may be resisted by males if they threaten the structure of sex roles.[31]

The commitment of resources to maintenance of a cultural system rather than the immediate increase of food and other basic material goods need not, of course, be seen as an indication of low productivity rates. Much of what Africans, particularly males, did with the supposed 'leisure' provided by the limited exploitation of subsistence opportunities must also be considered a form of economic investment. Most obviously the elaborate artefacts, particularly wood carvings, for which many African societies are famous represent immediate evidence of productivity. Likewise the negotiation and ritual enactment of complex social relationships demanded time and energy.[32]

In their material form such goods even had an important role in stimulating market exchange within the domestic economy. Their ideological content, however, supported in various ways the conservatism of the system as a whole. Insofar as the beliefs articulated through these media claimed to provide preternatural control over the environment or simply lent spiritual legitimacy to the existing order, they reinforced practices which might otherwise have been treated more flexibly. By now scholars have come to appreciate that 'primitive' belief systems are also sensitive to the paradoxes in the natural and human world and such an understanding helps to explain why Africans do not behave as rigidly as earlier interpretations of their culture would lead one to expect. Nonetheless, even in their most subtle representations of contradictions in social norms, African ideologies do not recognize the possibility of systematic alternatives to the existing order.[33] Change is seen as possible and even necessary at times but not therefore desirable; after all, in its most dramatic forms it has been associated with crises of subsistence. In the concluding section of this chapter we will examine more positive incentives for intensified productivity which are themselves not without elements of danger as well as opportunity.

The mature domestic economy: market relationships

Market-economic analysis has tended to play down the role of institutional inhibitions and even risk-aversion strategies in hampering African growth because it seems far easier to attribute such retardation to the absence of effective exchange opportunities. There can be little doubt that demographic and transport factors did limit the incentives for producing surpluses throughout the continent. Low population densities allowed the continuation of extensive herding and agriculture while negating the most essential element of any market: concentrations of buyers and sellers. The geography of Africa also presents serious barriers to long-distance transport. Water travel is limited by the small amount of indented shoreline relative to the size of the interior surface of the continent, as well as the disrupted navigability of most rivers, due to rapids and seasonal shallows. The wheel was introduced into northern Africa for overland travel during ancient times but then abandoned because the terrain and distances to be covered could not feasibly be provided with the necessary roads. Even pack-animal carriage is impossible over critical bush and forest zones infested with disease-bearing tse-tse flies. The disutility of the wheel in transport may also explain the virtual absence of transformations from linear to rotary motion in such African technologies as irrigation and (see Chapter 2) cotton-spinning.[34]

In the modern period Western technology has provided Africa with conditions for population increase and mechanized transport which have helped spur a great acceleration of economic growth. Yet such technology also brought new risks, ultimately reflected in the various structural problems of colonial and post-colonial African development, to be discussed in later chapters. The corollary to viewing more critically the market factors generated from outside Africa is to question their simple absence as an explanation for limitations on indigenous growth. Markets, even if restricted in spatial range, did exist in many – probably most – sectors of the African domestic economy. The examination of their development is necessary to complete the historical survey of this economy.[35]

Our ability to reconstruct the details, and especially the scale, of the earliest African marketing systems is hampered by the fact that most historical evidence comes from periods and places where such exchanges of subsistence staples were influenced in one way or another by extra-continental commerce in other types of commodities. Nonetheless, we can at least identify the situations where exchange developed autonomously within the domestic economy.

The forms of exchange relevant to the concept of African markets are those involving surpluses (and sometimes unevenly distributed shortages) in mutually complementary systems of specialized production. It is the possibility of acquiring new types of commodities which provides the incentive for surplus production in the first place. Not all systems of African domestic exchange fit this pattern.

Transactions of goods within household units and (as will be seen) through hierarchical structures of prestation-redistribution reflect social rather than market relations and do not necessarily involve an intensification of production. Even exchanges between communities can, in some instances, involve commodities which either group could (or even did) produce with equal efficiency. The motives for such transactions again involve the maintenance of stable relations between the groups involved and, by artificially (and in explicitly ritual terms) relegating certain goods to an importation sphere, may actually handicap productivity.[36]

The situations where more-dynamic exchange systems developed in the domestic African economy are those involving differing patterns of producing food and food-related commodities, usually at strategically located ecological frontiers. The types of exchanges may be usefully categorized in terms of three sets of complementarities: forager–domesticator, agriculturalist–pastoralist, and organic–mineral goods.

The first of these dyads, the relationship between hunting/gathering and cultivating/herding societies, appears to have been stimulating only in the presence of one specialized form of foraging: fishing. The skills of exploiting terrestrial game and wild plant life were retained by most domesticating African societies for supplementary, emergency and – in the case of male hunting – even prestige-political purposes. Those populations which remained firmly committed to a hunting and gathering way of life were either restricted to marginal areas where they retained limited economic relationships with the dominant and often rather sparse domesticators in immediately neighbouring zones or, in some cases, appear to have been entirely exterminated, thus providing a possible basis for the accounts of aboriginal 'little people' in many African mytho-histories. Some foragers survived within the core areas as clients of the dominant pastoral and agricultural groups as was the case in the earlier history of the South African Bushmen/San, and in more recent times the various pygmies of the equatorial forests and the 'Dorobo' peoples of the Kenya-Tanzania plains. In the case of the early San and pygmies the services offered to patrons centre around hunting and gathering; more commonly the foragers have been transformed into herdsmen, farm labourers, and metalworkers and ritual specialists.[37]

Fishing has already been noted as a relatively late stone-age mode of foraging which provided one of the demographic preconditions for domestication. In more recent times fishing groups and pastoral/agricultural food producers have maintained very vigorous exchange of their mutual specialities around a number of inland waterways such as the Niger River bend, Lake Chad, and Lake Victoria as well as sites on the ocean, especially in West Africa.

Cultural evidence from those inland fishing groups whose prehistory has been studied indicates that they are linked to the aquatic civilization which was once spread throughout this part of Africa, although the present sites were probably occupied in later neolithic or early iron-age times. Both the movement to new settlements and their exploitation for exchange along with direct food production suggests that the market relationships developed out of a response to the same subsistence crises which led to agricultural domestication elsewhere.[38]

In the waterways east of the Atlantic Ocean delta of the Niger it is possible to trace the movement of farming populations early in the second millennium AD to coastal sites where poor soil conditions forced them to specialize in fishing and depend for starch staples on inland exchanges. In modern times these regions have become quite densely populated, but it is difficult to know if this demographic situation was a cause of the decision to begin exploiting fish or a response to the opportunity of new maritime enterprises.[39]

Because of their wide distribution across the continent, agriculturalist–pastoralist complementarities provide more frequent, and often more complex stimuli for trade than do forager–domesticator links. Reference has already been made to seasonal movements of cattle into cultivation regions of West Africa. These contacts extend beyond feeding and manuring to include direct exchanges of dairy products, leather, and meat for agricultural and handicraft goods. There is also considerable evidence in the interlacustrine zone of East-Central Africa for cattle being accumulated by cultivators in order to trade them for grain during periods of local famine.[40]

Nevertheless, a number of factors tend to limit the economic impact of such exchanges. Many African pastoralists are concentrated in regions – particularly the diagonal dry belt extending south of the Sahara from the Senegal River to northern Kenya – where no other form of subsistence can be practised. Moreover, to the degree that their homelands are suitable for more varied food production, it is often the pastoralists themselves who supplement the sustenance from their herds by engaging in fishing or allowing their women or slaves to practise agriculture. Conversely in the more densely settled zones of East and Southern Africa, Bantu agriculturalists long ago took up cattle-keeping as a usually secondary, but quite extensive, form of subsistence.

Finally in those still significant areas where predominantly pastoral peoples do maintain the most regular contacts with cultivators owning little or no large stock, the latter have been made dramatically aware of the risks accompanying such complementarity. Pastoralists in many parts of Africa, as elsewhere in the world, practise more-or-less institutionalized marauding upon each other's herds as well as the property of more settled populations. The threat of such raids, added to the natural hazards of African environments (especially the drought-ridden savanna zones most likely to be close to pastoral areas), has the effect of discouraging intensive cultivation. It is precisely the key elements in such an agricultural system – multi-annual investments in land preparation, draught animals, and valuable tools – which are likely to be lost or abandoned because of raids.

In the sahel (desert edge) zone of West Africa and the interlacustrine regions of East Africa the military interaction of pastoral and sedentary peoples eventually spurred the formation of centralized states. The security provided by such political organization protected cultivators against depredations and eventually provided the focus for wide-ranging exchanges of goods. However states in these regions were in no sense the emanations of either agriculture or trade; ideologically they tended to identify themselves with the militaristic dimension of pastoral society or with hunting bands. They thus institutionalized the linkage between market opportunities and threats of violence on the broadest of Africa's ecological frontiers.[41]

Mining and other extractive industries produced another set of staple commodities – iron, salt and copper – which circulated within domestic African exchange systems. Among these goods iron is the most widely distributed, since most regions of Africa contain surface ore deposits sufficient for the manufacture of hand tools and weapons. Given the durability of such implements (one of their major advantages over wood), many societies have been able to meet their needs without resort to specialists or more than reciprocal exchange; during the dry season, farmers simply become their own or their immediate neighbours' smelters and blacksmiths. Within many regions, however, both iron and the skills required for its use are unevenly located. Moreover, the demand for iron implements may exceed the possibilities of unspecialized supply and supplementary fuel resources, particularly when there is a large need for weapons. Such a situation was the source of active market trade among a number of pre-colonial communities.[42] Unfortunately, for most cases we have direct evidence about intensive commercialization of ironworking only when it accompanied long-distance trade oriented overseas. Moreover, in a number of African societies, most notably the highly commercialized West African Sudan, blacksmiths were subjected to the sort of ritual and social stigmatization noted in the earlier discussion of metallurgy. This collective status allowed smiths to move across the geographical and political boundaries which separated various agricultural communities, thus creating a wide area of circulation for their skills. At the same time the most prestigious workers attached themselves in client relationships to local rulers and other elites, thus concentrating much of their production in enclosed systems of tribute and reward rather than the open market.[43]

In Equatorial Africa blacksmiths are ritually identified with members of the royal dynasties themselves, although the actual manufacture of ordinary ironware in this region appears to have been widely spread among common cultivators.[44] Copper, on the other hand, enjoyed a special status. Worked into non-utilitarian goods from as early as the fifth century AD, it circulated the region (along with shells from the Atlantic coast and palm mats from the northern Congo forest), and served as a kind of special purpose currency, controlled by elites and initially used in transactions involving changes of status rather than the purchase of staple goods. Nonetheless, the circulation of such items mobilized food production to some extent: the carriers of prestige commodities would require provisioning outside their home areas and salt (but apparently not fish) was included in the inventory of caravans coming from the coast. The complete transformation of Central African copper currency into 'general purpose money' appears to have occurred only from the sixteenth century on, in the context of long-distance trade.[45] Under such circumstances, as will be seen below, monetization penetrated many African economies.

Salt, unlike iron, is very unevenly distributed throughout Africa. Many societies can only supply themselves with sufficient quantities of this substance – so necessary in a tropical climiate, particularly for a population on a cereal diet – by inefficent methods of distilling vegetable ashes. Thus access to major sources of salt – a variety of desert mining centres, lake and desert potash deposits, brine springs and oceanic ponds – provides a basis for trade covering very large distances. Most of the early African salt-trade routes about which we know were joined with other types of complementarity: fish and shells from the sea, pastoral products from the desert edge, and metal goods from the vicinity of inland springs. Perhaps the most important of these systems linked the Sahara Desert, containing excellent but often remote rock-salt resources, with the agricultural centres of the Western and Central Sudan. This market required early concentrations of labour – often coerced – in both the desert mines and the sahelian centres of exchange. Moreover, even when the Sahara became a major link between West Africa and the Mediterranean, salt production continued to play a major role in regional commerce.[46]

Outside the highly unattractive conditions of a few key sites in the Sahara, salt production does not appear to have involved great risks to African food producers.

It was typically undertaken as a dry-season activity by groups of men who would be farmers during the rest of the year. It also appears that the longer and more active salt routes of East Africa depended – like iron – upon the stimulus of overseas trade for their full development. In West-Central Africa salt blocks sometimes appear to have functioned as currency in the state-controlled prestige exchange circuits but it is difficult, from available evidence, to estimate the scale of this movement.[47]

Conclusion: dynamics and limitations of subsistence

If viewed simply in terms of survival, the history of African food-production systems presents a picture of very active, varied and complex adaptation to often difficult environments. The outer boundaries of this growth process are, to a considerable extent, explicable by the obstacles of the environment. At the same time, the institutionalization of concerns with survival inhibited the fullest possible exploitation of existing resources and market opportunities.

As indicated by the production and exchange systems which did develop, African subsistence producers were not unwilling to respond to incentives for material betterment provided that accompanying risks could be limited relative to the potential new gains. But, historically, the most powerful of such incentives derived not from developments within the food-production sectors themselves, but through the arrival of non-African traders seeking more specialized commodities, especially gold, slaves, and wild-forest goods. The location and organization of this new form of trade depended heavily upon the earlier development of market centres within the domestic sphere, particularly at the major areas of exchange between fishermen, pastoralists, and agriculturalists. But the demands now to be made upon the African economy placed only secondary emphasis on the further intensification and integration of food-production systems.

The discussions of international trade which occupy the next several chapters will introduce new institutions and relationships between Africans and aliens in what often became, from the viewpoint of the continent as a whole, only marginal enclaves of growth. Each of these chapters will, however, stress the linkages between the new frontiers and their respective hinterlands. Whether these ties remained weak or developed significantly along either positive or negative lines depended both upon relationships with outsiders and the continuing dynamics and limitations of the local domestic African economies.

Notes

1. Goody (1976); Hindess and Hirst (1975); Meillassoux (1981).
2. The following discussion draws very heavily upon the various contributions to Harlan, De Wet and Stemler (1976); and on Sutton (1974). Several points on technology are discussed in greater detail in Austen and Headrick (1983). For more universal and comparative analysis of the origins of food production, see Cohen (1977), Reed (1977).
3. Sahlins (1968); Meillassoux (1960, 1973, 1981).

4. Lee (1979); see also various analyses of pygmy food production in Harding and Teleki (1981); also Fagan (1976); Gabel (1965).
5. Sutton (1974).
6. Clark (1971).
7. Sutton (1974).
8. Howell (1979); Wilmsen (1979). For contemporary evidence on fertility restraints elsewhere in Africa, see Caldwell and Caldwell (1977).
9. De Wet (1977); Ehret (1975).
10. Gabel (1974); Odner (1972); Phillipson (1977); Sutton (1981).
11. Munson (1976); McIntosh and McIntosh (1981).
12. Clark (1976).
13. Coursey (1976); Flight (1976).
14. Amborn (1976); Andah (1981) pp. 610–14; Herbert (1984) p. 10 f.; Posnansky (1981) pp. 542–6; Schmidt (1978); Shaw (1981); Shinnie (1971); Tylecote (1975).
15. Goucher (1981) and Van der Merwe (1980) give the argument for African steel as well as some evidence which can be used to defend a contrary viewpoint (see Austen and Headrick, 1983); on non-African steel, see Forbes (1956) and for a knowledgeable comparison, Forbes (1933) and Panseri (1966).
16. Maddin, Muhly and Wheeler (1977); Herbert (1984) passim.
17. Vansina (1979–80).
18. Raulin (1967) pp. 50–1; Hay (1972).
19. Herbert (1984) p. 32 f.; Levine (1974) pp. 56–197, passim; Olivier de Sardan (1969) pp. 36–7, 114–15; Pollet and Winter (1971) pp. 215–37; Wente-Lukas (1972).
20. Forbes (1933); Goucher (1981).
21. Phillipson (1977) especially p. 216 f.; Guy (1980).
22. Coursey (1976); Buddenhagen and Persley (1978).
23. Schmidt (1978) pp. 293–4; Sutton (1981) p. 579 f.
24. Jones (1959); Miracle (1966).
25. There are extensive analyses of swidden agriculture in Allan (1965); Boserup (1965); Harris (1972); Hart (1982); Miracle (1967); Spooner (1972) (largely a discussion of Boserup's influential thesis that swidden is a function of low population-to-land ratios).
26. Deshler (1965); Rutman and Werner (1973).
27. Stenning (1957); Webster (1979).
28. Hart (1982) pp. 73–6.
29. Bronson (1972).
30. Meillassoux (1973) vs. Pilling (1968); Sahlins (1976).
31. Austen (1968) p. 193; Beinart (1982) pp. 19–26; Guyer (1981) pp. 100–1.
32. Ingham (1979).
33. Horton (1967).
34. Law (1980); Austen and Headrick (1983).
35. For general discussion of domestic African markets, see Good (1973); Gray and Birmingham (1969); Hodder (1965).
36. Muller (1972).
37. Althabe (1965); Elphick (1977) p. 23 f.; Leacock and Lee (1982) pp. 189–305; see also above, n. 19.
38. McIntosh and McIntosh (1981); Munson (1980); Tymowski (1971).
39. Alagoa (1970); Horton (1969).
40. Cohen (1983).
41. Bronson (1972); Munson (1980); Steinhart (1979).
42. Herbert (1984) pp. 47–81; Sutton and Roberts (1968).
43. Meillassoux (1969).
44. Vansina (1973) pp. 140–2.
45. Herbert (1984) pp. 187–91; Maret (1981).
46. See below, Chapter 2.
47. Sutton and Roberts (1968); Thornton (1983) pp. 33–4.

Bibliography

Alagoa, E.J. (1970), 'Long-distance trade and states in the Niger Delta', *Journal of African History*, vol. 11, no. 3, pp. 319–29

Allan, William (1965), *The African Husbandman* (New York: Barnes & Noble)

Althabe, Gerard (1965), 'Changements sociaux chez les pygmées Boka de l'Est-Cameroun', *Cahiers d'Etudes Africaines*, vol. 5, no. 4, pp. 561–92

Amborn, Hermann (1976), *Die Bedeutung der Kulturen des Nilentals fur die Eisenproduktion in subsaharischen Afrika* (Wiesbaden: Steiner)

Andah, B. Wai (1981), 'West Africa before the seventh century, in Mokhtar (ed.), pp. 593–619

Austen, Ralph A. (1968), *Northwest Tanzania under German and British Rule* (New Haven: Yale University Press)

Austen, Ralph A. and Daniel Headrick (1983), 'The role of technology in the African past', *African Studies Review*, vol. 26, nos. 3/4, pp. 163–84

Beinart, William (1982), *The Political Economy of Pondoland, 1860–1930* (Cambridge: Cambridge University Press)

Boserup, Ester (1965), *The Conditions of Agricultural Growth* (Chicago: Aldine)

Bronson, Bennet (1972), 'Farm labor and the evolution of food production', in Spooner (ed.), pp. 190–218

Buddenhagen, I.W. and G.J. Persley (eds) (1978), *Rice in Africa* (London: Academic Press)

Caldwell, J.C. and Pat Caldwell (1977), 'The role of marital sexual abstinence in determining fertility: a study of the Yoruba in Nigeria', *Population Studies*, vol. 31, no. 2, pp. 193–217

Clark, J. Desmond (1971), 'A re-examination of the evidence for agricultural origins in the Nile Valley', *Proceedings of the Prehistoric Society*, vol. 37, no. 2, pp. 34–79

Clark, J. Desmond (1976), 'Prehistoric population and pressures favoring plant domestication in Africa', in Harlan, De Wet and Stemler (eds), pp. 67–106

Cohen, David (1983), 'Food production and food exchange in the precolonial Lakes Plateau region', in Robert I. Rotberg (ed.), *Imperialism, Colonialism, and Hunger: East and Central Africa* (Lexington: D.C. Heath), pp. 1–18

Cohen, Mark Nathan (1977), *The Food Crisis in Prehistory: Overpopulation and the Origins of Agriculture* (New Haven: Yale University Press)

Coursey, D.G. (1976), 'The origins and domestication of yams in Africa', in Harlan, De Wet and Stemler (eds), pp. 383–408

Deshler, W.W. (1965), 'Native cattle-keeping in eastern Africa', in Anthony Leeds and Andrew P. Vayda (eds), *Man, Culture, and Animals* (Washington, DC: American Association for the Advancement of Science), pp. 153–68

De Wet, J.M.J. (1977), 'Domestication of African cereals', *African Economic History*, no. 3, pp. 15–32

Ehret, Christopher (1975), 'On the antiquity of agriculture in Ethiopia', *Journal of African History*, vol. 20, no. 2, pp. 161–77

Elphick, Richard (1977), *Kraal and Castle: Khoikhoi and the Founding of White South Africa* (New Haven: Yale University Press)

Fagan, Brian M. (1976), 'The hunters of Gwisho: a retrospective', in G. de G. Sieveking (ed.), *Problems in Economic and Social Archaeology* (London: Duckworth), pp. 15–24

Flight, Colin (1976), 'The Kintampo Culture and its place in the economic prehistory of West Africa', in Harlan, De Wet and Stemler (eds), pp. 211–21

Forbes, R.J. (1933), 'The black man's industries', *Geographical Review*, vol. 2, pp. 230–47

Forbes, R.J. (1956), 'Metallurgy', in Charles Singer et al. (eds), *A History of Technology*, Vol. 2 (London: Oxford University Press), pp. 41–80

Gabel, Creighton (1965), *Stone Age Hunters of the Kafue* (Boston: Boston University Press)

Gabel, Creighton (1974), 'Terminal food collectors and agricultural initiative in eastern and southern Africa', *International Journal of African Historical Studies*, vol. 7, no. 1, pp. 56–68

Good, Charles M. (1973), 'Markets in Africa: a review of research themes: the question of market origins', *Cahiers d'Etudes Africaines*, vol. 13, no. 4, pp. 769–80

Goody, Jack (1976), *Production and Reproduction: A Comparative Study of the Domestic Domain* (Cambridge: Cambridge University Press)

Goucher, Candice L. (1981), 'Iron is iron 'til it is rust: trade and ecology in the decline of West African iron-smelting', *Journal of African History*, vol. 22, no. 2, pp. 179–89

Gray Richard and David Birmingham (eds) (1969), *Pre-colonial African Trade: Essays on trade in Central and Eastern Africa before 1900* (London: Oxford University Press)

Guy, Jeff (1980), 'Ecological factors in the rise of Shaka and the Zulu kingdom', in Shula Marks and Anthony Atmore (eds), *Economy and Society in Pre-Industrial South Africa* (London: Longman), pp. 102–19

Guyer, Jane I. (1981), 'Household and community in African studies', *African Studies Review*, vol. 24, nos. 2/3, pp. 87–137

Harding, Robert S.O. and Geza Teleki (eds) (1981), *Omniverous Primates: Gathering and Hunting in Human Evolution* (New York: Columbia University Press)

Harlan, Jack R., J.M. De Wet, and Ann Stemler (eds) (1976), *Origins of African Plant Domestication* (The Hague: Mouton)

Harris, David R. (1972), 'Swidden systems and settlements', in Peter J. Ucko (ed.), *Man, Settlement and Urbanism* (London: Duckworth), pp. 243–62

Hart, Keith (1982), *The Political Economy of West African Agriculture* (Cambridge: Cambridge University Press)

Hay, Margaret Jean (1972), 'Economic change in Luoland: Kowe, 1890–1945' (Unpublished PhD dissertation, University of Wisconsin)

Herbert, Eugenia W. (1984), *Red Gold of Africa: Copper in Precolonial History and Culture* (Madison: University of Wisconsin Press)

Hindess, Barry and Paul Q. Hirst (1975), *Precapitalist Modes of Production* (London: Routledge & Kegan Paul)

Hodder, B.W. (1965), 'Some comments on the origins of traditional markets in Africa south of the Sahara', *Transactions and Papers of the Institute of British Geographers*, vol. 36, pp. 97–105

Horton, Robin (1967), 'African traditional thought and Western science', *Africa*, vol. 37, no. 1, pp. 51–71; vol. 37, no. 2, pp. 155–87

Horton, Robin (1969), 'From fishing village to city state: a social history of New Calabar', in Mary Douglas and Phyllis M. Kaberry (eds), *Man in Africa* (London: Tavistock), pp. 37–58

Howell, Nancy (1979), *Demography and the Dobe !Kung* (New York: Academic Press)

Ingham, Barbara (1979), 'Vent for surplus reconsidered with Ghanaian evidence', *Journal of Development Studies*, vol. 15, no. 3, pp. 19–37

Jones, William O. (1959), *Manioc in Africa* (Stanford: Stanford University Press)

Law, Robin (1980), 'Wheeled transport in precolonial West Africa', *Africa*, vol. 50, no. 3, pp. 249–62

Leacock, Eleonore and Richard Lee (1982), *Politics and History in Band Societies* (Cambridge: Cambridge University Press)

Lee, Richard B. (1979), *The !Kung San: Men, Women, and Work in a Foraging Society* (Cambridge: Cambridge University Press)

Lee, Richard and Irven DeVore (eds) (1969), *Man the Hunter* (Chicago: Aldine)

Levine, Donald N. (1974), *Greater Ethiopia: The Evolution of a Multiethnic Society* (Chicago: University of Chicago Press)

McIntosh, Roderick J. and Susan Keech McIntosh (1981), 'The inland Niger delta before the empire of Mali: evidence from Jenne-Jeno', *Journal of African History*, vol. 22, no. 1, pp. 1–22

Maddin, Robert, James D. Muhly and Tamarra S. Wheeler (1977), 'How the Iron Age began', *Scientific American*, vol. 237, no. 4, pp. 122–31

Maret, Pierre de (1981), 'L'évolution monétaire du Shaba Central entre le 7e et le 18e siècle', *African Economic History*, 10, pp. 117–49

Meillassoux, Claude (1960), 'Essai d'interprétation du phénomène économique dans les sociétés traditionelles d'autosubsistence', *Cahiers d'Etudes Africaines*, vol. 1, no. 1, pp. 38–67

Meillassoux, Claude (1969), 'A class analysis of the bureaucratic process in Mali', *Journal of Development Studies*, vol. 6, pp. 97–110

Meillassoux, Claude (1973), 'On the mode of production of the hunting band', in Pierre Alexandre (ed.), *French Perspectives in African Studies* (London: Oxford University Press), pp. 187–203

Meillassoux, Claude (1981), *Maidens, Meal, and Money: Capitalism and the Domestic Community* (Cambridge: Cambridge University Press)

Miracle, Marvin P. (1966), *Maize in Tropical Africa* (Madison: University of Wisconsin Press)

Miracle, Marvin P. (1967), *Agriculture in the Congo Basin: Tradition and Change in African Rural Economies* (Madison: University of Wisconsin Press)

Mokhtar, G. (ed.) (1981), *UNESCO General History of Africa*, Vol. 2, *Ancient Civilizations of Africa* (London: Heinemann)

Muller, J.-C. (1972), 'Quelques réflexions sur l'auto-restriction technologique et la dépendance économique dans les sociétés d'auto-subsistence', *Cahiers d'Etudes Africaines*, vol. 12, no. 2, pp. 659–65

Munson, Patrick J. (1976), 'Archaeological data on the origins of cultivation in the south-western Sahara and their implications for West Africa', in Harlan, De Wet and Stemler (eds), pp. 187–209

Munson, Patrick J. (1980), 'Archaeology and the prehistoric origins of the Ghana empire', *Journal of African History*, vol. 21, no. 4, pp. 457–66

Odner, Knut (1972), 'Excavations at Narosura, a Stone Bowl site in the southern Kenya Highlands', *Azania*, vol. 7, pp. 25–92

Olivier de Sardan, Jean Pierre (1969), *La système des relations économiques et sociales chez les Wogo (Niger)* (Niamey: IFAN)

Panseri, Carlo (1966), 'Damascus steel in legend and reality', *Gladius*, vol. 4, pp. 5–66

Phillipson, D.W. (1977), *The Later Prehistory of Eastern and Southern Africa* (New York: Africana Publishing)

Pilling, Arnold R. (1968), 'Southeastern Australia: level of social organization', in Lee and De Vore (eds), pp. 138–45

Pollet, Eric and Grace Winter (1971), *La société Soninke (Dyahunu, Mali)* (Brussels: Université Libre)

Posnansky, M. (1981), 'Introduction to the later prehistory of sub-Saharan Africa', in G. Mokhtar (ed.), pp. 533–50

Raulin, Henry (1967), *La dynamique des techniques agraires en Afrique tropicale du nord* (Paris: CNRS)

Reed, Charles A. (ed.) (1977), *The Origins of Agriculture* (The Hague: Mouton)

Rutman, Gilbert L. and David J. Werner (1973), 'A test of the "uneconomic culture" thesis: an economic rationale for the "sacred cow" ', *Journal of Development Studies*, vol. 9, pp. 566–80

Sahlins, Marshall (1969), 'Notes on the original affluent society', in Richard Lee and Irven DeVore (eds), pp. 85–9

Sahlins, Marshall (1976), *Culture and Practical Reason* (Chicago: University of Chicago Press)

Schmidt, Peter R. (1978), *Historical Archeology: a Structural Approach via African Culture* (Westport, Connecticut: Greenwood)

Shaw, Thurstan (1981), 'The Late Stone Age in West Africa and the beginnings of African food production', in Colette Roubet *et al.* (eds), *Préhistoire africaine* (Paris: ADPF), pp. 213–35

Shinnie, P.L. (1971), 'The Sudan', in P.L. Shinnie (ed.) *The African Iron Age* (Oxford: Clarendon)

Spooner, Brian (ed.) (1972), *Population Growth: Anthropological Implications* (Cambridge: MIT Press)

Steinhart, Edward I. (1979), 'The kingdoms of the March: speculations on social and political change', in Webster (ed.), pp. 189–213

Stenning, Derrick J. (1957), 'Transhumance, migratory drift, migration: patterns of pastoral Fulani nomadism', *Journal of the Royal Anthropological Institute*, vol. 87, pp. 57–73

Sutton, J.E.G. (1974), 'The aquatic civilization of Middle Africa', *Journal of African History*, vol. 15, no. 4, pp. 527–46

Sutton, J.E.G. (1981), 'East Africa before the seventh century', in Mokhtar (ed.), pp. 586–92

Sutton, J.E.G. and A.D. Roberts (1968), 'Uvinza and its salt industry', *Azania*, vol. 3, pp. 45–86

Thornton, John K. (1983), *The Kingdom of the Kongo: Civil War and Transition, 1641–1718* (Madison: University of Wisconsin Press)

Tylecote, R.F. (1975), 'The origins of iron smelting in Africa', *West African Journal of Archaeology*, vol. 5, pp. 1–9

Tymowski, Michael (1971), 'La pêche à l'époque du Moyen Age dans la boucle du Niger', *Africana Bulletin*, vol. 12, pp. 7–26

Van der Merwe, Nikolaas J. (1980), 'The advent of iron in Africa', in Theodore A. Wertime and James D. Muhly (eds), *The Coming of the Age of Iron* (New Haven: Yale University Press), pp. 463–506

Vansina, Jan (1973), *The Tiyo Kingdom of the Middle Congo* (Madison: University of Wisconsin Press)

Vansina, Jan (1979–80), 'Bantu in the crystal ball', *History in Africa*, vol. 6, pp. 287–333; vol. 7, pp. 293–325

Webster, J.B. (ed.) (1979), *Chronology, Migration, and Drought in Interlacustrine Africa* (London: Longman)

Wente-Lukas, Renate (1972), 'Eisen und Schmied in südlichen Tschadraum', *Paideuma*, vol. 18, pp. 112–43

Wilmsen, Edwin M. (1979), *Diet and Fertility among Kalahari Bushmen* (Boston: Boston University Press)

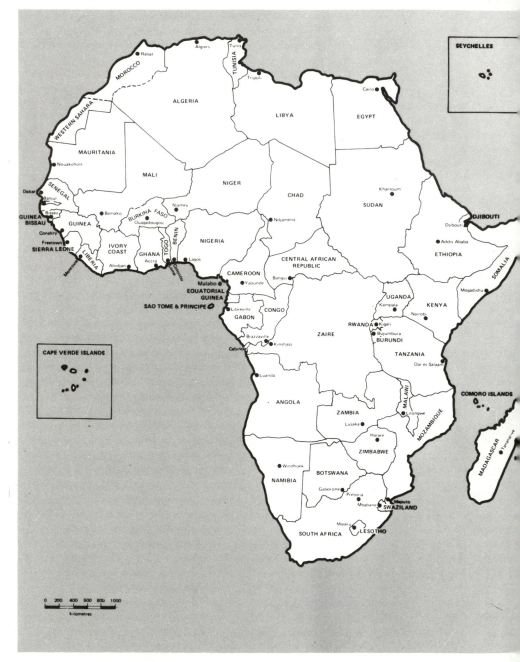

Map 1   *Africa 1986*

2

Commercial Frontiers
and Contact Economies: I
The West African Sudan and the Sahara

The region of Africa which provides the earliest evidence of a domestic economy organized around agriculture also offers the fullest case of internal economic development stimulated by external contact. The integration of the West African Sudan into the world economy was propelled by the same paradoxical combination of disadvantages and advantages which explain its early shift from foraging to domesticated food production. No other region of Africa, moreover, experienced in quite so explicit a manner the simultaneous process of internal growth and marginalization in its relationship to the international economy.

In geographical terms, the savanna and sahelian (desert edge) belt extending from Senegal to Lake Chad hardly appears an ideal centre for the emergence of long-distance trade and concentrated commercial production. Contacts between the region and the outside world are restricted by the Sahara Desert to the north and dense forest zones to the south. The desert environment threatens neighbouring agricultural areas with recurrent drought and the more humid southern savanna and forests inhibit the integration of cattle into agriculture or transport, as well as blocking the diffusion of cereal cultivation.

However, as has already been argued in Chapter 1, pressure from these conditions contributed significantly to the early emergence of agriculture in the Sudanic zone. They likewise encouraged a more autonomous pattern of economic response to long-distance trade than in the regions of Africa (to be discussed in the following chapters) with easier access to external commerce and better-watered, more homogeneous ecological conditions. The Sahara, which formed the earliest and most important link between the Sudan and outside trading partners, could only be traversed by slow and inefficient camel caravans. This situation greatly raised transport costs in comparison to sea routes but provided Sudanese domestic markets with a natural protection which encouraged the development of local industries in competition with imports. Likewise, the internal ecological boundaries of the region stimulated economic complementarities which became even more pronounced when market networks, created for the procurement of export goods, provided a medium for intensified local exchanges.

In the medieval period, when its only long-distance commerce depended upon the precarious Saharan caravan routes, the Sudanic zone played a vital role in the world economy as the key supplier of gold to the core Mediterranean markets. Conventional historiography of the region long suggested that once European navigation to the Atlantic coast of West Africa had diverted most of this gold flow southward, the Sudanic economy went into a major decline.[1] More recent studies indicate, on the contrary, that Sudanic trade and industry reached its peak after 1600, when the region was integrated into both desert and oceanic commercial systems. However, the loss of control over bullion supplies did deprive the Sudan of its crucial role in the international economy.

The pages which follow will trace the pre-colonial development of the Sudanic economy from a local perspective. But they will also suggest how the extent and limitations of this development provide a model for comparison with other areas of Africa and for the distinctions between the growth patterns of the continent as a whole and those of its external trading partners.

Trade routes and export commodities: the ancient and medieval era

When the desiccation of the northern portion of the African continent first produced the Sahara Desert, it created an ecological barrier which, to this day, is treated as the main boundary between black Africa and the outside world. At its northern edge the Sahara was penetrated by representatives of ancient Mediterranean civilizations – Egyptians, Greeks, Carthaginian/Phoenicians, Romans, Vandals, and Byzantines – but none were able to establish regular or direct economic relationships with the growing concentrations of agricultural populations in the Western and Central Sudan.

Egyptian contacts along the Nile are the best known of these early penetrations. They produced major urban centres at Napata and Meroe in the northern portions of the modern Republic of Sudan. However, despite attempts by earlier historians to trace a general 'Sudanic civilization' south and westward from this Egyptian-Nubian connection, it now appears that the Nile Valley (like the equally 'Mediterraneanized' Ethiopian coast) remained isolated from the rest of the continent until medieval times. The traverse of the Sahara in a lateral direction is an even more formidable undertaking than a north–south crossing and could only take place within the context of previously established routes over shorter distances.[2]

The beginnings of such routes appear to have been organized by Carthaginian, Roman, and possibly Greek chariot and ox-cart drivers who entered the Sahara from North Africa between 500 BC and the early centuries of the Christian era.[3] Rock drawings of chariots within the Sahara indicate two lines of penetration, a central one from Libya and Tunisia through the Fezzan and south-eastern Algeria, the other further west from Morocco into Mauritania. While the pictorial evidence suggests movements to the extreme southern edge of the Sahara, literary accounts and the distribution of Mediterranean artifacts indicate contacts only into the centre of the desert.

Whatever the degree of penetration, it appears to have been of only minuscule economic significance to North Africa and the ancient Mediterranean in general.[4] The most detailed descriptions and archaeological records of Mediterranean influence in the Sahara focus on Roman relations with a people of the Fezzan known as the Garamantes. Roman concerns here appear to have been largely defensive – to keep the pastoral Garamantes from threatening the intensive agriculture of North Africa – rather than commercial. Trade did take place, but involved only small numbers of slaves, ivory tusks and other wild-animal products, along with mysterious precious stones called carbuncles. Much less is known about the Moroccan–Mauritanian routes since they were more remote from the centres of colonization in North Africa. Herodotus makes the tantalizing statement that the Carthaginians sailed there via a short Atlantic route to trade for gold, but no other reliable ancient author refers to Africa as a source for this commodity, which would become the mainstay of medieval trans-Saharan trade.[5]

The agricultural societies of the Western and Central Sudan are never mentioned in pre-Islamic North African sources nor do they appear to have received any Mediterranean goods during this period. Nonetheless, communities dense enough to carry on regular regional or even long-distance trade existed south of the Sahara by this time and, in the case of Tichett and Tegdaoust in Mauritania, provide a connection between chariot paintings and the later centres of medieval trade, Ghana and Awdaghast.[6] What can be inferred at this point is that the northernmost regions of the Sudanic zone (including the then more fertile Mauritania as well as the upper Niger Bend) were in indirect contact with the Mediterranean via the common denominator of trade into the Sahara. The ancient literary and archaeological evidence for the Sahara does suggest the production of some goods – copper and salt – which might have been of as much interest for southern as for northward trade. Moreover the diffusion of iron metallurgy to West Africa can probably be attributed to these Saharan contacts.[7]

The major limitation of ancient Saharan trade was transport. The horse and ox-drawn vehicles used to travel into the desert could never have achieved regular crossings to the Sudanic zone. Direct commercial connections would have to await the seemingly retrograde abandonment of the wheel for a pack animal, the camel.[8]

The camel entered North Africa from the Middle East at about the same time as the Roman replacement of Carthage, in the first centuries BC. From a Mediterranean perspective, however, this innovation first appeared as more of a threat than a benefit. The Romans made some efforts to employ camels in agriculture, but their greatest concern was for the advantages that this animal would give the desert nomads in their incursions against cultivated regions. As the Roman defence system declined and Roman rule in North Africa gave way, after 429 AD, to the far less effective Vandal and Byzantine regimes the region was invaded from the south by camel-riding Berbers. Similar raids appear to have been directed against agricultural centres to the south of the Sahara, although here the results were ultimately more positive in stimulating the development of local states and later providing protected entrepôts for trade between the Sudan and the desert.[9]

It is difficult to ascertain precisely when the disorder of late Roman and Byzantine North Africa receded enough to allow the initiation of regular trans-Saharan trade. One set of evidence from Byzantine coinage records and Arab accounts of gold seizures in the conquest period (including a c.734 expedition into 'the Sus [southern Morocco] and the "Sudan" '[10]) suggests that major commerce in the precious metal may have begun as early as the sixth century. However, it is only in the mid-eighth century, with the establishment north of the desert of Muslim communities fully adapted to the camel as an instrument of both war and trade, that a clear record of caravan traffic to the Western and Central Sudan can be traced.[11]

It was the camel, with its unique capacity for carrying heavy loads over lengthy, waterless tracts, which made trans-Saharan trade possible; at the same time the conditions of camel transport imposed major limitations on trade between the Sudanic zone and the north. These conditions help explain why the caravan system did not act as more of an engine of growth for the entire Islamic world economy but they also account for the relatively small developmental gap between its metropolitan centres and peripheral areas such as the Sudan.

By comparison with modern but also with alternative pre-industrial modes of transport, the camel caravan was a rather inefficient instrument (see Appendix, Table A1). It travelled slowly, only 30 to 45 km per day, and required attendants to load and unload the animals on a daily, and often twice daily, basis. Each beast could only carry 120 to 150 kg and because of the great length of time required to cross the desert – often over two months – much of the cargo consisted of provisions for the voyage itself. Even with well-organized caravan routes, the crossing was highly dangerous and many travellers perished in sandstorms or simply through delay or losing their way.[12]

From its first introduction to its replacement in the twentieth century by motor vehicles, the technology of camel transport in North Africa underwent only one major innovation: the introduction during Roman times of the North Arabian saddle, which added nothing to the efficiency of commercial operations but did allow camel nomads a fateful military advantage over any other groups who entered the desert.[13] The Sahara thus remained under the political control of its pastoral Berber and later Arabian inhabitants who could impose heavy protection costs upon merchant caravans. The consequence of this entire situation for urban Muslim caravan merchants was that they exercised little control over the transport system upon which their entire prosperity depended. This handicap not only limited the degree of such prosperity but also the very structures within which the trade was organized, a condition whose consequences will be examined below.

The geography of trans-Saharan trade was complicated at all times and shifted frequently during the medieval period following political, demographic, and ecological changes in the desert and its adjacent zones. It is thus not possible to give a definitive historical account here but rather only to indicate the general features of the routes with selected references to representative specific locales (see map).

The Mediterranean destinations of Sudanic goods did not necessarily determine the patterns of desert transport since it was often easier to bring goods to the sea by the quickest possible means and then use more efficient water transport to get them to their ultimate consumers. Gold, the most critical of the Sudanic exports, generally entered the desert at the west and often exited via North African ports, even passing into the hands of European merchants. But the major destination of all this metal in medieval times was Egypt, where it would arrive either by sea or traverse overland routes. Egypt would pass gold through the Red Sea to its final destination, the 'abyss' of India, as payment for the spices and silks sought by Mediterranean commerce. West African slaves, the second major trade item, followed a more direct route since most came from the Central Sudan and were sent to Tunisia or Libya and would either be deployed locally (as were Western Sudan slaves in Morocco) or shipped no farther east than Egypt. As will be seen, the demand for slaves in the countries bordering the Indian Ocean could be met more efficiently by exports from eastern Africa.

Caravans for crossing the Sahara were assembled at the towns founded by Muslims along the northern frontier of the desert: Sijilmasa near Morocco, Wargla in south-eastern Algeria, Ghadames in Tunisia and Zawila and Murzuk in the Libyan Fezzan. The itineraries led through various strategic points in the middle of the Sahara some of which, like Awdaghast and Tedmekka, were simply oases for provisioning caravans; others, like Teghaza and Tekedda, produced major commercial goods such as salt or copper. Smaller North African caravans might terminate here, exchanging their goods for products brought north from the Sudan.

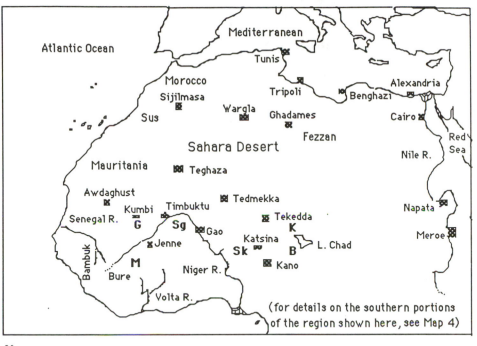

Key:
Centres of Sudanic Empires

B = Borno   **K** = Kanem   **Sg** = Songhai

G = Ghana   **M** = Mali   **Sk** = Sokoto

Map 2   *The Sudan–Saharan commercial frontier*

The populations of the desert centres thus carried on what was probably a pre-Islamic function of arbitrage between Saharan, Mediterranean and Sudanic commodities as well as engaging in strictly regional trade and even sending their own caravans to the Mediterranean.

The final destination of the major caravans and the southern terminus of the entire trans-Saharan system was the Sahel: the northern 'shore' of the Sudan. The cities of this zone – Kumbi in ancient Ghana, Timbuktu, Jenne and Gao on the Middle Niger, Katsina, Kano and other centres in Hausaland, Njima and Guzargamu in Kanem-Borno – were the ports and most often the political capitals of medieval Sudanic empires. However, for the most lucrative export items they served merely as entrepôts, gathering goods from regions beyond the reach of the camel and its masters.

For reasons to be discussed below, North African merchants did not regularly travel beyond the Sahel. We therefore have little literary evidence about the routes by which medieval Sudanic products entered the Saharan network. During the first centuries of the trans-Saharan trade its key commodity, gold, could definitely be procured in two areas not far from the centres of the Ghana and Mali empires: Bambuk between the upper Senegal and Faleme rivers and Bure in the north-west of the present-day Republic of Guinea. It is also likely that Lobi, in present-day Burkina Faso, was exploited at this date by merchants from the autonomous centre of Jenne on the middle Niger.[14] With increases in the demand for gold arising out of the growing commercial life of both the southern and northern Mediterranean in the fourteenth and fifteenth centuries, Jenne became the main centre of trade in gold, which was now brought over a greater distance from the richest ore-producing region of West Africa, the Asante (Ashanti) region of modern Ghana.[15]

The sources for slaves are even more elusive than those for gold since most were captured in a wide range of military activities. Because it was a process which disturbed the normal order of the region, we have documentation on raids for slaves into the Sudanic zone by Saharan groups allied with Mediterranean exporters. More commonly it was the Sudanic rulers themselves who supplied the slaves from among neighbouring, probably more southerly, populations. The Central Sudan controlled by Kanem-Borno seems to have sold more slaves than the Western Sudan according to both the impressionistic evidence of various visitors and the logic of its geographical situation. This region was closest to the major Arab lands and dense African populations, but far from the gold mines, without which slaves offered the only source of highly profitable exports.[16]

Other commodities are mentioned in various sources on the Saharan trade but none figures with any regular importance. Kola nuts from the West African forest zone apparently enjoyed some market in the Mediterranean but, as will be seen below, their main consumers were in the Sudan itself. Other West African 'spices', perfumes and resins are mentioned in various Arab texts but it is improbable that any were produced in sufficient quantities to play a significant role in long-distance trade. Finally it is surprising that wild animal products – particularly ivory – seem so insignificant in medieval trans-Saharan trade.[17] A key factor here may have been bulk, which made ivory too costly to ship out of West Africa by camel when Mediterranean and South Asian or East Asian markets could be supplied more cheaply from East Africa by sea.

If gold and slaves were the only major Sudanic exports in medieval trans-Saharan trade, both did at least reach the Mediterranean in significant quantities. The records of the trade itself do not provide us with any reliable statistics on either of these commodities. However modern estimates based on projections from more recent data suggest that at the high point of the medieval gold trade it was delivering well over a ton of the precious metal to the Mediterranean each year, while the trans-Saharan slave trade (including the desert routes of the Nilotic Sudan) took about six million Africans towards the Islamic world between 650 and 1600 (see Appendix, Tables A2, A3).

The gold figures do not appear impressive compared with twentieth-century production figures of hundreds of tons, and their limited scale helps explain why, even by the seventeenth century, Africa became eclipsed as a producer of bullion by the silver mines of the New World. However, West African gold was absolutely vital for the monetization of the medieval Mediterranean economy and the maintenance of its balance of payments with South Asia.[18]

The numbers of slaves exported are large, although again they represent only about half of those shipped by Europeans via the Atlantic in less than half the number of years. West African slaves were employed by Muslims mainly for domestic and military purposes rather than commodity production, although the operation of agriculture and mining within the Sahara and on its northern edge depended very heavily upon servile black labour.[19]

Routes and commodities: the era of European expansion

Within the Sudanic zone, the period from the ninth to the sixteenth centuries was both literally and figuratively a golden age. Not only did the export of gold dust make West Africa a critical adjunct to the world economy of the time, but this era also witnessed the flourishing of the first Sudanic empires: Ghana, Mali, and Songhai succeeded one another in the Western Sudan while Kanem and then Borno dominated the Central Sudan.

By the end of the sixteenth century, a number of crucial factors in this situation had shifted. European exploration of the Atlantic opened up routes to the coast of West Africa which challenged the commercial role of the Sahara and Sudan. The same process of oceanic expansion opened up the New World as a richer source of precious metals than West Africa and an unprecedented consumer of what had previously been very much the second-ranking African export: slaves.

Within the Sudan itself, these changes made themselves immediately felt in the 1590s when the Moroccan Sultan al-Mansur launched a trans-Saharan military campaign into the region of the Niger Bend. The Moroccan invasion failed in its major long-term goal of outflanking the Europeans by establishing direct control over Sudanic gold sources. Nonetheless, it succeeded in destroying the Songhai empire, leaving in its place a succession of smaller-scale, mutually competing, and internally unstable political authorities. Such disorder was obviously a hindrance to long-distance trade. It has also been blamed for the severe outbreaks of famine and disease reported in the Western Sudan during the seventeenth and eighteenth centuries.[20]

Until relatively recently, historians of Africa have been seduced by the neat pattern of these events into paying little attention to the post-1600 Sudanic economy. With the opening up of the Atlantic frontier, regions nearer the coast seem more dynamic and the Sudan comes back into focus only with the Islamic religious wars of the late eighteenth and nineteenth century, which seem to provide evidence of local awareness that the inland regions had declined.[21]

As will be seen below, there is now plentiful evidence that, in both external trade and – more significantly – the linkage of such exports and imports with internal commerce and production, the period after the opening of the Atlantic frontier was one of major growth for the Sudanic economy. However, the documentation of this trend cannot take the form of precise commercial statistics since we have so little direct data from the medieval era to compare with figures from later times. The estimates for the trans-Saharan gold and slave trade used above were based upon projections from European commerce in the Atlantic and North African records of the eighteenth and nineteenth centuries, which is the first period to give us anything like hard numbers for this region. The only indicators from outside of Africa which allow us to compare Sudanic economic activity in medieval and more modern times are accounts of general conditions affecting the volume of trans-Saharan trade.

The seventeenth and eighteenth centuries did constitute a period of demographic and economic stagnation and probably even decline for the Islamic Middle East.[22] However, the resulting negative effects on trans-Saharan trade would be more than compensated for by the increased presence in North Africa of European merchants who, even in the late medieval period, had constituted an important market for Sudanic goods. Moreover the vast acceleration of European overseas commerce which accompanied the nineteenth-century industrial revolution not only augmented this direct demand for desert-borne goods but also stimulated a revival of productivity in Mediterranean Islamic societies, which in turn sought more West African commodities.

The ability of the Sahara to compete with the Atlantic as an avenue of long-distance trade depended upon two conditions: the supply of commodities for such trade from the savanna rather than the forest; and a lower cost of communication with the Sudan across the desert rather than via the southern coasts. The first condition could be met because gold, which was not produced in the Sudan itself, was replaced in outward-bound caravans by a mixture of other goods. The second condition prevailed as long as transportation between the Sudan and the Atlantic relied upon donkeys, oxen, and human porterage, all even less efficient than the camel.[23] Only in the early twentieth century, with the advent of colonial railways, was it cheaper to reach the Sudan from the south or west rather than from the north.

West African gold had been a major objective of European Atlantic exploration and once entrepôts were established on the coast, most of this metal left the continent by the shorter route to the sea. Gold never disappeared entirely from the trans-Saharan trade and continued to be a standard of monetization in such Western Sudanic centres as Timbuktu. But the quantities reported as reaching nineteenth-century Morocco (which, because of its location must have accounted for at least half the North African import) are measured in tens of kilograms rather than the tons of the projected medieval (and documented Atlantic) trade.[24]

The trans-Saharan slave trade appears never to have diminished during this period and finally reached its highpoint in the nineteenth century. Between 1600 and 1800 demand may have fallen away in the shrinking cities and farmlands of Tunisia, Egypt and the Fertile Crescent but there was some compensation in both military and civilian sectors of Morocco in the Muslim far west and the Ottoman regions of the north-eastern Mediterranean. After 1800 all Islamic areas needed increased numbers of servile African immigrants for domestic service, military manpower, and agricultural labour, particularly when supplies from the competing Caucasus regions were cut off by Russian expansion. Despite the huge Atlantic demand, slave supply in Africa was never a problem, as the traders skimmed off the increase from what appears to have been a generally growing population, aided in the Sudan by the violence of secular and religious warfare. Somewhat over three million Africans (most via the Central and Eastern Sudan) entered the desert slave trade in these three hundred years, i.e. about half the quantity of the preceding near-millennium.[25]

Along with gold and slaves, accounts of the post-1600 Saharan trade give great prominence to Sudanic exports which appear to have been very marginal to the medieval commerce, such as leather goods, gum arabic, wax, ivory, and ostrich plumes. In part the visibility of these new items may be only an apparent change, resulting from the improved descriptions of commerce available in later periods, particularly the nineteenth century. However, the existence of such records itself reflects the enlarged role of Europeans in North African commerce and the consequently increased demand for the commodities in question, particularly the seemingly frivolous but very valuable ostrich plumes.[26]

Apart from the trans-Saharan trade, Sudanic commerce could, during the period of European presence on the Atlantic coast, profit from an increased flow of intra-African exchanges. The import of salt from the Sahara which, in medieval time, had probably come to depend upon the export of gold and slaves destined for the Mediterranean, now rested to a much greater extent upon the supply of goods consumed by the desert dwellers themselves. Farmers in the Sudan were, by at least the nineteenth century, producing export surpluses not only of traditional grain crops, but also onions and tobacco which entered the northern markets. Furthermore a number of the key manufactured goods used in the Sahara – leather bags and harness, cotton cloth and wooden sword handles – now came from Sudanic cities.[27] The West African forest societies which traded directly with Europe via the Atlantic appear at the same time to have enlarged their commercial ties to the Sudan. Despite oceanic competition, a market still existed in the south for Mediterranean commodities brought across the Sahara. A considerable portion of the slave population destined for the Atlantic also reached the coast through the hands of Sudanic traders. With its increased prosperity, the forest region also purchased a growing quantity of goods produced in the Sudan and Sahara: salts of various kinds, cattle products and Sudanic cloth. In return the forest supplied relatively few goods for trans-Saharan export but could pass through to Sudanic consumers a portion of their oceanic imports. These included a variety of manufactured items but most especially cowry shells, so vital to internal Sudanic marketing (see below) and so costly to ship across the Sahara. Moreover, at or near the very areas which had previously attracted Sudanic merchants seeking gold supplies – the western coasts south of the Senegal Valley and the Volta region – a substitute commodity was found in the kola nut, whose export to the Sudan appears to have increased after the medieval period and particularly in the nineteenth century.[28]

The changes in Saharan trade after 1600 are reflected in a shift – but the very opposite of an overall decline – in the pattern of Sudanic marketing centres. In geographical terms, the movement was in a southern and eastern direction, away from the concentration on Niger Bend gold trade and toward the Central Sudanic areas of more dense population and greater opportunities for combining trans-Saharan with regional and Atlantic trade.

Timbuktu and Jenne may therefore have suffered an absolute economic loss in the seventeenth and eighteenth centuries, although the very existence of local historians lamenting the troubles of the region in lengthy written chronicles attests to a level of luxury culture comparable to that of the medieval period.[29] Moreover the Niger Bend continued during this latter period to serve as the focus for all Sudanic trade with the western Maghreb. Even the absence of a stable imperial structure in the region was compensated for to some extent by the growing influence of the Kunta sheikhs, who combined the roles of religious and commercial leadership in a fashion which foreshadowed the new order which would emerge from the jihadist states further south.[30]

The most effective political consolidation of a growing market zone occurred in the Central Sudan rather than the Western Sudan. Here gold had never been the major item of trans-Saharan trade so that the dominant desert-side state of the region, the Borno empire, did not suffer any major losses from the European coastal presence. Borno was not, however, as well-positioned to profit from the positive advantages of coastward trade as the more southerly and densely populated Hausa region.[31]

The Hausa were relative latecomers to the Sudanic commercial systems, having been overshadowed throughout the later medieval period by both Borno to the north-east and Songhai to the west. By the eighteenth century, however, Hausa traders and urban handicraft manufacturers had established one of the most prosperous networks of exchange in all of West Africa. The major weakness in this system – its subjugation to the various costs of endemic warfare among the mutually independent Hausa city states – was finally overcome after 1805 when a relatively unified empire was established in Hausaland under the Fulani Muslim reformer, Usuman dan Fodio. Historians of the post-medieval-decline persuasion have often interpreted the Fulani jihad (along with a parallel set of religious wars in the eighteenth- and nineteenth-century Western Sudan) as a reaction against the general economic and religious decline of the region by particularly impoverished pastoralists. However, the evidence we now have of general Hausa development in the immediately preceding period as well as the emergence of reformist Muslim leadership from a wealthy – if socially alienated – Fulani sedentary elite suggests that this movement, like most successful political revolutions, represented less a reversal than a fulfilment of the prevailing economic processes.[32]

The prosperity of the Sudan during this last pre-colonial phase must also be attributed to favourable trends in climatic cycles. After repeated failures of rainfall in the seventeenth and early eighteenth centuries, few major droughts are recorded for the region from the mid 1700s until the eve of the First World War.[33] The latter date also coincides broadly with the extension of newly constructed colonial railways from the Atlantic coast into the Sudanic savannas, thus eliminating the last transport advantages of the desert routes to the Mediterranean. At the same time, imposition of European political rule in both West Africa and the Maghreb brought violent disruption of many local societies as well as a finally effective suppression of the trans-Saharan slave trade.

In the ensuing colonial economy the Sudanic regions became something of a backwater as opposed to adjacent coastal areas of West Africa. Yet, even under these unfavourable conditions Sudanic entrepreneurs demonstrated – as will be seen in a subsequent chapter – impressive capacities for expanding their economic operations, often on a far more autonomous basis than Africans closer to the new centres of overseas influence. To understand the resiliency of the Sudanic economy through all these changes we must now look closely at the internal structure of local markets and production systems.

The developmental impact: commercial organization

As on all the frontiers of African international trade, the relationship between the Mediterranean and Sudanic economies which met at the Sahara was initially very asymmetrical. Mediterranean merchants monopolized the caravan traffic between the two regions and the Sudan essentially supplied raw materials in return for Mediterranean manufactured goods. The structure of this linkage is embodied in the type of knowledge each society had of the other: Mediterranean Muslims wrote geographical works on the Sudan which contained information useful for carrying on trade but conveyed little but scorn for the indigenous culture of the 'Land of the Blacks'. The Sudanese who travelled north were pilgrims and students rather than merchants, and returned with increased appreciation for both religious and secular elements of Islamic urban life styles (and thus a taste for imports) but no systematic understanding of the 'metropolitan' economy.[34]

Yet, unlike similar relationships elsewhere in Africa, the development of the Saharan trading system over time resulted in a narrowing rather than a widening of the economic gap between its own poles. While the Mediterranean Islamic economy stagnated from the later medieval period onward, the Sudan witnessed the emergence of a vigorous indigenous merchant estate and an urban manufacturing sector which could compete with imported goods on a wide range of regional markets.

The critical reasons for this shift lie only partially in the model of development provided by the Mediterranean to the Sudan; indeed, such 'international demonstration effects' are analysed as the very basis for dependency and underdevelopment at other points on the map of African economic history.[35] Instead further explanations must be sought in the limitations placed upon Mediterranean penetration of the Sudan and the structures of local economic complementarity which preceded – and profited from – the growth of international trade.

This movement towards structural, if not quantitative, parity can be seen first in the relationship between Mediterranean and Sudanic merchant groups. The Muslim traders who came to the Sudanic zone from North Africa benefited from the most advanced system of commercial institutions available in the medieval world. Islam, in its Arabian origins, was essentially the creation of an urban merchant society. Its subsequent development as a cultural and legal system supported long-distance trade through such devices as the keeping of written accounts, the formation of business partnerships, and the formalization of banking and credit systems.[36] Although indigenous merchants of the Sudan also converted to Islam they did not assimilate the full model of Mediterranean merchant enterprise, in part because they lacked access to the necessary material and cultural resources but also because the model was of limited effectiveness.

If compared with European commercial organization on the Atlantic and even Muslims operating in the Indian Ocean, the caravan merchants of the Sahara do appear to have worked under severe handicaps: their firms were small and essentially restricted to family members; they did not survive over long periods of time; and they could not integrate effectively the wide range of operations linking the entire desert system. Much of the explanation offered by historians for this weakness is unrelated to West African trade: the fragile resource endowment of the Middle East and the emergence, in the Islamic heartlands, of militarist regimes hostile to merchant values.[37] However, a major contributing factor was the overdependence upon intractable overland caravan routes, of which the Sahara is a typical example. The general insecurity and inefficiency of desert transport made it virtually impossible to undertake the kinds of planning necessary to maintain large-scale enterprises.[38] Accounts we have of partnerships and letters of credit extended in the Sudan indicate linkages extending no farther away than the northern entrepôts of the Sahara itself such as Sijilmasa, Murzuk, or Ghadames. In medieval Tunisia or Egypt, the Sudan was considered too remote for merchants there to be held to the terms of contracts or given bank drafts.[39]

More specifically, the structure of the camel caravan offered an obstacle to Mediterranean control over trans-Saharan commerce. The major fixed capital asset of this system, the camel, as well as the territory through which trade passed, remained in the hands of desert Bedouin populations who guarded their own share of the profits and identified no more strongly with their northern than with their southern partners. Furthermore the technical inefficiency of the caravan system meant that large numbers of northern merchants and their entourages had to spend a considerable period of time in the Sudanic zone where they were dependent upon the local economy for their support.

The Sudanic merchants who operated from the desert-side entrepôts of West Africa functioned, in the first instance, as dependent feeders into the trans-Saharan trade. They supplied their Mediterranean partners with export goods (most significantly, gold) while distributing the less valuable imports (the most precious items tended to be consumed by the Sahelian urban elites) to the outlying markets.[40] All evidence indicates that the profit earned from these efforts by the Sudanic merchants was far below that realized by trans-Saharan traders and it was the latter who controlled the relationship by means of credit advances. Sudanese traders were needed as partners initially because camel transport could not be utilized far beyond the desert edge: the local substitutes – oxen, donkeys, and human porterage – were, however, even slower and more fragmented and thus unlikely to attract direct Mediterranean investment. There is some evidence, from both political relations at the entrepôts and the myths of gold producers so savage that they could only be dealt with through 'silent barter', which suggests deliberate attempts by Sudanese to block the penetration of their region by Mediterraneans. But it is not likely that incursions were ever a serious economic threat, even during the immediate aftermath of the Moroccan invasion.

The ultimate strength of the Sudanic merchants, however, came from their ability to organize elaborate networks of trade which did not depend directly upon trans-Saharan exchange. Although individual traders could not gain as much wealth and prestige from these transactions as did caravan merchants from the Mediterranean, their aggregate impact upon the economy of the Sudan was far greater. Quantitative research has indicated that by the late nineteenth century the net value of internal Sudanic commerce vastly exceeded that of exports across the Sahara.[41] The role of local trade in mobilizing and integrating regional resources was also, as will be indicated below, of critical consequence.

The immediate base for this autonomous exchange system was the complementarity of West Africa's major ecological zones: desert, savanna and forest. As already noted, exchange between these zones preceded the introduction of international trade. With the establishment of specialized traders moving over long distances in search of gold, however, the circulation of traditional foodstuff goods extended its range, and entirely new forms of production came into existence. By the time European traders arrived on the Atlantic coasts of West Africa, Sudanic merchants had already made their way overland to this frontier and were well prepared to exploit its new international dimensions.[42]

The role of merchants, as an occupational group spread throughout the Sudan and distinguished by its own Islamic ritual, fitted relatively easily into the pluralistic pattern of the region, which already separated artisan castes from the majority cultivator population.[43] At least one recently formed group of Western Sudanic merchants, the Korooko, trace their descent directly from a blacksmith caste.[44] More commonly, however, the Sudanic identity of indigenous Muslim merchants was based on multiple levels of ethnicity, beginning with their use of specific West African languages and receding into their consciousness of descent from various population groups strategically placed to enter the occupation of trade. By tracing out these identities, it is possible to reconstruct the spread of integrated market structures through the Sudan from west to east and north to south.

The two major groups of West African merchants are the Juula of the Western Sudan and the Hausa of the Central Sudan.[45] Both these terms refer to the languages spoken by the traders which, in each case, is that of the largest local savanna cultivator group, the Manding in the west and the Hausa farther east. The Juula emerged at a much earlier period and clearly began as gold traders; Hausa merchants emerged later in history and have always concentrated upon internal markets although also dealing in ivory and some slaves for trans-Saharan export.

The earliest Juula groups appear not to have been Manding but rather Soninke, the people of the ancient Ghana empire who moved south and east, first in search of gold and then as refugees from the political collapse and physical desiccation of their Mauritanian homeland. These groups took on their Manding linguistic identity (along with a probable Sonrai one) during the height of the medieval Mali and Songhai empires. The search for gold in the Volta basin, possible political-religious quarrels with Songhai rulers, as well as an interest in more direct routes eastward for purposes of Islamic pilgrimage, brought them into the Central Sudan during the fourteenth and fifteenth centuries where they founded the first Hausa-speaking merchant lineages. The Hausa network then began to grow on its own, recruiting not only Hausa cultivators but also groups from other culture areas with links to the immediate north: Kanuri salt and fish traders from Borno; and Tuareg-speaking cultivators who appear to have migrated from the savanna at a still earlier period to take up profitable positions in the Sahel under the domination of camel nomads.

While the common denominator of this entire system of trade was the Muslim adherence of its members, Islam did not provide a formal pattern for its internal organization.[46] The rules of Islamic law were useful in maintaining stable relations between Mediterranean and Sudanic traders at the Sahelian entrepôts as well as regulating affairs along the Juula and Hausa inland networks. The enforcement of these rules as well as other cultural concerns of metropolitan Muslims and Sudanic elites created a parallel diaspora of clerical specialists who did not always demand strict religious adherence on the part of the local lay Muslim community, to say nothing of the surrounding pagan majority. The major social function of Islam was to provide merchants with an identity which reinforced their occupational role. As Muslims, Sudanic merchants could relate more easily to one another. They also gained respect from other West African peoples as both political neutrals and the representatives of a cult which had material and spiritual connections to a universe larger than the parochial world of local villages, or even savanna empires.

The limitations of Islam in defining the Sudanic commercial system are revealed by the fact that most merchants, despite some training in Quranic liturgy, remained functionally illiterate. Only in the later eighteenth or early nineteenth century did the largest Hausa traders within the Sokoto Caliphate begin emulating their Mediterranean brethren by keeping business records in written form.[47] Specific arrangements for the distribution of goods thus ignored Islamic rules of partnership, credit and inheritance and depended almost entirely upon arrangements made within a modified version of the secular kinship idiom. A partial exception is the critical figure of the landlord/broker, established at various market centres to provide services and contacts between travelling merchants and local customers. This occupation was defined in Islamic legal terms and could function on a relatively impersonal basis (although the broker was often a kinsman of his client) but its major role in many areas was to mediate with the non-Muslim local authorities.

The traditional forms of Sudanic kinship did not, of course, provide a better model for commercial organization than Islamic commercial codes. However in the Sudan, as elsewhere in Africa, descent could be manipulated by recruiting junior partners into a trading organization as clients or even slaves. The most effective and trustworthy of such dependents might then be promoted to higher positions by receiving wives from the patron's own biological family or through payment of bride price. Arrangements like this could promote considerable flows of working capital and transmit the expertise and goodwill necessary to maintain a trading enterprise over a considerable period of time. In fact it is not so radically different from the metropolitan Islamic system as the differing idioms would suggest, since the latter also suffered from Quranic inheritance rules which dispersed business assets and merchants here also made frequent use of servile agents in key roles.[48]

The developmental impact: changes in production

The essential test for measuring the effect of trans-Saharan trade upon the West African economy consists of examining the linkage between an expanding system of markets and merchants and local systems of production. Certain aspects of the trade – its control by an ethnically/ritually distinct 'stranger' group and its emphasis on exports marginal to the local agricultural enterprise and imports of consumer/state luxuries – would suggest a substantivist model of 'peripheral markets' whose linkages and subsequent impact were minimal or even negative.[49] If the system did indeed contribute positively to local development, it is necessary to demonstrate that the movement of goods through the region stimulated productive processes by mobilizing a wide range of local factors, introducing commodities which could be incorporated into West African production, and allowing the assimilation by Sudanic entrepreneurs of some of the more intensive production systems of the Mediterranean metropoles.

Not only did the exports of the Sudan across the Sahara consist of raw materials, they also represented shrinking assets: gold, and the output of predatory enterprises; slaves and wild-animal products. Their impact was thus predominantly, although not purely, negative.

The most intensive of the processes involved here was gold mining which generally profited traders far more than it did producers. The information we have from relatively recent times concerning Bambuk and Bure, the gold zones in the Western Sudanic region, suggests that either medieval demand had exhausted the richest ore deposits or the industry was always one of relatively low intensity. Gold in this area is mined in relatively shallow open pits, usually under 3 m deep, although sometimes as deep as 18 m. The labour units are extended family groups, working for relatively small regular rewards (plus the rare chance of finding a large nugget) during the season of the year too dry to afford any opportunities for agricultural production. Bure, as a more attractive zone, has continued to attract a flow of seasonal immigrant miners who, along with trading settlements, created some market for local food producers. The mines in the Volta region developed later and continued, into the nineteenth century, to operate on a larger scale, stimulating some secondary economic activity. Shafts here, while still open at the top and untimbered, and thus dangerous, might go as deep as 30 m. While labour was organized by family heads around individual excavations, sometimes as many as forty men might be needed to bring ore to the surface. To maintain and provision this effort considerable additional labour, usually in the form of slaves, was required along with the services of blacksmiths specialized in producing mining tools.[50]

Less needs to be said, from a strictly economic viewpoint, about slave and wild-produce exports. Almost all the slaves we know about in the trans-Saharan trade were war captives from outside the exporting societies. Slave trading thus strengthened the military orientation of Sudanic society at an indirect cost to more productive activities and a direct but undeterminable demographic cost to the regions immediately victimized.[51] The gathering of ostrich feathers and gum arabic – the two best-documented wild-produce exports – was a more peaceful process than slave capture but was restricted to small groups of mainly Berber entrepreneurs and their retainers operating on the desert-edge fringes of the Senegambia and Central Sudan desert frontiers with little impact on the rest of the region.[52]

The commodities imported into West Africa were, for the most part, manufactured or processed goods designed for luxury consumption or military purposes, such as fine cloths, weapons, armour, and North African horses. 'Barbary steeds' were a particularly sought after commodity which could not be duplicated by the animal husbandry sectors of the Sudan because of climatic conditions and the absence of further export markets as inducements to undertake the necessary skilled efforts. The costly imported horses were thus used almost exclusively for display and warfare rather than ploughing or commercial transport.[53]

But the goods coming across the desert also included true raw materials such as copper and cowry shells: the former was used by artisans in the Sahelian cities as well as the creators of the famous bronze/brass castings of the Nigerian and Cameroonian forest.[54] Cowry currency played an important role in facilitating the market exchange – and therefore production – of food and other lesser commodities. One major indicator of the growth of the Sudanic economy during the post-1600 period is its ability to absorb a vastly increased local money supply. Cowries were now far more plentiful in West Africa because European shippers could import them at a greatly reduced cost from the Indian Ocean.[55]

Finally paper and books – another very prominent set of imports – were incorporated into the local process of Islamic learning, which may appear to belong among the items of imitative urban consumption but did assist the organization of commerce and, as will be seen, agricultural production.

The consumer tastes aroused by the trans-Saharan trade for even the most unproductive or destructive commodities could have a stimulating effect on the Sudanic economy if some opportunities arose for the replacement of these goods by local manufactures. The conditions of the Saharan frontier both encouraged such import substitution for an important range of Mediterranean goods and limited the scope of commodities which could be produced in the Sudan.

The positive incentive to local handicrafts came from the high cost of overland transport, whether across the Sahara or through the forests and savanna. Thus Sudanic artisanal products easily competed in price with foreign goods.

The major cities of the Sahel – Timbuktu in the medieval period and Kano during later times – consequently became centres for manufacturing as well as commerce. Cotton textiles were woven, dyed and manufactured into garments; leather was transformed into a wide variety of goods for household use and the equipment of horses and camels; sword blades, imported from the north, were fitted with wooden handles, scabbards, and other finishing elements. Even imported silk was incorporated into local cloth manufacturing.[56] The mosques and palaces of the cities throughout the region, originally designed by imported Mediterranean architects, were soon adapted by indigenous artisans to local conditions of climate and building materials, creating a distinctive and widespread Sudanic urban profile.[57]

Impressive as these industries were, they never transcended the systemic technological limitations of the inherited domestic economy. The main source of power
in all manufacturing activities remained human muscle, never transformed in any
regular and efficient fashion from linear to rotary motion. It must be remembered
that the Mediterranean Islamic world which served as a model for the Sudan also
carried on cloth-making and metallurgy without harnessing animal, water, or
wind power through the use of wheels and gears. However such energy transformations were employed in medieval northern Africa and the Middle East for
irrigating fields and processing grains and sugar.[58] The absence of this technology
in the Sudanic economy must thus be explained by a combination of chronological, ecological, cultural, and market factors.

By the time of the fullest Sudanic medieval development and contact with the
Middle East, Muslim technology was already in decline and far less a subject of
Arabic writing than in the early centuries of Islam.[59] Irrigated agriculture had, in
particular, been over-extended and is, under any circumstances, quite difficult to
adapt to West Africa, as subsequent colonial and post-colonial development projects (see Chapter 9) have amply demonstrated. The sugar culture of the Mediterranean was imported into the Sudan, but without any success, while the grinding
of grain remained restricted to the female sphere of individual households. The
demand for marketed food in Sudanic cities would probably not have justified
establishing central milling facilities, even had oxen or streams to power wheels
been more readily available.

Finally, whether or not Sudanic blacksmiths ever attempted to extend their
enterprises into regular steel production and larger-scale iron manufacturing, such
efforts faced two major obstacles. First, by the fifteenth century European metal-
lurgists had developed large, water-powered furnaces and forges which allowed
them to produce steel goods on a far cheaper basis than Muslims, even for the
trans-Saharan market. Second, the limited role of draught animals in the Sudan
and the fact that local horses were ridden unshod meant that a major market for
blacksmiths in both Europe and the Middle East – supplying horseshoes and their
nails, heavy harness, and ploughs – was absent in West Africa. The dependent,
yet very active, role of Sudanic metalworkers is perhaps best illustrated by the
major annual function of Kano blacksmiths in the nineteenth century: setting
thousands of imported sword blades into locally manufactured wood handles.[60]

In the rural sectors of the Sudanic economy, far more activity was linked to the
servicing of growing regional markets than to the supply of goods for trans-
Saharan trade. The most important of the commodities which entered these
regional circuits – salt and kola – do not incorporate a very complex production
process. Salt mining and panning probably changed very little from ancient times;
however its scale and the use of servile working forces must have increased
considerably to meet the growing demand, since salt was sold on all the markets
extending from the Sahara into the deepest forest belt. Kola, until the twentieth
century, appears to have been a 'protected' rather than cultivated crop although
again, its constantly enlarging market required new inputs of gathering and care-
ful preparation for transport.[61]

At a less prominent but more pervasive level, the pull of the long-distance
trading systems also brought about changes in the basic processes of livestock and
agricultural production. This change can be seen most easily in the introduction of
new crops which were cultivated often by merchant groups themselves for trading
purposes, particularly cotton, indigo, onions and tobacco.[62]

It is most difficult to trace the shifts in the allocation of land and labour factors for the production of either novel or long-established staple goods. While the majority of the Sudanic population remained rural and self-sustaining in food supplies, increasing surpluses did have to be provided for the more urbanized groups specializing in trade, handicrafts, and state affairs. There is no precise way of measuring either this change in output nor the degree to which rural people utilized commercial circuits for improving their own consumption of complementary agricultural goods or manufactured items. Agricultural land only became a negotiable commodity in the vicinity of the great commercial cities. Even here there was no open market in real estate but rather a system of redistribution by political rulers, who rewarded their major officials and supporters through the granting of estates in particularly valuable cultivation sites.[63]

During the nineteenth century there was a major proliferation of such landholdings throughout the Sudan, especially in the Sokoto Caliphate. They were owned by both state elites and merchants, often extended over very wide areas, and deployed a labour force consisting mainly of slaves, often numbering in the hundreds. Considerable debate has arisen among scholars as to whether the resulting agricultural organization should be properly labelled a 'plantation': that is, a form of cultivation clearly different from traditional household production and similar to the type of intensive rural labour exploitation embodied in the more familiar European slave estates of the New World.[64]

The most plantation-like characteristic of the large Sudanic farms was their assembling of large groups of slaves as a single work force under the supervision of the owner or his representative on demesne land (fields belonging directly to the master). Capital, land, and labour were thus combined on a new scale under a single owner who retained complete rights to the proceeds.

When their internal organization is examined more closely, however, even the most extensive and commercially oriented of the Sudanic estates bear more resemblance to traditional African farms than to the cotton and sugar plantations of the Americas. The coercive power which brought slaves together on the demesne undoubtedly increased the quantity of labour which was devoted to marketable commodities. But otherwise there is no evidence of economies of scale: that is, arrangements of the factors of production on a more efficient basis than could be achieved by smaller agricultural units. Although the presence of large numbers of workers on a single field under the supervision of an overseer theoretically allowed a different assignment of tasks to that in traditional farming systems, this opportunity does not seem to have been exploited. Instead, the large slave gangs were divided into smaller units of about twenty-five individuals, whose work routines replicated the customary division of labour between men, women, and children in family-based farms.[65] The larger group might work together during periods of more concentrated effort, such as harvest or planting times, but this also represented no innovation since such seasonal aggregation of labour – usually in the form of voluntary male youth groups – was normal for most African savanna cereal cultivation.

The Sudanic slave estate made no use of new technology in either cultivation or processing of harvested crops. Fields were worked by hand hoes and cotton (the product with the widest potential market) was spun into thread by slave women on distaffs (wooden spindle-whorl shafts). Indeed, it is often argued that in the absence of technological innovation from other sectors of the economy, agricultural slavery functioned as a disincentive to change, since it allowed the dominant classes of the Sudan to increase production without undertaking the risks entailed by new devices or novel work organization. The obstacles to animal-drawn plough cultivation in the West African grasslands have already been noted in Chapter 1 and the imposition of unfamiliar work routines upon slaves might have increased their propensity (already quite widespread in the nineteenth century) to run away and even join hostile forces in neighbouring states.[66]

Given these limited economic advantages to plantation agriculture as well as the social inhibitions upon coercion, there was a tendency for most captive farm labourers in the Sudan – even those who initially worked on demesne land – to be employed in village cultivation. Under the latter circumstances slaves devoted all or most of their time to family plots and were only required to turn over a specified portion of each year's production to their masters. Agricultural slavery could, for the individual who experienced it, eventually evolve into a status little different from the tributary obligations of nominally 'free' peasants. Village slaves in well-situated areas often sold enough crops and handicrafts on their own accounts to be considered relatively prosperous. In other cases slave-produced goods did not enter the market at all but were used instead to support the households and retinues of the masters, or even the slaves themselves, who would thus remain available for service outside agriculture, particularly in warfare.[67]

It is important to understand the distinctions between Sudanic servile agriculture and plantations outside Africa but such a comparison should not obscure the process of change which the slave estate represents within the Sudan. First of all, merely by relocating large numbers of farmers, no matter how their labour was organized, the slave system furthered market development. Secondly, the deployment of slaves in agriculture rather than (or in addition to) exporting them represents a recognition by Sudanic elites that investments in production were as important as exchange or political power. Finally, precisely because it did not, like its New World counterpart, represent a radically different form of production to that of the surrounding environment, the Sudanic plantation or slave village was not an enclave but rather a stimulus to the general growth of the regional economy.

A second type of rural labour concentration which appeared throughout the Sudan consisted of settlements established by Muslim clerics far from the major cities. For such groups (like the medieval European monasteries which they resemble) commercial agriculture was intended only as a means for supporting a commitment to scholarship and a strictly orthodox Islamic life style. The labour force combined slaves, who had been received as gifts or payment for clerical services, with free pupils, whose work was seen as a form of tuition payment and devotional exercise. But the economic outcome was the further intensification of rural production and the creation of new centres of wealth which could also be reinvested in local commerce.[68]

Conclusion: the Sudanic economy in African perspective

For all its limitations, the Sudanic contact economy represents something of an ideal African development pattern: continuous and pervasive regional growth with a minimum of dependence upon foreign partners for the provision of critical goods and services. By contrast, the commercial frontiers to be discussed in Chapters 3 and 4 were less effectively articulated with their hinterlands, and less autonomous in their relations with external trading partners. The greater exposure of such oceanic contact points to the technology of Asia and Europe suggests possibilities for economic transformation far more radical than those of the Sudan. But, as will be seen, few such potentialities were ever realized.

But this comparison does not allow us to use the Sudan as a standard against which to measure general African development. Given its own ecological vulnerability and the inevitability of fuller incorporation into an expanding European world system, the Sudan could not provide a viable historical alternative to the dilemmas of growth and dependency at other points in the continent's economic path. Nonetheless, the abstract notion of growth mobilizing a wide range of local material and social resources and maintaining a high degree of regional self-sufficiency can at least be kept in mind when contemplating the more problematic experiences which constitute the rest of African economic history.

Notes

1. E.g. Bovill (1968).
2. Oliver and Fage (1962) pp. 44–62 (on 'Sudanic civilization'). An excellent analysis of historical caravan geography is Devisse (1972).
3. Law (1967); Mauny (1970) pp. 60–131.
4. Swanson (1975); Milburn (1979).
5. Swanson (1975). For a critique of evidence concerning Phoenician voyages south of Morocco, see Mauny (1970), pp. 18ff., 210–21.
6. Devisse (1970); Munson (1980).
7. Lambert (1971); Herbert (1984), pp. 16–19; Williams (1969).
8. Bulliet (1975); Demougeot (1960).
9. Bulliet (1975) pp. 138–40; Munson (1980).
10. Ibn Abd-el-Hakam (1922). The strongest claim for a pre-Islamic gold trade is made by Garrard (1982) but see the critique in Kaegi (1984).
11. Lewicki (1962, 1964) provides the earliest solid evidence of such trade.
12. There are good accounts of Saharan trade conditions in Boahen (1962); Godhino (1969) pp. 99–124; Goitein (1967) p. 277f.
13. Bulliet (1975) p. 87f.
14. Curtin (1973) (on Bambuk); Balandier (1949); Rivière (1972) (on Bure); Arhin (1970) (on the Volta region); McIntosh (1981) (on Jenne) disputed by Hunwick (1981).
15. Posnansky (1971); Wilks (1971).
16. Austen (1979); Lovejoy (1983) pp. 25–6.
17. There is no mention of trans-Saharan ivory trade in Heyd (1879); Hopkins and Levtzion (1981) or Mauny (1961). Dyer (1979) makes an interesting argument for such a commerce but his evidence is unconvincing.
18. See calculations in Garrard (1980) p. 149f.; Godhino (1969) p. 202f. On the importance and destination of Sudanic gold, Day (1979); Richards (1983) pp. 3–26; Watson (1967).
19. Austen (1979); McDougall (1983).
20. Abitbol (1979) passim; Cissoko (1968); Tymowski (1974).
21. Boahen (1962) is a classic case of such an assumption within a serious economic account.
22. Bergeron et al. (1973); Cook (1970) passim; Udovitch (1981) passim.
23. Meniaud (1912) pp. 118–19; Ogunremi (1982) pp. 103–14.
24. Miège (1961) p. 361; Newbury (1966).
25. Austen (1979) and see Appendix, Table A2 on p. 275, below.
26. Johnson (1976); Lovejoy (forthcoming); Miège (1961) *passim*; Newbury (1966).

27. Lovejoy and Baier (1975); Johnson (1973).
28. Agiri (1972); Howard (1972); Lovejoy (1980).
29. Abitbol (1979); Saad (1983).
30. Batran (1971); Willis (1971) (both these sources somewhat exaggerate the, nonetheless important, role of the Kunta).
31. Adamu (1978); Lovejoy (1974).
32. Coquery-Vidrovitch (1985) p. 43; Johnston (1967) p. 29, For a contrasting view, see Azarya (1978) pp. 21–2.
33. Lovejoy and Baier (1975); a modified picture of this relatively favourable era is given in Watts (1983) p. 104.
34. Hopkins and Levtzion (1981) for Mediterranean Islamic views of the Sudan; Hunwick (1978); Zouber (1977) for the content of classical Islamic learning in the Sudan.
35. Felix (1974).
36. Goitein (1964); Labib (1969); Rodinson (1974); Udovitch (1970).
37. Ashtor (1976) p. 331f.; Issawi (1970).
38. Steensgaard (1974) pp. 42–59.
39. Goitein (1967) pp. 242–5; Levtzion (1968); Pérès (1937); Idris (1962) pp. 675–6.
40. Brenner (1971).
41. Farias (1974).
42. Lovejoy (forthcoming).
43. Teixeira da Mota (1972); Wilks (1962).
44. Amselle (1977).
45. Curtin (1984) pp. 38–59; Perinbam (1972) (on the Juula); Adamu (1978); Lovejoy (1980) (on the Hausa).
46. Cohen (1971).
47. Goody (1968); Lovejoy (1980) p. 102 (the periodization is still very unclear; see descriptions of caravan scribes in Lovejoy's main source, Mischlich (1942) pp. 92–4); Cohen (1971) reports that the level of functional literacy is still very low today among Hausa traders; however Curtin, private communication, insists that the Juula kept written commercial records well before the eighteenth century although the absence of surviving documentary evidence (explainable by lack of interest in preserving or copying such mundane texts under destructive climatic conditions) leaves this contention in doubt.
48. Baier (1980) pp. 175–88. On slaves/clients as the agents and heirs of commercial firms in the Mediterranean Islamic world, see Brunschvig (1960) p. 33; Raymond (1975) p. 295.
49. Malowist (1966); Perinbam (1972).
50. See note 14 above.
51. Lovejoy (1983) pp. 60–73; Panikkar (1963) p. 287 for a strongly negative argument; see Chapter 4, below, for further discussion of the impact of the slave trade on supply areas.
52. There seem to be no modern studies of ostrich feather production although we can grant considerable authority to the statement of the nineteenth century explorer, Gustav Nachtigal (1971, p. 373) that grazing or incubating the birds was far less common than hunting them; on gum-gathering, see Curtin (1975) pp. 215–18.
53. Harris (1982); Law (1980).
54. Herbert (1984) pp. 113–21.
55. Hogendorn and Gemery (1981); Johnson (1970); Lovejoy (1974).
56. There are no extensive economic histories of these cities but see useful indications in Lovejoy (1980) especially pp. 66, 72; Miner (1953); Monteil (1932).
57. Prussin (1973) p. 155f.
58. Ashtor (1981); Rabie (1981).
59. See note 58 and Watson (1983) p. 139f.
60. Law (1980) p. 104; Jagger (1978); see also, note 15 in Chapter 1, above.
61. Bernus and Bernus (1972); Lovejoy (1980) p. 14; McDougall (1983).

62. Hill (1968); Lewicki (1974) pp. 58–61.
63. Tymowski (1970); Hill (1976).
64. Lovejoy (1983) pp. 206–9 (see also references in Lovejoy's book to previous articles in which he has taken a much stronger position on the 'plantation' character of Sudanic slavery); for strong anti-plantation arguments, see Mason (1981); Olivier de Sardan (1975).
65. Hogendorn (1977).
66. Irwin (1981) p. 145; Lovejoy (1983) pp. 147–8, 275. On the general problem of weak police power over runaway slaves, see Austen (1986).
67. Klein and Lovejoy (1979).
68. Hunter (1977); Sanneh (1979); Stewart (1973) p. 109f.

Bibliography

Abitbol, Michel (1979), *Tombouctou et les Arma* (Paris: Maisonneuve)

Adamu, Mahdi (1978), *The Hausa Factor in West African History* (Zaria: Ahmadu Bello University Press)

Agiri, Babatunde Aremu (1972), 'Kola in Western Nigeria, 1850–1930' (Unpublished PhD dissertation, University of Wisconsin)

Ajayi, J.F.A. and Michael Crowder (eds) (1971), *History of West Africa*, Vol. 1 (London: Longman)

Amselle, Jean-Loup (1977), *Les négociants de la savanne: histoire et organisation sociale des Kooroko (Mali)* (Paris: Anthropos)

Arhin, Kwame (1970), 'Succession and gold mining at Manso-Nkwata', *Research Review* (Institute of African Studies, University of Ghana), vol. 6, no. 3, pp. 101–9

Ashtor, Eliyahu (1976), *A Social and Economic History of the Near East in the Middle Ages* (Berkeley: University of California Press)

Ashtor, Eliyahu (1981), 'Levantine sugar industry in the Late Middle Ages: a case of technological decline', in Udovitch (ed.), pp. 91–132

Austen, Ralph A. (1979), 'The trans-Saharan slave trade: a tentative census', in Gemery and Hogendorn (eds), pp. 23–76

Austen, Ralph A. (1986), 'Social bandits and other heroic criminals: a European concept and its application to Africa', in Donald Crummey (ed.), *Banditry, Rebellion and Social Protest in Africa* (London: Currey), pp. 89–108

Azarya, Victor (1978), *Aristocrats Facing Change: the Fulbe in Guinea, Nigeria, and Cameroon* (Chicago: University of Chicago Press)

Baier, Stephen (1980), *An Economic History of Central Niger* (Oxford: Clarendon Press)

Balandier, Georges (1949), 'L'or de la Guinée française', *Présence Africaine*, vol. 4, pp. 539–48

Batran, Abd-al-Aziz (1971), 'Abdallah Sidi al-Mukhtar al-Kunti and the recrudescence of Islam in the Western Sahara and the Middle Niger: ca. 1750–1811' (Unpublished PhD dissertation, University of Birmingham)

Bergeron, C. et al. (1973), *L'ankylose de l'économie méditerranéenne au XVIIIe siècle: le rôle de l'agriculture* (Nice: Centre de la Méditerranée Moderne et Contemporaine)

Bernus, Edmond et Suzanne Bernus (1972), *Du sel et des dattes: introduction à l'étude de la communauté d'Ingall et de Tegidda-u-tesemt* (Niamey: Etudes Nigériennes)

Boahen, Adu (1962), 'The caravan trade in the nineteenth century', *Journal of African History*, vol. 3, no. 3, pp. 349–59

Bovill, E.W. (1968), *The Golden Trade of the Moors* (London: Oxford University Press)

Brenner, Louis (1971), 'The North African trading community in the nineteenth century Central Sudan', in Norman R. Bennett and Daniel F. McCall (eds), *Aspects of West African Islam* (Boston: African Studies Centre, Boston University), pp. 137–50

Brunschvig, Robert (1960), 'Abd', in *The Encyclopedia of Islam*, new edition, Vol. 1 (Leiden: Brill), pp. 24–40

Bulliet, Richard (1975), *The Camel and the Wheel* (Cambridge: Harvard University Press)

Cissoko, Sèkéné-Mody (1968), 'Famines et épidémies à Toumbouctou et dans la boucle du Niger du XVIe au XVIIIe siècle', *Bulletin de l'Institut Fondamental d'Afrique Noire*, vol. 30, no. 3, pp. 806–21

Cohen, Abner (1971), 'Cultural strategies in the organization of trading diasporas', in Claude Meillassoux (ed.), *The Development of Indigenous Trade and Markets in West Africa* (London: Oxford University Press), pp. 266–81

Cook, M.A. (ed.) (1970), *Studies in the Economic History of the Middle East* (New York: Oxford University Press)

Coquery-Vidrovitch, Catherine (1985), *Afrique noire: permanences et ruptures* (Paris: Payot)

Curtin, Philip D. (1973), 'The lure of Bambuk gold', *Journal of African History*, vol. 14, no. 4, pp. 623–32

Curtin, Philip D. (1975), *Economic Change in Precolonial Africa: Senegambia in the Era of the Slave Trade* (Madison: University of Wisconsin Press)

Curtin, Philip D. (1984), *Cross-Cultural Trade in World History* (Cambridge: Cambridge University Press)

Day, John (1979), 'The great bullion famine of the fifteenth century', *Past and Present*, no. 79, pp. 3–54

Demougeot, Emilienne (1960), 'Le chameau et l'Afrique du Nord romaine', *Annales ESC*, vol. 15, pp. 209–47

Devisse, Jean (1970), 'La question d'Audagust', in Denis Robert, Serge Robert, and Jean Devisse (eds), *Tegdaoust*, Vol. 1 (Paris: Arts et Métiers Graphiques), pp. 109–56

Devisse, Jean (1972), 'Routes de commerce et échanges en Afrique occidentale en relation avec la Méditerranée: un essai sur le commerce africaine médiévale du XIe–XVIe siècles', *Revue d'Histoire Economique et Sociale*, vol. 50, pp. 42–73, 357–97

Dyer, Mark (1979), *Central Saharan Trade in the Early Islamic Centuries (7th–9th Centuries AD)* (Boston: Boston University Press)

Farias, P.F. de Moraes (1974), 'Silent trade: myth and historical evidence', *History in Africa*, vol. 7, pp. 9–24

Felix, David (1974), 'Technological dualism in late industrializers: on theory, history, and policy', *Journal of Economic History*, vol. 34, pp. 194–238

Garrard, Timothy F. (1980), *Akan Goldweights and the Gold Trade* (London: Longman)

Garrard, Timothy F. (1982), 'Myth and metrology: the early trans-Saharan gold trade', *Journal of African History*, vol. 23, no. 4, pp. 443–61

Gemery, Henry A. and Jan S. Hogendorn (eds) (1979), *The Uncommon Market: Essays in the Economic History of the Atlantic Slave Trade* (New York: Academic Press)

Godhino, Vitorino Maghalaes (1969), *L'économie de l'empire portugaise du XVe–XVIe siècles* (Paris: Mouton)

Goitein, S.D. (1964), 'Commenda and family partnerships in medieval Islam', *Islamic Studies*, vol. 3, pp. 315–37

Goitein, S.D. (1967), *A Mediterranean Society: Jewish Communities of the Arab World*, Vol. 1, *Economic Foundations* (Berkeley: University of California Press)

Goody, Jack (1968), 'Restricted literacy in northern Ghana', in Jack Goody (ed.), *Literacy in Traditional Societies* (Cambridge: Cambridge University Press), pp. 198–264

Harris, Rosemary (1982), 'Review article: the horse in West African history', *Africa*, vol. 52, no. 1, pp. 81–5

Herbert, Eugenia (1984), *Red Gold of Africa: Copper in Precolonial History and Culture* (Madison: University of Wisconsin Press)

Heyd, Wilhelm (1879), *Geschichte des Levanthandels im Mittelalter* (Stuttgart: J.G. Cotto)

Hill, Polly (1968), 'Notes on the history of the northern Katsina tobacco trade', *Journal of the Historical Society of Nigeria*, vol. 4, no. 3, pp. 477–81

Hill, Polly (1976), 'From slavery to freedom: the case of farm slavery in Hausaland',

Comparative Studies in Society and History, vol. 18, pp. 395–426

Hogendorn, Jan S. (1977), 'The economics of slave use on two "plantations" in the Zaria emirate of the Sokoto Caliphate', *International Journal of African Historical Studies*, vol. 10, no. 3, pp. 369–83

Hogendorn, Jan S. and Henry A. Gemery (1981), 'Abolition and its impact on monies imported to West Africa', in David Eltis and James Walvin (eds), *The Abolition of the Atlantic Slave Trade* (Madison: University of Wisconsin Press), pp. 99–116

Hopkins, J.F.P. and Nehemiah Levtzion (1981), *Corpus of Early Islamic Sources for West African History* (Cambridge: Cambridge University Press)

Howard, Allen Marvin (1972), 'Big men, traders, and chiefs: power, commerce and spatial change in the Sierra-Leone–Guinée Plain, 1865–1895' (Unpublished PhD dissertation, University of Wisconsin)

Hunter, Thomas Charles (1977), 'The development of an Islamic tradition of learning among the Jahanke of West Africa' (Unpublished PhD dissertation, University of Chicago)

Hunwick, John O. (1978), 'A sixteenth century African scholar: Muhammad Baghoyogho' (Unpublished ms.)

Hunwick, John (1981), Private communication

Ibn Abd-el-Hakam (1922), *The History of the Conquest of Egypt, North Africa, and Spain* (New Haven: Yale University Press)

Idris, Hady Roger (1962), *La Berbérie orientale sous les Zirides: 10e–12e siècles* (Paris: Maisonneuve)

Irwin, Paul (1981), *Liptako Speaks: History from Oral Tradition* (Princeton: Princeton University Press)

Issawi, Charles (1970), 'The decline of Middle Eastern trade, 1100–1850', in D.S. Richards (ed.), *Islam and the Trade of Asia* (Oxford: Cassirer), pp. 245–66

Jagger, Philip John (1978), 'The blacksmiths of Kano City: a study in tradition, innovation, and entrepreneurship' (Unpublished MPhil dissertation, University of London)

Johnson, Douglas L. (1973), *Jabal al-Akhdar, Cyrenaica: An Historical Geography of Settlement and Livelihood* (Chicago: University of Chicago Geography Department)

Johnson, Marion (1970), 'The cowry currencies of West Africa', *Journal of African History*, vol. 11, no. 1, pp. 17–50, vol. 11, no. 2, pp. 331–50

Johnson, Marion (1976), 'Calico caravans: the Tripoli–Kano trade after 1880', *Journal of African History*, vol. 17, no. 1, pp. 95–117

Johnston, H.A.S. (1967), *The Fulani Empire of Sokoto* (London: Oxford University Press)

Kaegi Jr, Walter Emil (1984), 'Byzantium and early trans-Saharan gold trade: a cautionary note', *Graeco-Arabica*, vol. 3, pp. 95–100

Klein, Martin and Paul E. Lovejoy (1979), 'Slavery in West Africa', in Gemery and Hogendorn (eds), pp. 181–212

Labib, Subhi Y. (1969), 'Capitalism in medieval Islam', *Journal of Economic History*, vol. 29, no. 1, pp. 79–96

Lambert, Nicole (1971), 'Les industries sur cuivre dans l'ouest saharien', *West African Journal of Archaeology*, vol. 1, pp. 9–21

Law, R.C.C. (1967), 'The Garamantes and trans-Saharan enterprise in classical times', *Journal of African History*, vol. 8, no. 2, pp. 181–200

Law, Robin C. (1980), *The Horse in African History* (London: Oxford University Press)

Levtzion, Nehemiah (1968), 'Ibn Hawqal, the cheque, and Awdaghost', *Journal of African History*, vol. 9, no. 3, pp. 213–33

Lewicki, Tadeusz (1962), 'L'état nord-africaine de Tahert et ses relations avec le Soudan occidentale à la fin du VIIIe siècle et au IXe siècle', *Cahiers d'Etudes Africaines*, vol. 2, pp. 513–35

Lewicki, Tadeusz (1964), 'Traits d'histoire du commerce trans-saharien: marchands et missionaires ibadites en Soudan occidentale et centrale au cours des VIIIe–XIIe siècles', *Ethnographia Polska*, vol. 8, pp. 291–311

Lewicki, Tadeusz (1974), *West African Food in the Middle Ages According to Arabic*

Sources (Cambridge: Cambridge University Press)

Lovejoy, Paul E. (1974), 'Interregional monetary flows in the precolonial trade of Nigeria', *Journal of African History*, vol. 15, no. 4, pp. 563–86

Lovejoy, Paul E. (1980), *Caravans of Kola: the Hausa Kola Trade, 1700–1900* (Zaria: Ahmadu Bello University Press)

Lovejoy, Paul E. (1983), *Transformations in Slavery: A History of Slavery in Africa* (Cambridge: Cambridge University Press)

Lovejoy, Paul E. (forthcoming), 'The trans-Saharan trade and the salt trade of the Central Sudan: a comparison of nineteenth century patterns', in Habib El-Hesnawi (ed.), *A History of the Trans-Saharan Trade Routes* (Tripoli)

Lovejoy, Paul and Stephen Baier (1975), 'The desert-side economy of the Central Sudan', *International Journal of African Historical Studies*, vol. 8, no. 4, pp. 551–81

McDougall, E. Ann (1983), 'The Sahara reconsidered: pastoralism, politics and salt from the eighth through the twelfth centuries', *African Economic History*, vol. 12, pp. 263–86

McIntosh, Susan Keech (1981), 'A reconsideration of Wangara/Palolus, island of gold', *Journal of African History*, vol. 22, no. 2, pp. 145–58

Malowist, Marian (1966), 'The social and economic stability of the Western Sudan in the Middle Ages', *Past and Present*, No. 37, pp. 3–15

Mason, Michael (1981), 'Production, penetration and political formation: the Bida state, 1857–1901', in Donald Crummey and Charles Stewart (eds), *Modes of Production in Africa: The Precolonial Era* (Beverly Hills: Sage), pp. 204–26

Mauny, Raymond (1961), *Tableau géographique de l'ouest africaine au moyen âge* (Dakar: IFAN)

Mauny, Raymond (1970), *Les siècles obscurs de l'Afrique noire, histoire et archéologie* (Paris: Fayard)

Meniaud, Jacques (1912), *Haut-Sénégal-Niger (Soudan Français): géographie économique* (Paris: Larose)

Miège, Jean Louis (1961), *Le Maroc et l'Europe, 1830–1894* (Paris: PUF)

Milburn, Mark (1979), 'On Libyan and Saharan chariots and "Garamantes" ', *Maghrib Review*, vol. 4, pp. 45–8

Miner, Horace (1953), *The Primitive City of Timbuctoo* (Princeton: Princeton University Press)

Mischlich, Adam (1942), *Über die Kulturen in Mittel-Sudan* (Berlin: Reimer)

Monteil, Charles (1932), *Une cité soudanaise: Djenne* (Paris: Anthropos)

Munson, Patrick J. (1980), 'Archaeology and the prehistoric origins of the Ghana empire', *Journal of African History*, vol. 21, no. 4, pp. 457–66

Nachtigal, Gustav (1971), *Sahara and Sudan*, Vol. 4, *Wadai and Darfur* (Berkeley: University of California Press)

Newbury, C.W. (1966), 'North African and Western Sudan trade in the nineteenth century: a re-evaluation', *Journal of African History*, vol. 7, no. 2, pp. 233–46

Ogunremi, Gabriel Ogundeji (1982), *Counting the Camels: The Economics of Transportation in Precolonial Nigeria* (New York: Nok)

Oliver, Roland and J.D. Fage (1962), *A Short History of Africa* (Harmondsworth: Penguin)

Olivier de Sardan, P. (1975), 'Captifs ruraux et esclaves impérieux du Songhai', in Claude Meillassoux (ed.), *L'esclavage en Afrique précoloniale* (Paris: Maspero), pp. 99–134

Panikkar, H. Madhu (1963), *The Serpent and the Crescent: A History of the Negro Empires of Western Africa* (New York: Asia Publishing House)

Pérès, Henri (1937), 'Relation entre le Tafilalet et le Soudan à travers le Sahara, du XIIe au XIVe siècle', in *Mélanges de géographie et d'orientalisme offerts à E.-F. Gautier* (Tours: Arrault), pp. 409–14

Perinbam, B. Marie (1972), 'Trade and society in the Western Sahara and the Western Sudan: an overview (since 1000 AD)', *Bulletin de l'Institut Fondamental de l'Afrique Noire*, vol. 34, pp. 778–801

Posnansky, Merrick (1971), 'Ghana and the origins of West African trade', *Africa Quarterly*, vol. 11, no. 2, pp. 111–14

Prussin, Labelle (1973), 'The architecture of Djenne: African synthesis and transformation' (Unpublished PhD dissertation, Yale University)

Rabie, Hassanein (1981), 'Some technical aspects of agriculture in Medieval Egypt', in Udovitch (ed.), pp. 59–90

Raymond, André (1975), *Artisans et commerçants au Caire* (Cairo: Institut Français)

Richards, J.F. (ed.) (1983), *Precious Metals in the Late Medieval and Early Modern World* (Durham: Carolina Academic Press)

Rivière, Claude (1972), 'L'or fabuleux du Bouré', *L'Afrique Littéraire et Artistique*, vol. 5, pp. 41–5

Rodinson, Maxime (1974), *Islam and Capitalism* (New York: Pantheon)

Saad, Elias N. (1983), *Social History of Timbuktu: The Role of Muslim Scholars and Notables, 1400–1900* (Cambridge: Cambridge University Press)

Sanneh, Lamin O. (1979), *The Jahanke: History of an Islamic Clerical People of the Senegambia* (London: Oxford University Press)

Steensgaard, Niels (1974), *The Asian Trade Revolution of the Seventeenth Century: the East India Companies and the Decline of Caravan Trade* (Chicago: University of Chicago Press)

Stewart, Charles C. (1973), *Islam and Social Order in Mauritania* (Oxford: Clarendon Press)

Swanson, John T. (1975), 'The myth of the trans-Saharan trade during the Roman era', *International Journal of African Historical Studies*, vol. 8, no. 4, pp. 582–600

Teixeira da Mota, A. (1972), 'Mande trade in the Costa da Mina according to Portuguese documents until the mid-sixteenth century' (Unpublished paper delivered to Conference on Manding Studies, London)

Tymowski, Michel (1970), 'Les domaines des princes du Songhai (Soudan occidentale)', *Annales ESC*, vol. 25, pp. 1637–58

Tymowski, Michel (1974), *Le développement et la régression chez les peuples de la boucle du Niger a l'époque précoloniale* (Warsaw: University of Warsaw)

Udovitch, Abraham L. (1970), *Partnership and Profit in Medieval Islam* (Princeton: Princeton University Press)

Udovitch, Abraham L. (ed.) (1981), *The Islamic Middle East, 700–1900: Studies in Economic and Social History* (Princeton: Darwin Press)

Watson, Andrew M. (1967), 'Back to gold – and silver', *Economic History Review*, vol. 20, pp. 1–34

Watson, Andrew M. (1983), *Agricultural Innovation in the Early Islamic World: the Diffusion of Crops and Farming Techniques, 700–1100* (Cambridge: Cambridge University Press)

Watts, Michael (1983), *Silent Violence: Food, Famine, and Peasantry in Northern Nigeria* (Berkeley: University of California Press)

Wilks, Ivor (1962), 'A medieval trade route from the Niger to the Gulf of Guinea', *Journal of African History*, vol. 3, no. 3, pp. 337–41

Wilks, Ivor (1971), 'The Mossi and Akan states, 1500–1800', in Ajayi and Crowder (eds), pp. 344–86

Williams, D. (1969), 'African iron and the classical world', in L.A. Thompson and J. Ferguson (eds), *Africa in Classical Antiquity* (Ibadan: Ibadan University Press), pp. 62–80

Willis, John Ralph (1971), 'The Western Sudan from the Moroccan invasion (1591) to the death of al-Mukhtar al-Kunti (1811)', in Ajayi and Crowder (eds), pp. 441–83

Zouber, Mahmoud A. (1977), *Ahmad Baba du Tombouctou (1556–1627): sa vie et son oeuvre* (Paris: Maisonneuve)

3

Commercial Frontiers
and Contact Economies: II
East Africa and the Indian Ocean

The eastern coast of the continent, with its opening to the active commercial currents of the Indian Ocean, provided pre-modern Africa with its earliest link to the international economy. Like the Sahara, the Indian Ocean joined sub-Saharan Africa to a system of trade and production dominated, at its medieval highpoint, by Muslims and characterized by forms and levels of economic organization closely related to those of the contemporary Mediterranean. The patterns of commodity exchange across the two frontiers were also broadly similar. However the impact of cosmopolitan trade upon East African development turned out to be very different from the parallel zones of the Western and Central Sudan.

The key to these differences must be sought first in the internal articulation of the two regions; second in the market consequences of external linkage by sea rather than land routes; and third, in direct contact with Europeans, which intensified, rather than displaced the Muslim-Asian economic presence.

The conditions of development

As already noted in Chapter 1, all of the factors making for regional market exchange were present in pre-contact East Africa, although in quantitatively and structurally less favourable terms than in West Africa. The movement from foraging to domesticated food production in the former area depended upon the migration of peoples and techniques from other parts of the continent. However, the spread of Cushitic pastoralists and Bantu cultivators into East Africa was extremely uneven, leaving large areas still under the control of thin hunter-gatherer populations up to relatively recent times.[1]

It is not only the aggregate low density which distinguishes the East African demographic situation from that of contemporary West Africa, but also the pattern of population distribution. Along the latitudes between the northern and southern boundaries of the Great Lakes, the largest demographic concentrations were found in the interior. Between these areas and the East African coast lay a thinly inhabited zone, the *nyika* or wilderness. Again, along the coast of the entire region settlement was more dense. Only in the extreme south, around the Zambezi Valley, were the coast and interior joined by continuous belts of heavy population. Both the coastal Swahili peoples and the Zambezi Valley Shona are Bantu-speaking and probably did not arrive in their present areas until contacts with the Indian Ocean trading system had already been established.[2]

Even a longer period of pre-contact settlement would probably not have produced a very wide-ranging system of long-distance trade within the region because

56

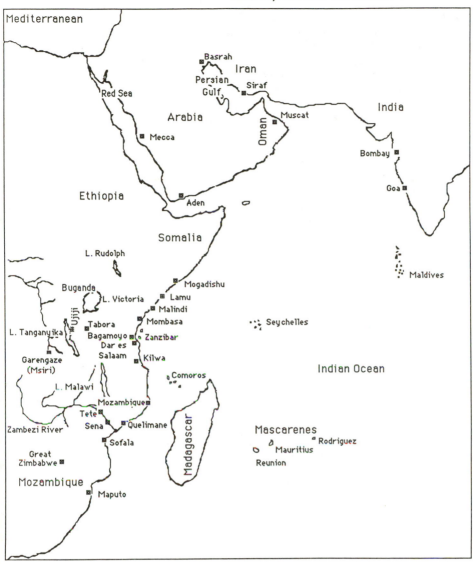

Map 3   *The Indian Ocean commercial frontier*

of the distribution of its complementary resources. Unlike in West Africa, cattle here are spread throughout cultivating areas. Only in certain pockets – rather than a continuous belt – of Tanzania, Kenya and other regions still further north can one find predominantly pastoral peoples and even these, for the most part, practise some agriculture.[3] Trading relations, as well as violent confrontations, did take place from early times between East African agriculturalists and pastoralists, acccounting for some of the impressive centralized states of the interlacustrine zone. But these are particularly far from the coast as well as any other frontier offering possibilities for more extensive commerce, so that they were only 'discovered' by the outside world in the nineteenth century.

As in West Africa, salt and copper deposits formed the basis for indigenous long-distance trade routes at fairly early periods; but these resources are also located in the interior zones of already dense population, thus providing no incentive for penetration of the *nyika* to the east and very little linkage with coastal trade until the nineteenth century.[4]

The instrument by which East Africa retained ties to international markets was the Indian Ocean sailing vessel, generally – if somewhat inaccurately – referred to in Western literature as the dhow.[5] Compared with the process of technological innovation undergone by European sailing vessels the dhow may appear as something of a seagoing camel, i.e. a mode of transport subject to little change and relatively low fixed capital inputs. The feature that fundamentally defines such craft – a lateen sail allowing for limited adjustments against prevailing winds on open oceans – has been retained since its first introduction in ancient times. Up to 1500, moreover, the hulls of dhows were sewn rather than nailed together, thus limiting their size and durability.

However, even with no technological innovations, waterborne traffic in this pre-mechanized era enjoyed immense efficiency advantages over carriage by land. A dhow could cross the Indian Ocean in about one-third the time required by a Sahara camel caravan to travel the same distance; one such boat carried a load equivalent to one-thousand camel loads; only one dhow crew member was needed for several cargo tons versus two or more men to each ton in the desert trade (see Appendix, Table A1). Moreover, as will be seen in more detail below, dhow navigation did undergo some technological innovation during both the medieval period and the later era of European entry into the Indian Ocean. The fixed and human capital of such a transport system could also be tied far more directly into the urban world of the Indian Ocean merchant than was ever the case with desert caravan traffic.

Entrepôts and exports: the pre-European period, AD 150–1500

The key factor shaping the East African commercial frontier was thus a coastal region more isolated from its hinterland and more integrated into an international system than were the Sahelian 'ports' of West Africa. Nonetheless, the ocean did not provide infinite possibilities for external contact. Dhow trade tended to follow limited patterns based upon the juxtaposition of populated areas around the Indian Ocean perimeter and the direction and rhythm of the annual monsoon winds. Thus the earliest overseas contacts with East Africa were from the Red Sea by ancient voyagers who never strayed far from the sight of the African and West Arabian coastlines.[6] Later exploitation of the south-east–north-west monsoon pattern allowed ships to come from as far away as the Indian shores of the Persian Gulf. Evidence also exists of Indonesian and Chinese navigation to East Africa; but all economically significant contacts with these areas passed through India to the entrepôts of the Persian Gulf.[7]

There was no one location in ancient or medieval East Africa situated so as to remain for long the focal point of overseas trade. The internal geography of the region favoured the coast south of the Zambezi Valley, where contact with the interior was most feasible and, because of local gold deposits, most profitable. However the path of the monsoons influenced shippers from the Persian Gulf to favour the northern ports. In response to this incongruity an entire string of towns developed, mainly on offshore islands stretching from the southern Somali coast to Sofala in Mozambique. Each of these ports exported products from its own hinterland and also (except for Sofala) functioned to some degree as an entrepôt for goods (particularly gold) originating farther to the south.[8]

Given the greater efficiency of sea transport, the commodities involved in this trade cover a wider range of exports and are far less restricted to 'luxuries' than was the case in the Sahara. The product indicated as of greatest value from the earliest (*c.* second century AD) Egyptian accounts of East African trade is ivory, which retained its paramount position right up to the end of the nineteenth century.

Slaves are constantly mentioned in medieval sources on East African trade but inferences concerning orders of magnitude are even harder to come by than for Sudanic West Africa. Demand for East African slaves varied with the shifting needs of Persian Gulf agriculture and pearl fishing and the servile military forces of Arabia, Iraq and India. By projecting the relatively precise slave trade figures of the nineteenth century upon the known supply-and-demand factors of the earlier centuries we can estimate a total slave trade from 650 to 1500 of about 5 million. But at least half of these slaves came from the countries bordering the Red Sea, leaving only 2 million to 2.5 million as the approximate number taken from the Swahili coast over an 850-year period (see Appendix, Table A2).

A more consistent mainstay of the dhow trade was mangrove tree poles which provided a basic material of house construction – even dictating its dimensions – throughout the southern Persian Gulf. Also iron – a commodity whose local scarcity helps account for the persistence of sewn-boat construction – was sent northward from East Africa.[9]

Gold, the great staple of the trans-Saharan trade, could be found in East Africa only south of the Zambezi. Estimates of productive capacities in this area suggest that at the high point of the trade – between the twelfth and fifteenth centuries – as much as one and a half tons were exported annually (see Appendix, Table A3). However output had already gone into irreversible decline immediately before the Portuguese arrival.[10]

Like the larger and steadier supply of West African gold, this bullion eventually found its way to India. On the way, however, it had to pass through several coastal ports, first Sofala in Mozambique, then Kilwa in southern Tanzania, and finally northern towns like Mombasa and Malindi in Kenya. At the peak of East African gold production Kilwa enjoyed a period of near monopoly over its export and thus achieved impressive internal development which will be discussed below. But by the fifteenth century Indian merchants began to trade with the coast in larger vessels whose seasonal voyaging patterns would not allow them to venture south of Kenya. Mombasa and Malindi thus began to compete with Kilwa and one another for shares in the gold traffic.[11]

Entrepôts and exports:
the era of Portuguese and Omani control, 1500–1885

The political independence which the East African coastal towns had enjoyed during the first period of their integration into the world economy was also a factor in collective economic weakness. With the temporary exception of Kilwa, no centre within the region had been able to concentrate foreign commerce in such a way as to provide the basis for more intensive local development. It was only with the forceful establishment of external commercial powers on the coast – the Portuguese from Europe and the Omanis from South-east Arabia – that a few entrepôts established stable domination over the others. From this point on the interior could become more effectively linked with the coast and major shifts began to take place in the production of commodities for the market.

The Portuguese were the first and most ambitious in bringing about such changes but, largely for this reason, they achieved relatively little. The Omanis reacted to, and borrowed from, European initiatives but ultimately adapted these to East African and Indian Ocean conditions on a basis which allowed a greater degree of local development.

Behind these economic shifts in East Africa lay a larger struggle for control of the maritime trade routes of the Indian Ocean, South-east Asia, and East Asia. Although the Swahili coast was never a primary goal of Portuguese overseas expansion, Vasco da Gama, in his epoch-making voyage of 1498, was able to make use of the rivalry among local cities to obtain, at Malindi, a navigator for the crossing to India. In the system later established by the Portuguese for the Indian Ocean, Goa in India was to be the administrative centre, Mozambique on the extreme southern African coast would be a major provision station and Mombasa, controlled by the monumental Fort Jesus, provided a means of dominating the northern Swahili coast.[12]

Portuguese attempts to police and tax – but by no means restrict – the trade of East Africa led to numerous local rebellions. However, in contrast to India, South-east Asia, and East Asia, no rival European powers attempted to displace Portugal here. Instead, this role was left to the Persian Gulf Arab state of Oman.

During the pre-Portuguese period Oman, like Siraf on the Persian side of the Gulf, had sent merchant vessels to East Africa without seeking any political control over the area. In response to a period of Portuguese control over their home base, however, the Omanis adapted the construction and armament of their shipping to European styles and then undertook to counter-attack against the Portuguese at Mombasa.[13]

Fort Jesus at Mombasa fell to the Omanis in 1698 and representatives with small garrisons were soon sent to other coastal towns as far south as Kilwa. The Portuguese remained in control of the Mozambique coast and even threatened the shaky Omani position to the north several times during the early eighteenth century. However the Omanis finally established their own East African capital on the island of Zanzibar and became a firm fixture on this part of the coast. Further economic development would thus centre upon the two poles of external hegemony.

The Portuguese approach to exploiting Mozambique consisted of bold and heavy-handed state initiatives which generally backfired. The most spectacular of these undertakings was an expedition sent in 1569 to conquer the Shona state of Mutapa, which was erroneously thought to control the entire local production of gold. The venture proved to be very costly in military terms and gained the Portuguese only the limited economic benefit of rights to participate directly in rather small-scale interior markets. With the rise, in the late seventeenth century, of a more dynamic and protectionist successor state to Mutapa, the Rozvi kingdom of Changamire, even this privilege was curtailed.[14]

Along the Zambezi itself the Portuguese took over the trading post established slightly inland at Sena by their Muslim predecessors and then expanded still further west to found major entrepôts at Tete and Zumbo. The entire expanse of the lower Zambezi Valley was claimed as crown land and distributed in the form of *prazo* estates to various Portuguese subjects with the hope of promoting more stable and intensive production of agricultural and mineral goods. The legal form of the *prazo* belied its social and economic realities: many of the estate holders were simply confirmed in the possession of lands which they had already taken; often the *prazo* founders and more frequently their descendants were Indians or Afro-Europeans rather than Portuguese immigrants and they governed their domains much like African chiefs, making considerable use of servile military retainers known as *chikunda*.

The *prazos* failed completely to establish any form of commercial agriculture and used their female slaves to mine gold in the established local fashion with only modest results. The *prazos* ultimately shifted from the role of producing trade goods to that of gathering commodities from the surrounding areas. During the late eighteenth century, when first French and then Brazilian demand for slaves began to make itself felt in East Africa, the *prazos* proved well adapted to supplying this commodity but in the process became even less amenable to control from the coast.[15]

On the coast itself the island of Mozambique, and Quelimane, a port immediately in the Zambezi delta, gradually replaced Sofala as the main outlets for the produce of their mutual hinterland. This trade no longer passed north, either through the East African towns or the Persian Gulf, but went directly to India. Portuguese commerce profited from this system only indirectly, since the East African gold and ivory never reached Europe but was used in India to purchase spices and other Asian goods. However the Portuguese crown still felt compelled to ensure – through taxes and restrictive licensing – that a substantial share of the direct profits from Mozambique trade went to the state and to Portuguese citizens. The result of this effort was constant conflict between Portuguese authorities and the Indian merchants who dominated Mozambique trade.

Up until the mid-eighteenth century this system continued to work reasonably well for the Portuguese since they were able to maintain some control over the export of gold, which remained at the level to which it had declined just before their arrival: somewhat under a half ton per annum. However, during the later 1700s, annual gold output (for reasons to be discussed below) dropped to a little over 100 pounds. Ivory and slaves now dominated the overseas trade of Mozambique, and these were drawn mainly from regions north of the Zambezi.[16] The stage was thus set for the rise of Zanzibar as an alternative and more effective entrepôt for the general East African hinterland.

The Omani establishment in Zanzibar enjoyed two advantages over Mozambique: its location and the more relaxed policy of its rulers towards foreign traders. While the impact of the Portuguese incursion in the Indian Ocean had impelled the Omanis to adopt European methods of ship construction, the administrative apparatus of their government – both in Arabia and as later developed in East

Africa – did not allow for elaborate control over merchants. Moreover the trading interests of the Omanis complemented, rather than competed with, those of other groups arriving on the coast. The Omanis brought mainly Persian Gulf goods (particularly dates) to East Africa and sought in return mainly slaves. Indian traders specialized in the exchange of textile goods for ivory. The first Europeans to enter the local market on a regular basis after the Portuguese were the French who, in the late eighteenth century, sought slaves at Mozambique and Kilwa for their Indian Ocean sugar islands of Bourbon and Ile-de-France (now Réunion and Mauritius). The supply was more than sufficient for them and the Omanis who had not yet undertaken major East African plantations of their own.[17]

In the nineteenth century Britain, as an extension of its Indian empire, established an informal political hegemony over both the Persian Gulf and the East African coast. The commercial consequences included persistent, although only partially effective, interference with slave traffic, but otherwise simply a formalization of the prevailing free-trade system. Britain, France, Germany, and the United States all signed 'most favoured nation' treaties with the Omani government at Zanzibar and proceeded to import ever-increasing quantities of manufactured goods in exchange for ivory, resins, cloves, and other 'legitimate' products. The dhow trade with other Indian Ocean regions also flourished, including half a million slaves exported during the nineteenth century. Indians in East Africa, while no longer able to import South Asian cottons, still exported goods (especially ivory and cloves) to their homeland and played a major role as agents and financiers of international commerce.[18]

By the early nineteenth century the Omanis of Zanzibar had become an East African rather than an Arabian power when one branch of the ruling Busaidi dynasty made Zanzibar its permanent residence. Establishment of control over the other coastal towns did require force but the burden, once accepted, was relatively light: a small garrison, a 5 per cent ad valorem export duty (administered by Indian customs 'farmers'), and the willingness to let goods designated for major foreign shippers pass through the port of Zanzibar.

Zanzibari commercial penetration of the East African interior was almost entirely a matter of spontaneous private entrepreneurship, based on a combination of more concentrated capital resources on the coast and new initiatives by expanding inland populations. On the more northern part of the coast from Mombasa in Kenya to Mogadishu in Somalia, Zanzibar influence was, until well after the mid-nineteenth century, felt only superficially and the overall extension of trade routes remained limited. This was the area in which physical obstacles to inland movement had always offered major obstacles to commerce. Moreover the modest but still significant patterns of trade established here since ancient times suffered a major setback between the sixteenth and eighteenth centuries because of the disorders created by pastoral Oromo (Galla) invaders, whose influence extended from Somalia to the north of Mombasa. By the late eighteenth century, however, the Oromo were receiving small trading caravans from the Somali and Kenya coasts and even organizing their own trading ventures across short zones of the interior. Behind Mombasa, the Kamba peoples had also become linked to coastal trading networks and in their turn were penetrating inland as far as Mount Kenya and the foothills of Mount Kilimanjaro. However, after the 1850s all of these routes would be placed in the shadow of Zanzibari caravans emanating from the northern Tanzania coast.[19]

In southern Tanzania a far more flourishing trade was able to arise without

direct Zanzibari organization. From the late eighteenth century Kilwa (now significantly shifting its main site from an island to the mainland) enjoyed a major
commercial revival. As E.A. Alpers has amply documented the key explanation
for this development must be sought in the motivations of Yao inland traders who
transferred their entrepôt for ivory and slaves from Mozambique during the later
eighteenth century, largely in response to better opportunities for French and
Omani-Indian commerce. The overland routes from Kilwa led into the densely
populated regions around Lake Malawi (or Nyasa as it was then known) and
provided the bulk of the slaves sold on the East African coast. During the nineteenth century these amounted to well over one million, although somewhat more
than half were retained locally for use on coastal plantations.[20]

The most dramatic change in inland–coastal relations took place on the 'central'
route linking the 'Mrima' mainland just opposite Zanzibar with the rich territories
near and beyond Lake Tanganyika and Lake Victoria. Population growth and
commercial initiative among the Nyamwezi peoples of west-central Tanzania
made the development of this linkage possible. However coastal merchants soon
became its main exploiters and by the mid-nineteenth century had established
major urban settlements at Tabora in the Nyamwezi homeland, and Ujiji on Lake
Tanganyika. From this artery coastal commercial centres spread north-west to
Uganda, westward to Zaire, and south-west into Zambia and Malawi. A second
movement inland on a more northern axis led representatives of the Zanzibari
system to the Mount Kilimanjaro area and from there into central Kenya, the
eastern shores of Lake Victoria and finally as far as Lake Rudolf on the present-day
Kenya–Ethiopia border.[21]

The Mrima ports of Bagamoyo, Pangani and Tanga emerged from obscurity
during the 1800s to serve as major entrepôts for Zanzibari long-distance caravans.
However, like towns and islands on other parts of the coast, including Zanzibar
itself, these centres also exported a considerable quantity of goods produced by
local agricultural enterprise. The nineteenth century thus witnessed a vast expansion and acceleration of trade which affected not only the traditional international
staples such as ivory (still the leading single export), slaves (now at their peak) and
timber but also commodities circulating within the interior, such as foodstuffs,
iron (and iron implements), copper and salt and adding to these a whole new range
of major export goods: cloves, cowries, gum copal, copra and cereals (to name
only the most important).[22] The development implications of such a shift are more
radical than contemporary changes on the Saharan frontier of West Africa but
they also remain more difficult to analyse in anything approaching a conclusive
manner.

The developmental impact: commercial organization

Because the East African coast was so accessible from the sea and cut off (until the
nineteenth century) from its hinterland, commerce in the region could much more
easily than in Sudanic West Africa come under the control of foreign merchants.
Nonetheless one cannot, as some dependency theorists have argued, simply cate-
gorize the economic process resulting from this relationship as proto-imperialist
underdevelopment.[23] The structure of trade in the region and the resulting changes
in production were complex and include varying elements of growth and decline,
dependency and autonomy.

Although the Indian Ocean commercial system was, in most respects, considerably more efficient than the trans-Saharan caravan trade it was based initially on the same Islamic mercantile institutions. The study of how these institutions affected East Africa is complicated, however, by the fact that the region was only of very secondary importance in the Indian Ocean trade as a whole and that the entire commercial system experienced significant changes with the arrival of European ships in the sixteenth century.

The general material available to us on medieval Muslim and Indian commercial history indicates that the trading firms associated with Indian Ocean trade were more efficient and stable than those organizing caravans across the Sahara.[24] The most obvious reasons for this distinction are the already noted advantages in speed, capacity and manpower enjoyed by water over land transport. Dhow carriage could also be incorporated into the structure of urban mercantile enterprise in a way which was not possible for camel caravans. Merchants thus invested part of their capital in the permanent ownership of ships. Even when goods were assigned to vessels belonging to other merchants (often for purposes of spreading the still very high risk of loss) or *nakhodas* (captains) who specialized in operating dhows, the individuals involved still belonged to the same urban society and could thus more effectively organize their common interests than could traders dealing with desert camel nomads. Even the pilots of Indian Ocean ships, although usually separate from either *nakhodas* or merchants, were also men of the city and often highly literate, a quality which allowed cumulative improvements in what must be regarded as a formal science of navigation.[25]

At the beginning of the medieval period the indigenous populations of the East African coast had none of the capacities required for active participation in this maritime culture. Indeed, the urban centres which did appear during this period all traced their founding elites back to the regions of Arabia and the Persian Gulf and thus literally present the appearance of colonies.

Culturally, biologically and politically, however, the 'Swahili' society of the East African coast is not a simple extension of the Middle Eastern world but an amalgam of foreign and indigenous elements. The Swahili language, which became not only the lingua franca but also the mother tongue for most of these merchant groups, is purely Bantu in structure with an enormous input of Arabic vocabulary. Physically, the majority of the populations are of African descent, the more so, of course, as their alleged alien origin (the Persian Gulf for the earliest 'Shirazis') is placed in the distant past.[26] The Portuguese and Omani Arabs who entered the area later also proceeded to assimilate into the local population and culture but always retained, at least at their ruling levels, closer political and social ties to their respective metropoles. The most alien group of all merchants were the various Muslim and Hindu groups of Indians (native Christians from Portuguese Goa appear to have assimilated more fully to at least Mozambique African society); but even these communities might have become more indigenized had they not been caught up in the status-racial categories of modern European colonialism relatively early in the nineteenth century as an extension of the British regime in India itself.[27]

However 'foreign' the coastal merchants groups of East Africa may or may not have been, their role as economic colonialists must initially be defined in terms of competition for domination of trade: trade between the region and the outside world and between the coast and the interior. It was virtually impossible for any East African merchants to achieve control over long-distance shipping on the Indian Ocean and adjoining seas. The concentration of capital, skills and even raw materials (i.e. teakwood) required to build, maintain and operate large vessels was located in the Persian Gulf and could not be replicated in such a peripheral region as East Africa. Sayid Sa'id, the first Omani ruler to settle permanently in Zanzibar did, in fact, maintain a fleet of large ships which he sent as far afield as Europe and the United States but, despite an effort to develop a local shipbuilding industry, the entire undertaking ultimately remained dependent upon the boatyards of India. Swahili craftmen regularly constructed their own dhows, but these seldom exceeded twenty-five tons and were used almost entirely for shipping along the coast.[28]

Political competition for control of, or at least access to, the East African coast appears to have been intensive among the various Swahili towns before 1500, with little serious intervention from outside. Portuguese intervention after 1500 was certainly colonialist in intent but did not succeed in any of its major goals regarding the control of trade. The Omani centralization of the main coastal trade upon Zanzibar also required extensive coercion through warfare, intrigue, and some appeal for British assistance. However, the economic system which eventually grew out of this 'empire' soon cut off all political ties to Oman and provided sufficiently broad benefits to the coastal area so that it could be maintained with a minimum of continuous repression.[29]

Competition between alien and indigenous merchant groups appears most meaningful in discussing the organization of inland, as opposed to oceanic, commerce in East Africa. Both the Portuguese and the Omanis broke most sensationally with previous trade patterns by establishing themselves at points in the interior far beyond the previous coastal frontier. Portuguese colonization of the Zambezi Valley, however, affected only limited shifts in the direction of Mozambique trade, especially when it is remembered that some Arab-Swahili groups had made direct contact with the Shona gold-producing societies even before 1500.

The Zanzibar-based network, on the other hand, reached almost every point of commercial interest in the East and East-Central African interior, including some which had been specifically denied the Portuguese such as the copper-producing Kazembe state of Katanga (Shaba) in present-day Zaire.[30] In despatching their caravans over these extensive routes the Omanis had to compete with a number of mainland peoples who had previously controlled the carriage of goods to and from the coast: most notably the Kamba, behind Mombasa in the north, the Nyamwezi along the central Tanzanian axis and the Yao behind Kilwa.

The weapons used by the coastal traders in this effort represent a mixture of economic, political and military devices. On the coast, customs duties charged at differential rates discriminated against inland traders. In the interior, Arab-Swahili caravans generally offered a better array of import goods than their competitors since they alone received extensive credit from Indian financiers.

These advantages proved sufficient to reduce the Kamba and Nyamwezi to a secondary position in the organization of caravans to the coast. But the Yao, with a much longer history of coastal trade, retained control of the routes between Kilwa and Lake Malawi despite competition and assault from the Bisa and Ngoni peoples of the interior and the emergence of Zanzibar trading settlements linking the lake with northern trading routes.[31]

The Zanzibari traders established in the East African interior, even at their points of greatest strength, represented less an imposition of the Indian Ocean commercial system upon indigenous society than an accommodation between the two. It is significant that Indian merchants – clearly the most wealthy and sophisticated business men on the coast with the best connections to overseas centres of capital – did not generally accompany the caravans inland. Their exclusion may have been partly a result of deliberate protectionism on the part of Arab-Swahili merchants, as well as a function of Indian disinclination to live outside the bounds of close communal ties.[32] However the economic conditions of trade in the interior did not favour such a specialized group. Commercial organization in these regions could not be separated from political organization and the latter required considerable adaptation to local society.

At those points in the interior where indigenous states were particularly strong, as among the interlacustrine Bantu (especially Buganda), the Nyamwezi, and the Shambaa, rulers demanded a share of profits and often exclusive access to the sources of trade goods.[33] Where states were weak or non-existent, as in the area west and south of the Nyamwezi, coastal traders such as the famous Tippu Tip could intervene or take over power themselves. Their main political instruments here were servile or freebooting military forces, known as *ruga-ruga* and very similar to the *chikunda* of the Portuguese *prazo* estates on the Zambezi.[34] However the Zanzibaris had no monopoly on this kind of politics, as indicated by the cases of Mirambo, a Nyamwezi warlord who successfully fought off Arab-Swahili assaults on his position in the critical trading area west and north of Tabora, and Msiri, a Nyamwezi (actually of related Sumbwa origin) trader who overthrew the local Kazembe rulers to form his own state in the copper-rich region of Katanga (Shaba).[35]

The fact that ultimate economic control over East African export trade remained in the hands of coastal Indian creditors and oceanic merchant-shippers provides a major qualification to the notion of interior commercial autonomy. However the awareness of such financial dependence combined with a physically and politically separate sphere of operation generated an effort by inland traders to exploit local means of capitalization. Arab-Swahili caravan merchants did not, therefore, return speedily to the coast but often spent years in the interior amassing large export stocks at a minimal cost in borrowed import goods. Political force, which depended only to a limited extent upon imported firearms, can be seen as one major method of self-financing. Another low-cost method of covering maintenance costs and also generating export commodities was participation in internal market systems for the exchange of foodstuffs, salt, local cloth, copper, iron and iron goods.[36]

In summary the organization of East African commerce up to the late nineteenth century displayed a number of weaknesses compared to that of the contemporary Sudanic zone of West Africa. The gap between alien and indigenous firms was greater: the latter, whether semi-alien Arab-Swahili or purely local peoples, depended upon outside credit and operated in a relatively unspecialized manner, combining political and commercial functions. However, the contrasts should not be exaggerated, especially in anticipation of comparisons with the far more abrupt commercial frontier of the Atlantic. For East Africa, the chain of intermediaries between the industrial centres of Europe, the merchant-artisan capitalists of the Indian Ocean metropoles, the Arab-Swahili society of the coast and caravan routes, and the indigenous participants in long-distance trade is more clearly hierarchical than in the Sudan; but the presence of so many links in the chain allowed considerable mutual adaptation at each point of contact. The result was both the integration of a very wide region into a single market and the maintenance of a certain degree of autonomy by those agencies further down the hierarchy. The problems of dependency and even dynamic underdevelopment in the pre-colonial East African economy are more acute in the sectors of production than in those of exchange.

The developmental impact: production

Contemplation of the relationship between the export trade of East Africa and domestic productive capacities has moved even historians not identified with dependency perspectives to view the pre-colonial economic history of the region as 'progress towards an inevitable dead end'.[37] Such a pessimistic analysis is suggested by three factors: the demographic impact of large-scale slave trading and the diseases spread by nineteenth-century caravan contacts; the generally violent nature of both slave and ivory procurement; and the increasing specialization of the region in unprocessed raw material exports at the expense of indigenous manufacturing capacities. As these issues are examined in turn it will be suggested that the Indian Ocean frontier was, indeed, more threatening to internal East African development than was the Sahara for the Sudan, but in terms which provided at least some counterbalancing stimulus to continuous regional growth.

POPULATION CHANGES AND TRADE

The demographic questions have to be dealt with first, because they are so essential. They do not belong directly to the realm of economic history and, given the limited available evidence, remain a matter of controversy even among those who have examined population issues most closely.[38] In certain respects the expansion of external contacts increased the capacity of the East African ecology to support larger populations. First of all, new staple food crops such as rice, maize, manioc, and peanuts (groundnuts) were diffused throughout the interior by coastal merchants. Secondly, the regional distribution of food and food-related commodities (especially iron hoes) was facilitated by the movement of caravans carrying long-distance goods and the introduction of new forms of currency, such as beads and cowry shells, for purchases of food, salt and other domestic products.

The export of slaves from East Africa (excluding Ethiopia and the Nilotic Sudan) remained consistently at a lower level than the traffic across the Sahara or the Atlantic, although it did accelerate greatly during the nineteenth century (see Appendix, Table A2). Even during this latter peak period, the areas seriously affected remained limited to a zone bounded on the coast by Kilwa and Quelimane and extending inland just beyond Lake Malawi. The parts of this area nearest the coast did show signs of depopulation by the mid-nineteenth century but the major supply source, the Chewa-speaking 'Nyasa' peoples west of Lake Malawi, remained thick on the ground right up to the twentieth century, when they continued to export labour to surrounding and more distant centres of economic activity.[39] Moreover it must be kept in mind that a large proportion of the slaves forcibly taken from the interior were not removed from East Africa but rather relocated at various points on the coast. The impact of this population redistribution can thus be understood only by examining (as will be done below) the process rather than the level of enslavement and the linkage of coastal slave labour to the regional economy.

The population of all of East Africa – including present-day Kenya, Malawi, Tanzania, Uganda, Zambia and Zimbabwe – clearly suffered a drastic decline from the late 1880s to the end of the 1920s. The difficult question to answer concerning this demographic disaster is whether it represents a continuation of

trends set in motion by the nineteenth-century caravan trade or was a new phenomenon peculiar to the ensuing colonial situation.

Caravan traffic did influence the disease ecology of the region, most obviously
by introducing in a rather abrupt manner virulent ailments from the outside
world. Deaths from smallpox and cholera are reported along the entire caravan
system throughout the nineteenth century. Accelerated commercial activity also
linked pockets of diseases previously endemic in restricted areas, such as sleeping
sickness and tick-borne relapsing fever, thus infecting populations which had no
natural immunities or social practices to shield them from these illnesses.
Unfortunately the available evidence is too impressionistic to allow any precise
measurement of either the absolute numbers of people affected by epidemics or the
demographic impact relative to previous rates of population change.[40]

For the end of the nineteenth century we have better records of what may be
entirely new factors: jiggers brought in via the west coast of Equatorial Africa and
destroying the limbs of initially unprepared East Africans; rinderpest devastating
cattle herds throughout the eastern and southern portions of the continent; and
finally sleeping sickness and respiratory fever spreading on an entirely unprecedented scale. The arrival of the jigger and rinderpest epidemics and the imposition of European rule were purely coincidental. The effect the rinderpest epidemic
had in limiting the areas devoted to grazing also helps explain the spread of
sleeping sickness, which is carried by tse-tse flies who need the shelter of undisturbed 'bush'. However, colonial demands upon African populations for labour
(particularly porterage services), for cash crops at the expense of food, and for
resettlement in easily controlled villages account for much of the increased stress
and disease among East Africans. At the same time this region became the site of
pioneering research and public health efforts by British and German tropical
medicine experts.[41]

Demography is therefore an important element in the process of economic
change experienced by East Africa through its incorporation into the Indian Ocean
market but whether external contacts increased or decreased the local population,
thus either aiding or hampering more growth, is simply not clear from presently
available historical data. But the issues raised by inquiries into demography must
be kept in mind when considering the more visible linkages between production
and international trade.

PREDATION AND GATHERING
In the early stages of its development, the overseas trade of East Africa involved a
similar range of products to that of the Sudanic zone of West Africa, with gold and
ivory predominant and slaves in a position of much less prominence. However by
the nineteenth century ivory and slaves came to dominate the export production of
the region as indicated in the proportions of various goods listed for the Mozambique port of Quelimane in Table 3.1. The figures for Zanzibar in Table 3:2
suggest a greater role for agricultural goods but it must be remembered that these
came mainly from the coast (which will be discussed separately below). For the
interior served by Zanzibar, ivory and slaves had become the overwhelmingly
most important commodities exported.

Given the kinds of goods it sent abroad, East Africa in the nineteenth century is
often referred to as a classical example of a *Raubwirtschaft*, a robber or predatory
economy dependent on forcible appropriation of non-renewable assets. The
regions which supplied these goods received little in return and often suffered
serious damage.

Table 3.1 *The changing distribution of Mozambique (Quelimane) exports*[1]

Commodities	1806 Quantity	1806 Percentage of total value	1821 Quantity	1821 Percentage of total value
Gold	0.04 tons	9	0.02 tons	2.9
Ivory	65.6 tons	48	23.1 tons	4.2
Slaves	1 484	18	5 040	85.6
Wheat	92.1 tons	5	4.8 tons	2.4
Rice	211.8 tons	10	25.4 tons	1.5
Other		9		3.4

[1]Adapted from Isaacman (1972) p. 88.

Table 3.2 *Zanzibar exports, 1859–84*

Commodities	1859[1] Quantity	1859[1] Percentage of total value	1883–4[2] Quantity	1883–4[2] Percentage of total value
Ivory	488 660 lbs	40	500 000 lbs	38
Cloves	4 860 100 lbs	15	1 050 000 lbs	26
Cowries	8 016 000 lbs	14		
Copal	875 875 lbs	10	196 850 lbs	5
Coconut[3]	4 452 000 lbs	5	'important'	4–5(?)
Hides	95 000 lbs	7	122 749 lbs	5
Sesame	8 388 360 lbs	6		
Rubber			750 000 lbs	19
Slaves	7 300	1	'at an end'	
Other		1		2–3(?)

[1]Adapted from Austen (1977b); Nicholls (1971) p. 370.
[2]Adapted from Bennett (1973) pp. 119–22.
[3]Includes all coconut products.

The demographic aspects of the slave trade have already been discussed. Ivory hunting at points receding ever more deeply west and north-west from the coast had no such immediate impact upon the indigenous economy. A relatively small group of specialists – largely Nyamwezi – undertook the work of killing the elephants and transporting their tusks back to the points of export. The indirect effects of this activity, however, were very similar to slave trading. In order to coerce local populations to supply them with ivory, particularly west of Lake Tanganyika, and to assure the control of trade routes, ivory traders as well as allied inland rulers engaged in constant violence.[42] The atmosphere in much of the region resembled a process of armed invasion; indeed, in explaining much of the local violence, it is difficult to distinguish between the effects of slave and ivory trading and the actual in-migration of militarized Zulu-related Ngoni peoples out of Southern Africa and gun-bearing displaced peasants moving southward from the northern Nilotic Sudan.[43]

For the populations living in the path of these predatory trades, survival required a shift towards closer, more easily defensible patterns of village settlement. The need to produce food in these restricted areas explains some of the readiness to adopt new crops such as maize and rice and to integrate animal husbandry more closely with crop cultivation. However for many regions the shift involved an abandonment of lands previously devoted to shifting agriculture and cattle-grazing, a practice which appears to have anticipated the rinderpest epidemic as a cause for the spread of tse-tse flies and thus sleeping sickness.[44]

The rise and decline of goldmining in East Africa also represents the export of a wasting natural resource, but here the problem, at least initially, centres less on demography and violence than on technology. Gold seams occur in scattered sites on the plateau of present-day north-eastern Zimbabwe and western Mozambique. They are most concentrated in quartz reefs which were effectively identified by early Shona miners and excavated at considerable depth and length with iron tools adapted from agriculture and warfare. The techniques were similar to those used for the construction of the granite buildings of Great Zimbabwe and, as will be seen below, the rise of this urban centre is closely associated with the high point of gold exports between the twelfth and fifteenth centuries.

Even in this relatively prosperous phase, however, exploitation of reefs was limited by the inability of miners to control flooding and the time-consuming and wasteful methods of separating gold from earth and crushed quartz. By the mid-fifteenth century the richest reefs had been worked to the limits of this technology and East African gold production concentrated more on alluvial deposits. These were tapped by the panning of streams or shallow excavations, mainly carried on by women. Scholars relying on archaeological evidence have assumed that this technological shift led to a major decline in gold output.[45] However, Portuguese trade records suggest that production levels up to the late eighteenth century remained only about half a ton below the previous peak[46] (see Appendix, Table A3). The decline in efficiency at individual sites was apparently counterbalanced by the active presence of the Portuguese, both as merchants on the eastern plateau and as organizers of alluvial mining expeditions into new areas north of the Zambezi. The sharp drop in gold exports from Mozambique at the end of the eighteenth century is partially explained by a continuing depletion of accessible mineral resources but the most decisive factor was undoubtedly the diversion of human capital, in its various forms, to the suddenly expanding slave trade. The immediate rewards of predatory enterprise now overtook the laborious gathering of inanimate products.

Copper mining played a less important role in the East African export economy than did gold since there was little external demand for this metal until late in the nineteenth century. At this time Msiri, the Sumbwa-Nyamwezi trader who had installed himself in Katanga, attempted to accelerate the processing and transport of copper for foreign markets but the crudeness of his methods as well as the costs which would have faced any non-mechanized enterprise of this kind doomed his effort to failure.[47]

Nearer to the coast, the gathering of wild export goods remained so closely under the control of foreign merchants as to have virtually no impact at all on the local economy. Mangrove poles, a major item in the trade from East Africa to Arabia and Iran from the earliest times, were cut down in the rivers and estuaries close to the coast by occasional work teams organized around the crews of the boats which ultimately exported them.[48] Cowry shells were originally the exclusive product of the Maldive Islands in the eastern Indian Ocean but when demand in West Africa exceeded this traditional supply source in the early nineteenth century, European merchants began taking shells from the Kenya coast. Here too the shippers could act as their own producers leaving almost no role for the local population.[49] Indigenous coastal peoples, indeed often rural non-Muslims, did monopolize the gathering of copal, a wild resin used in nineteenth century varnish production and accounting for over 10 per cent of registered Zanzibar exports in this period. However in its raw form, as a deposit in the ground near old or preferably extinct sandarusi trees, copal fetched a low price. Most of the cost paid at Zanzibar went to traders rather than producers and the major value-adding process of cleaning the gum was undertaken by foreign merchants or even over-seas manufacturers.[50]

PLANTATION AGRICULTURE

Up to the nineteenth century fully commercial agriculture had been virtually non-existent in any part of East Africa. Coastal towns were surrounded by slave cultivated farms producing a great variety of goods; but the urban populations were too small (4000 to 10 000 is an estimate for fifteenth-century Kilwa) and the overseas merchant traffic too efficient to provide a major stimulus to market production. A small quantity of local agricultural goods went overseas, most notably grain to the Somali coast and various coconut products (particularly coir fibre) to the Persian Gulf.[51]

After 1800, plantation agriculture experienced a take-off which, in its rate of growth if not its absolute quantity, surpassed all other sectors of the export economy. For the Kenya coast grain (mainly millet and rice) as well as sesame and coconut products appear to have become the most important of all products, although exact trade statistics are not available. In the nineteenth century Zanzibar became a net importer of food crops but increased its export of coconuts and added the valuable new crop of cloves. Experiments with sugar plantations were also undertaken on Zanzibar and the northern Tanzania mainland, although these never proved successful.[52]

The impact of this plantation system upon the East African economy has gener-ally been perceived by historians as limited or even negative. In the first place the entire phenomenon was closely linked to the expansion of European influence on the coast and dominated locally by Asian foreigners from Oman and India. Secondly, the linkages of the plantations to the rest of the region's economy can be questioned: they were at once enclaves which, like their analogues in the New World, provided goods only for overseas markets; at the same time they retained a traditional African tendency to reproduce themselves as self-sufficient social units oriented less towards any market production than to maintaining the status of their owners.[53]

While all of these conditions did exist, the plantations still constituted a major force for economic development in East Africa. The analogy to the New World is suggested by the European role in initiating the plantation system. More speci-fically, France, in the later eighteenth and early nineteenth century, established sugar plantations in the Mascarene Islands. This venture increased the flow of slaves from East Africa, provided a model for their local exploitation through intensive commercial agriculture, and served as a conduit for the introduction from Indonesia of cloves, later the principal plantation crop of Zanzibar. How-ever, as with the earlier Portuguese attempts to impose a European pattern of exploitation upon East Africa, the French initiatives essentially accelerated the integration of East Africa into an already operative Middle East–Indian Ocean economy.[54]

French labour demands were too small to account for the scale of the Muslim slave trade from East Africa in the nineteenth century, especially when the traffic from Mozambique to Brazil is taken into account (see Appendix, Table A2). Instead we must keep in mind the substantial slave trade which existed before the French arrival and also its destination – a Persian Gulf region which was already incorporating servile African immigrants into commercial date planting and pearl fishing. By expanding the general dimensions of world trade the Europeans increased the market for such Asian products mainly within the Indian Ocean region. Likewise the cloves produced at Zanzibar found their main market in India and Arabia rather than in Europe or America.

Its integration into the nearby Indian Ocean economy rather than the remote Western one allowed the East African plantation system to survive the frequent fate of specialized agricultural production: a hectic expansion in its early years followed by a sharp decline in prices once the relatively inelastic limits of world demand had been met. The onset of this latter condition in the clove market during the 1850s produced a certain degree of stagnation in the Zanzibar plantations, thus shifting many of them towards subsistence rather than commercial farming. But at the same time other planters, particularly along the Kenya coast, increased their outputs of lower-value commodities such as coconuts, cereals, and sesame, for which there were still buyers in neighbouring regions.

Within East Africa the Omani planter elite had cut its economic ties to Arabia and invested the profits from both trade and plantations into the local economy. Nonetheless a certain distance from indigenous society was maintained on the central island of Zanzibar by the largest landowners, who stressed their pure Arabian-immigrant descent, spoke Arabic, and adhered, without proselytizing others, to the dissident Ibadi sect of Islam. The smaller clove plantations of Zanzibar's twin island, Pemba, as well as the grain and coconut farms of the Kenya mainland, were as often owned by Swahilis, the mixed-blood, Bantu-speaking, long-settled coastal population which followed orthodox Sunni Islam. It is not clear how long these barriers could have been maintained, especially since Arabian immigrants of the mid-nineteenth century included impoverished Sunni Hadramautis. Even the separate role of Indians as financiers and merchants rather than planters might have shifted had Britain not restricted the Indians, as British subjects, from owning slaves.

Finally, the nineteenth-century East African coastal economy resembles the plantation regions of the New World in the contrast between relatively intensive agricultural production and an urban sector which depended upon imports for most of its manufactured goods. The degree of control over servile labour was somewhat greater than in the Western and Central Sudanic zones of West Africa. The greatest number of slaves were concentrated in export crops and they worked almost exclusively on demesne land. Indeed the planting of permanent clove and coconut trees added a form of value to local estates which allowed them to be bought, sold, and mortgaged against debts rather than exploited simply through tribute collection.

Work regimes on the coconut plantations, however, remained relatively lax and even the clove estates, which required intensive, closely supervised labour during the harvesting season, left their workers to their own devices (which did not include significant handicraft production) for much of the year. The most rigorous discipline was maintained at Malindi in Kenya where millet and sesame were cultivated throughout the year by slave forces often numbering over a hundred each, although divided into working gangs of only five to twenty men.[55]

As in Sudanic West Africa (and the more closely related Red Sea and Persian Gulf commercial agriculture) East African plantation slavery did not yoke human labour to new scales of mechanized or even animal-powered production. The basic work routines were still organized around the hand tools and small groupings characteristic of family and village agriculture. Again, as in the Sudan, and despite the insular location of many of the plantation regions, slaves in East Africa frequently managed to escape and in some instances raid the communities of their former masters. This condition may have acted as a constraint upon innovative deployment of servile labour and may also account for the fact that slaves on plantations did not live at a level of comfort radically different from that of the landowners. Many were employed in occupations more prestigious than that of field-hand and most, through eventual emancipation, could look forward to entering the mainstream of coastal society. One of the major potential factors for regional economic growth derived from slavery was the constant flow of freedmen, along with other, more voluntary, immigrants into the local urban population.

URBAN SECTORS

Population data, even for the much-observed coastal cities of East Africa in the nineteenth century, is imprecise and unreliable. Nonetheless, there is clear evidence of growth through the course of the century, with Zanzibar reaching a population of somewhat over 50 000, Kilwa slightly below this (although a large proportion was always slaves in transit), Bagamoyo (the main Zanzibar entrepôt on the Tanganyika coast) attaining about 20 000 and Mombasa over 15 000. Populations also clustered around the inland caravan centres such as Tabora and Ujiji in central Tanzania but these remained within the medieval coastal range of 5 000. The inland centres were particularly susceptible to depopulation through epidemics, as illustrated by the largest of these settlements, Msiri's ill-fated (and poorly sited) capital at Garengaze.[56]

Despite their increasing size, East African coastal cities lacked anything like the level of handicraft industries found in contemporaneous urban centres adjacent to the Sahara. The explanation for this difference lies essentially in the geographic location of the region. The Indian Ocean gave advanced overseas manufacturing systems easy entrée to the main local markets and contained no significant intermediate populations – comparable to the Saharan pastoralists – who would be accessible on competitive terms to local urban producers. Indeed as the merchant shipping system increased in efficiency and scale the autonomy of East African artisanship seems to have declined.

The peak of this local development is probably represented by the situations of Kilwa on the coast and Great Zimbabwe in the southern interior in the period just before the arrival of the Portuguese that is between the thirteenth and fifteenth centuries.[57] The most striking artisanal achievement of both these centres is their monumental architecture. In the case of Kilwa this borrowed techniques from the Middle East, but in both areas architecture made refined use of local materials, as well as adding impressive and original decorative detail to the basic structures. Both sites contain evidence of significant local cloth-producing (but not dyeing) industries. Kilwa also manufactured beads for local trade purposes and its sultans struck their own copper coinage. At Great Zimbabwe copper was drawn into wire, to be used for jewelry.

The decline of the two centres in the fifteenth century can be explained by new economic factors although not specifically the presence of the Portuguese. Kilwa, as already noted, enjoyed a pre-eminent position in the East African gold trade during the period of its urban splendour; subsequent internal shifts coincided with successful commercial competition from more northerly ports.[58] Great Zimbabwe was abandoned by its inhabitants in the same period for reasons most evidently related to the food-carrying capacity of the local environment but undoubtedly tied also (at least insofar as much smaller structures were erected at later settlement sites) to the simultaneous exhaustion of the richest gold-bearing reefs in the region.

After the fifteenth century neither Kilwa nor any other coastal towns ever regained a comparable level of architectural expression or maintained significant capacities for cloth, bead, or coin production. The interior, however, did produce manufactured goods which could compete with overseas imports, particularly the rough *manchilla* cotton cloth of the Zambezi region, as well as the copper goods originating farther to the west. With the development of the caravan routes and still more efficient overseas supply systems in the nineteenth century, cheap American cloth and large quantities of imported copper wire began to find their way into the interior, cutting into yet another refuge of local manufacturing. The same period witnessed, however, a vastly increased circulation of East African-produced iron goods, both weapons and agricultural implements.[59] Thus the oceanic frontier could always provide some market opportunities to replace those it removed but apparently the tendency from the fifteenth to the late nineteenth century was to substitute imports for the more sophisticated local goods.

Conclusion

The development of the East African economy displays more elements of dependency and underdevelopment than the Sudanic West African case. The most immediate indicators of this distinction are the urban sectors of the two areas, those in the Sudan having attained a level of artisanal manufacturing which could substitute for and compete with goods from the Mediterranean, while towns in the coast and interior of East Africa remained (or even degenerated into) little more than entrepôts for raw material exports and manufactured imports. However it must be kept in mind that the most dynamic sectors of the East African economy – the caravan trade to the far interior and the commercial plantations of the coast – emerged only in the nineteenth century. They were still growing at the point when the imposition of European colonial rule cut them off. It can be argued with equal plausibility that a continuation of this growth would have stimulated either greater demographic crises and destruction of local resources and institutions or more autonomous development in the secondary economy of the expanding urban centres. In its subsequent colonial and post-colonial development, East Africa would also contrast with the western portion of the continent in its openness to alien penetration and the widely varied indigenous experience of the resulting economic changes.

Notes

1. Gabel (1974).
2. Chittick (1975).
3. Deshler (1965).
4. Sutton and Roberts (1968); Herbert (1984), pp. 12–13.
5. Hornell (1946); Hourani (1953); Moreland (1939); Villiers (1948).
6. Datoo (1970); Mathew (1975).
7. Wheatley (1975); Sauvaget (1954).
8. Datoo (1975).
9. Chittick (1970); Ricks (1970); Whitehouse (1979).
10. Curtin (1983); Duncan (n.d.); see below for an extensive discussion of fluctuations in the Mozambique gold trade.
11. Datoo (1975).
12. Axelson (1960, 1973); Freeman-Grenville (1963).
13. Bathurst (1972); Johnston and Muir (1962).
14. Beach (1980), p. 34f.; Sutherland-Harris (1969).
15. Isaacman (1972); Newitt (1973).
16. Alpers (1975), pp. 39–171.
17. Filliot (1974); Austen (1977b); Austen(1981) and Appendix, Table A2 below for assessments of the impact of French slave trading vs. Alpers (1975), pp. 94–5 and Sheriff (1971), who assign it a major role.
18. Nicholls (1971); Sheriff (1971).
19. Abir (1968); Ehret (1974); Lamphear (1969).
20. Alpers (1975), p. 172f.; Austen (1977b).
21. Roberts (1969); Smith (1963).
22. Nicholls (1971), p. 324f.; Sheriff (1971) (see below for more detailed discussions of these commodities).
23. Alpers (1975), pp. 201–3, 264–7; Ehret (1974); Sheriff (1975).
24. Das Gupta (1976); Labib (1978); Goitein (1980); Pearson (1976).
25. Ferrand (1928); Lewis (1973); Tibbets (1971); Villiers (1948).
26. Allen (1981); Pouwels (1974).
27. Sheriff (1971), p. 427f.; Landen (1967), pp. 149–50.
28. Nicholls (1971), p. 367; Prins (1965).
29. Nicholls (1971), 295–323; Walter T. Brown (1971).
30. Cunnison (1961, 1966).
31. Roberts (1969); Lamphear (1969); Alpers (1975) pp. 243–52.
32. Amiji (1971); Bennett (1971), pp. 150–1.
33. Fallers (1969); Feierman (1974), p. 65f.; Hartwig (1976); Unomah (1973); Were (1967) pp. 123–50. For parallel developments among Oromo peoples of the Ethiopian interior connected to the Red Sea trade, Abir (1965).
34. Brode (1907); Page (1974); Wright and Lary (1971).
35. Bennett (1971); Shorter (1968); Verbeken (1956).
36. Beverly Brown (1971); Wright and Lary (1971).
37. Roberts (1969) p. 73.
38. Hartwig (1979). The most contentious position (in favour of positive demographic development before the colonial period) is Kjekhus (1977); for a general assessment, see Coquery-Vidrovitch (1985), pp. 46–51.
39. Alpers (1975), p. 239–43; Chanock (1977); Cooper (1977) pp. 240–1.
40. Good (1972, 1978); Hartwig (1978).
41. Beck (1977), pp. 17–22, 37f.; Ford (1971), pp. 110–82.
42. Beachey (1967); Roberts (1969).
43. Omer-Cooper (1966), pp. 66–85; Uzoigwe (1969).
44. Alpers (1969); Iliffe (1978) pp. 67–77.

45. Huffman (1972); Phimister (1976); Summers (1969) p. 195f.
46. Duncan (n.d.); Randles (1975) pp. 76–81. Curtin (1983) contains a valuable synthesis of data available at that time but with lower post-1500 figures than suggested by Duncan's sources.
47. Verbeken (1956) pp. 124–7; Herbert (1984) pp. 45, 73–4, 159–60.
48. Curtin (1981); Prins (1965/66); Burton (1860) Vol. 2, p. 542.
49. Allen (1974).
50. Burton (1860) Vol. 2, p. 542.
51. Coupland (1938) pp. 320–1; Freeman-Grenville (1962) pp. 31, 106, 109.
52. Austen (1977b); Cooper (1977); Ylvisikar (1979) p. 51f.
53. This is the principal thesis of Cooper's excellent 1977 study, which also provides data for an alternative interpretation; for a Marxist variant on Cooper, see Sheriff (1985).
54. Austen (1981).
55. Cooper (1977) pp. 81–97, 170–3.
56. Cooper (1977) p. 56; Brown and Brown (1976); Nicholls (1971) pp. 267, 319; Freeman-Grenville (1962) p. 192; Verbeken (1956) pp. 80–3.
57. Chittick (1974); Garlake (1973); Huffmann (1972).
58. Datoo (1975); Sheriff (1975). For a claim that Swahili urban culture in Kenya reached a peak under conditions of 'benign neglect' in the eighteenth century, see Allen (1974).
59. Herbert (1984) p. 172–4; Isaacman (1972) pp. 73–5; Roberts (1969); (1973) p. 209.

Bibliography

Abir, Mordechai (1965), 'The emergence and consolidation of the monarchies of Enarea and Jimma in the first half of the nineteenth century', *Journal of African History*, vol. 6, no. 2, pp. 205–19

Abir, Mordechai (1968), 'Caravan trade and history in the northern parts of East Africa', *Paideuma*, vol. 14, pp. 103–20

Allen, James de Vere (1974), 'Swahili culture reconsidered: some historical implications of the material culture of the northern Kenya coast in the eighteenth and nineteenth centuries', *Azania*, vol. 9, pp. 104–38

Allen, James de Vere (1981), 'Swahili culture and the nature of East Coast settlements', *International Journal of African Historical Studies*, vol. 14, no. 2, pp. 303–25

Alpers, Edward A. (1969), 'Trade, state and society among the Yao in the nineteenth century', *Journal of African History*, vol. 10, no. 4, pp. 405–20

Alpers, Edward A. (1975), *Ivory and Slaves: Changing Patterns of International Trade in East Central Africa to the Later Nineteenth Century* (Berkeley: University of California Press)

Amiji, Hatim M. (1971), 'Some notes on religious dissent in nineteenth century East Africa', *African Historical Studies*, vol. 4, no. 3, pp. 603–16

Austen, Ralph A. (1971), 'Patterns of development in nineteenth century East Africa', *African Historical Studies*, vol. 4, no. 3, pp. 645–57

Austen, Ralph A. (1977a), 'Abushiri et le lutte contre la domination allemande en Tanzanie', in Charles André Julien et al. (eds), *Les Africains*, Vol. 1 (Paris: Présence Africaine), pp. 51–81

Austen, Ralph A. (1977b), 'The Islamic slave trade out of Africa (Red Sea and Indian Ocean): an effort at quantification' (Unpublished paper, Conference on Islamic Africa: Slavery and Related Topics, Princeton University)

Austen, Ralph A. (1981), 'From the Atlantic to the Indian Ocean: European abolition, the African slave trade, and Asian economic structures', in David Eltis and James Walvin (eds), *The Abolition of the Atlantic Slave Trade* (Madison: University of Wisconsin Press), pp. 117–39

Axelson, Eric (1960), Portuguese in South-East Africa 1600–1700 (Johannesburg: Struik)

Axelson, Eric (1973), Portuguese in South-East Africa, 1488–1600 (Johannesburg: Struik)

Bathurst, R.D. (1972), 'Maritime trade and imamate government: two principal themes in the history of Oman to 1728', in Derek Hopwood (ed.), *The Arabian Peninsula* (London: Allen & Unwin), pp. 89–106

Beach, D.N. (1980), *The Shona and Zimbabwe, 900–1850: An Outline of Shona History* (Gwelo: Mambo, London: Heinemann, New York: Africana)

Beachey, R.W. (1967), 'The East African ivory trade in the nineteenth century', *Journal of African History*, vol. 8, no. 2, pp. 269–90

Beck, Ann (1977), *Medicine and Society in Tanganyika, 1890–1930* (Philadelphia: American Philosophical Society)

Bennett, Norman R. (1971), *Mirambo of Tanzania, ca. 1840–1884* (New York: Oxford University Press)

Bennett, Norman R. (ed.) (1973), *The Zanzibar Diaries of Edward D. Ropes, Jr., 1882–1892* (Boston: Boston University Press)

Bennett, Norman R. (1978), *A History of the Arab State of Zanzibar* (London: Methuen)

Brode, Heinrich (1907), *Tippoo Tib* (London: Arnold)

Brown, Beverly (1971), 'Muslim influence on trade and politics in the Lake Tanganyika region', *African Historical Studies*, vol. 4, no. 3, pp. 617–29

Brown, Beverly and Walter T. Brown (1976), 'East African towns: a shared growth', in W. Arens (ed.), *A Century of Change in Eastern Africa* (The Hague: Mouton), pp. 183–200

Brown, Walter T. (1971), 'The politics of business: relations between Zanzibar and Bagamoyo in the late nineteenth century', *African Historical Studies*, vol. 4, no. 3, pp. 631–43

Burton, Richard F. (1860), *The Lake Regions of Central Africa* (New York: Harper)

Chanock, Martin (1977), 'Agricultural change and continuity in Malawi', in Robin Palmer and Neil Parsons (eds), *The Roots of Rural Poverty in Central and Southern Africa* (Berkeley: University of California Press), pp. 396–409

Chittick, Neville (1970), 'East African trade with the Orient', in D.S. Richards (ed.), pp. 97–104

Chittick, Neville (1974), *Kilwa: An Islamic Trading City on the East African Coast* (Nairobi: British Institute in Eastern Africa)

Chittick, Neville (1975), 'The peopling of the East African coast', in Chittick and Rotberg (eds), pp. 16–43

Chittick, Neville and Robert I. Rotberg (eds) (1975), *East Africa and the Orient* (New York: Africana Publishing)

Cooper, Frederick (1977), *Plantation Slavery on the East Coast of Africa* (New Haven: Yale University Press)

Coquery-Vidrovitch, Catherine (1985), *Afrique noire: permanences et ruptures* (Paris: Payot)

Coupland, Reginald (1938), *East Africa and its Invaders: From the Earliest Times to the Death of Sayyid Said* (Oxford: Clarendon Press)

Cunnison, Ian (1961), 'Kazembe and the Portuguese, 1798–1832', *Journal of African History*, vol. 2, no. 1, pp. 61–76

Cunnison, Ian (1966), 'Kazembe and the Arabs to 1870', in Eric Stokes and Richard Brown (eds), *The Zambezian Past* (Manchester: Manchester University Press), pp. 226–37

Curtin, Philip D. (1981), 'African enterprise in the mangrove trade: the case of Lamu', *African Economic History*, no. 10, pp. 23–33

Curtin, Philip D. (1983), 'Africa and the wider monetary world, 1250–1850', in J.F. Richards (ed.), *Precious Metals in the Later Medieval and Early Modern Worlds* (Durham, NC: Carolina Academic Press), pp. 231–68

Das Gupta, Ashin (1976), 'Trade and politics in 18th century India', in Richards (ed.), pp. 181–214

Datoo, Bashir Ahmed (1970), 'Rhapta: the location and importance of East Africa's first port', *Azania*, vol. 5, pp. 65–75

Datoo, Bashir Ahmed (1975), *Port Development in East Africa: Spatial Patterns from the Ninth to the Sixteenth Centuries* (Nairobi: East African Literature Bureau)

Deshler, Walter W. (1965), 'Native cattle-keeping in eastern Africa', in Anthony Leeds and Andrew P. Vayda (eds), *Man, Culture, and Animals* (Washington, DC: American Association for the Advancement of Science), pp. 153–68

Duncan, T. Bentley (n.d.), Unpublished ms. on Indian Ocean trade, University of Chicago

Ehret, Christopher (1974), 'Nineteenth century roots of economic imperialism in Kenya', *Kenya Historical Review*, vol. 2, no. 2, pp. 260–83

Fallers, Lloyd A. (1969), *The King's Men: Leadership and Status in Buganda on the Eve of Independence* (New York: Oxford University Press)

Feierman, Steven (1974), *The Shambaa Kingdom: A History* (Madison: University of Wisconsin Press)

Ferrand, Gabriel (1928), *Introduction à l'astronomie nautique arabe* (Paris: Geuthner)

Filliot, J.M. (1974), *La traite des esclaves vers les Mascareignes au XVIIIe siècle* (Paris: ORSTOM)

Ford, John R. (1971), *The Role of the Trypanosomiases in African Ecology: A Study of the Tsetse Fly Problem* (Oxford: Clarendon Press)

Freeman-Grenville, G.S.P. (1962), *A Medieval History of the Coast of Tanganyika* (Berlin: Akademie)

Freeman-Grenville, G.S.P. (1963), 'The coast, 1498–1840', in Oliver and Mathew (eds), pp. 125–68

Gabel, Creighton (1974), 'Terminal food collectors and agricultural initiative in eastern and southern Africa', *International Journal of African Historical Studies*, vol. 7, no. 1, pp. 56–68

Garlake, Peter S. (1966), *The Early Islamic Architecture of the East African Coast* (Nairobi: Oxford University Press)

Garlake, Peter S. (1973), *Great Zimbabwe* (London: Thames & Hudson)

Goitein, S.D. (1980), 'From Aden to India: specimens of correspondence of India traders of the twelfth century', *Journal of the Economic and Social History of the Orient*, vol. 23, no. 1, pp. 43–66

Good, Charles M. (1972), 'Salt, trade and disease: aspects of development in Africa's northern Great Lakes region', *International Journal of African Historical Studies*, vol. 5, no. 4, pp. 543–86

Good, Charles M. (1978), 'Man, milieu and the disease factor: tick-borne relapsing fever in East Africa', in Hartwig and Patterson (eds), pp. 46–87

Gray, Richard and David Birmingham (eds) (1969), *Pre-colonial African Trade: Essays on Trade in Central and Eastern Africa before 1900* (London: Oxford University Press)

Hartwig, Gerald W. (1976), *The Art of Survival in East Africa: The Kerebe and Long-Distance Trade, 1800–1895* (New York: Africana Press)

Hartwig, Gerald W. (1978), 'Social consequences of epidemic diseases: the nineteenth century in East Africa', in Hartwig and Patterson (eds), pp. 25–45

Hartwig, Gerald W. (1979), 'Demographic considerations in East Africa during the nineteenth century', *International Journal of African Historical Studies*, vol. 12, no. 4, pp. 653–72

Hartwig, Gerald W. and K. David Patterson (eds) (1978), *Disease in African History* (Durham, NC: Duke University Press)

Herbert, Eugenia (1984), *Red Gold of Africa: Copper in Precolonial History and Culture* (Madison: University of Wisconsin Press)

Hornell, James (1946), 'Sailing craft of western India', *Mariners' Mirror*, vol. 32, pp. 195–217

Hourani, George Fodio (1953), *Arab Seafaring in the Indian Ocean in Ancient and Medieval Times* (Beirut: Khayats)

Huffman, T.N. (1972), 'The rise and fall of Zimbabwe', *Journal of African History*, vol. 13, no. 3, pp. 353–66

Iliffe, John (1978), *A Modern History of Tanganyika* (Cambridge: Cambridge University Press)

Isaacman, Alan F. (1972), *Mozambique: The Africanization of a European Institution: the Zambezi Prazos, 1750–1902* (Madison: University of Wisconsin Press)

Johnston, T.M. and J. Muir (1962), 'Portuguese influences on shipbuilding in the Indian Ocean', *Mariners' Mirror*, vol. 48, pp. 58–63

Kjekhus, Helge (1977), *Ecology Control and Economic Development in East Africa: The Case of Tanganyika, 1850–1950* (London: Heinemann)

Labib, Subhi Y. (1978), 'Karimi', in *The Encyclopedia of Islam*, new edition, Vol. 4 (Leiden: Brill), pp. 640–3

Lamphear, John (1969), 'The Kamba and the northern Mrima coast', in Gray and Birmingham (eds), pp. 75–101

Landen, Robert Geran (1967), *Oman since 1856* (Princeton: Princeton University Press)

Lewis, Archibald (1973), 'Maritime skills in the Indian Ocean, 1368–1500', *Journal of the Economic and Social History of the Orient*, vol. 16, pp. 238–64

Mathew, Gervase (1975), 'The dating and the significance of the *Periplus of the Erythrean Sea*', in Chittick and Rotberg (eds), pp. 147–63

Moreland, W.H. (1939), 'The ships of the Arabian Sea about A.D. 1500', *Journal of the Royal Anthropological Society*, vol. 69, pp. 63–74, 173–92

Newitt, M.D.D. (1973), *Portuguese Settlement on the Zambesi: Exploration, Land Tenure and Colonial Rule in East Africa* (New York: Africana Publishing)

Newitt, M.D.D. (1978), 'The southern Swahili coast in the first century of European expansion', *Azania*, vol. 13, pp. 111–26

Nicholls, C.S. (1971), *The Swahili Coast: Politics, Diplomacy and Trade on the East African Littoral, 1798–1856* (London: Allen & Unwin)

Oliver, Roland and Gervase Mathew (eds) (1963), *History of East Africa*, Vol. 1 (Oxford: Clarendon Press)

Omer-Cooper, J.D. (1966), *The Zulu Aftermath: A Nineteenth Century Revolution in Bantu Africa* (London: Longmans)

Page, Melvin (1974), 'The Manyema hordes of Tippu Tip', *International Journal of African Historical Studies*, vol. 7, no. 1, pp. 69–84

Pearson, Michael N. (1976), *Merchants and Rulers in Gujarat* (Berkeley: University of California Press)

Phimister, Ian (1976), 'Pre-colonial gold mining in Southern Zambezia: a reassessment', *African Social Research*, vol. 21, no. 1, pp. 1–31

Pouwels, Randell L. (1974), 'Tenth century settlement of the East African coast: the case for Qarmatian/Ismaili connections', *Azania*, vol. 9, pp. 65–74

Prins, A.H.J. (1965), *Sailing for Lamu* (Assen: Van Gorcum)

Prins, A.H.J. (1965/66), 'The Persian Gulf dhows: two variants in maritime enterprise', *Persica*, vol. 2, pp. 1–18

Randles, W.G.L. (1975), *L'Empire du Monomotapa du XVe au XIXe siècle* (Paris: Mouton)

Richards, D.S. (ed.) (1970), *Islam and the Trade of Asia* (Oxford: Cassirer)

Ricks, Thomas M. (1970), 'Persian Gulf seafaring and East Africa: ninth to twelfth centuries', *African Historical Studies*, vol. 3, no. 2, pp. 339–58

Roberts, Andrew (1969), 'Nyamwezi trade', in Gray and Birmingham (eds), pp. 39–74

Roberts, Andrew (1973), *A History of the Bemba* (London: Longman)

Sauvaget, Jean (1954), 'Les merveilles de l'Inde', (trans. and ed.), in *Memorial Jean Sauvaget*, Vol. 1 (Damascus: Institut Français de Damas), pp. 187–309

Sheriff, Abdul M.H. (1971), 'The rise of a commercial empire: an aspect of the economic history of Zanzibar, 1710–1873' (Unpublished PhD. dissertation, University of London)

Sheriff, Abdul M.H. (1975), 'Trade and underdevelopment: the role of international trade in the economic history of the East African coast before the sixteenth century', in B.A. Ogot (ed.), *The Economic and Social History of East Africa* (Hadith, no. 5) (Nairobi: EAPH), pp. 1–23

Sheriff, Abdul M.H. (1985), 'The slave mode of production along the East African coast,

1810–1873', in John Ralph Willis (ed.), *The Slave Estate in Islamic Africa* (London: Cass), pp. 161–81

Shorter, Aylward (1968), 'Nyungu-ya-Mawe and the "Empire of the Ruga-Rugas" ', *Journal of African History*, vol. 9, no. 2, pp. 235–59

Smith, Alison (1963), 'The southern section of the interior, 1840–84', in Oliver and Mathew (eds), pp. 253–96

Summers, Roger (1969), *Ancient Mining in Rhodesia and Adjacent Areas* (Salisbury: National Museum of Rhodesia)

Sutherland-Harris, Nicola (1969), 'Trade and the Rozwi Mambo', in Gray and Birmingham (eds), pp. 243–64

Sutton, J.E.G. (1973), *Early Trade in Eastern Africa* (Nairobi: EAPH)

Sutton, J.E.G. and Andrew Roberts (1968), 'Uvinza and its salt industry', *Azania*, vol. 33, pp. 45–86

Tibbets, G.R. (1971), *Arab Navigation in the Indian Ocean before the Coming of the Portuguese* (London: Royal Asiatic Society)

Unomah, A.C. (1973), 'Economic expansion and political change in Unanyembe, ca. 1840–1900' (Unpublished PhD dissertation, University of Ibadan)

Uzoigwe, G.N. (1969), 'Kabalega's Aburusura: the military factor in Bunyoro' (Nairobi: Makerere Institute of Social and Economic Research, Conference Papers, mimeo)

Verbeken, Auguste (1956), *Msiri, roi du Garenganze* (Brussels: Cuypers)

Villiers, Alan (1948), 'Some aspects of the Arab dhow trade', *Middle East Journal*, vol. 2, pp. 399–416

Were, Gideon (1967), *A History of the Abuluyia of Eastern Kenya* (Nairobi: EAPH)

Wheatley (1975), 'Analecta Sino-Africana Recensa', in Chittick and Rotberg (eds), pp. 76–114

Whitehouse, David (1979), 'Maritime trade in the Arabian Sea: the ninth and tenth centuries A.D.', *South Asian Archeology* (Naples: Istituto Universitario Orientale), pp. 865–85

Wright, Marcia and Peter Lary (1971), 'Swahili settlements in northern Zambia and Malawi', *African Historical Studies*, vol. 4, no. 3, pp. 547–73

Ylvisikar, Marguerite (1979), *Lamu in the Nineteenth Century: Land, Trade and Politics* (Boston: Boston University Press)

4

Commercial Frontiers
and Contact Economies: III
Western Africa and the Atlantic

The opening of sea routes between Europe and the South Atlantic affected the economic development of all parts of Africa. In the preceding chapters we have seen how pre-existing patterns of international commerce in the West African Sudan and East Africa were altered after the sixteenth century. The most important changes, however, came in zones where European seafarers established themselves as the primary, and often the first, regular link to the outside world.

This change occurred along a coastline extending from Senegambia to Angola, around the Cape of Good Hope and Natal, through to Mozambique. The last of these European-dominated regions was discussed along with the Asian-oriented Indian Ocean frontier; the second will be treated in a separate section concentrating on colonial Southern Africa; the first, including the coast and immediate hinterland of what are generally known as the regions of Guinea and Equatorial Africa, is the subject of the present chapter.

The experience of the Atlantic frontier is distinguished by three critical factors: the technological gap between Europeans arriving via the ocean and the Africans with whom they dealt; the persistence of multiple, competing centres of trade all along the coast; and finally the intensity and variety of European demand for local export goods. The combination of these features made West and West-Equatorial Africa at once the most dynamic and the most disadvantaged of all the African contact economies.

Trade routes: European control of the ocean

Before the European voyages of discovery, the Atlantic coast of Africa had been integrated into international trade only in part, and that as the outer periphery of Sudanic commercial systems. A few products from this region – mainly spices – found their way into trans-Saharan trade and others – such as kola and sea salt – reached the interior savanna. The most active exchange, however, seems to have been regional, as the ocean offered excellent opportunities for obtaining fish and salt supplements to the starch diets of the immediately adjacent populations.

In theory at least, the sheltered waterways linking various river estuaries from the Congo northwards to present-day Ghana provided the means of a wide-ranging West African coastal trade in such specialized items as beads, copper and slaves. Unfortunately, the only evidence we have for commerce of this kind derives from a period when Europeans were exploiting the intra-coastal connections which they had themselves possibly initiated.[1] In any case, African oceanic trade could not have been organized as anything more than a loose system of relays, most of which would have resembled the scope and structure of the markets linking each coastal zone with its immediate hinterland.

A number of more dramatically revisionist historians have argued that various navigators – Phoenician, Arab or African – had established Atlantic connections between tropical West Africa and both the Mediterranean and the New World prior to the Portuguese explorations of the fifteenth century. The weaknesses of these contentions help to explain the significance of the modern European achievement as both event and process. The event is, at the very least, unlikely since ancient and medieval rowing and sail technology was incapable of sustaining any recurrent navigation of the South Atlantic. Moreover, whatever conclusions about navigation may be drawn from evidence of biological and cultural similarities between African and New World peoples, there is no indication of any continuous economic relations between these regions before the fifteenth century.[2]

The maritime ventures of Portugal thus opened up an entirely new dimension of African intercontinental commerce. Unlike the medieval frontiers of the Sahara and the Indian Ocean, moreover, the Atlantic was an arena of continuous and accelerating innovation in the technology of transport. From the fifteenth to the nineteenth centuries ships were equipped with ever-larger and better-designed sails, new steering devices, improvements in the size and structure of hulls, and more effective instruments and manuals of navigation.[3] The abandonment of sails and wood structures for steam and iron in the mid-nineteenth century brought this process to a climax which, as will be seen in the next chapter, helped prepare the way for colonial occupation. But the factor of constantly increasing efficiency was already important in determining the character of African–European economic relations well before this time.

The effect of such a transport system was to carry to an extreme the independence of external merchants from intermediate and ultimate supply zones already observed in the comparison of Saharan and Indian Ocean commerce. The Atlantic Ocean contained no important stopping points, and voyages were made directly from Europe (or North America) to Africa on ever-shortening schedules. Some of the trade, particularly in the first centuries, involved carriage of local goods between African coastal centres, but these ventures simply eliminated the potential or actual operation of African canoes in these same markets.

One measure of the growing efficiency of European transport was the steady decrease in the ratio of crews to the tonnage of goods carried: by the end of the sailing era only one man was needed for each 9–14 tons, a gain of two to three-fold over the Indian Ocean dhow system and fifteen to thirty-fold over Saharan camel caravans (see Appendix, Table A1). Most provisions needed for Atlantic voyages could be carried from home, to be supplemented only by such basic items as fresh water, cereals and fruit at selected points in Africa. The only transport facilities required from Africans were pilotage into sheltered harbours or canoe lighterage where ships had to anchor beyond surf and sand bars.

The settlements at African Atlantic ports reflected the limited needs of the shippers as opposed to the structures generated by more socially dense systems of African linkage to the hinterland. Often Europeans carried on their trade directly from shipboard without developing any permanent agencies on land. Where 'factories' (permanent trading posts) were established, they did not require large settlements and often had the net effect of limiting European dependency still further, since they were designed essentially to reduce the time spent by ships in

African waters before turning around to complete their voyages to the more comfortable western or northern shores of the Atlantic.

Trade routes: African supply zones

The critical factor in understanding the internal situation of African suppliers in the Atlantic trade is not transport technology – which was here neither innovative nor widely encompassing – but rather the autonomous integration of the new oceanic frontier into pre-existing regional market structures. European shippers concentrated their trading efforts on a series of coastal areas all of which were already functioning as centres of at least local market exchange. A major variant between these zones was their degree of articulation into the older Sudanic system of intercontinental trade. This commercial experience, as well as independent demographic and political factors, determined the form in which Africans organized control over the routes between the coast and interior sources of export goods. Finally, the nature of the European presence differed radically from one zone to another, reflecting the interplay of African and external factors.

For the purposes of the present analysis, the Atlantic coast of Africa may be divided into six major zones (see map): 1) Senegambia–Upper Guinea; 2) the Gold Coast; 3) the Bight of Benin; 4) the Bight of Biafra; 5) Gabon–Congo; 6) Angola. The ascending order of these zones represents a directly decreasing level of integration into the Sudanic commercial world. Zone 1 is, for the most part, a direct extension of the Western Sudanic savanna although somewhat distant from its main economic and political centre of the Middle Niger. Zones 2 and 3 are forest areas which were strongly linked to the Sudanic economy but never fully assimilated to it. Finally, east and south of the Niger River and its coastal delta, Sudanic contacts disappear entirely.

Organization of commerce between these coasts and the interior again falls into three basic patterns although these do not correspond precisely to the degree of integration with the Sudanic zone. In the Senegambia–Upper Guinea zone, long-distance carriage of goods remained under the control of Sudanic Muslim Juula merchants who required only protection and other landlord services from the relatively small and weak states occupying the coast and its immediate hinterland.[4]

In the forest zones linked to the Sudan, major inland states – Asante, Dahomey, Oyo and Benin – controlled traffic to the coast, using their own subjects as merchants. State systems here had developed partially in response to Sudanic trade and continued, even after the opening of the Atlantic frontier, to maintain major commercial ties to the savanna and even the Sahara. Their inland position allowed them both to profit from arbitrage between the northward and southward trading systems and to protect themselves from the dangers of too close proximity to the seagoing Europeans.[5]

A similar pattern of interior middlemen states (but lacking their own long-distance merchants) emerged in Angola, where no connections existed with the Sudan. These states (the best known of which are Matamba and Kasanje) were themselves entirely new formations, based upon migrations of Lunda peoples from the interior and Mbundu groups from the coast. The threats of Portuguese domination, as will be seen, provided a more immediate explanation for the location of these commercial centres than did positive commercial factors; but they also enjoyed opportunities for exploiting multiple trade routes, in this case playing off the Angolan coast against Dutch, British and French traders north of the Congo.[6]

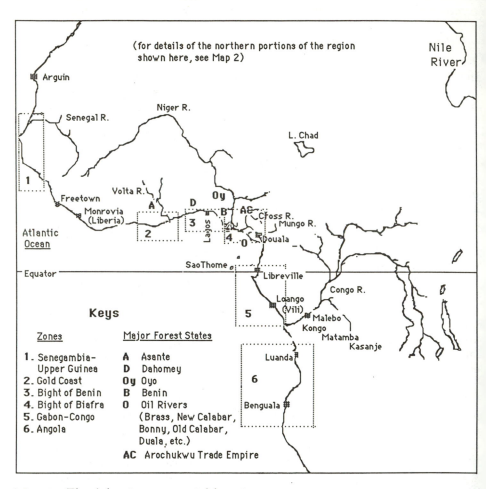

(for details of the northern portions of the region shown here, see Map 2)

Keys

Zones

1. Senegambia–Upper Guinea
2. Gold Coast
3. Bight of Benin
4. Bight of Biafra
5. Gabon–Congo
6. Angola

Major Forest States

A   Asante
D   Dahomey
Oy Oyo
B   Benin
O   Oil Rivers
    (Brass, New Calabar, Bonny, Old Calabar, Duala, etc.)
AC Arochukwu Trade Empire

Map 4   *The Atlantic commercial frontier*

Between the Niger and the Congo the major commercial partners of Europeans were African states located directly on the coast. These entities managed the carriage of goods from the interior, whether by navigating the rivers and estuaries of the Niger, Calabar, Cameroon, and Gabon areas or by the overland caravans of the Vili Loango kingdom along the Congo coast. Control over the more distant inland regions from which trade goods ultimately originated belonged to peoples usually connected to the coastal merchants only by a complex chain of further intermediaries.[7]

The trading factories established by Europeans along the western African coast from the fifteenth century onwards provided the bases from which the interior of the continent would eventually be colonized. However, up until the nineteenth century (and for most areas not until after the 1880s) these establishments remained decidedly modest. The nature of the European presence varied considerably, ranging from the small Portuguese colony of Angola to the fortified towns and trading posts of Senegambia, Upper Guinea and the Gold Coast, to the unfortified posts, moored hulks and trade from the decks of passing ships in the Bight of Benin and Biafra and the Gabon–Congo coasts.

This variation was not determined by differences in the volume, value, or composition of trade – often the greatest quantities of staple goods came from the coastal zones with the most minimal permanent European presence – but rather resulted from political and cultural factors. The largest centres can be explained by competition among Europeans in the more accessible Senegambia–Gold Coast regions and the inability of the Kongo and Mbundu coastal states in Angola to handle the abrupt initiation of international contacts by Portugal (other areas without the experience of Sudanic contacts were brought more gradually into the Atlantic system). Whatever the scale and structure of the European factories, their major function was always to receive goods for immediate shipment from the coast rather than to collect or produce them in the interior. Nonetheless, the varying types of foreign penetration would have some effect upon the development of African commercial and productive activities.

Commodities: the shifting composition of exports

The establishment of transport linkages between the bustling economies of the North Atlantic and western Africa created opportunities for exchanges of a wide range of goods. African exports into this system always included such staples as ivory, dyewoods and hardwoods, gum, wax, etc. However the major phases of this trade were each marked by the preponderance of a single commodity or set of commodities. In the beginning the key object of European trade was gold, later it became slaves, and in the final pre-colonial phase vegetable oils and wild rubber predominated. Historians have often been tempted to ascribe too much change in the western African economy to these export shifts. Nonetheless, they are important and in order to comprehend both the extent and limits of their impact, it is necessary to delineate their often rather fuzzy chronology.

Renaissance Europeans were well aware that West Africa was the main source of the gold which had become so important to their commercial system. The most important single object of the Portuguese discoveries, therefore, was to achieve access to this precious metal independently of the Muslim-controlled Sudan–Saharan caravan system.[8] The Portuguese thus established their first West African trading centre at Arguin, on the barren Mauritanian coast, where they could tap directly into the desert trade. This position was abandoned after a few years in favour of trading stations on the Senegambia–Upper Guinea coast which sustained themselves more easily and established direct ties to the western centres of gold mining at Bambuk and Bure. Finally in present-day Ghana (significantly called El Mina – 'the mine' – by the Portuguese and the Gold Coast by their Dutch, British, and Danish successors) the Europeans found themselves in proximity to the most productive of the gold-bearing zones in western Africa.

The search for gold explains not only the concentration of Europeans in those areas already integrated into the Sudanic trade but also the initial motivations for entry into less-developed markets. Thus on the coast of the Bight of Benin, where Sudanic connections had existed but in an apparently rather indirect form, the Portuguese and Dutch initially traded for beads, cloth and slaves which they exchanged on the Gold Coast for gold. Likewise early Portuguese expansion in Angola can be explained by the desire for slaves to send to the Gold Coast as well as the illusion that the interior of this region also contained precious metals.[9]

The export of West African gold via the Atlantic appears to have been considerably more efficient than the series of overland routes needed to reach the Mediterranean (see Appendix, Table A3). Historians have thus calculated a flow of three-quarters to one and three-quarter tons per annum to Europe and America despite the continuing movement of at least some bullion into the Sudan and Sahara.[10] This trade reached its peak in the sixteenth and seventeenth centuries and then began to drop off sharply, recovering only when new techniques of extraction were introduced into the mining industry of the Gold Coast by European entrepreneurs in the colonial period. It is possible that the decline in exports was caused by depletion of gold sources which were accessible through existing African technology. Another explanation, as with Mozambique, lies in the competition between gold production and the new demands of the slave trade.[11]

Europeans sought slaves in Africa almost entirely for a single purpose: the working of plantations in the tropical regions of the New World. As with the gold trade this form of entreprise grew out of the late medieval European economy. The basic model of what later became the Atlantic plantation complex had its origins in the eastern Mediterranean where Europeans began cultivating sugar on large landholdings with gangs of imported labourers. Initially this work force had been white, recruited from the Caucasus and Eastern Europe by Italian slave traders. However with the closing off of commercial access to these areas through Ottoman expansion in the fifteenth century, and the simultaneous shift of the sugar plantation system to Iberia and the islands off the north-western African coast, it became logical to employ black Africans. At first a number of these slaves came by way of the trans-Saharan trade but very quickly after the establishment of commercial centres on the western African coast Europeans began acquiring their black labour via the Atlantic.[12]

During its first century and a half the Atlantic slave trade remained relatively small since the sugar system was still restricted to the Old World and the coast of Brazil. After 1600, however, Brazilian production expanded and the Dutch, British and French began to open up further New World areas (particularly the Caribbean Islands) for plantation production. The system reached its peak in the eighteenth century when slaves constituted by far the most important item of export from Africa (see Appendix, Figure A1). Between 1810 and 1870 the slave trade became illegal for Europeans and North Americans, but continuing demand from Brazilian, Cuban and (to a far lesser extent) United States plantations encouraged the legal and illegal evasion of mainly British suppression policies. The rate of Atlantic slave traffic therefore attained its greatest level during this last phase, although 'legitimate' export goods were beginning to reach an even higher scale of value.

Estimates of the total number of human beings who were shipped in the Atlantic slave trade still remain controversial but the amount and quality of research already devoted to this topic (itself a function of the business efficiency of the European trade, with its elaborate record-keeping) indicates that the range of results would not fluctuate too widely from 11 million to 12 million (see Appendix, Table A2). This is a huge number, particularly in the light of the short period of time in which it was attained. By comparison, as already noted, total Islamic slave trade by both desert and sea routes was about one-third larger but, even in its peak periods, far less intensive. It must be noted, however, that the impact of the Atlantic slave trade was relatively spread out in space, if not in time. During its final and most intensive phase in the nineteenth century, as many as 15 per cent of the slaves came not from the Atlantic coast of Africa but rather from Mozambique. Within western Africa, the sources of slaves constantly shifted, with the share of Senegambia–Upper Guinea and the Gold Coast peaking early and then declining while that of the Bight of Biafra and the Gabon–northern Congo coast rose.[13]

The specific damage inflicted by the Atlantic slave trade in the development of African commercial and productive capacities will be discussed below but in general it does not appear to have hampered a shift into other forms of export activity once the opportunity for these was presented.

The European industrial revolution of the nineteenth century, with its simultaneous increase in the demand for imported raw materials and decrease in the cost of procuring them, provided precisely such an opportunity. The acceleration of Atlantic trade during this period affected all African commodities: ivory and other staples, gold, and slaves. However the most significant area of growth was in widely abundant vegetable products which had previously enjoyed only a limited export market.

Until the nineteenth century the only significant long-distance exchange of cultivated or 'protected' crops occurred within the Sudanic economy where kola, cotton, and even cereal grains moved between forest, savanna and desert zones. This commerce, as already seen, increased considerably during the nineteenth century, in large part because of favourable long-term rainfall conditions. Agricultural goods exported overseas during the first centuries of Atlantic trade had consisted mainly of peppers which never achieved either a major market in Europe or new levels of production in western Africa. There was thus no direct precedent for the nineteenth-century European interest in two categories of African goods: vegetable oils and wild rubber.

The sources of African vegetable oils were two crops: the oil palm, a long established indigenous food source, and the peanut, a plant introduced from the New World after 1500.[14] Palm oil and palm kernels became a mainstay of trade in the entire Guinea and equatorial forest area from the early decades of the nineteenth century onward, when Europeans used them, first as lubricants and a source of candles, and then as a component of soap manufacture. Peanuts, used both for soap and domestic European food preparation, came mainly from the coastal savanna regions of Senegambia and Angola (see Appendix, Figures A2, A3).

The market for rubber developed relatively late in the nineteenth century with the perfection of the vulcanization process and the growing demand for rubber footware, mechanical parts and fittings of various kinds, and bicycle tyres. Rubber was found in wild form in most African forest areas but by the early 1880s it enjoyed a particular boom in Upper Guinea, present-day Ghana, the northern Congo coast, and Angola.[15]

During the early and mid-nineteenth century there were also attempts by both Europeans and Africans to transfer the plantation crops of the New World and Asia to western Africa. For the most part these experiments failed – cotton, in particular, never took hold nor did sugar, tobacco and indigo. However, in two places under direct Portuguese control, northern Angola and even more so the island of São Thomé (which had been the world's greatest centre of sugar production during the early sixteenth century), coffee and cocoa were very successfully planted.[16] But the major expansion of such new exports would await the changed conditions of the colonial period.

The commercial impact:
Europeans, Afro-Europeans and Afro-Muslims

Given the low intensity of the primary processes through which exports were supplied, the economy of the Atlantic coast, Africa's other commercial frontier, was dominated by merchants rather than producers. What distinguishes this zone from the regions considered previously is the coupling of a much higher intensity of export and import exchanges with a low level of assimilation between external and internal trading institutions. Europeanized African merchants thus played a far less significant role on the Atlantic coast than did the Islamic Juula and Hausa in the Sudan or even here. Europeans also restricted their own trading ventures to the coast in contrast to the Arab-Swahili caravans and military commercial establishments which penetrated the East African interior (for the non-commercial sources of proto-colonial and colonial penetration, see Chapter 5).

The explanation for this contrast lies, first of all, in the insulation between Europeans and Africans provided by the former's complete control of maritime technology – a control which would later facilitate colonial conquest. Second, but of more direct interest to the discussion which will immediately follow, was the factor of wide competition between merchant organizations on both the European and African sides of the frontier. The reasons for competitiveness, as opposed to the concentration of points of exchange on the trans-Saharan and Indian Ocean frontiers, will be indicated below but its effect was to spread the impact of the trade over a wide variety of participants, none of whom could, or needed to, undertake major social or cultural transformations.

Europeans began their commercial operations in western Africa with the conscious aim of stifling competition by erecting elaborate terrestrial establishments at key centres along the coast. In the evolution of this trade from the earliest Portuguese ventures to the British, French, and German domination of the nineteenth century, it became obvious that entry into trans-oceanic shipping was possible for a great number of European merchants whose activities on the western African coast escaped all efforts at central control. Official entrepôts thus gave way to a system of virtually free trade. In East African terms, the movement was backwards: from the nineteenth-century Zanzibar staple to the scattered Swahili towns of the medieval period.

The Portuguese in the fifteenth and sixteenth centuries treated West African trade as an exclusive state enterprise run by officers of the crown at fortified colonial enclaves. In the seventeenth century, when the Portuguese position was challenged by Holland, England and France (and to a lesser extent, Denmark, Sweden and Brandenburg), European governments no longer took direct responsibility for commercial operations but nonetheless sought to enforce monopolies which were granted to officially chartered companies. These various West African (or Royal African, Guinea, Senegal, West Indian, etc.) companies were perceived as necessary in order to encourage individual merchants to enter a trade which was highly risky and required military operations against not only the established Portuguese but also other newcomers. Given the eventual effective competition (which even extended to interlopers from the same nations as the companies), none of the monopoly organizations were able to maintain profitable operations. By the time the slave trade reached its peak in the eighteenth century, the major powers had officially opened up western African trade to all merchants and continued to maintain the forts and factories of the companies as public services, available at low cost to any ships which wished to reduce the time necessary to bulk full export cargoes.[17]

During the nineteenth century, various political and ideological factors (see Chapter 5) contributed to the retention and even piecemeal expansion of these small colonial holdings by Portugal, Britain, and France, although Holland, Denmark and the other smaller powers now abandoned all territorial claims in western Africa. Most of the firms involved in the slave trade disappeared after 1800, to be replaced by a much larger number of merchants who exported the expanded bulk of 'legitimate' African goods. The even greater ease of entry into such commerce encouraged extensive competition in each port but provided little incentive to enlarge the scale of individual firms or extend operations into most areas of the interior. The major innovation of the mid-nineteenth century, the introduction of steam to Atlantic transport, created new concentrations in the shipping concerns serving western Africa. However, until the colonial period (and with the exception of the German Woermann interests), the ownership of firms operating steamships tended to remain separate from merchant enterprise and actually created new opportunities for small coastal operators to enter the export–import trade.[18]

The major beneficiaries of these changes in the later nineteenth century were not new arrivals from Europe but rather locally born members of what are usually called Afro-European or creole societies. The biological origins of such groups and even of individuals within each group varied considerably. Many were descended from unions between European merchants and African women. The majority, however, entered the orbit of the European commercial centres by other routes. They or their ancestors had often been slaves, adopted children, or voluntary employees of Europeans, mulattos or already Europeanized Africans. During the nineteenth century many thousands of Africans were taken off illegal slaving vessels by the British Royal Navy (and to a much lesser extent the French and American navies) and then resettled in Sierra Leone, The Gambia, Liberia and Gabon under missionary tutelage to form sizeable creole communities. In some of these places, as well as in Dahomey and Lagos, slaves emancipated while still off the African coast were joined by others who had gained their freedom in Brazil or North America.[19]

The raison d'être of the earliest Afro-European communities had been to provide permanent services on land for European shippers. In the older centres of their original settlement, Senegambia, Upper Guinea and the Gold Coast, many of these agents had developed sufficient means to trade locally on their own account, usually from politically autonomous communities near the main European centres. By the nineteenth century, the most attractive areas for Afro-European commerce were the small European colonies in Senegal, Sierra Leone, the Gold Coast, Lagos, Gabon and Angola. However the increased size and new sources of these communities meant that their commercial activities spread out to coastal centres without permanent European political supervision, such as Dahomey, the Bight of Biafra and the northern Congo coast.

Even under conditions most favourable to their enterprise, creole merchants remained a relatively weak intermediary group between the external European economy and the internal African suppliers of export goods. None of the Afro-Europeans ever became wealthy enough to establish an economic base in Europe or even became significant owners of ocean-going vessels. Because of their limited capital, they tended to specialize in import and retail trade rather than the more risky business of exporting local commodities. On this basis the creoles could compete with the smaller expatriate European firms on the coast and sometimes take over the assets of failing foreign merchants, as occurred on the nineteenth-century Gold Coast.

Even the most successful Afro-European firms generally preferred to maintain informal bookkeeping and extended family forms of property rights rather than taking on the organizational and legal structure of modern European businesses.[20] This pattern cannot be explained by lack of education or legislative provision: both were available by the nineteenth century in the colonial enclaves where most Afro-Europeans were based. One explanation, as with the Afro-Muslim merchants of the Sudanic zone, is that indigenous relationships of kin and slavery provided the only reliable basis for organizing firms in a society where the wage labour market was still very weak. A simultaneous and equally compelling motive was the protection of property from the legal claims of Europeans, given the tendency of Africans to depend upon external advances of capital which they often could not repay on schedule. Such defensive tendencies were reinforced during the course of the late nineteenth century when vegetable-oil export prices declined (a by-product of the transport revolution associated with steam navigation), making coastal trade more economically precarious than ever.

Insofar as they did rely upon control of local social resources, creole merchants enjoyed no advantage over non-Europeanized African middleman groups. The major assets of the Afro-Europeans were their access to European import goods, modern forms of river transportation, and information about external markets. Had coastal trade been more concentrated in a few areas, such a position might have provided the means for building up long-distance trading systems of the type created by Afro-Muslims in the Sudan and East Africa. In the competitive situation which existed, however, efforts towards this end were constantly frustrated, as illustrated by the case of the Afro-Europeans who penetrated most deeply into the western African hinterland, the *pombeiros* of Angola.[21]

The *pombeiros* represented large Portuguese merchant firms firmly established in the most developed of the European commercial centres of western Africa. *Pombeiro* caravans travelled from Luanda on the coast to remote markets at Kasanje in central Angola and to Malebo (Stanley Pool) in the Congo. To achieve this access the Portuguese had destroyed the Mbundu and Kongo states which had previously controlled coastal trade and had also come to terms with the equally expansive Imbangala of Kasanje, who established an eastern limit to *pombeiro* movement. Even on this basis, the system fell apart by the later eighteenth century because unlicensed *pombeiros* began trading with interloping ships on the northern Angola coast while the Imbangala and Malebo suppliers fed a major portion of their slave and ivory exports to a competing trade network emanating from the northern Congo coast, where British, Dutch and French shippers made regular calls. The groups who organized caravans from this latter region – essentially Vili peoples of Loango and related local states – achieved more effective penetration of the interior than did the *pombeiros* since the Vili alone were able to establish permanent, politically neutral agencies at various points along the routes.[22]

The Vili are, in fact, a unique phenomenon in western Africa since elsewhere it was only Muslim trading groups from the Sudanic zone who managed to maintain direct and autonomous caravan connections between the Atlantic seaboard and the distant interior. At the moment of the European discoveries, Juula merchants from the Western Sudan were already established on the coasts of Senegambia and present-day Ghana, as buyers of gold, kola, salt and dried fish. In Senegambia the establishment of European trading factories brought no basic change to this system: Juula traders continued to move goods between the coast and their home-lands in the region of the upper Niger. In all likelihood the rate of traffic was now vastly accelerated, since Europeans provided a major market for Sudanese slaves without competing for any coastal goods except the already much-diminished gold supplies.[23]

In present-day Ghana, the major source for the late-medieval Sudanic gold trade, Juula and Europeans did initially compete with one another. Once the European centres at the 'Gold Coast' had been set up, however, Sudanic traders confined their sphere to the centres of what became the Asante empire, slightly over 150 km from the ocean. While gold from this region flowed mainly to Euro-peans, Juula, and later Hausa, traders flourished as – among other things – suppliers of slaves and buyers of European goods. When the European demand for slaves from this region declined in the nineteenth century and gold was apparently not available in sufficient quantities to replace it, the elevated import expectations of Asante were maintained by a major increase in northern trade, particularly the export of kola through Hausa caravans.[24]

To the east of present-day Ghana the Sudanic merchant networks had never reached the coast in medieval times and, throughout the period of pre-colonial European trade, a watershed between coastal and savanna commercial zones continued to exist. It is much more difficult in these areas than in Asante to establish the balance between complementary and competitive factors linking such zones. Slaves always appear to have moved in response to demand in either direction but ivory in nineteenth-century Cameroon and Gabon represents a scarcer commodity whose price to European shippers may have been somewhat raised by the existence of an alternative outlet to the north. In all these areas Sudanic trade – particularly that of the Hausa – continued to grow from 1500 to 1900 so that the European coastal presence, where not demonstrably helpful, certainly appears to have done little damage.[25]

The commercial impact: African ethnic relays

Between the domain of the Europeans and Afro-Europeans on the seaboard and the Muslim caravan routes from the north lay a large region of Guinea and equatorial forest and southern savanna where export commerce was controlled by the indigenous population. With the already noted exception of the Loango Coast Vili, the traders here failed to develop market networks and merchant estates which transcended geographical and cultural boundaries. Goods moving to or from the coast were therefore not carried by single caravans or agents of the same organization over wide distances, but instead passed by a system of relays from one ethnic group to another across territories often defined by shifts from overland to water routes.[26]

The geographical obstacles suggested by references to forests and rivers navi-gable over only limited stretches, often for limited seasons, provide part of the explanation why relays rather than network systems should dominate long-distance commerce in this portion of Africa. The fact that gold gave way to slaves and the products of foraging and small-scale agriculture as the principal export is also important: the latter commodities came from scattered areas, thus encour-aging a multiplicity of supply routes.

However, similar conditions along various sections of the routes feeding Sudanic and Indian Ocean frontiers did not prevent integrated caravan networks from dominating these systems. The critical factor determining the segmented structure of the Atlantic supply routes was competitiveness among coastal outlets. Africans in direct contact with Europeans thus enjoyed certain advantages in the Atlantic trade but these were lessened by the possibility of their interior partners exploiting the choice between alternative oceanic markets.

The core of the Atlantic trading system is thus much more fragmented and unstable than the hinterland of either of the two commercial frontiers previously discussed. Nonetheless it was held together by two, not always distinguishable, sets of institutions. The first were the instruments of exchange which linked each sphere of the relay system (including the European one) to the next: accounting units, credit arrangements, and partnership alliances. The second were the social formations within each sphere which transported and stored goods and provided the necessary conditions of market access.

Units of account are complicated in western Africa because, given the political and cultural autonomy of African trading groups and the relative unimportance of bullion in local exchanges, no currency existed which had the same value to both partners. Forms of money existed in many of the African societies involved but these – whether palm oil, cotton cloths, cowries, copper ingots, brass or iron bars, or brass horseshoe-shaped 'manillas' – were used mainly for internal exchanges and figured in international trade essentially as import goods. International accounts thus had to be settled through barter equivalencies often expressed in terms of stable commodity-monetary units (iron/copper bars, gold ounces, cases of gin, etc.) but actually embodying very flexible exchange values (the 'bar value' of a real iron bar could shift radically according to supply/demand factors). The changing barter terms of trade for African commodities on the European market are thus accurately reflected in prices paid on the coast and passed along to the hinterland.[27]

Exchanges of import for export goods, whether on the coast or in the interior, often could not be made immediately, and thus required the advancement of credit by one partner or the other. The advances in almost all cases (the major exceptions involved Juula merchants in Senegambia dealing with temporarily isolated European posts) went from Europeans to coastal Africans and from these along the chain of intermediaries leading to ultimate interior suppliers. The direction of this credit flow reflected the superior access of Europeans to a capital market. In specific cases it often subjected foreign merchants to losses from default or fraud, but in the aggregate it allowed a degree of external control over prices, which normally provided very high gross profit rates at each point of transaction.

In order to ensure that trade took place when merchants arrived at a market controlled by an alien society and that credit arrangements were respected, it was necessary to establish regular relations with individuals from the host group. Europeans often dealt with this problem in their own terms, using Afro-European agents on the coast, disbursing credit books to Africans who had received advances (even if the latter were themselves illiterate), or publishing information among themselves about the reliability of various African partners and exploiting the mobility of sailing vessels to avoid those who proved difficult. For Africans travelling inland and for some European traders, more complex social alliances were required. These might include mutual residence of one entire household in the compound of the 'host' trading partner, entry into pledges of 'blood brotherhood', or some comparable ritual pact, and intermarriage. The latter, a very frequent and effective device, often reflected the same asymmetry as credit flows: Europeans and traders nearer the coast took wives from their debtor partners, but did not give their own women to these groups.[28]

The decision to enter partnership alliances already indicates the degree to which commercial relations in western Africa might become imbedded in diffuse social relationships. This feature is even more pronounced in the maintenance of trading organizations within each relay sphere. The variants in these organizations follow essentially three different models: a lineage/village system of collective mobilization; a political model based on the authority of centralized rulers or segmented big men; and a ritual model centred around membership in regional cults. It must be stressed that these categories are analytic abstractions, designed to help understand the dominant characteristics of various trading systems; any one historical system often had elements of two or more such models.

The simplest means for an African society to enter into a trading system was to mobilize the local male population during the non-agricultural season for commerce with neighbouring regions. This practice is not unique to either western Africa or international trade; it was the device by which the Nyamwezi built up their caravan system in East Africa and is a common means everywhere of carrying on regional exchange. The basic organization of such trade is the normal village/lineage structure of age groups and kin groups. Both the authorities and the work force are the same ones that function in the food-producing activities of the society. The territory to which such organization gave access was constrained by the seasonality of the commercial expeditions and the size of the groups involved. In western Africa outside the Sudan the dry seasons suitable for travel are not as long as in East Africa. Small caravans of villagers would thus suffice for defending routes through friendly or neutral territory, but could not readily deal with competition from outsiders who wished to retain commercial control over their own areas. In fact, systems of village-based relays tended to be very fragmented and characteristic of remote sources of primary goods or the immediate hinterlands of coastal entrepôts such as the Ivory Coast, where the total volume of trade – and therefore the incentive to build up more specialized organizations – was not great.[29]

Along the major Atlantic trade routes not fed directly by Juula merchants – that is, from the Ivory/Gold Coasts east and southward – most merchants were organized around specialized political authorities. This model would even best describe the coastal trading groups in those areas whose interior relays were based on village/lineage structures. Here the nucleus of men engaged in long-distance commerce were retainers of local rulers and did not usually engage in regular food production. The immediate supervision or leadership of trading expeditions was always the responsibility of individuals close to the centre of power – sometimes the ruler himself – but a large portion of the work force, particularly porters and canoe paddlers, usually consisted of slaves recruited especially for such purposes.

The politically organized trading organizations of western Africa varied considerably in their structure. For purposes of general analysis they may be classified as centralized and decentralized systems, although many actual cases fall somewhere between these poles. The great inland Guinea states of Asante, Dahomey, Oyo, and Benin, along with the Portuguese colony of Angola and its Mbanda, Imbangala, Matamba and Kasanje trading partners fall into the centralized category, at least during their periods of effective operation.[30] In each of these states a single political authority controlled access to commerce by establishing effective administrative-military authority over the key trading areas and regulating the entry of indigenous and foreign merchants into the market. In most (but not all) cases the ruler himself maintained a corps of official merchant-chiefs who enjoyed special rights with regard to supplies of public capital and opening trade, exemption from market taxes, etc., but never a total monopoly over international exchanges. Important merchants were therefore not necessarily part of the state apparatus but their activities were subject to political control and often privileged competition from state traders.

Decentralized trading polities controlled the canoe-borne commerce of coastal waterways in the Ivory Coast, eastern Nigeria, Cameroon and Gabon, as well as the inland Congo River and its tributaries.[31] Political authority in these systems never extended beyond a single urban settlement and its immediate hinterland (e.g. the Niger Delta 'city states') and was sometimes confined to a village which only recognized bonds with its neighbours when defending common territory from outsiders. Trade was organized through wards or 'houses': the kin and slave retinues of single enterprising individuals. The ward/house was not an entirely specialized unit since it provided much of its own food supply, but the subsistence model here was a form of fishing which already encompassed expeditions away from home settlements for the acquisition and exchange of marketable goods. In the transition from fishing to trade in overseas export commodities the wards/houses became real capitalist firms, investing in the fixed assets of canoes and slaves to maximize profits, and rising or falling according to their degree of economic success.

Ultimately all western African trading polities proved incapable of organizing economies over more than a limited territorial scale. The centralized states, particularly Asante and Oyo in the late eighteenth century, could expand into very wide areas but control over these regions ultimately created political crises and declining economic returns. The decentralized states were less stable but more flexible; it was difficult to reconcile even a minimal notion of paramount authority with the competitive character of the trading units. In fact the logic of social mobility often allowed an ex-slave to assume leadership, as illustrated by the well-known case of Ja-Ja at Bonny in the late-nineteenth-century Niger Delta.[32] Such conflicts could be resolved by establishing new settlements with different authorities (Ja-Ja moved from Bonny to Opobo), so that the system as a whole endured. However the economic range of canoe-based enterprises was limited by the navigability of the rivers and creeks on which they operated. Beyond these they were dependent on relays from other kinds of middlemen.

It can be argued that if western African states had possessed more effective military and administrative technology – as was perhaps becoming the case in Asante by the mid-nineteenth century – they might have succeeded in integrating larger trading areas and have even eventually created more effective markets for internal production. This contention, as will be seen, provided an economic justification for European colonialism; but its converse, the over-preponderance of the state, will also be examined as one of the principal criticisms of the colonial and post-colonial African economy. For pre-colonial Sudanic and East Africa, states were important in concentrating external access to the products of long-distance trade – something which proved impossible on the Atlantic coast – but did not establish political hegemony over the interior networks. The most effective of these networks in western Africa were operated by Juula and Hausa merchants as political neutrals, relying for their internal cohesion upon a shared Muslim ritual identity. Within some of the trading systems of the western African forest zones indigenous cults could provide a parallel (if less effective) basis for wide-ranging, non-political market organization.

Non-Muslim ritual trading networks are known to have operated in three areas of western Africa: central Igboland (the Aro system); the Cross River of Nigeria-Cameroon (the Ekpe system); and southern Cameroon-Gabon (the *bilaba* system).[33] In the Aro case, merchants dispersed themselves over a wide area on the basis of their unique identification with a shrine which had some claim to transcendence over other local spiritual forces (the Chukwu – 'Great Spirit' – oracle of the Aro homeland). In the other cases (as was also partially true of the Aro), ritual organizations only facilitated access to market territories for merchants more explicitly organized as village/lineage groups or trading houses from decentralized states.

In one sense, these ritual systems simply provided the basis for partnership-alliances between individual traders of different societies. Such alliances existed in less elaborate forms at all points of juncture between western African relay spheres. Once linked to widely accepted ritual structures, however, alliances could allow a single group of traders to move across a number of local spheres to establish a wider range of trade. While centralized state trading systems tended to control access to the coast from the interior, ritual systems moved in the opposite direction, although only the Ekpe system began directly on the coast. The groups through whom this trade passed accepted the legitimacy of external penetration first because they shared the beliefs associated with the traders: the Aro oracle, the Ekpe leopard force, and the prestige of the successful gift donor in *bilaba* (a form of potlach). By so doing most societies also received an assured return of imported goods for the exports they produced.

Even at their most successful level, ritual trading systems remained nothing more than extended relays. The Aro and *bilaba* traders cut across the political segments of single ethnic groups while the Efik merchants could use the Ekpe cult to move over ethnic boundaries along the Cross River, but not much beyond (the Mungo River route feeding into the same West Cameroon hinterland was controlled by a competing coastal group, the Duala). The Juula/Hausa traders who used their Muslim cult identity in comparable ways had thus created not only much wider-ranging commercial networks but also a merchant role which was more specialized and efficient in its divorce from political and even ritual functions. The indigenous western African ritual trade systems demonstrate an impressive ability of local peoples to overcome, on a completely autonomous basis, some of the fragmenting elements of a competitive situation.[34] They also indicate, however, the failure of these societies to draw on their overseas partners for institutions and techniques which would create some correspondence of economic capacity on the two sides of the Atlantic frontier.

The developmental impact: export production

The production systems which fed the Atlantic trade of Africa – mining, pre-datory gathering, and agriculture – are not essentially different from those linked to other frontiers of external commerce and thus do not have to be described in detail. The evolution of these activities within western Africa did, nonetheless, bear the distinctive stamp of both the Atlantic economy and the local physical-cultural landscape.

The similarity to other regions is most marked in the production of goods which constituted the earliest export staples: ivory and other wild products and gold. Gold, as already noted, came from the identical sources which supplied the trans-Saharan trade. Its export overseas had no impact on production other than to increase its scale. The opening of the Atlantic did vastly increase the demand for gathered wild products, culminating in the massive export of rubber (mostly the *Landolphia* vine variety) in the late-nineteenth century. These enterprises paralleled the search for ivory in nineteenth-century East Africa; in the equatorial portions of western Africa there was even a similar movement inland of coastal ivory traders-hunters, especially in the case of the Cokwe in Angola and south-eastern Zaire.[35]

The Cokwe undermining of Lunda political authority resembles the violence and disorder engendered in immediately neighbouring areas by Arab-Swahili-Nyamwezi ivory traders from Tanzania. But, for all the range of their penetration, the Cokwe lacked the sense of cohesion which Swahili culture and a Zanzibar base gave to East-coast traders. Moreover, in most of western Africa the density of populations and/or local control over trading relays prevented any merchant group from seizing control over a wide area of export gathering. The impact of such activities was thus diffused and far less significant, in either a positive or negative sense, than in East Africa.

The slave trade represents a special category of predatory commerce which affected western Africa with far greater intensity than any other region, especially when it is considered that the same populations often fed both the Atlantic and the trans-Saharan markets. As already noted, the demographic impact of the Atlantic demand for slaves was distributed fairly widely along the western (and even eastern) African coast and hinterland. The demographic effect of human exports was also somewhat balanced by the positive impact on population of New World food crops (see Chapter 1). Of those areas most heavily drawn upon, some, like the interior of Dahomey (present-day Benin) and the 'Middle Belt' of Nigeria, show clear evidence of depopulation. However, the Igbo hinterland of the Bight of Biafra has always – like the Malawi area of East Africa – been recognized as a major exporter of population both in the slave trade era and after it. Even the territories of the former Kongo kingdom in north-western Angola, once thought to have been devastated by direct Portuguese slave raids, now appear to have experienced slight demographic gains. This finding is explained by the fact that the Angola coast was tapped exclusively by the Atlantic slave trade, which sought mainly adult males, thus leaving in Africa most of the female population,[36] who are the key determinant of reproduction in any human population.

None of this evidence indicates that the slave trade had a positive impact upon western Africa; it only suggests that the costs to productivity and internal market integration must be relegated to the realm of the potential rather than the actual. Had the population lost through both the violence of the trade and the actual export of living men, women and children been retained in the region, they might have stimulated more intensive economic development in their home regions or helped to settle (as groups from Igboland and the slave-producing Cameroon Grassfields ultimately did in the colonial period) the relatively empty equatorial forest stretches separating the densely inhabited regions of western Africa.[37] In structural terms, therefore, the aspect of the slave trade which had the most negative effects on development is not the direct destruction of population, but rather the exploitation of population surpluses for the strengthening of overseas exchange linkages at the expense of internal trade and productivity.

The costs that the slave trade imposed upon general economic activities were, nevertheless, relative rather than absolute since other forms of market production did develop in western Africa, often not only simultaneously with slave exporting but also dependent upon local slave exploitation. The notion of 'legitimate' trade goods as opposed to slaves is thus a Western ideological concept (see Chapter 5) that tells us little about changes in African production processes. Nonetheless, the shifts in, and high levels of world demands for, western African raw materials in the nineteenth century does provide a unique opportunity for comparing the impact of differing groups of exports.

The new patterns of trade brought about shifts of some kind in the immediate organization of production, the linkages between export processes and other sectors of the economy, and the social composition of export enterprise. In evaluating all of these changes it must, however, be kept in mind how important a role predatory production – of slaves, ivory, rubber, timber, etc. – continued to play in nineteenth-century western African exports.

Palm oil and palm kernels represent only a limited movement beyond such *Raubwirtschaft*. Oil-palm trees grew wild, although mainly around cleared areas, where they could be maintained continuously by some clearing and weeding efforts on the part of neighbouring farmers who wished to harvest the fruit. Fairly intensive labour was required to extract the oil or kernel and bring it to a local market, although most of this work could be done by women in the homestead without disturbing the rhythms of normal food-production activities. The major entrepreneurial activity in the palm trade continued to be the bulking of produce at major inland market centres, its transport to the central coastal markets, and the various military-political efforts required to maintain competitive control of such routes.[38]

Peanut production marked more of a 'revolution' in the western African economy since this crop required the full effort of farmers during their main cultivation season. In order to take advantage of the demand for peanuts at Atlantic ports, many Africans migrated each year from the Senegambian interior to agricultural lands within reach of the coast. Once having decided to grow peanuts for export, however, the farmer did not have to change any of hs cultivation techniques or acquire new capital goods since this crop had already been adopted into local food-production systems several centuries earlier.[39]

Even where technical inputs and investments or even the balance between producer and merchant/transporter had not changed much, the export economy of the nineteenth century did link together a wider sector of the western African economy than had its predecessors. The predatory export systems of this area had always demanded some level of provisioning – mainly in the form of foodstuffs – from the local economy. In the nineteenth century, as the total value of overseas trade rose and the bulk of goods which had to be brought to the coast to produce each unit of import value increased – 'legitimate' commodities being less precious than gold and slaves – the demand for such secondary linkages to the export economy expanded. The primary producers of the new export goods, particularly peanuts and palm goods, also represent a new factor brought into the main market system, although the rewards which finally reached them through the chain of intermediaries was always small.

The degree to which the nineteenth-century export system mobilized such producers can perhaps best be perceived by examining the social formations within which they now worked. Roughly speaking, commercial agricultural production was divided among peasants and slaves, although the distinction between these two categories is sometimes difficult to discern. Peasants were those farmers living on their own land and producing goods for the world market as well as local consumption. In the palm-exporting regions, the commitment to export production remained rather marginal and, in the periods of falling prices towards the end of the nineteenth century, farmers here could simply withdraw from the market. Senegambian peanut growers, on the other hand, had invested a far greater portion of their efforts in export crops. Moreover, they found themselves in serious conflict with the military elites of the earlier slave-trading regime, who were not needed for bulking and transport services (these continued to be provided, as in the past, by autonomous Juula merchants) but regularly confiscated large portions of peasant wealth. The result of this conflict was a Senegambian social revolution, in which peasants rallied around Muslim clerics to form new political units. Once achieved, however, this new regime adopted many of the forms of the order it had overthrown, including a military apparatus and trade in slaves for both export and local deployment.[40]

The striking social innovation in the Senegambian economy of the nineteenth century is therefore not the market-oriented peasant producer but rather the use of slaves as a major factor in export agriculture. Even here, the concept of redirecting such human capital from a commercial to a producer role is more radical than the historical process on the ground. Slaves are, in fact, found in almost all of the western African communities involved in the Atlantic trade of the nineteenth century but in most cases they were used in even less-concentrated and innovative forms of cultivation than on the Sudanic and Indian Ocean frontiers.

Agricultural slaves in the Atlantic zone were most often incorporated into individual households to work alongside their masters or settled in satellite compounds or villages with tributary obligations, in labour or kind, to the owner groups. The only evidence of any special functions connecting such slaves to the export economy is the assertion in some areas that they climbed palm trees to cut fruit – a task too dangerous to appeal to free males, and too arduous and sexually undecorous for the women who undertook most of the extra work demanded by palm production.

Slaves were more prominent in the canoe crews and military formations which controlled access to export goods than they were in the production sectors. However in a few areas of nineteenth-century western Africa local elites placed their servile labourers on large estates which may be described as agricultural plantations. Some of these were controlled by the new Muslim leadership of Senegambia and thus resemble both the slave-pupil farming units which had always surrounded centres of Islamic learning in this area, as well as the new agricultural formations of contemporaneous northern Nigeria. More-isolated plantations grew up adjacent to coastal trading centres which shifted from slaves to legitimate goods, such as Dahomey and the rivers of Guinea, Sierra Leone and the Congo. Even in the largest-scale units there is no evidence of more-intensive cultivation techniques or labour discipline connected with the use of slaves. While slavery is related to the commercialization of agriculture in western Africa, it remains even further than the Swahili coast and Sudanic models from constituting a distinctive production system.[41]

The developmental impact: manufacturing

The expanded pace of market participation by western African cultivators in the nineteenth century therefore did not alter the relatively diffuse structure of commercial enterprise developed in this region from the earliest periods of Atlantic trade. This feature helps to explain – but is also explained by – the relative weakness of local urban centres as foci of both commerce in rural goods and handicraft manufacturing.

Before the opening of the Atlantic, various forms of manufactured goods had circulated within the internal markets of western Africa. Cloth was probably the most widespread since cotton-weaving had spread from the Sudan into Senegambia and Guinea while woven raphia-palm textiles played a major role in the indigenous exchange systems of the Congo region. Metal and metal goods were also traded, especially copper, which is known to have been incorporated into the paraphernalia of early Nigerian ritual and circulated very widely as currency in western equatorial Africa.[42]

The further development of these industries was threatened, however, by the exposure of western Africa to direct competition with European manufactures. Unlike the Sudanic or East African contact economies, the Atlantic frontier offered neither natural protection against imported goods nor the concentration of trade and real or potential artisanal activities in a few major entrepôts. Instead, European shippers, with easy access to supply sources from Asia and the Americas as well as their own continent, could bring trade articles directly to whichever African port might offer the best barter prices. Moreover, the prime cost of imported manufactures went down steadily as Europeans subjected the production of textile and metal goods first to the proto-industrial revolution of water and wind power and then to the more dramatic one of steam-driven factories.

The effect of this competition on African manufacturing was complex, although generally inhibitive of any positive technological transformations. Whether African handicraft production declined or expanded depended upon the position of specific artisans within the geography of Atlantic markets and the hierarchy of local manufacturing processes. Because of the continued high costs of internal transportation, western African industries located more than about one hundred and fifty kilometres from the coastal entry points of European goods still enjoyed a significant cost advantage over imports. Of still greater consequence, however, was the division between producers of intermediate and final-use manufactured goods.

At the trading ports Europeans sold Africans certain categories of commodities which went directly to consumers without further processing. These included plain white and dyed cotton cloth, metal vessels, blades, guns, jewelry, and alcoholic beverages. However, an even wider market existed for European goods which could be incorporated into subsequent African artisanal activities: yarn, or cloth to be unravelled for yarn (particularly if dyed in certain colours); and iron and copper bars. The attraction of these goods was that they overcame certain bottlenecks in the African manufacturing system: the spinning of yarn (always much slower without the use of the wheel than weaving); and dyeing in colours not available from local plants (mostly just blue indigo in West Africa); and the smelting of iron (copper mainly came to areas where it had always been imported).

African artisans enjoyed an advantage over Europeans in producing final goods from these materials because they could direct their efforts towards specific and varied local demands such as the types of blades favoured on hoes or woodworking instruments, the patterns of design sought in fancy cloths, and the prestige–ritual needs of metal statuary. Even without direct statistical evidence, we can infer an increase in African artisanal activity from the volume of intermediate goods imported, from archaeological evidence, and from the increased demand for the objects in question under the conditions of export-based prosperity.[43] However, we must also recognize a disincentive to make changes in the very areas of African technology which hampered long-term competition with Europeans. Cotton-weavers no longer had any reason to bring spinning up to their own pace by adopting the wheel (but the presence of female slaves in abundant numbers seem to have disinclined even Europeans supervising cotton cloth manufacture on the West African coast from using spinning wheels).[44] African blacksmiths made tools and weapons from inferior imported bar iron rather than developing capacities for working their own high-carbon bloom more efficiently.[45]

That such changes would have taken place without the presence of imported substitutes for the relevant intermediate goods cannot, of course, be assumed. However, it does appear ironic that the region of Africa most actively involved in contact economic growth should have undergone a development process in many respects more limited than that of the West African Sudan or East Africa. The summation of this experience raises some general questions about autonomous African economic change in an international context.

The direction of contact economic change: development, stagnation, or crisis?

The frontiers of international commerce undoubtedly provided the major stimulus to growth in the pre-colonial African economy. However, the meaning of such experiences for African development and dependency remains ambiguous. The historical sequel to the contact economies was the takeover of African territory by European colonial regimes whose impact on further internal change was, as will be seen below, profound. Historians of modern Africa have thus had to ask themselves how the onset of colonialism can be linked to previous economic patterns. Did the new regimes represent a disruption of real or potential indigenous development, an exogenous solution to insurmountable African stagnation, or a logical outcome of processes already at work in the contact economies? Arguments for all three of these positions can be formulated from the various perspectives which have been used to analyse African economic history. An image of development is suggested by studies which stress the market opportunities offered by the frontiers of extra-continental contact and the dynamism with which Africans responded to such incentives. However, even from this perspective, it is clear that actual development did not extend to the transformation of production organization and technology in agriculture and manufacturing. Nonetheless, it can still be asserted that the growing concentration of trade, production, and population in such centres as Kano, Zanzibar, and Asante might eventually have provided the basis for more radical economic change. Moreover, these centres could have imported European technology – as some did with only limited success – for incorporation into their own systems of development.[46]

It is perhaps easier to assert that African economies in this period were simply expanding the capacities of their domestic structures without real possibilities for changes beyond those which historically occurred. The explanations for such stagnation have been treated at some length in the preceding sections: ecological barriers to animal power and the wheel; the substitution of servile labour for capital-intensive technology in areas of high population concentration; the inscription of risk-averse strategies into the cultures of many African groups closely engaged in market activities; and the effect of already-developed European technology in delivering manufactured goods to Africa more cheaply than Africans could produce substitutes for them.

The arguments for development or stagnation in African contact economies assume that the external frontiers represent nothing more than markets to which Africans could respond with whatever resources appeared most appropriate. Scholars convinced that Africa was entering a crisis in the late nineteenth century assert instead that the particular form of market relationships with Europe did not allow Africans to maintain true autonomy. One form of the crisis argument, presented by liberal-market historians such as A.G. Hopkins and David Fieldhouse claims that the possibilities for the exchange of a wide range of local goods undermined the archaic organization of African societies, creating conflicts between new classes of merchants and peasant producers on the one side, and slave-owning political elites on the other. According to this view, only a radical reorganization of these societies in a form and on a scale compatible with the structure and technology of the truly modern external world could resolve the African dilemma and such a change was only historically possible through colonialism.[47]

Another version of the crisis theory, from a Marxist/dependency perspective, stresses the demands of European trading partners who could not allow Africans to remain either outside the world system as inefficient operators of traditional economies nor would let them enter that system on any terms but that of 'peripheral' producers of raw materials in exchange for Western manufactured goods.[48] The common denominator of both these versions is that the presence of Europeans on Africa's economic frontiers dictated internal changes which were not assimilable to ongoing patterns of either development or stasis. The first form of the crisis argument addresses the internal African patterns more directly and needs to be reviewed briefly in the light of the evidence already presented. The second refers to European concerns with Africa, which will be the main topic of Chapter 5.

The kind of crisis which Hopkins and Fieldhouse identify is difficult to apply to the contact economies of either the West African Sudan or East Africa. The former was sufficiently sheltered from any direct economic encounter with Europeans so that its development processes suffered no disruption until the actual arrival of colonial rulers. In East Africa there were colonial and proto-colonial interventions in the local economy by the Portuguese, the French, and the British. But these influences either accelerated or slowed down the evolution of long-distance trade and slave-based agriculture without imposing any alternative pattern on a region whose most immediate external ties still bound it to Asia rather than to Europe.

It is thus western Africa which provides the real test for the notion of an indigenous socio-economic crisis as a prelude to colonialism. Certainly this was the region most fully exposed to European influence. Moreover, the transition from slave to 'legitimate' exports was closely tied here to the chronology of European industrialization. Likewise, the worldwide depression from the 1870s to the 1890s is reflected in a fall of vegetable-oil prices (see Appendix, Figure A2), leading to numerous West African 'palavers' over credit, barter rates, and trade stoppages.

But it is not at all clear how deeply these crises in external trade touched the

African societies involved. The shift from slave exports created little problem since it did not diminish the total regional market for servile labour and allowed essentially the same or (in the case of Senegambia) very similar social formations to take over the supply of vegetable-oil products. Declining prices for palm products and peanuts caused profound problems for European trading firms in West Africa, since their entire existence depended upon the continuation of such commerce. But African producers and merchants could (as many did) simply drop out of the market until conditions provided better incentives for commercial efforts. Further, for societies such as Asante and the Upper Guinea Coast, which were the most committed to some form of long-distance trade, the decline of Atlantic markets could be compensated for by kola trade with the Sudan.[49] In short, the flexibility and in some respects limited development of the African economy allowed it to confront shifting European market demands without any evidence of systemic breakdown.

Whether or not the Europeans could tolerate these African solutions to common economic problems remains another issue. It has been argued throughout this book that Africa was becoming less significant to the world economy at the same time as it involved itself more closely in international commercial relationships. Why then did Europeans take over African economies at the end of the nineteenth century? To answer this question we must turn temporarily away from Africa itself to consider how the continent was perceived from the centre of the expanding Atlantic economy.

Notes

1. Fage (1962); Herbert (1974); Patterson (1975) p. 23.
2. Van Sertima (1976) (for the pre-European Atlantic connections thesis). Mauny (1971) p. 18f. offers a good summary of the negative evidence.
3. Gemery and Hogendorn (1978); North (1968).
4. Curtin (1975); Rodney (1970).
5. The literature here is huge but among the key works: on Asante and its predecessors, Daaku (1970); Wilks (1975); on Benin, Ryder (1969); on Dahomey, Argyle (1966); Ross (1967); Peukert (1978); on Oyo, Law (1977).
6. Birmingham (1966); Miller (1983); Thornton (1983).
7. Again, a huge bibliography represented incompletely by Alagoa (1970); Augé (1969); Austen (1983a); Harms (1981); Jones (1963); Latham (1973); Northrup (1978); Patterson (1975); Vansina (1973).
8. Godhino (1969) pp. 39–41, 176f.
9. Garfield (1971) pp. 34–45; Ryder (1969) p. 34f.
10. Curtin (1983) pp. 238–50 whose calculations are based particularly upon Godhino (1969); Vogt (1979).
11. Bean (1974); Rodney (1969).
12. Craton (1984); Curtin (1971).
13. Curtin (1969); Inikori (1982) 'Introduction' (critique of Curtin). For a discussion of the demographic impact of the slave trade upon western Africa, see below.
14. Stilliard (1938); Brooks (1975).
15. Woodruff (1958) especially p. 68f.; Dumett (1971); Howard (1972) p. 43f., p. 363.

16. Gemery and Hogendorn (1979); Hardy (1921) pp. 35–9, 128–302, 230–46; Pallinder (1974); Garfield (1971); Wheeler and Pélissier (1971) p. 64.
17. Curtin (1975) pp. 100–5; Davies (1957); Rodney (1970) pp. 122–51; Vogt (1979), p. 93f.
18. Davies (1973) pp. 29–30; McPhee (1926) pp. 72–3.
19. Curtin (1975) pp. 95–100; Daaku (1970) p. 96f.; Priestley (1969); Rodney (1970) p. 200f.; Turner (1975).
20. Dumett (1973); Hopkins (1966); Reynolds (1974).
21. Miller (1973).
22. Martin (1972) pp. 33–92, 118–31.
23. Curtin (1975) pp. 68–91; Wright (1977).
24. Teixeira da Mota (1972); Wilks (1971); Lovejoy (1980).
25. Johnson (1978b); Wirz,(1972), pp. 148–65, 193f.
26. Meillassoux (1971) 'Introduction'.
27. Curtin (1975) pp. 233–53; Johnson (1966); Jones (1958).
28. Austen (1983a); Newbury (1972).
29. Meillassoux (1964); Terray (1971).
30. See note 5 above; Miller (1973).
31. See note 7 above; Horton (1969); Ikime (1968); Ogadengbe (1971).
32. Cookey (1974); Jones (1963) pp. 127–32, 159f., 186–7. For similar cases in the Congo basin, see Harms (1981) passim; Vansina (1973) pp. 310–12.
33. Austen (1983b); Dupré (1972); Northrup (1978) pp. 114–45; Ottenberg (1958); Ruel (1969).
34. Possibly the most significant aspect of these cults was their ability to ward off accusations of witchcraft against successful merchants, an issue which cannot be pursued here (but see brief discussion in Chapter 10).
35. Miller (1969).
36. Fage (1975); Manning (1981–2); Thornton (1977).
37. Coquery-Vidrovitch (1985) pp. 32–42 (summary of research); Inikori (1982) for an articulate overstatement of the case for a major destructive economic impact.
38. Martin (1956); Oriji (1982); Oyewumi (1972).
39. Brooks (1975); Pélissier (1966).
40. Klein (1972); but see qualifications in Curtin (1981).
41. Lovejoy (1983), pp. 159–83. Most published studies of coastal West African slavery (including Austen, 1977) give little detail on agricultural production so most of the above is based on Austen (1975); Isichei (1975); Reynolds (forthcoming).
42. Herbert (1984) p. 123f.
43. Johnson (1978a); Pitts (1978); Fagg (1963) pp. 35–8.
44. Duncan (1972) pp. 218–22.
45. Goucher (1981).
46. Wilks (1975) p. 640f.
47. Fieldhouse (1973) pp. 83, 141; Hopkins (1973) pp. 142–66. For an argument closer to the one followed here, see Ehrensaft (1972).
48. Amin (1971); Wallerstein (1973, 1976).
49. Wilks (1971); Howard (1972) p. 43f.

Bibliography

Alagoa, E.J. (1970), 'Long-distance trade in the Niger Delta', *Journal of African History*, vol. 11, no. 3, pp. 319–29
Amin, Samir (1971), 'La politique française à l'égard de la bourgeoisie sénégalaise commerçante (1820–1960)', in Meillassoux (ed.), pp. 361–76

Argyle, W.J. (1966), *The Fon of Dahomey* (Oxford: Clarendon Press)

Augé, Marc (1969), 'Statut, pouvoir, et richesse: relations lignagières, relations de dépendance, et rapports de production dans la société alladien', *Cahiers d'Etudes Africaines*, vol. 9, no. 3, pp. 469–81

Austen, Ralph A. (1975), Cameroon Littoral fieldnotes

Austen, Ralph A. (1977), 'Slavery among coastal middlemen: the Duala of Cameroon', in Igor Kopytoff and Suzanne Miers (eds), *Slavery in Africa* (Madison: University of Wisconsin Press), pp. 305–33

Austen, Ralph A. (1983a), 'Metamorphoses of middlemen: the Duala, Europeans, and the Cameroon hinterland, ca. 1800–ca. 1960', *International Journal of African Historical Studies*, vol. 16, no. 1, pp. 1–24

Austen, Ralph A. (1983b), 'Cult organizations and trading networks in non-Muslim West Africa' (African Studies Association Meetings Papers)

Bean, Richard (1974), 'A note on the relative importance of slaves and gold in West African exports', *Journal of African History*, vol. 15, no. 3, pp. 351–6

Birmingham, David (1966), *Trade and Conflict in Angola: The Mbundu and their Neighbours under the Influence of the Portuguese, 1483–1790* (Oxford: Clarendon Press)

Birmingham, David and Phyllis Martin (eds) (1983), *History of Central Africa* (2 vols, London: Longman)

Brooks, George (1975), 'Peanuts and colonialism: consequences of the commercialization of peanuts in West Africa, 1830–70', *Journal of African History*, vol. 16, no. 1, pp. 29–54

Chamberlain, Christopher (1979), 'Bulk exports, trade tiers, regulation and development: an economic approach to the study of West Africa's "legitimate trade" ', *Journal of Economic History*, vol. 39, no. 2, pp. 419–38

Cookey, Sylvanus (1974), *King Ja Ja of the Niger Delta: His Life and Times, 1821–1891* (New York: Nok)

Coquery-Vidrovitch, Catherine (1985), *Afrique noire: permanence et ruptures* (Paris: Payot)

Craton, Michael (1984), 'The historical roots of the plantation model', *Slavery and Abolition*, vol. 5, no. 3, pp. 189–221

Curtin, Philip D. (1969), *The Atlantic Slave Trade: A Census* (Madison: University of Wisconsin Press)

Curtin, Philip D. (1971), 'The Atlantic slave trade 1600–1800', in J.F.A. Ajayi and Michael Crowder (eds), *History of West Africa*, Vol. 1 (London: Longman), pp. 240–68

Curtin, Philip D. (1975), *Economic Change in Precolonial Africa: Senegambia in the Era of the Slave Trade* (Madison: University of Wisconsin Press)

Curtin, Philip D. (1981), 'The abolition of the slave trade from Senegambia', in David Eltis and James Walvin (eds), *The Abolition of the Atlantic Slave Trade* (Madison: University of Wisconsin Press), pp. 83–97

Curtin, Philip D. (1983), 'Africa and the wider monetary world, 1250–1850', in J.F. Richards (ed.), *Precious Metals in the Late Medieval and Early Modern Worlds* (Durham, NC: Carolina Academic Press), pp. 231–68

Daaku, Kwame Yeboa (1970), *Trade and Politics on the Gold Coast, 1600–1720* (Oxford: Clarendon Press)

Davies, K.G. (1957), *The Royal African Company* (London: Longmans)

Davies, P.N. (1973), *The Trade Makers: Elder Dempster in West Africa, 1852–1972* (London: Allen & Unwin)

Dewey, Clive and A.G. Hopkins (eds) (1978), *The Imperial Impact: Studies in the Economic History of Africa and India* (London: Athlone Press)

Dike, K. Onwuka (1956), *Trade and Politics in the Niger Delta, 1830–1885* (Oxford: Clarendon Press)

Dumett, Raymond E. (1971), 'The rubber trade of the Gold Coast and Asante in the nineteenth century: African innovation and market responsiveness', *Journal of African History*, vol. 12, no. 1, pp. 79–101

Dumett, Raymond E. (1973), 'John Sarbah, the elder, and African mercantile entrepreneurship on the Gold Coast in the late nineteenth century', *Journal of African History*, vol. 14, no. 4, pp. 653–79

Duncan, T. Bentley (1972), *Atlantic Islands: Madeira, the Azores, and the Cape Verdes in the Seventeenth Century* (Chicago: University of Chicago Press)

Dupré, Georges (1972), 'Le commerce entre sociétés lignagières: les Nzabi dans la traite à la fin du dix-neuvième siècle (Gabon-Congo)', *Cahiers d'Études Africaines*, vol. 13, no. 4, pp. 616–58

Ehrensaft, Philip (1972), 'The political economy of informal empire in pre-colonial Nigeria, 1807–1887', *Canadian Journal of African Studies* vol. 6, no. 3, pp. 451–90

Fage, John D. (1962), 'Some remarks on beads and trade in Lower Guinea in the sixteenth and seventeenth centuries', *Journal of African History*, vol. 3, no. 2, pp. 343–7

Fage, John D. (1975), 'The effect of the export slave trade on African populations', in R.P. Moss and Richard Rathbone (eds), *The Population Factor in African Studies* (London: University Press), pp. 15–23

Fagg, William (1963), *Nigerian Images* (New York: Praeger)

Fieldhouse, D.K. (1973), *Economics and Empire, 1830–1914* (Ithaca: Cornell University Press)

Fynn, John K. (1975), *Asante and its Neighbours, 1700–1807* (London: Longman)

Garfield, Robert (1971), 'A history of São Thomé Island, 1470–1655' (Unpublished PhD dissertation, Northwestern University)

Gemery, Henry A. and Jan S. Hogendorn (1978), 'Technological change, slavery, and the slave trade', in Dewey and Hopkins (eds), pp. 243–58

Gemery, Henry A. and Jan S. Hogendorn (1979), 'Comparative disadvantage: the case of sugar cultivation in West Africa', *Journal of Interdisciplinary History*, vol. 9, no. 3, pp. 429–49

Godhino, Vitorino Magalhaes (1969), *L'économie de l'empire portugaise au XVe–XVIe siècles* (Paris: Mouton)

Goucher, Candice L. (1981), 'Iron is iron 'til it is rust: trade and ecology in the decline of West African iron smelting', *Journal of African History*, vol. 22, no. 2, pp. 179–89

Guilbot, J. (1951), 'Le Bilaba', *Journal de la Société des Africanistes*, vol. 21, no. 4, pp. 163–74

Hardy, Georges (1921), *La mise en valeur du Sénégal de 1817 à 1854* (Paris: Larose)

Harms, Robert W. (1981), *River of Wealth, River of Sorrow: The Central Zaire Basin in the Era of the Slave and Ivory Trade, 1800–1891* (New Haven: Yale University Press)

Herbert, Eugenia (1974), 'Portuguese adaptation to trade patterns, Guinea to Angola (1443–1640)', *African Studies Review*, vol. 17, no. 2, pp. 411–23

Herbert, Eugenia (1984), *Red Gold of Africa: Copper in Precolonial History and Culture* (Madison: University of Wisconsin Press)

Hopkins, A.G. (1966), 'Richard Beale Blaize, 1854–1904: merchant prince of West Africa', *Tarikh*, vol. 1, no. 2, pp. 70–9

Hopkins, A.G. (1973), *An Economic History of West Africa* (New York: Columbia University Press)

Horton, Robin (1969), 'From fishing village to trading state: a social history of New Calabar', in Mary Douglas and Phyllis M. Kaberry (eds), *Man in Africa* (London: Tavistock), pp. 37–58

Howard, Allen Marvin (1972), 'Big men, traders, and chiefs: power, commerce and spatial change in the Sierra Leone–Guinée plain, 1865–1895' (Unpublished PhD dissertation, University of Wisconsin)

Ikime, Obaro (1968), *Merchant Prince of the Niger Delta: The Rise and Fall of Nana Olomu, Last Governor of the Benin River* (London: Heinemann)

Inikori, J.E. (ed.) (1982), *Forced Migration: The Impact of the Export Slave Trade on African Societies* (London: Hutchinson)

Isichei, Elizabeth (1975), private communication

Johnson, Marion (1966), 'The ounce in eighteenth-century West African trade', *Journal of African History*, vol. 7, no. 2, pp. 197–214

Johnson, Marion (1970), 'The cowrie currencies of West Africa', *Journal of African History*, vol. 11, no. 1, pp.17–50, vol. 11, no. 2, pp. 331–53

Johnson, Marion (1978a), 'Technology, competition, and African crafts', in Dewey and Hopkins (eds), pp. 259–69

Johnson, Marion (1978b), 'By ship or by camel: the struggle for the Cameroons ivory trade in the nineteenth century', *Journal of African History*, vol. 19, no. 4, pp. 539–49

Jones, G.I. (1958), 'Native and trade currencies in southern Nigeria during the eighteenth and nineteenth centuries', *Africa*, vol. 28, no. 1, pp. 43–53

Jones, G.I. (1963), *Trading States of the Oil Rivers: A Study of Political Development in Eastern Nigeria* (London: Oxford University Press)

Klein, Martin A. (1972), 'Social and economic factors in the Muslim revolution in Senegambia', *Journal of African History*, vol. 13, no. 3, pp. 419–41

Latham, A.J.H. (1973), *Old Calabar, 1600–1891: The Impact of the International Economy upon a Traditional Society* (Oxford: Clarendon Press)

Law, Robin (1977), *The Oyo Empire c. 1600–c. 1836* (Oxford: Clarendon Press)

Lovejoy, Paul E. (1980), *Caravans of Kola: The Hausa Kola Trade, 1700–1900* (Zaria: Ahmadu Bello University Press)

Lovejoy, Paul (1983), *Transformations in Slavery: A History of Slavery in Africa* (Cambridge: Cambridge University Press)

McPhee, Allan (1926), *The Economic Revolution in British West Africa* (London: Routledge)

Manning, Patrick (1981–2), 'The enslavement of Africans: a demographic model' followed by comments, *Canadian Journal of African Studies*, vol. 15, no. 3, pp. 499–526; vol. 16, no. 2, pp. 127–39

Manning, Patrick (1982), *Slavery, Colonialism and Economic Growth in Dahomey, 1640–1960* (Cambridge: Cambridge University Press)

Martin, Anne (1956), *The Oil Palm Economy of the Ibibio Farmer* (Ibadan: University of Ibadan)

Martin, Phyllis (1972), *The External Trade of the Loango Coast, 1576–1870* (Oxford: Clarendon Press)

Mauny, Raymond (1971), *Les siècles obscurs de l'Afrique noire, histoire et archéologie* (Paris: Fayard)

Meillassoux, Claude (1964), *Anthropologie économique des Gouro du Côte d'Ivoire* (Paris: Mouton)

Meillassoux, Claude (ed.) (1971), *The Development of Indigenous Trade and Markets in West Africa* (London: Oxford University Press)

Miller, Joseph C. (1969), 'Cokwe trade and conquest in the nineteenth century', in Richard Gray and David Birmingham (eds), *Pre-colonial African Trade: Essays on Trade in Central and Eastern Africa before 1900* (London: Oxford University Press), pp. 175–201

Miller, Joseph (1973), 'Slaves, slavers, and social change in nineteenth century Kasanje', in Franz-Wilhelm Heimer (ed.), *Social Change in Angola* (Munich: Weltforum), pp. 9–29

Miller, Joseph (1983), 'The paradoxes of impoverishment in the Atlantic zone', in Birmingham and Martin (eds), pp. 118–59

Newbury, Colin W. (1972), 'Credit in early nineteenth century West African trade', *Journal of African History*, vol.13, no. 1, pp.81–95

North, Douglas (1968), 'Sources of productivity change in ocean shipping, 1600–1800', *Journal of Political Economy*, vol. 76, pp. 53–67

Northrup, David (1978), *Trade Without Rulers: Precolonial Economic Development in South-eastern Nigeria* (Oxford: Clarendon Press)

Ogadengbe, Kingsley Oladipo (1971), 'The Aboh kingdom of the lower Niger, 1650–1900' (Unpublished Ph D dissertation, University of Wisconsin)

Oriji, J.N. (1982), 'A re-assessment of the organization and benefits of the slave and palm produce trade amongst the Ngwa Ibo', *Canadian Journal of African Studies*, vol. 16, no. 3, pp. 523–48

Ottenberg, Simon (1958), 'Ibo oracles and intergroup relations', *Southwestern Journal of Anthropology*, vol. 14, pp. 295–317

Oyewumi, J.A.O. (1972), 'Development and origin of palm kernel production in Nigeria, 1807–1960' (Unpublished M Soc. Sci. dissertation, University of Birmingham)

Pallinder, Agneta (1974), 'Aborted modernization in West Africa? The case of Abeokuta', *Journal of African History*, vol. 15, no. 1, pp. 65–82

Patterson, K. David (1975), *The Northern Gabon Coast to 1875* (Oxford: Clarendon Press)

Pélissier, Paul (1966), *Les paysans du Sénégal* (St Iriex, Haute-Vienne: Fabergue)

Peukert, Werner (1978), *Der atlantische Sklavenhandel von Dahomey (1740–1797)* (Wiesbaden: Steiner)

Pitts, Delia Carol (1978), 'An economic history of cotton production in Senegal' (Unpublished Ph D dissertation, University of Chicago)

Priestley, Margaret (1969), *West African Trade and Coast Society* (London: Oxford University Press)

Reynolds, Edward (1974), 'The rise and fall of an African merchant class on the Gold Coast, 1830–1874', *Cahiers d'Etudes Africaines*, vol. 14, no. 2, pp. 253–64

Reynolds, Edward (forthcoming), *Chiefs, Farmers and Preachers: Tradition and Modernization in Akuapem*

Rodney, Walter A. (1969), 'Gold and slaves on the Gold Coast', *Transactions of the Historical Society of Ghana*, vol. 10, pp. 13–28

Rodney, Walter A. (1970), *A History of the Upper Guinea Coast, 1545–1800* (Oxford: Clarendon Press)

Ross, David (1967), 'The autonomous kingdom of Dahomey' (Unpublished PhD dissertation, University of London)

Ross, David (1969), 'The First Chacha of Wydah: Francis Felix De Souza', *Odu* (N.S.), vol. 2, pp. 19–28

Ruel, Malcolm (1969), *Leopards and Leaders: Constitutional Politics among a Cross River People* (London: Tavistock)

Ryder, Alan C. (1969), *Benin and the Europeans* (London: Longman)

Stilliard, N.H. (1938), 'The rise and development of legitimate trade in palm oil with West Africa' (Unpublished MA dissertation, University of Birmingham)

Teixeira da Mota, A. (1972), 'Mande trade on the Costa da Mina according to Portuguese documents until the mid-sixteenth century' (Unpublished paper delivered to Conference on Manding Studies, London)

Terray, Emmanuel (1971), 'Commerce pré-colonial et organisation sociale chez les Dida de Côte d'Ivoire', in Meillassoux (ed.), pp. 145–67

Thornton, John K. (1977), 'Demography and history in the kingdom of the Kongo, 1550–1750', *Journal of African History*, vol. 18, no. 4, pp. 517–30

Thornton, John K. (1983), *The Kingdom of Kongo: Civil War and Transition, 1641–1718* (Madison: University of Wisconsin Press)

Turner, J. Michael (1975), 'Les brésiliens: the impact of former Brazilian slaves in Dahomey' (Unpublished Ph D dissertation, Boston University)

Van Sertima, Ivan (1976), *They Came before Columbus* (New York: Doubleday)

Vansina, Jan (1973), *The Tio Kingdom of the Middle Congo* (London: Oxford University Press)

Vogt, John (1979), *Portuguese Rule on the Gold Coast, 1462–1682* (Athens: University of Georgia Press)

Wallerstein, Immanuel (1973), 'Africa in a capitalist world', *Issue*, vol. 3, no. 3, pp. 1–11

Wallerstein, Immanuel (1976), 'The three stages of African involvement in the world-economy', in Peter C.W. Gutkind and Immanuel Wallerstein (eds), *The Political Economy of Contemporary Africa* (Beverly Hills: Sage), pp. 30–57

Wheeler, Douglas and René Pélissier (1971), *Angola* (New York: Praeger)

Wilks, Ivor (1962), 'A medieval trade route from the Niger to the Gulf of Guinea', *Journal of African History*, vol. 3, no. 2, pp. 337–41

Wilks, Ivor (1971), 'Asante policy towards the Hausa trade in the nineteenth century', in Meillassoux (ed.), pp. 124–41

Wilks, Ivor (1975), *Asante in the Nineteenth Century* (Cambridge: Cambridge University Press)

Wirz, Albert (1972), *Vom Sklavenhandel zum Kolonialenhandel: Wirtschaftsraüme und Wirtschaftsformen in Kamerun vor 1914* (Zurich: Atlantis)

Woodruff, William (1958), *The Rise of the British Rubber Industry during the Nineteenth Century* (Liverpool: University of Liverpool Press)

Wright, Donald R. (1977), 'Darbo Jula: the role of a Mandinka Jula clan in the long-distance trade of the Gambia and its hinterland', *African Economic History*, no. 3, pp. 33–45

 *5*

From Slave Trade to Imperialist Partition
Africa in the Economy of
Early Industrial Europe

One of the many burdens which economic dependency imposes upon Africa is the need to explain already complex internal developments by reference to the domestic concerns of Europeans. Despite the greater prominence and thus, for most students, greater familiarity of European affairs, this task is not an easy one. The paradox of Africa's simultaneous involvement and marginalization in the world economy also operates in the opposite direction. Europe's increasing involvement in the African economy, which reached a climax with the imperialist partition of the late nineteenth century, is also at odds with the decreasing economic importance of Africa for Europe (see Appendix, Table A4).

This paradox cannot be resolved; as will be seen, it is at the heart of the dilemmas Africa would continue to face in its entire twentieth-century development. However, the problem can be understood better if distinctions are drawn between different dimensions of European economic relationships with Africa. First, there is the question of material need, defined by the ongoing market exchanges between the two continents and those exchanges which, with detached hindsight, appear likely to have developed. Second, there are the perceptions of those relationships by contemporary European policy-makers influenced, like the economic behaviour of Africans or anyone else, by a wide range of ideological and social concerns not directly related to the market. Finally, there is the technical capacity for penetration of overseas areas achieved by Europeans during the early industrial era which must be linked both to the benefits of previous economic relationships with Africa, and the cost of future ones. The often incongruous combination of these needs, perceptions, and capacities created the basis for Africa's role in the world economy of the eighteenth and nineteenth centuries.

At the beginning of the industrial age, in the late eighteenth century, Africa served Europe mainly as a supplier of slaves for sugar plantations in the West Indies. Until recently historians have seen little economic paradox alongside the more obvious moral contradictions of this phase in Europe's past. The slave-sugar complex was evaluated in the same terms as those used by contemporary observers: a highly prosperous affair, making a major contribution to the eventual take-off into full industrial development.[1] More recent research has suggested, however, that the slave trade itself was a risky business, yielding, at best, moderate profits (from just under 10 per cent per annum at its high point in late-eighteenth-century Britain to between 1 and 7 per cent in continental Europe.[2] Private returns on West Indian plantation investments were much higher, but in order to determine their role in the national economy, account must be taken of the high social costs incurred through protective tariffs, military expenditure and administration.[3] For Britain the total sum of these profits does not figure very prominently in the national income of the time and in particular seems to have played little role in providing the investment capital for early industrialization.[4]

Eighteenth-century European statesmen, on the other hand, believed that the slave system was of immense importance to their economies. In almost perfect correspondence with prevailing mercantilist theory it produced a commodity with high resale value (sugar) in return for just the kind of skilled enterprise and manufactured trade goods which home governments wished to use for procuring foreign exchange. The plantation islands of the Caribbean were thus the subject of elaborate protectionist legislation and constituted a major prize in the frequent wars of the period. However, despite major increases in the quantity and prices of slaves exported from Africa (the former more than doubled, the latter more than tripled in the course of the eighteenth century[5], see Appendix, Figure A1) efforts to control this trade by political means had been virtually abandoned. In contrast to the era of the gold trade, Africa was now recognized as a secondary, if still very critical, element in Europe's search for overseas wealth.

As already indicated, it is difficult to consider the capital accumulated from Atlantic slave and sugar enterprise as vital for the industrial revolution. Nonetheless, certain economic institutions developed through the pursuit of long-distance tropical trade – centralized capital markets, insurance, mass marketing, and improved shipping capacities – became crucial during the nineteenth century in transforming factory commodity production from its regional beginnings to its ultimate scale and complexity. Trade with Africa played a role in these developments, but the most important impetus came from the larger and more persistent Dutch and British East India companies. Monopolies of this kind could not survive, as has already been noted, in the more open and low-capital commerce with Africa. Indeed, the one last attempt to finance the slave trade on a major and officially sponsored scale, the notorious South Sea Bubble of 1720, inhibited the operation of the London stock market for almost a century afterwards.[6]

It may thus be argued that the capacities of the proto-industrial and early industrial economy in Europe not only gained relatively little from African trade, but actually displayed its power by pursuing the Atlantic sugar complex at considerably greater expense than it was probably worth. One, admittedly very imperfect, demonstration of this relationship can be made from a comparison of French and British experience in the late eighteenth century. The involvement of both powers in the trade with Africa and the Caribbean was broadly equivalent and in each case this connection stimulated manufacturing of inexpensive export goods around the relevant port cities. However, for the French this enterprise proved to be a dead end because it was not, as in Britain, articulated into a broader domestic and world market.[7]

The abolition of the slave trade

As a consequence of its initial advantage in the production and marketing of factory-made textile and iron goods, Great Britain sought, during the nineteenth century, to convert tropical commerce from the 'old colonial system' of mercantilism to one of free trade.[8] This attack on various forms of monopolistic restrictions coincided with the campaign against the slave trade and in the minds of many contemporaries, as well as modern historians, the two causes are closely identified. In economic terms, both theoretical and practical, such an identification is illogical and the tensions between its two components played a major role in shaping European policy towards Africa in the nineteenth century.

Abolitionists were fond of citing passages from that Bible of market economics, Adam Smith's *Wealth of Nations*, which noted the relative inefficiency of slave labour as opposed to free workers spurred by incentives for personal gain. However the rationality of tropical slavery was not lost on such eighteenth-century contemporaries of Smith as the French economist and statesman Turgot nor on British liberal economists of the nineteenth century who specialized in colonial questions. All were agreed that under conditions of land surplus and labour scarcity, capitalist farming could only develop if workers were somehow constrained – whether by slavery or other restrictive devices – to work in integrated units.[9]

The validity of this analysis is demonstrated by the expansion of slave plantations during the nineteenth century both in Africa and the Middle East (as seen above) and in the African-worked export economies of the New World. Contrary to what historians have long believed, the British sugar-production system continued to prosper right through the period of ultimately successful anti-slavery agitation (1780s to 1807) declining only after abolition and the 1833 emancipation of all British slaves had dealt it a direct blow.[10] Meanwhile Cuba and Brazil, which remained practically if not legally free to import African slaves did so in large numbers and even integrated their forced labour with great success into the steam-powered mechanization of sugar-processing.[11] Moreover the key raw material for the booming British textile industry, cotton, was produced on slave plantations, first in the West Indies but later in the southern United States, although the servile labour force here was able to reproduce itself with very limited imports from Africa.[12]

Given this positive linkage between tropical slavery and the industrial capitalism of the European metropoles, how did abolition become such a widely accepted cause, especially in Britain? In market-economic terms, the only answer is that the interests most immediately affected – slave-traders, sugar planters, and merchants – had become marginal to the major trends of the new industrial economy. They could no longer block a policy which other sectors of society wished to pursue. These other groups were not the new manufacturing interests of the industrial era (especially cotton spinners) since they had little role in the initial anti-slavery movement and were later very dubious about interference – through action in Africa and elsewhere – with the slaving interests of such commercial partners as Brazil and the United States.[13] Atlantic slavery and British capitalism may thus have grown together, but the relationship was such that the abolition of the first would not threaten the larger development of the second. This characteristic of the nineteenth-century world economy provided the conditions which made abolition possible, but it does not indicate why it should have been actively sought.

Many modern historians of abolition, faced with the weakness of existing economic explanation for its success, have returned to an emphasis on 'moral' motivations. It is clear from their researches that, except for the minority of actual slave-traders and owners, most influential sectors of Western society had become thoroughly convinced by the late eighteenth century that slavery was a reprehensible institution. Moreover this abstract notion of secular enlightenment philosophy had also become an article of faith in the most dynamic religious movements of Anglo-American Protestantism, and was taken up later in the nineteenth century by important sectors of the continental Catholic Church.[14] Abolitionist pressure groups thus became a real factor in the formulation of European and especially British policy towards Africa, although their demands for active steps in suppressing the trade on the high seas and at its source met with sporadic opposition from free-trade ideologues and the business community.

Abolition cannot, therefore, be treated as a mere instrument of British or other market interests. Its prevalence in early industrial Europe suggests, however, that it articulated with the general perceptions held by Europeans of their economic relationship with Africa. These perceptions are rather complicated because they are based less upon the experience of trade and plantation enterprise overseas than upon concern with the domestic social consequences of transition to a modern social order. Nonetheless, we must briefly pursue the source of this posture because anti-slavery ideology is so important in shaping European economic action in Africa during both the nineteenth and the twentieth centuries.

For Europeans anti-slavery represented at once a critique and an affirmation of the world engendered by industrial capitalism. It was a critique because it attacked a condition for which European enterprise was held responsible. Moreover it did so through institutions – the churches – and in the name of values – divine command, appeals to personal conscience, and paternalistic concern for the downtrodden – which the new industrial system seemed to threaten. At the same time, abolitionism stressed the contrast between an archaic institution – slavery – and certain conditions of modernization – individual liberty and the sanctity of the nuclear family – which supposedly benefited both bourgeoisie and workers in industrial Europe. It is not at all clear to what extent this outward projection of domestic tensions contributed to maintaining social stability within Europe, but the impulse to do so imbued all commercial relationships in Africa with a meaning which transcended the rational calculation of material benefits.[15]

Free/legitimate trade and political expansion

In the course of the nineteenth century, the scale of African–European commerce increased dramatically and, until the 1860s, so did the terms of trade for African exports. As in the previous slave trade, Europeans were paying higher monetary amounts for African products, and doing so with barter goods whose production cost in Europe constantly went down, thus providing Africans with greater quantities of exports at each price level (see Appendix, Figures A2, A3).

At the same time the relative value of African trade within the Atlantic economy was decreasing, in both quantitative and structural terms (see Appendix, Table A4). The world economy as a whole was growing at a more rapid rate than African commerce, which was no longer linked to other areas which might be considered critical. None of Africa's exports provided critical components or fuels for the main manufacturing and tertiary sectors (textiles, iron, and transport) of the Industrial Revolution. Even those goods for which there was a growing demand in Europe (particularly vegetable oils) competed with alternative supplies from non-African areas which became constantly more accessible as the world market expanded. Within this market, the capacity of Africans to purchase the growing output of European products remained limited compared to more populous and accessible portions of the world.[16]

In terms of strict market logic, the policy to be pursued by Europeans in such a situation would appear to be one of minimal investment. As seen above, African societies were quite capable of adapting themselves to the changes required by termination of the slave trade and increasing demand for non-human exports. European merchants operating on the African coasts did not, in general, press for expansion into the interior where they could not hope to compete on a profitable basis with the bulking functions of African 'middlemen'. In Europe, major commercial interests and liberal economic theorists looked with disfavour upon any public expenditures on African ventures and even attempted periodically to cut back on existing colonial commitments.

An explanation of why, for at least Britain and France, these commitments continued to grow throughout the nineteenth century and expanded so dramatically for all of Europe in the 1880s and 1890s must thus be sought, as with the anti-slavery movement, in the larger context of the European economy and its links with the metropolitan social and political order. One major factor in this explanation is again the capacity of an economic system as flourishing as the European one to indulge itself in apparently wasteful efforts. Despite criticisms questioning the value of naval squadrons and colonies in Africa during the mid-nineteenth century, the sums required for maintaining these undertakings did not represent a very heavy charge upon the national budgets of the time.[17] Moreover the process of industrialization in the West was accompanied by the development of new technological capacities – in transport, medicine, and firearms – which lowered the costs of further involvement in Africa to the point where the continent could become the object of 'exploration' with no immediate economic goals.[18]

The most literal form of this exploration was acted out by adventurous individuals or small expeditions who travelled to the interior of Africa seeking systematic knowledge of the physical and cultural landscape. The obsession of these explorers with the inland courses of various rivers indicates at once a need to justify their efforts in economic terms and a romantic remoteness from the concerns of their countrymen actively involved in African commerce. The rivers were uncharted precisely because their limited navigability rendered them useless for trade between inland regions and the coast. The costs of exploration were thus borne by governments along with academic and philanthropic (including missionary and anti-slavery) establishments rather than the for-profit private sector. Nonetheless the explorers did provide a base of experience and information which made possible the eventual, more practical, penetration of the continent.[19]

For a time in the nineteenth century steam transport and medical science appeared to supply the only other ingredients necessary for an expanded European presence on the continent. As already seen, the introduction of steam into the shipping system linking Europe, Africa and Asia had an important impact upon coastal commerce. Two of the pioneers in such oceanic transport, McGregor Laird and William Mackinnon were sufficiently inspired by abolitionist concerns to pursue major schemes for trade with the interior. However, even when disease factors had been brought at least potentially under control, efforts to send steamers inland along rivers ran into the obstacles of the rivers themselves. The deepest penetration, on the White Nile almost to Uganda, was achieved by Muslims, involved in slave trading, rather than European entrepreneurs. By the 1880s European steamers operated mainly on an experimental basis (with missionary sponsorship) on the East-Central African Great Lakes, on short commercial trajectories up the Senegal and Gambia rivers, and as a major challenge to African coastal traders exclusively on the lower Niger (but this only after great and unprofitable missionary and military investment).[20]

In the military sphere, steam navigation augmented a coastal hegemony already effectively achieved by Europeans in the era of sail. But modern firearms and increased experience in tropical military organization did give Europeans a potential means of vastly increasing their control on the land. Before the 1880s, however, this power was deployed on a large scale only at the fringes of the continent, in Algeria and South Africa for reasons not directly related to commerce. In Senegal and on the Gold Coast, France and Britain had fought smaller campaigns which helped strengthen both their hold on these trading centres and their confidence in contemplating more aggressive undertakings. But it was precisely the cost of wars in such peripheral areas which the civilian authorities at home constantly attempted to avoid.

The balance between a negative commercial evaluation of expansion in Africa and an increasing technological capacity for effecting such expansion was tilted in the direction of 'free trade imperialism' by the influence of the sectors in the European economy which calculated their returns in the form of long-term systemic benefits rather than immediate private profits. The representatives of these sectors were not primarily merchants or manufacturers but, rather, abolitionists, ideologues or public servants. The role of such groups cannot be set aside as 'non-economic' because they believed themselves to be motivated by a vision of world economic transformation transcending the short-sighted perspective of the petty groups actually engaged in African trade. Moreover it was this brand of economics – or meta-economics – which would most immediately shape the development of twentieth-century Africa.

The anti-slavery movement was directly, if not solely, responsible for most British efforts to change the basis of commercial activity in Africa. In order to enforce the abolition of the slave trade, Britain maintained small but significant naval squadrons on both the Atlantic and Indian Ocean coasts of the continent. These forces were constantly used to intervene in local commercial affairs, thus constituting the basic sanction of British 'informal empire'. While abolitionists themselves were divided for some decades over the value of such violent enforcement methods, the expenses of the squadrons were attacked in Parliament mainly on economic grounds and survived because even their most fervent opponents did not dare actually to defend the slave trade.[21]

More consistent with the unanimously held abolitionist views of the links between 'Christianity, Commerce, and Civilization' were the missionary ventures launched from various points along the African coast during the nineteenth century. Efforts by missionaries to modernize African economies met with little success. A few of their trading ventures prospered, but not in terms radically different from those of secular European firms. Missionary attempts to introduce new forms of organization and technology into the producer sections of local economies almost all failed. The one technical function which independent African elites inevitably demanded of them was the repair and maintenance of firearms, an activity which had few positive linkages with the rest of the economy, to say nothing of the spiritual goals of church work. Missionaries in coastal enclaves did succeed in training a creole elite which absorbed many of the middle-class values embodied in anti-slavery ideology. In West Africa these groups were able – as indicated in Chapter 4 – to compete on roughly equal terms with smaller European coastal merchants, but had little impact on the economies of the interior. The major alternative career to trading for these Western-educated Africans was not modern agriculture or manufacturing but rather entry into the embryonic local cadres of colonial civil servants, doctors, lawyers, clergy, and teachers.[22]

If the missions could achieve relatively little on their own to convert Africa from the 'barbarity' of slave-trading to the modern 'work ethic', their presence drew the British government into undertakings which could never have been justified on purely commercial grounds. The establishment of crown colonies and protectorates in West Africa (Sierra Leone in 1808, the Gold Coast 1843, Lagos in 1861), along with a series of anti-slavery treaties granting Britain rights of intervention in the affairs of many more states in West Africa and the Zanzibar sultanate, can all be traced to some degree of local mission influence. Likewise government subsidies and naval support for trading ventures up the Niger between 1841 and 1869 depended upon the missionary concern for these very controversial efforts.

Such government–missionary–commercial collaboration required a belief on the part of state officials themselves that the risks of African ventures would eventually pay dividends. The domestic risk – that unwarranted expenditures might expose a government to serious censure – was balanced by the strong commitment of politically influential blocs to the ideology of abolitionism. The key British foreign policy shapers of the mid-century era, Palmerston and Russell, were themselves convinced abolitionists and further believed that with the proper public initiatives – including occasional military intervention – Africa could be converted into a major economic partner of Britain. On a still wider scale such statesmen felt responsible for maintaining a strategic presence in tropical areas, even without immediate economic reward, merely to ensure access to more remote sources of potential or actual commerce.[23]

Strategic concern for protecting positions in the world market network naturally became most acute when rival powers threatened to interrupt such access. For Britain in the mid-nineteenth century, threats of this kind remained small because no other nation yet enjoyed a comparable level of industrial development or naval strength. Moreover, even for the bellicose Palmerston, Africa ranked far lower in strategic priority than other regions of the world.

Up until the 1870s France remained Britain's only potential African rival and much of the activity of both British and French imperialists in Africa must be attributed to fear of exclusion, particularly on the part of France. The French anti-slavery movement during this period was not nearly as active or influential as that of Britain. Nonetheless France, in order not to be overshadowed by British initiatives – which were never accepted as entirely philanthropic – was forced to maintain its own anti-slavery naval patrol in West Africa and to found new settlements both for receiving liberated slaves and to provide merchants with strategic *points d'appui*.[24]

For Africa as a whole French ventures never attained the same level of intensity and coherence as British ones because of the even lower levels of trade involved, the weaker general and missionary support for anti-slavery (damaged further by rather extensive illegal slaving on the part of French East and West Indian sugar planters), and the ideological isolation of the navy which continued to pursue forward policies without close support from either abolitionist or economic interest groups.[25] Only in Senegal did French commercial and official representatives combine to create an effective new economic base. A key motivation for this alliance was the limitation of administrative and military initiatives to a level and geographic scale consistent with the coastal peanut trade; however, the rhetoric of various local campaigns often suggested French ambitions to advance up the Niger Valley across the Western and Central Sudan. This French threat helps to explain some of the British initiatives in the Lagos region. Moreover an ultimate inability of either power to surrender existing holdings so as to consolidate their mutual West African holdings meant that petty rivalries concerning trade outlets and tariff regulations would continue to plague local commercial relations.[26]

Up to the 1870s, however, the Anglo–French rivalry in Africa was manageable since the two powers shared a sense of the limited value of African investment and could regularly assure one another that no immediate steps towards major expansion were planned. Such restraint disappeared in the late nineteenth century when both the diplomatic great-power game and the world economy had moved in directions which appeared far more difficult to control.

No topic in African history has received more attention from scholars than the late-nineteenth-century European imperialist 'scramble'. It is not proposed here to review, even in outline, the complex events and motivations involved in this process. Chapter 7 will deal in some detail with the partition of Southern Africa because in this region international political action and the resulting colonial frontiers were closely linked with local European economic interests. The general diplomacy of the partition, however, must be seen in the context of changes in Europe resulting from developments – particularly the unification of Germany – which go far beyond the confines of this book.

It has, in fact, been relatively easy for historians attacking a largely straw-man 'Marxist' interpretation of the partition to demonstrate that neither economic interest groups nor immediate concerns for the exploitation of Africa influenced the 'official minds' of those statesmen who made the decisions about creating new colonies in Africa. Yet, once again such a distinction between the 'political' and the 'economic' is too facile. Pervading the minds of even the most lofty diplomatists were powerful, if demonstrably unrealistic, anxieties concerning the links between great-power status and economic imperialism. The new powers, both Germany and Italy, identified the earlier economic ascendancy of Britain with the substance of empire rather than the ideology of free trade. The older powers, Britain, France, and most anxiously of all, Portugal, saw themselves humiliated or, at the very least, overshadowed by the emergent role not only of Germany but also the massive United States and Russia. African colonies represented a surviving economic asset which, if not critical in the glories of the past, might now be expanded to assure meaningful status in the future. Within this general context of intense and multi-faceted international competition, the economic rationale behind African colonization was to a considerable extent pre-emptive – designed to assure access to potential rather than actual markets and commodities, as well as trade routes to the always larger prize of Asia.[27]

During the period of the African colonial scramble – roughly the last quarter of the nineteenth century – Europe also experienced a set of market crises which collectively constituted something like a twenty-year 'Great Depression'.[28] Because the fall in world commodity prices particularly affected the most important African exports – especially palm oil and peanut oil (see Appendix, Figure A2) – Africa's significance for the European economy appeared even smaller during this period than it had previously. On the other hand some European merchants in West Africa reacted to the local crises resulting from price declines by demanding that metropolitan governments intervene on their behalf against 'unfair' African competitive practices. Given the marginal position of such merchants in the European economy and also their lack of internal agreement as to what form of imperialist intervention they wanted, it is hard to see this exercise of economic pressure as a major cause of the Scramble.[29] Nonetheless it reflects a broader abandonment of previous confidence in the unimpeded market.

The link between the Great Depression and African partition must therefore be sought in the perceptions of total economic policy at the metropolitan centres of European decision-making. Here imperialist initiatives could be planned not as a form of assistance to existing economic enterprises but rather as the creation of entire new markets and production bases. Statesmen were deliberately acting in independence of market forces so as to counter the cyclical disorders which seemed to be an inevitable result of laissez-faire liberal economics. The major ideology competing with liberalism on the domestic European scene at this time was socialism, whose more radical Marxist visions appeared to be vindicated by depressions such as those of the 1870s–1890s period. By creating colonies in Africa, European governments were attempting to chart a third solution, one which drew upon nationalist loyalties, neo-mercantilist policies, and abolitionist sentiment and harnessed them to an essentially conservative group of political leaders.[30] It was this complex of forces which would continue to guide European economic policy in Africa during the period of formal colonial rule.

Conclusion

Seen in the broadest perspective of world economic development, some form of economic imperialism in Africa appears to have been inevitable. The rate of growth in industrializing Europe so far outstripped development within Africa that the commercial frontier between the two economies would eventually have to be penetrated from the outside. The historical circumstances of the nineteenth century, however, determined that the form of this penetration would embody more of the contradictions than the achievements of the contemporary European system. Given the movement of world trade and the cost of the technologies available for deployment within African at the time, it was not feasible for the private sector of the European economy to effect such penetration on its own (the disastrous results of attempts at licensing private 'parastatal' realms in colonial Africa will be seen in Chapter 6). Instead, the initiative for expansion had to come from the state, supported by an ideology which drew its image of the non-Western world from the anti-slavery tradition and the continuing dilemmas of domestic modernization.

Africa now entered fully into the periphery of Western industrial society not because that society needed direct control of African resources to continue its own growth but rather because the path of this growth had become too broad and incomprehensible to exclude any options which offered at least an illusion of significance. As will be seen in the discussion of neo-mercantilism and decolonization in Chapter 8, Africa did provide certain sectors of the Western economy with valuable returns for their investments although, on the aggregate, the colonial venture remained of questionable value. For Africa, however, it is not the balance sheets but the structures of colonialism which were the most critical determinants of change. The economic history of twentieth-century Africa represents a struggle to find a pattern of development which could effectively harness the forces so ambiguously imposed upon the continent by nineteenth-century European imperialism.

Notes

1. Mantoux (1928); Williams (1944) p. 105f. For a more recent, but not very convincing, restatement of this thesis, see Mandel (1968) pp. 108–10; Darity (1982a, 1982b).
2. Anstey (1975) pp. 328–48. This conclusion has been challenged by Inikori (1981) but see Anderson and Richardson (1983); Inikori (1983).
3. Thomas (1968); Coelho (1974); but see Sheridan (1965, 1968); (Ward) 1978.
4. Bairoch (1973); Crouzet (1980); Engerman (1972, 1975); O'Brien (1982); but see Wallerstein (1983).
5. Bean (1975) pp. 68–78.
6. Dickson (1967) p. 189f.; Kindleberger (1984); Morgan and Thomas (1962) p. 12f.; Smith (1984).
7. Boulle (1972, 1975); Engerman (1975).
8. Schuyler (1945); for a more nuanced account, Kindleberger (1975).
9. Davis (1975) pp. 132–3; Curtin (1977); Engerman and Eltis (1980); Winch (1965) pp. 96–101.
10. Beiguelman (1978); Drescher (1977); Ward (1978).
11. Scott (1984).
12. Curtin (1969) p. 232f.; Fogel and Engerman (1974) pp. 20–9.
13. Gallagher (1950); Temperly (1972) pp. 44–66, 170f.
14. Davis (1975); Drescher (1980); Renault (1971) p. 225f.; Walvin (1980).
15. Davis (1975) pp. 346–85. For evidence of British working class hostility to anti-slavery ideology, see Ellison (1972); Hollis (1980).
16. Austen (1970); Platt (1973).
17. Temperly (1972) p. 182f.; Ward (1961) p. 193f.
18. Headrick (1981).
19. Hallet (1965); Rotberg (1970) (the historical literature on European explorers in Africa still tends to treat the economic rhetoric of its subjects rather uncritically).
20. Headrick (1981) pp. 73–6; Gray (1961) pp. 16–19f.
21. See note 17 above.
22. De Gregori (1969) pp. 152–8. For a more critical analysis of missionary transformation efforts, see Austen and Headrick (1983).
23. Gavin (1958); Robinson and Gallagher (1961) pp. 1–26.
24. Daget (1979); Schnapper (1961).
25. Brunschwig (1971).
26. Barrows (1974); Hargreaves (1963).
27. Austen (1975); Robinson and Gallagher (1961). For modified restatements of the 'economic' thesis, see Cain and Hopkins (1980); Hynes (1979); Owen and Sutcliffe (1972).
28. Rosenberg (1967); the questioning of the reality of such an extended trade decline by Saul (1969) does not undermine its importance in the perception of contemporaneous European policy-makers.
29. Ajayi and Austen (1972) (vs. Hopkins, 1968); Ratcliffe (1979).
30. Wehler (1969); see critique by Eley (1976).

Bibliography

Ajayi, J.F. Ade and Ralph A. Austen (1972), 'Comment on A.G. Hopkins, "Economic imperialism in West Africa: Lagos 1880–1892" ' and 'Reply', *Economic History Review*, vol. 25, no. 2, pp. 303–12

Anderson, B.L. and David Richardson (1983), 'Market structure and profits of the British

African trade in the late eighteenth century: a comment', *Journal of Economic History*, vol. 43, no. 3, pp. 713–21

Anstey, Roger (1975), *The Atlantic Slave Trade and British Abolition, 1760–1810* (London: Macmillan)

Austen, Ralph A. (1970), 'The abolition of the overseas slave trade: a distorted theme in West African history', *Journal of the Historical Society of Nigeria*, vol. 5, no. 2, pp. 257–74

Austen, Ralph A. (1975), 'Economic imperialism revisited: late nineteenth century Europe and Africa', *Journal of Modern History*, vol. 47, no. 3, pp. 519–29

Austen, Ralph A. and Daniel Headrick (1983), 'The role of technology in the African past', *African Studies Review*, vol. 26, nos. 3/4, pp. 163–84

Bairoch, Paul (1973), 'Commerce internationale et genèse de la révolution industrielle anglaise', *Annales ESC*, vol. 28, pp. 541–71

Barrows, Leland (1974), 'The merchants and General Faidherbe: aspects of French expansion in Senegal in the 1850's', *Revue Française'd' Histoire d'Outre-Mer*, vol. 61, pp. 236–83

Bean, Richard Nelson (1975), *The British Transatlantic Slave Trade, 1650–1775* (New York: Arno)

Beiguelman, Paula (1978), 'The destruction of modern slavery: a theoretical issue', *Review: Fernand Braudel Center*, vol. 2, no. 1, pp. 71–80

Bolt, Christine and Seymour Drescher (eds) (1980), *Anti-Slavery, Religion, and Reform* (Folkstone: Dawson)

Boulle, Pierre H. (1972), 'Slave trade, commercial organization, and industrial growth in eighteenth century Nantes', *Revue Française d' Histoire d'Outre-Mer*, vol. 59, no. 214, pp. 70–112

Boulle, Pierre H. (1975), 'Marchandise de traite et développement industriel dans la France et l'Angleterre du XVIIIe siècle', *Revue Française d'Histoire d'Outre-Mer*, vol. 62, nos. 226/227, pp. 309–30

Brunschwig, Henri (1971), 'Anglophobia and French African policy', in Prosser Gifford and Wm Roger Louis (eds), *France and Britain in Africa* (New Haven: Yale University Press), pp. 3–34

Cain, P.J. and A.G. Hopkins (1980), 'The political economy of British overseas expansion, 1750–1914', *Economic History Review*, vol. 33, no. 4, pp. 463–90

Coelho, Philip R.D. (1974), 'The profitability of imperialism: the British experience in the West Indies, 1768–1772', *Explorations in Economic History*, vol. 10, pp. 253–80

Crouzet, François (1980), 'Towards an export economy: British exports during the Industrial Revolution', *Explorations in Economic History*, vol. 17, pp. 48–93

Curtin, Philip D. (1969), *The Atlantic Slave Trade: A Census* (Madison: University of Wisconsin Press)

Curtin, Philip D. (1977), 'Slavery and empire', in Vera Rubin and Arthur Tuden (eds), *Comparative Perspectives on Slavery in the New Plantation Societies* (New York: New York Academy of Sciences), pp. 3–11

Daget, Serge (1979), 'British repression of the illegal French slave trade: some considerations', in Henry Gemery and Jan Hogendorn (eds), *The Uncommon Market: Essays in the Economic History of the Atlantic Slave Trade* (New York: Academic Press), pp. 419–42

Darity Jr, William A. (1982a), 'A general equilibrium model of the eighteenth century Atlantic slave trade: a least likely test for the Caribbean School', *Research in Economic History*, vol. 7, pp. 287–326

Darity Jr, William A. (1982b), 'Mercantilism, slavery and the Industrial Revolution', *Research in Political Economy*, vol. 5, pp. 1–21

Davis, David Brion (1975), *The Problem of Slavery in the Age of Revolution* (Ithaca: Cornell University Press)

Davis, David Brion (1984), *Slavery and Human Progress* (New York: Oxford University Press)

De Gregori, T.R. (1969), *Technology and the Economic Development of the Tropical African Frontier* (Cleveland: Press of the Case Western Reserve University)

Dickson, P.G.M. (1967), *The Financial Revolution in England: A Study in the Development of Public Credit, 1688–1756* (London: Macmillan)

Drescher, Seymour (1977), *Econicide: British Slavery in the Era of Abolition* (Pittsburgh: University of Pittsburgh Press)

Drescher, Seymour (1980), 'Two variants of anti-slavery: religious organization and social mobilization in Britain and France, 1780–1870' in Bolt and Drescher (eds), pp. 43–63

Eley, Geoff (1976), 'Social imperialism in Germany: reformist synthesis or reactionary sleight of hand?', in Joachim Radkau and Immanuel Geiss (eds), *Imperialismus im zwanzigsten Jahrhundert* (Munich: Beck), pp. 71–86

Ellison, Mary (1972), *Support for Secession: Lancashire and the American Civil War* (Chicago: University of Chicago Press)

Engerman, Stanley (1972), 'The slave trade and British capital formation in the eighteenth century: a comment on the Williams thesis', *Business History Review*, vol. 46, no. 4, pp. 430–43

Engerman, Stanley (1975), 'Comment on Richardson and Boulle and the "Williams thesis" ', *Revue Française d' Histoire d'Outre-Mer*, vol. 62, nos. 226/227, pp. 331–6

Engerman, Stanley L. and Eltis, David (1980), 'Economic aspects of the abolition debate', in Bolt and Drescher (eds), pp. 272–93

Fogel, Robert William and Stanley L. Engerman (1974), *Time on the Cross: The Economics of American Negro Slavery* (Boston: Atlantic-Little, Brown)

Gallagher, John (1950), 'Fowell Buxton and the new African policy, 1838–1842', *Cambridge Historical Journal*, vol. 10, pp. 36–58

Gavin, R.J. (1958), 'Palmerston's policy towards East and West Africa, 1836–1865' (Unpublished PhD dissertation, Cambridge University)

Gray, Richard (1961), *History of the Southern Sudan, 1839–1889* (London: Oxford University Press)

Hallet, Robin (1965), *The Penetration of Africa: European Exploration of North and West Africa to 1815* (New York: Praeger)

Hargreaves, John D. (1963), *Prelude to the Partition of West Africa* (London: Macmillan)

Headrick, Daniel (1981), *The Tools of Empire* (New York: Oxford University Press)

Hollis, Patricia (1980), 'Abolition and British working class radicalism in the years of reform', in Bolt and Drescher (eds), pp. 294–313

Hopkins, A.G. (1968), 'Economic imperialism in West Africa: Lagos, 1880–1892', *Economic History Review*, vol. 21, pp. 580–606

Hynes, William G. (1979), *The Economics of Empire: Britain, West Africa, and the New Imperialism, 1870–1895* (London: Longman)

Inikori, J.E. (1981), 'Market structures and the profits of the British African trade in the eighteenth century', *Journal of Economic History*, vol. 41, pp. 745–76

Inikori, J.E. (1983), 'Rejoinder', *Journal of Economic History*, vol. 43, no. 3, pp. 723–8

Kindleberger, Charles P. (1975), 'The rise of free trade in Western Europe, 1820–1875', *Journal of Economic History*, vol. 35, no. 1, pp. 20–55

Kindleberger, Charles P. (1984), 'Financial institutions and economic development: a comparison of Great Britain and France in the eighteenth and nineteenth centuries', *Explorations in Economic History*, vol. 21, pp. 103–24

Mandel, Ernst (1968), *Marxist Economic Theory* (New York: Monthly Review Press)

Mantoux, Paul (1928), *The Industrial Revolution of the Eighteenth Century* (New York: Harcourt Brace)

Mathieson, William Law (1929), *Great Britain and the Slave Trade, 1839–1865* (London: Longmans)

Morgan, Edward Victor and W.A. Thomas (1962), *The Stock Exchange: Its History and Functions* (London: Elek)

O'Brien, Patrick (1982), 'European economic development: the contribution of the periphery', *Economic History Review*, vol. 25, no. 1, pp. 1–18

Owen, Roger and Bob Sutcliffe (eds) (1972), *Studies in the Theory of Imperialism* (London Longman)

Platt, D.C.M. (1973), 'Further objections to an "imperialism of free trade" ', *Economic History Review*, vol. 26, no. 1, pp. 77–91

Ratcliffe, Barry M. (1979), 'Commerce and empire: Manchester merchants and West Africa', *Journal of Imperial and Commonwealth History*, vol. 7, no. 3, pp. 293–320

Renault, François (1971), *Lavigerie, l'esclavage africaine, et l' Europe, 1869–1892* (Paris: E. de Boccard)

Robinson, Ronald and John Gallagher (1961), *Africa and the Victorians: The Official Mind of Imperialism* (London: Macmillan)

Rosenberg, Hans (1967), *Grosse Depression und Bismarckzeit* (Berlin: Gruyter)

Rotberg, Robert I. (ed.) (1970), *Africa and its Explorers: Motives, Methods, and Impact* (Cambridge: Harvard University Press)

Saul, Samuel Berrick (1969), *The Myth of the Great Depression* (London: Macmillan)

Schnapper, Bernard (1961), *La politique et le commerce français dans le Golfe de Guinée de 1838 à 1871* (Paris: Mouton)

Schuyler, Robert Livingston (1945), *The Fall of the Old Colonial System: A Study in British Free Trade, 1770–1870* (New York: Oxford University Press)

Scott, Rebecca J. (1984), 'Explaining abolition: contradiction, adaptation, and challenge in Cuban slave society, 1860–1886', *Comparative Studies in Society and History*, vol. 26, no. 1, pp.83–111

Sheridan, Richard B. (1965), 'The wealth of Jamaica in the eighteenth century', *Economic History Review*, vol. 18, pp. 292–311

Sheridan, Richard B. (1968), 'The wealth of Jamaica in the eighteenth century: a rejoinder', *Economic History Review*, vol. 21, pp. 46–61

Smith, Woodruff D. (1984), 'The function of commercial centers in the modernization of capital: Amsterdam as an international exchange in the seventeenth century', *Journal of Economic History*, vol. 14, no. 4, pp. 984–1005

Temperly, Howard (1972), *British Anti-Slavery, 1833–1870* (Columbia: University of South Carolina Press)

Thomas, Robert Paul (1968), 'The sugar colonies of the Old Empire: profit or loss for Great Britain?', *Economic History Review*, vol. 21, pp. 30–61

Wallerstein, Immanuel (1983), 'European economic development: a comment on O'Brien', *Economic History Review*, vol. 35, no. 4, pp. 580–3

Walvin, James (1980), 'The rise of British popular sentiment for abolition, 1787–1832', in Bolt and Drescher (eds), pp. 149–62

Ward, J.R. (1978), 'The profitability of sugar planting in the British West Indies, 1650–1834', *Economic History Review*, vol. 31, pp. 197–213

Ward, W.E.F. (1961), *The Royal Navy and the Slavers* (London: Allen & Unwin)

Wehler, Hans Ulrich (1969), *Bismarck und der Imperialismus* (Berlin: Kiepenhauer u. Witsch)

Williams, Eric (1944), *Capitalism and Slavery* (Chapel Hill: University of North Carolina Press)

Winch, Donald (1965), *Classical Political Economy and Colonies* (Cambridge: Harvard University Press)

6

The Colonial Economies: I
Étatist-Peasant Regimes

For the conservative orthodoxy which once dominated the study of African economic history, it was the imposition of direct European rule which primarily brought about the transition from primitive, subsistence systems to modern, market-oriented production and exchange. A major purpose of the earlier sections in this book has been to demonstrate the degree to which such development had already taken place in the pre-colonial African economy through the stimulation of both domestic and external markets. Moreover, as was argued in Chapter 6, the establishment of European political control over Africa was motivated by very ambivalent and often confused understandings of modernization and market needs. It is therefore not surprising that the new European regimes not only failed to solve many of the problems which had previously inhibited African growth but also created important new sets of difficulties.

Despite all these reservations, it is impossible to deny that dramatic changes did take place in Africa as a result of colonialism; the economy in the late twentieth century is very different from that of the past. At the very least, the European governments created a new infrastructure of administration, transport, and social services which influenced all aspects of exchange and production. Under the new order foreign merchants were able to break across the frontiers which had characterized previous international trade and penetrated directly into the markets of virtually the entire continent. Finally colonial rule created the possibility for direct appropriation of African productive resources by Europeans and the relegation of Africans to the status of a proletariat.

This last possibility was only partially realized in most portions of the continent and thus provides a basis for organizing the present discussion of colonial economies. Unlike in previous sections, the basis for division between chapters here will not be points of contact with the outside world but rather forms of control over production, more particularly the ownership of land. The boundaries are partially geographic but more clearly analytic and thus require a brief explanation.

The regimes to be described in the present chapter are characterized as étatist because in them the major representatives of European interests and the dominant forces in organizing the new economy were bureaucrats representing the metropolitan state. The use of the term 'peasant' to identify African subjects of such a system may lead to some misunderstandings, which will be dealt with later in this chapter and in Chapters 7 and 9; but for want of any better label it is presented to indicate small-scale agriculture producers occupying their own land. The principal issue of analysis here is the rationale for such structures and their consequences for economic growth. Chapter 7 will deal with African economies in which private

European entrepreneurs competed directly with Africans and one another for control of land, labour, and political influence. These economies achieved more intensive forms of economic growth and the critical issue there will be to explain the relationship of such development to the subjugation and deprivation of indigenous Africans.

The geographical areas in which the respective systems were most dominant and characteristic are fairly readily identifiable but there is a shadowy middle ground presenting some analytical problems. West Africa, from Senegal through Nigeria, provides the classic situation of étatist-peasant development. The region presently encompassed by the Republic of South Africa exemplifies the most fully developed regime of competitive exploitation (Chapter 7 will offer an opportunity to review the entire post-contact history of the area, which was ignored in previous sections). The countries of East, Central, and even Southern Africa display at different times and places a variety of economic patterns. This chapter will treat the étatist-peasant sectors of all these economies together with West Africa. The major enclaves of settler farming, and expatriate-owned plantations and mines in these areas will be discussed in Chapter 7, although none of the regimes in the regions ever developed the full settler autonomy of South Africa.

There are thus obvious contradictions in the categories of étatist-peasant and competitive exploitation and to some extent they serve as convenient devices for presenting a large body of material rather than indicators of entirely distinct patterns of colonial development. The following chapters on decolonization and post-colonial economies will take up the question of convergence and continuing variation between the two types of regimes.

Infrastructure: the parastatal experiments

The inability of pre-colonial African economies to meet their oceanic partners on equal terms can most easily be explained as a problem of infrastructure. Given the natural obstacles to efficient communication on the continent, only major investments in modern transport could bring about significant acceleration of either internal or external commerce. A necessary condition for such investments – but one in turn dependent upon their results – was the establishment of larger and more stable political units. It is conceivable that even without colonial rule some of the more dynamic African states such as Asante, Sokoto, or even Buganda might eventually have provided the basis for such development.[1] Historically, however, they were never given the opportunity and the colonial regimes, representing European societies which already possessed modern capital resources, obviously had much greater possibilities of achieving rapid success.

The eventual installation of new transport networks, the establishment of an unprecedented pax, and the provision of various health and educational services constitute the clearest contribution of colonial regimes to African economic development. But, even for the major European powers of the late nineteenth century, creation of such an infrastructure in Africa involved what were initially perceived as prohibitive costs. Only after considerable hesitation and experimentation with various parastatal solutions did colonial governments finally undertake those investments which were to give them a central role in the development of all but the southernmost regions of the continent.

Through almost all of tropical Africa the diplomats' 'paper partition' of the 1880s and early 1890s was followed by years and sometimes decades of relative inactivity. Only the most rudimentary, if any, administration was established outside the capitals, few roads and hardly any railways were built, and for most Africans life had hardly changed. The reasons for these hesitations were financial: private European investors were uninterested in Africa, metropolitan legislatures opposed major public expenditures on colonies, and even the Western commercial firms already established at coastal entrepôts refused to move inland ahead of piecemeal government 'pacification'.[2]

In several areas of the continent, early colonial regimes sought solutions to the problems of staking out political claims against external European rivals and providing basic infrastructure for internal development through the recognition and even encouragement of concession companies. In return for exclusive rights to exploitation of the areas under their control, the companies would take upon themselves the major costs of initial modernization.

These parastal enterprises fall into two major groups. In a small number of cases – Northern Nigeria, German East Africa (present-day mainland Tanzania), British East Africa (Kenya, Uganda), and British South Central Africa (Zambia, Zimbabwe) – the companies received charters to rule entire territories without any direct involvement of metropolitan government officials. Elsewhere – throughout French Equatorial Africa, in Cameroon, King Leopold's Congo Independent State (present-day Zaire), and Mozambique – concessions were given only for selected regions, with overall responsibility for the colony theoretically remaining in the hands of a colonial civil service.

But even the lure of monopoly profits and the charismatic appeal of such company founders as Sir George Goldie, William McKinnon, Carl Peters, Cecil Rhodes, or the 'Portuguese Rhodes', Paivo de Andrada, could not raise the capital necessary for the infrastructural needs of the new colonies. With the partial exception of Rhodes's British South Africa Company, the parastatal system provided only a formula for disaster.

The first to go were the chartered company sovereignties whose inadequate resources were completely absorbed in unsuccessful attempts to establish their political position. Peters's East African regime collapsed in the anti-German coastal rebellion of 1888–9. A few years later, McKinnon's Imperial British East African Company declared bankruptcy in the course of its first major expedition to Uganda. Finally Goldie's Royal Niger Company, the best financed of the tropical chartered regimes, found itself faced with the task of conquering all of Northern Nigeria in direct competition with government military forces despatched by France. By 1900 each of these three charters had been revoked and only in the Southern African 'Rhodesias' (to be discussed in Chapter 7) was a private company still ruling over an entire African colony.[3]

The concessions granted *within* various territories would last longer and consequently inflict more serious damage upon African development. The beneficiaries of such monopoly privileges generally lacked both the vision – however misguided – of the chartered company imperialists and their political visibility. Equally deficient in the capital for their more limited undertakings, many of the concession companies nevertheless managed to obtain considerable financial benefits from their investments through various combinations of speculative fraud and crude impositions upon existing systems of predatory commodity acquisition.

The great model for concessionary regimes was the Congo Independent State, a territory owned privately by the Belgian King, Leopold II. Leopold himself was a grand imperialist visionary who invested large amounts of his vast personal wealth and energy in his colony. As constitutional monarch he also enjoyed the prestige required to induce the Belgian government to advance him large loans (up to 60 million francs) when, in the 1890s, the Congo approached bankruptcy. Leopold further used his influence to induce leading Belgian and foreign capitalists to risk their wealth in the Congo. To assure adequate returns on these funds, Leopold legislated a dual set of monopolies: one portion of the Congo was declared a state domain, closed to all private enterprise, and a second group of zones was parcelled out to private concessionary companies, in many of which the state (i.e. Leopold) was also a major shareholder. This system did succeed in its immediate infrastructural goals of financing a basic administrative apparatus, and an elementary rail and road network. Once this had been achieved, however, the rate of investment in the Congo dropped sharply and expatriation of profits rose to spectacular heights. As the world was also to learn after 1904, when conditions in the Congo became the subject of a major international scandal, the cost of such profits had been borne by the local population who were forced by the most brutal means to deliver wild rubber and ivory to European exporters.[4]

The concessionary regime in the Congo did at least provide significant levels of initial investment and tapped a territory which turned out to contain great mineral wealth. After Leopold's rule was replaced by that of the Belgian government (1908) the new regime could manage to reform previous abuses while still maintaining impressive levels of profit and reinvestment. Other concessionary systems may have been somewhat less guilty of atrocities but they also failed to provide any basis for later development. In Mozambique, the inspiration (and much of the capital) for concession companies came less from the Congo than from Rhodes's South African ventures. Between 1888 and 1892 the Mozambique, Zambesia, and Niassa companies were granted rights to vast territories, in the hopes of finding precious metals or diamonds. The only infrastructure left by these companies was a port and railroad system in southern Mozambique which mainly served the interests of neighbouring Southern Rhodesia. Otherwise, the concession regime simply represented an enlarged version of the centuries-old *prazo* system (see Chapter 3), abusing, and even exporting as contracted labour, the local work force. When the concessions were finally abolished by Antonio Salazar's attempted reforms of Portuguese colonial administration in the 1920s and 1930s, all they left behind was a continuous tradition of violent exploitation.[5]

The Congo model was most closely followed in neighbouring French Equatorial Africa and German Cameroon although in both these regions the limited amounts of capital invested, shortages of indigenous manpower, and the failure to find precious metals meant that virtually nothing was accomplished. In 1897 almost 80 per cent of the French Congo, Gabon, and Ubangi-Shari (present-day Central African Republic) was parcelled out to a total of forty companies, a number of whom made virtually no effort to develop their concessions. In Cameroon only two groups, the Gesellschaft Süd-Kamerun and the Gesellschaft Nordwest-Kamerun, received major concessions from the German government, but these amounted to about 50 per cent of the entire territory. In neither the French nor the German cases did the companies construct railways or contribute any significant infrastructure. Some of the concessions did make large profits up to 1913 (and in a few French cases for another decade or more) mainly through the export of wild rubber. As in Leopold's Congo, however, such success was accompanied by extreme mistreatment of Africans, giving rise to scandals in Europe and a number of local rebellions.[6]

Infrastructure: the state and railways

The assumption underlying both pre-scramble enthusiasm for African colonies and the ensuing parastatal experiments was that, once superficial obstacles to European penetration of Africa had been removed, a combination of private enterprise and modern technology would rapidly transform the economy of the continent. The early colonial years demonstrated the falsity of such beliefs: not only did responsible European investors refuse to take up African ventures but the African peoples of the interior, far from welcoming their liberation from coastal 'monopolistic middlemen', put up very vigorous resistance to European penetration.

The main task of the first colonial governments was therefore military conquest, often in the wake of failed parastatal regimes where these had first stirred up African violence but also in most regions of the continent where any kind of indigenous authorities saw their political and economic interests threatened by an outside force.[7] By metropolitan European standards the cost of the military apparatus required to control Africa remained minimal. However such expenditures vastly exceeded the current revenues of any African territories, thus cutting deeply into the public funds which any home government was willing to lay out for colonial development. The first economic priority in each colony therefore became the generation of tax receipts to maintain the very apparatus which was supposed to assure the conditions of growth.

Further planning embodied a major element of risk-avoidance, both in the negative sense of blocking initiatives which might stir up social disorder and the positive one of strengthening the ability of the state to maintain political-military control. Negative risk-avoidance was expressed in the protection by colonial governments of peasant production. The positive element – combined with a strategic imperative carried over from the scramble era – dictated the structure of tropical African railways.

Despite the fixation on rivers of the nineteenth-century European explorers and treaty-makers, no major breakthrough in the transport bottleneck of the African economy could be made without investment in new land arteries. Given the technology available to Europeans at the end of the nineteenth century, it was inevitable that this new transport system should take the form of railways, whose high cost, rigid orientation, and capital-intensive structure would leave a lasting imprint on twentieth-century African economies.[8]

The great financial burden of railway construction in tropical Africa was felt first through the role it gave the state in planning transport and second through the pressures it put upon African revenues. Except in the mining regions of the southern subcontinent there was little incentive for private European investors to participate in expensive, long-term railway projects. Thus it was left to colonial administrators in Europe and Africa either to undertake construction on their own, with funds borrowed from both public and private sources, or to subsidize private railway entrepreneurs by offering various combinations of land concessions and public guarantees on returns to their capital. The first pattern was prevalent in British and French West Africa and British East Africa, the second was followed by Belgian, German, Portuguese, and some British Central African regimes.

In either situation, the heavy involvement of the state meant that market considerations in planning railways could easily give way to potentially conflicting strategic concerns. Thus the main purpose of a railway project might be the military control of inland territories, as in the case of French expansion into the Sudanic zone of West Africa or German reactions to the Maji Maji rebellion in present-day Tanzania. Even the carriage of commercial goods became a strategic issue when governments grew concerned about dependence on the facilities of neighbouring territories ruled by another colonial power. Thus essentially the same markets were served by competing lines throughout the Anglo-French chessboard of West Africa, along the German–French–Belgian coasts of West Central Africa, in German and British East Africa, and through the various territories linking the Zambia–Zaire copperbelt to two oceans. Finally, there were the most grandiose schemes of all – the French trans-Saharan and Senegal–Sudan–Guinea *'Grande traverse'*, the British 'Cape to Cairo' route, and the German *'Mittelafrika'* design – none of which ever came to realization but all of which influenced the direction of actual railway construction.

Since most of the railways in tropical Africa were built by governments using borrowed funds, their immediate legacy to the territories through which they ran was a major load of indebtedness to the metropole. A significant portion of public revenues was therefore committed to meeting these obligations and diverted (until the major shifts in development financing of the 1940s – see Chapter 8) from either the private disposable incomes of Africans or other government projects. Moreover this repayment necessarily took the form of foreign exchange, thus adding another incentive for promoting export production at the expense of alternative types of economic enterprise. The railways reinforced this tendency even more dramatically by the geographical orientation they gave to transport flows.

African colonial railways are a classic element of what is called a dendritic market system, i.e. a leaflike network emanating from the outlets of international trade to the various regions of the African interior but not linking the latter to one another. In some cases the railways aided the development of internal trade, most spectacularly for kola merchants operating between southern and northern Nigeria, but for the most part they served only export and import commerce.[9]

Had Africa been partitioned a few decades later, infrastructure planners might have given greater attention to building motor roads, which are cheaper than railways to construct, provide at least comparable efficiencies of transport, and can be utilized more flexibly. Motor transport became important in Africa only after railways had already been built and colonial governments felt compelled to restrict them to uses which would protect their heavy existing investments. Roads were built as feeders to railways from hitherto inaccessible areas but competition was limited by construction allocations and legislation which taxed or even forbade motor transport along routes already served by rail.[10]

The conflict between rail and road transport policies raises the more complex issue of structural relationships between investments of this kind and internal African development. Given the bottlenecks in the pre-colonial economy, it is clear that railways could offset heavy capital cost by providing producers and consumers with significant 'social savings', i.e. reductions in transport expenses which made possible market relations that did not previously exist. For example, commercial cultivation of cotton and coffee in Uganda would have been impossible in 1900, when human porterage to the Indian Ocean cost $1,500 per ton and required three months of labour by a large group of poorly paid bearers. With the opening of the Kenya–Uganda Railway in 1902, costs dropped to under $200 per ton, the trip took only six days and several tons were carried for every man/day of labour expended. The labour market also benefited from the relative ease with which workers could now move to areas of employment opportunity, while the workers themselves enjoyed better wages and more access to consumer goods.

The Kenya–Uganda line is a case of a railway built from public funds essentially for strategic purposes: the British were anxious to protect the Suez Canal from the threat of a dam built across the Upper Nile which would cut off water supplies to Egypt! Nonetheless it tapped an inland region with real commercial potential. A number of the other transport projects constructed with less bizarre strategic motives in such areas as present-day Angola, Congo, Malawi, Mali, Tanzania, and even the generally prosperous Ghana failed to generate revenues which could repay their construction costs or, in some instances, even their operating expenditures.

But the historical problem of railway capital intensity cannot be reduced to a market equation of immediately measurable costs and benefits. The railways must be examined, as were earlier transport systems on Africa's pre-colonial commercial frontiers, in terms of the possibilities they provided for expanded and integrated activity within the indigenous sectors of the African economy. The outcome of such an examination is largely negative. We have already seen how the market impact of railways worked to promote exports rather than internal exchange. As entities in themselves the railways offered opportunities for transport enterprise, external capital inputs, and wage employment which excluded or severely restricted Africans in favour of Europeans.

We can best understand this outwardly oriented impact if we consider the concentration of capital embodied in railways to resemble the large and efficient ships with which Europeans achieved such a unique degree of autonomy on the Atlantic commercial frontier of pre-colonial Africa. Not only is there a technological connection between steam shipping and rail locomotives but the construction and administration of most African railways encompassed modernized harbour systems which directly linked the new land transport systems with older sea routes. The ownership of such enterprises or even the facilities to service them was completely beyond the means of African enterpreneurs, who were thus excluded from a dominant sector of the internal economy. It is not so much the modern character of the new transport technology which accounts for this situation but rather its indissolubly concentrated ('lumpy' as economists would say) capital structure. Africans easily adapted to mechanized transport in river traffic, with its limited range, and became very active in the ownership and maintenance of trucks, buses and taxis for road transport. The forces which first imposed and then defended the position of railways in African colonial transport thus attacked, whether deliberately or not, the interests of African entrepreneurs.

Africans also benefited very little from the types of material and human capital which entered into railway construction and maintenance; the 'backward linkages' of the new transport sector. Locomotives, rolling stock, rails, and other equipment as well as the steel with which they were produced were all manufactured in Europe and the engineering firms and even skilled workmen who built the new lines and harbour installations were also brought in from the colonial metropolises. Indeed, one of the motivations for undertaking colonial transport projects was to provide employment for metropolitan capital-goods industries, a consideration which sometimes placed additional cost burdens on African economies by excluding competitive bidding from other industrial countries which might offer more efficient services.[11]

The positive impact of railways in mobilizing the African labour market has already been noted. In the immediate period of railway construction, this benefit was offset by the tremendous numbers of unskilled workers required for railway construction. Thousands of men at a time were forcibly recruited, at low pay, often during peak periods of agricultural labour demand, to wield picks and shovels, saws, axes and sledgehammers on railway labour gangs. Under the worst conditions, as in the building of the French Equatorial Congo–Océan line from 1922 to 1934, workers were taken for long periods of time over great distances, subjected to unfamiliar climates and food staples, and kept in camps without adequate housing, nutrition, or health care. The resulting death rates reached epidemic proportions.[12]

Once railways were completed, they and the harbours offered relatively well-paid permanent employment to a small core of Africans whose skills could not easily be transferred to any other areas of the economy. The enclave character of railway capital is thus reflected in the division of African wage labour into a mass without any secure base in the modern sector and an elite (much like government clerks) modelling themselves on the situation of their immediate European predecessors and supervisors. The colonial state and its transport projects were supposed to release tropical African markets from the limitations of scale imposed by inherited geographical, social, and political conditions. In a literal sense, this goal was achieved but at a cost whose dimensions have already been suggested by looking directly at transport and whose further implications can be seen in the development of trade and production.

Commerce: from competition through oligopoly to étatism

At the moment of the colonial partition of Africa, the patterns of commercial organization on the continent indicated a movement toward more open market competition. As already seen, late nineteenth-century conditions had encouraged a growing number of European and African private merchant firms to establish themselves along the coasts of both West and East Africa. Access to the interior remained under the control of African states, many of which restricted trade to their own agents, but it was assumed that colonial rule would eliminate all such archaic-monopolistic obstacles to full economic development. What actually happened in the course of the colonial period was a virtual reversal of expectations. Competition among the most sophisticated private firms was radically reduced while the colonial state came to intervene in commercial affairs on a scale far surpassing that of its indigenous predecessors. Commerce did immensely increase and with it various opportunities for merchant enterprise but the tendency in the dominant sectors of trade was one of dependence not only upon external market forces but also upon local political agencies.

European trading firms had been ambivalent supporters of colonial partition and proved even more cautious about exploiting the opportunities offered by colonial annexation. Few established coastal merchants participated in – and most actively opposed – the parastatal charter and concession companies of the early years. Coastal firms did want European governments to support them in conflicts with African trading states, but when such states were suppressed Europeans hesitated to move beyond them into the interior, particularly the more distant hinterland of meta-economic fantasy. Direct European inland trade followed the flag – meaning, in most cases, the pacifying machine gun – and often the railway. Once established, however, white firms permanently displaced the African long-distance middlemen.

Not only traditional African competitors, but also most of the European and creolized African merchants who had striven against one another in the late nineteenth century were soon eliminated from the commercial scene. By the 1920s West Africa, the classical locus of trading rivalries, was dominated by three giant commercial conglomerates, the French Compagnie Française de l'Afrique Occidentale (CFAO) and Société Commerciale de l'Ouest Africain (SCOA) and the British United Africa Company (UAC). Shipping to this area was also controlled by 'conferences' in which the major British, German and French firms established uniform rates and penalized merchants who did not make regular use of their services. The frontier of this commercial empire was the boundary between French Equatorial Africa and the Belgian Congo (present-day Zaire). In the latter territory all merchants played only a minor role since the economy was dominated by major producer firms, especially the copper and diamond mines of Union Minière du Haut-Katanga and Forminière in Kasai along with Lever Brothers' large palm-oil plantations (see Chapter 7).[13] In East Africa, for reasons to be discussed, no European firms achieved a comparably preponderant position.

Economists and economic historians have devoted considerable effort to explaining the process of concentration among European firms in Africa.[14] From an international perspective, the phenomenon represents an extension of tendencies towards amalgamation-cartelization appearing at the same time among business organizations in the European-American metropoles. In Africa itself, the penetration of the interior by railways required firms possessing the capacity to maintain extended agencies with complex and relatively costly systems of bureaucratic integration, inventory storage, and calculation of long-term conditions. Moreover, the sharp fluctuations in world demand for African commodities – buoyant from the late 1890s to the disruption of the First World War, up again in 1919–20, down in 1922–3, up again until the crash of 1929 (see Appendix, Figures A2, A4) – made commercial survival extremely difficult for smaller enterprises which did not possess the resources to ride out periods of slump. Finally, the important role of colonial governments and single banking institutions in distributing contracts and credit to commercial firms tended to favour the largest, most established units whose reliability was most easily attested.

The linkage between problems of transport, market fluctuations, political and credit patronage on the one hand and monopolistic/oligopolistic trading firms on the other was not new to the African economy. It explains the domination of middleman states in many areas during the pre-colonial period. What is new in the colonial era is the transfer of business institutions developed in the most advanced sectors of the Western industrial world to manage the economy of relatively backward Africa. This seeming incongruity grew out of the capital-intensive character of the new technology brought in by the colonialist, most widely steamships and railways but also deep-level mining and plantations with mechanized processing facilities in the West Central region.

Such innovations shifted the control of the central economic sectors away from Africans and created the basis for self-perpetuating enclaves of external influence. Yet their presence did not eliminate the possibility of African commercial entrepreneurship or reduce the market situation to a direct relationship between African peasants and European merchants. The gaps between these two poles of the colonial economy needed to be filled by non-European trading groups able to operate outside their home areas. The candidates for such a role were European-ized Africans (creoles), Levantine and South Asian immigrants, and Muslim Africans.

Among these three groups the creoles were the least successful in adapting to the new commercial conditions. In their area of greatest strength, the coast of West Africa, they had constituted one element in the larger population of small merchant firms which found it difficult to survive under the dual pressure of fluc-tuating price conditions and competition from giant conglomerates. Some African entrepreneurs attempted to capture a major place in the export-import trade through ambitious oligopolistic schemes of their own, but these floundered on both the hostility of European governments and the unrealistic economic percep-tions of their founders.[15] More generally the creole merchant elite shifted its fields of enterprise during the early colonial period, sometimes pioneering the large-scale cultivation of new export crops (see below) but more often and lastingly turning to investments in urban real estate and the education of their children for professional and bureaucratic careers (the latter with large European companies as well as colonial governments).[16]

The major realms of opportunity for African trade lay in the areas which did not attract European firms: petty retailing in the urban centres and export-import dealing at rural centres away from the major transport routes. For the established creole elite such occupations represented a step downward in status and also, in the case of rural commerce, a sacrifice of comfort and social ties for initially limited income possibilities. This niche was partially filled by Africans migrating out of poorer rural areas, often those who had previously been purchased as slaves such as the Igbo in Nigeria or the Bamileke in Cameroon. However most rural migrants lacked the means or connections to enter trade independently and even the Igbo and Bamileke acquired their position as prominent commercial groups only late in the colonial period.[17] The opportunity for exploiting intermediary merchant roles was therefore taken up primarily by non-African immigrants: Levantines (Lebanese and some Greeks) in western Africa; South Asians in East Africa.

The commercial success of these immigrants resulted from their combination of advantages and disadvantages not found in any African group. Through the process of migrating, even from poor rural areas in their homelands, the immi-grants established connections with compatriots already established in metro-politan and colonial commercial centres and through them to Europeans. Once in Africa, there were few careers open to them other than trade (some East African Asians entered the lower ranks of the civil service but could not hope for much advance beyond this) so they were willing to undertake the hardships of itinerant peddling and village shopkeeping. Moreover all available assets, whether in the form of cash earnings, control of family labour and the services of new immi-grants, or influence over rural African clientele, were invested in furthering business interests, with the remote (and often unrealized) goal of comfortable retirement in the country of origin.

It is not necessary to argue, as some historians of the West African creoles have done, that the rise of immigrants resulted from either a lack of economic moti-vation on the part of Africans or a deliberate attempt by Europeans to undermine politically threatening indigenous entrepreneurs. Despite occasional tensions with both African and European commercial groups, immigrant entrepreneurs essentially filled a role for which there was no effective competition. Nonetheless, the occupation of such a critical position by an alien group indicates yet another disjuncture between the African economy and the international system into which it was now more closely integrated. Here again the development of a colonial market produced a structural problem, although the consequences in this case would not be felt until the emergence of independence.[18]

Despite its emphasis on overseas export-import trade, the colonial system also provided considerable opportunity for the expansion of Muslim trading networks essentially concentrating on internally produced and consumed goods such as kola, African cloth, cattle, salt, and fish. The new transport facilities eased the movement of these goods over long distances and colonial political barriers had little effect in restricting their circulation. Particularly in West and West-Central Africa, Juula and Hausa merchants profited from the growth of new urban centres and were joined in many of these locations by more recently mobilized trading groups, such as Muslim (and later Christian) Yoruba in present-day Ghana. The parallel and wide-ranging Somali cattle trade in colonial East Africa has not, unfortunately, been studied in any detail.[19]

Domestically oriented commerce of this kind grew directly out of the most dynamic sectors of the pre-colonial economy, particularly that of the Western and Central Sudanic zone of West Africa and is in many respects a unique model of African economic autonomy in the colonial period. Muslim merchants did not depend upon European credit or patronage for their main undertakings and had little interest in advancement into the white-collar sectors of the colonial hierarchy, as evidenced by their disdain for Western education. At the same time this sector of the economy must be seen as somewhat encapsulated within the dominant colonial order since it could neither aspire to control over the enterprises of greatest profitability nor mobilize production on a scale which challenged the major orientation towards raw-material exports and manufactured imports.

From commerce to manufacturing: the limits of transformation

Given the very apparent modernization in the infrastructural and commercial sectors of African economy, it appears at first blush paradoxical that metropolitan systems of large-scale production, using factories and power-driven machinery, were barely introduced into the colonies which are the subject of this chapter. For some Marxist theorists the critical distortion of twentieth-century African growth is precisely the disjuncture between a highly developed merchant capitalism and a very weak producer capitalism.[20] The disjuncture is real and significant, but it turns out to be easier to explain why major European commercial firms and governments did not invest in manufacturing than (as will be done in later chapters) to deal with efforts to develop an industrial base in settler colonies and late-colonial or post-colonial tropical regimes.

The success of large European trading firms in Africa resulted from their access to capital resources compatible with sophisticated technology in the infrastructural sectors; but the immediate context within which such advantages became decisive was one of market instability and risk. In surviving the various price fluctuations experienced by African commodities in the early twentieth-century world market, merchant firms became cautious rather than more enterprising. In particular, there was little incentive for them to shift from investments in import and export inventories – working capital which could be turned over quickly in good times and liquidated flexibly in bad times – to the fixed assets of manufacturing plants. Moreover the continued improvements of transport facilities connecting Africa with the European metropoles had its most immediate effect in lowering the cost of moving goods between the existing manufacturing centres of Europe (and later Asia) and the raw-material-producing regions scattered over a wide area not only of Africa, but the entire tropical world. The rising level of demand for manufactured goods in any one section of Africa was thus less likely than under the 'natural protection' conditions of the pre-colonial economy to justify industrial development.[21]

Finally, European colonial governments saw themselves primarily as the representatives of metropolitan economies which benefited from the existing pattern of trade. There is clear evidence of instances in which these attitudes were translated into policies which blocked efforts at local industrialization.[22] But for the most part such efforts simply did not exist and the major shortcoming of colonial regimes was their failure actively to promote them.

This failure can in turn be understood as a function of yet another absent factor: pressure from a local class of merchants and artisans, whether immigrant or indigenous, who identified their own interests with the development of internationally competitive industries. The lack of such pressure is not due to any lack of manufacturing enterprise on the part of commercial and artisan groups within the smaller sectors of the colonial African economy. It is rather explained by the structural barriers between such enterprise and the dominant sectors with which they were supposed to compete.

Local manufacturers – recruited from both African and Levantine-Asian merchant groups – did provide modern substitutes for some imported goods such as bottled beverages, soap, and cigarettes. These were items of relatively strong consumer demand, high transport cost in relation to price, and contained a large proportion of local materials. In a few cases international firms such as the Unilever soap interests were also induced to build factories in particularly strong colonial African markets, such as that of Nigeria, in order to maintain their local selling position.[23] But the impact of a few such undertakings was very limited.

African artisans were forced on a much broader scale to adjust their production systems to the new situation. On the one hand the easier access to imports virtually eliminated markets for such basic items as cheap textiles and locally smelted iron. At the same time imports included (as in the contact period) a large proportion of intermediate goods – finished yarn, chemical dyes, scrap metal and rubber – which could be converted for specific local needs by African craftsmen. Moreover the growth of the colonial economy increased the demand for all purchased goods, providing absolute benefits to local artisans even when the greatest share of this new market fell to imports.

Artisans thus functioned in a complementary rather than competitive relationship to the international sector and their adjustment took two forms. Some, paralleling the Muslim domestic merchants, operated in an encapsulated sector which was relatively independent of European or Asian activities. For artisans, such opportunities were found mainly in the areas of most refined skill, such as the weaving of fancy cloth and the carving of ritual objects. Rising incomes in the general African population increased the market for such items and they even found some external demand among tourists and Europeans or Americans interested in 'exotic' artifacts for their homes or museums.[24]

A second, more widely available but less autonomous option lay in the urban or village 'informal sector'. There growing numbers of artisans found employment either maintaining the less 'lumpy' imported European devices such as cars and trucks, bicycles, agricultural tools, etc., or producing their own commodities out of the scrap from these imports, particularly metal (now the basis, among other things, for hoe blades). The major expansion of this sector has taken place since the colonial period but its structural features were in evidence well before independence. As with guns and textiles in the pre-colonial period, the industries developed around imported goods and materials displayed tremendous vitality and ingenuity but were ultimately capable of forming only backward linkages with the international or 'formal' sectors. They successfully adapted their technology to deal with the products of modern mechanized industry but could not provide goods of their own which might substitute for complex imported commodities or even replace their vital working parts.[25]

The state and the market: monetization

If colonial governments did not concern themselves much with repressing or, conversely, encouraging a rather weak manufacturing sector, they showed considerable interest in the management of exchange relationships. This intervention took various forms, the most politically obvious being the regulation of markets. But the most pervasive, particularly in the early years of colonialism, was the imposition of a single, government issued, monetary currency.

Monetization had developed in African markets before the colonial period so that these measures can be seen as a stage in a spontaneous process of economic development. But it is important to understand the specific motives and methods of colonial currency policies and their impact across the varied situations of each territorial economy.

The earliest forms of African money – many of which survived well into the colonial period – consisted of consumable commodities which enjoyed special advantages as stores of value, media of exchange, or units of account. They include livestock, salt bars, metal bars, jewelry, or tools; cotton, palm leaf, or bark textiles; and shells. Often the items which physically most resemble modern coinage, such as small copper crosses in pre-contact Central Africa, might only be valid for ritual transactions involving political authority, a foreshadowing of some colonial money uses. The more widely negotiable currencies, especially cowry shells, were susceptible to extreme inflation during the late nineteenth century when improved European procurement and shipping supplied them on a vastly expanded scale.[26]

By the eve of the colonial period major centres of trade such as the West and Central Sudan and the Guinea and Swahili coast had shifted from 'commodity money' to silver coinage of various kinds, particularly the ubiquitous Maria Theresa or Spanish dollar (thaler) but also French five franc pieces, British sterling, and Indian rupees. This currency still had a potential commodity value for Africans, but was also acceptable as return payments by Europeans whose entry into African trade was thus eased. Its value was relatively stable, although not guaranteed by the issuing (really exporting) mints in Europe, Asia, and Latin America.[27]

During the first decades of their establishment all colonial governments replaced existing currencies within their territories by new, government-issued specie (coin) and paper tied at fixed rates to the metropolitan money system. Such a move was consistent with the general monetary orthodoxy of the period which held major world currencies to a stable gold standard and sought to limit the circulation of silver which, it was feared, might flow out of the colonies to cause local stagnation and metropolitan inflation. Within the colonies a universal monetary standard greatly eased the collection of taxes and payment of public expenditures. Finally, governments together with designated issuing banks could profit from the seigneurage of new coinage, i.e. the difference between their official value and the always lower cost of the metals from which they were made.

The effect of these monetary changes on African economies was mixed, although the balance of advantages and disadvantages shifted in a negative direction as the results percolated from the centre to the periphery of each colonial system. At the highest level, metropolitan government control over currency restricted the amount of money which might circulate in Africa at any moment and even forced each territorial treasury to maintain fairly generous reserve funds (for British colonies, deposited in London). Thus the financing of government and private development in Africa was inhibited, although it is likely that in a more open monetary system much locally generated capital would voluntarily have fled Africa into more promising investment climates and more secure currency systems.[28]

In the main centres of established trade, such as the Nigerian coast, African holders of pre-colonial currencies suffered some inconveniences, as such media were still needed for many local transactions and government hesitation about redeeming them resulted in a certain degree of hoarding and speculation. However, in the long run the stabilization of currency was a general benefit here and even improved market access for smaller entrepreneurs.

The greatest difficulties occurred in the rural hinterlands where, ironically, colonial officials had expected the most positive effects. Fiscal concerns were foremost in such calculations since these were the regions (as opposed to the coastal areas of British West Africa) where government revenues depended upon direct taxation. But it was also thought that cash payments would allow the gatherers and cultivators of export goods greater control over their discretionary income than the existing alternative of bartering for consumer goods at the 'company store' of the main (often monopolistic) local produce buyer.

The immediate reality as well as its long-term effects were often quite different. During early stages as well as later periods of export-price declines, cash incomes met little more than tax obligations. Moreover demands for payment in official currency could make conditions worse, especially if the initial revenue from produce took the form of paper (subject to deterioration, burning, and insect destruction) or base metal coins whose value especially in post-First World War Africa could decline sharply with metropolitan devaluations. Merchants and administrators with greater access to banks and information could manipulate the ignorance of peasants and the informed preference for silver of more sophisticated inland groups, thus skimming still more from local revenues. In many rural areas coins circulated relatively little but instead were hoarded against the 'special purpose' demands of taxation and other emergencies. The unproductive nature of such behaviour, as opposed to more traditional investments of temporary surpluses was widely articulated by Africans themselves through adages such as 'shillings do not breed'.[29]

The imposition of monetization and taxation beyond the boundaries of market centres probably speeded the expansion of the market economy but it also linked this process with an exercise of authoritarian intervention by the state and a mistrust of market mechanisms by peasants which would mark all future economic development in tropical Africa.

The state and the market: regulation of commerce

Official monetization had been imposed upon African colonies in a kind of Rousseauist gesture of forcing local markets to be free. The other forms of commercial regulation promulgated by colonial governments were undertaken with less pretension to liberalism but with an even greater mixture of motives, policies and results.

Across the various parts of the continent covered by this chapter, the distribution and timing of official market intervention were extremely varied. East and Central Africa experienced the most sustained activity; French West Africa witnessed regular but never overwhelming intervention and British West Africa moved from relatively limited to very severe forms of market control. Government justifications for such activities were also mixed, ranging from the promotion of metropolitan collective and individual interests, through the imposition of what was considered progressive economic behaviour upon insufficiently motivated Africans, to the protection of these same 'innocent natives' from the disruptive risks of an overly dynamic market.

During the period of the colonial partition, as already noted, many imperial enthusiasts hoped to incorporate African colonies into neo-mercantile market systems closed to the outside world by tariff barriers. Although much of the transport structures of the new African territories did link them on a mutually competitive basis to specific metropoles, the realities of limited contributions by Africa to world trade and the need to maximize the revenue potential of each colony inhibited the pursuit of strong exclusionary policies. Moreover various international colonial agreements, including the 1885 Berlin Treaty and the post-First World War League of Nations Mandate regulations, explicitly prohibited 'closed door' trade legislation. Even in the 1930s, when all European metropoles instituted systems of preferential tariffs and regulations in order to use their colonies as buffers against the effects of the Great Depression, the impact on African trade was not severe (the main result was to raise manufactured import prices by excluding the highly competitive products of Japan).[30]

Those regulatory policies which had the greatest effect concerned the transactions in export goods and internal markets. Here the full range of European attitudes towards African economic development found its expression. Governments thus granted buying monopolies to specified (usually European) firms while requiring costly licences for smaller (usually Asian/Levantine or African) produce buyers in order to assure a 'responsible' commercial presence in rural areas. Africans were often inhibited by law from receiving credit or selling certain foodstuffs so as to protect the subsistence base of the territory from the commercial sphere. Finally governments regulated the prices of exports through special agencies which held their own taxation powers.

As might be expected, intervention of this kind developed first in those regions least effectively integrated into the market during the pre-colonial and early colonial periods: French West Africa and Belgian, British, French, German and Portuguese East and Central Africa. In many of these areas the regulation of African marketing was closely linked to the competing interests of concessionary companies and European agricultural producers. For French West Africa, however, the regulation system arose entirely from relations between the state and peasant producers. The most persuasive form of official interventionism took the form of Sociétés Indigènes de Prévoyance (SIP) ('Native Provident Societies'). Despite their name, these organizations were run entirely by European district administrators for purposes of storing food supplies and financing local development projects (British administrators controlled comparable funds through the share of general taxation retained by 'Native Treasuries' under the indirect rule system). Since Africans were forced to contribute to SIPs, they perceived their contributions as a tax (*le petit impôt du commandant*) and not as a means of controlling markets. During the price falls of the early 1930s and again in the mid-1950s the French also established *caisses de stabilisation* (price stabilization funds) to guarantee minimum returns to African commodity producers. The *caisses* were supported by tariffs which did not directly affect growers but they also appear to have had little influence in a market already sheltered from world prices by special trading arrangements with the metropole.[31]

When British West African governments finally chose to intervene in marketing, they did so in a far more dramatic manner than colonial regimes in less-prosperous areas of tropical Africa. The initial impulse for such efforts came in the 1930s from the protests of Ghanaian and some Nigerian cocoa growers against European purchasing firms, which attempted to deal with Depression conditions by agreeing not to compete with one another in local markets. The government decided to intervene in this crisis by both guaranteeing prices and allocating shares in the market to a fixed list of firms. During the Second World War this arrangement was formalized and extended to all major export commodities throughout British West Africa as well as Uganda. In principle, the boards were to finance their subsidies during lean years by surpluses collected during periods when export prices exceeded the legislated maximums.

In practice, though, the boards never had to pay anything to farmers, since prices never dropped below the minimum for the remainder of the colonial period. Instead, the boards collected enormous reserves which were first deposited in London to help stabilize sterling currency and eventually provided African governments with a major source of development funding.[32] Thus, in the classic region of étatist-peasant colonial economies it was clearly the state which controlled the major share of market revenue. The controversy among students of British Africa about the impact of marketing policy rests ultimately upon perceptions of the actual and potential role of the producers at the base of the system, the peasants.

Peasant agriculture: the expansive phase

The designation of twentieth-century African farmers as 'peasants' has been a major point of contention between market and structural interpretations of African economic history. The term itself is usually employed by proponents of structural positions, although it has been attacked from both left and right as implying unrealistic models of rural situations and their dependency upon larger-scale economic and political institutions.[33]

In all this debate there still remains substantial agreement about some features of agriculture in those colonial territories which produced export crops on land under African control. First, the units of production were small and 'owned' (more accurately, occupied without significant rent payment or threat of displacement) by those who worked them. Second, such farmers were only partially integrated into the cash economy. They cultivated crops destined for remote markets and made some use of purchased tools and chemicals as well as wage labour. At the same time most continued to grow their own food supplies and organized their work around pre-colonial hoe-cultivation technology and the inherited social patterns of household, kinship and community. The commercial output of such agriculture usually expanded very rapidly in the first stages of export commercialization but afterwards grew more slowly, with little shift in the productivity of individual units.

Disagreements about the analysis of these systems centre around explaining the limitations of their growth. Liberal analysis tends to stress market imperfections caused by continuing ecological problems as well as misguided political intervention in the economy. Structural (and here these are mainly Marxist) historians insist that the survival of traditional 'modes of production' intrinsically inhibits growth and that these were deliberately preserved by the colonial agencies of capitalism to maintain their position of dominance over the African economy.[34] The relationship between the various dimensions of change in this critical sector of the colonial African economy can best be understood by somewhat artificially dividing the development of peasant agriculture into phases: a first one of entry into major export production and a second of adjustment to an established position in this role.

The entry phase has been the one most stressed by market-oriented historians in part because it seems to demonstrate so spectacularly the validity of their perspective.[35] The fact that such a range of export crops – palm oil and palm kernels, peanuts, cocoa, coffee, and cotton being the most significant – could be grown by autonomous African smallholders suggests that responsiveness to the market existed almost anywhere in the world so long as the necessary opportunities were presented. Moreover Africans often won their places in these markets to the surprise and consternation of European regimes, whose own economic plans were based on expatriate plantation agriculture or, in other cases, the promotion of smallholder crops quite different from the ones that Africans themselves decided they could best sell (e.g. cotton instead of the eventually successful peanuts in northern Nigeria).

This chapter will deal first and in most specific form with the initial stages of peasant export agriculture since the issues of later adjustment are to be pursued more fully in subsequent sections on decolonization and post-colonial economies. While liberal historians are justified in noting the role of African smallholder initiative in determining the character of this system, the historical process was never as simple as their model suggests. Market conditions were not uniform throughout the African colonies so that the costs of peasant integration varied considerably. Further, even in the most successful cases of smallholder entrepreneurship, political and social coercion often played as great a role in the development of commercial farming as did purely market factors. It is only by contemplating the interplay of a variety of market and institutional conditions that we can hope to capture some of the complex reality of African peasant agriculture under colonialism.

One set of market factors relevant to peasant cash-cropping has already been treated at some length earlier in this chapter: the lowering of distribution costs through the introduction of enlarged and more effective political regimes and, above all, mechanized overland transportation. The discussion which follows will focus on similar considerations less obvious from the vantage point of metro-politan or territory-wide decision-making: the costs to farmers themselves of cultivating specific commercial crops as balanced against the benefits derived from their sale.

The most critical cost faced by any group of rural Africans venturing into export farming was its effect upon domestic food supplies. In many cases this effect was not very great since the resources allocated to expanding commercial production did not come directly from food-producing activities. In some forest areas, where food crops were largely a female responsibility, men took up cash-cropping in lieu of essentially non-agricultural activities. Women, on the other hand, played a major role in the commercial preparation of palm products on a schedule which interfered very little with their other farm and household chores.[36] However we must not be too quick to adopt the classical economic argument of 'vent for surplus', i.e. that lowered transport costs simply created a market for land and labour resources which had previously been underutilized.[37] The degree to which the colonial market fitted existing subsistence patterns depended upon the varying material and social ecology of particular forms of cultivation.

The least disturbing export undertakings were those involving products which Africans themselves consumed, particularly palm oil and peanuts. First of all expanded cultivation of these commodities did not require any change in the organization of production; indeed they were crops whose export had already taken on major proportions in West and Central Africa during the nineteenth century. Both could also be expanded without any immediate risk to food sources. Oil-palm trees grow spontaneously around cleared areas in the forest zone without competing for land devoted to root crops. Peanuts are cultivated in the more precarious savannas, but in large portions of this zone they can be intercropped with cereals and initially even enrich the soil by fixing nitrogen in it. During periods of famine, increased proportions of both palm oil and peanuts can be held back from export markets and consumed at home, although neither is an adequate substitute for starch staples.[38]

Two other major export crops which added nothing of nutritional value to rural African diets – cocoa and coffee – nonetheless fitted easily into subsistence patterns. They are forest crops cultivated in the form of small trees which require the shade of leafier plants and these latter, at least in the early stages of commercial farming, tended to be the established food crops, such as plantains, cocoyams, or cassava.[39] Cotton, on the other hand, was a savanna crop adopted with consider-able reluctance by African farmers because of its high cultivation cost. The plant was not, of course, edible, and it occupied (and exhausted) soil which could not be interplanted with the local cereal staples. Moreover the seasonal labour demands of cotton are quite extensive and coincide with the time when both men and women are needed for planting, weeding, and harvesting savanna food crops.[40]

As already suggested with regard to palm oil and peanuts, one factor lowering the costs of entry into export cultivation for colonial Africans was familiarity with the crops on demand in the world market. Peanuts registered most positively on this scale: their commercial cultivation continued smoothly from the mid-nineteenth century through the colonial period. Palm oil and kernels also carried over from pre-colonial times although, in many of the former palm producing regions of West and West Central Africa, farmers shifted to commodities with a higher income yield particularly cocoa. Native African varieties of rubber, which sold well as gathered forest products in the immediate pre-colonial and early colonial period, began to be cultivated shortly after the turn of the century by some Africans (as well as Europeans) only to have the world price collapse just before World War I. Kola production expanded in various forest areas of West Africa with the improvement of rail and river communications to the Muslim savannas, but the scale of demand here could never compete with newer crops sold overseas.[41]

Cocoa and coffee were the major new crops introduced and their adoption took time because of unfamiliarity and lack of confidence that efforts at cultivating young trees over several years would eventually yield any profitable result. Even in regions of East Africa where coffee was indigenous, but consumed on a very small scale in rituals, peasants were hesitant for both economic and cultural reasons to commit themselves to the expansion of production.[42] Once accepted, these crops could spread very quickly, as in the much celebrated case of Ghanaian cocoa, but the early hesitancy should be kept in mind when considering the measures required to initiate production.

Finally, the entry of African peasants into new or expanded market production depended to a considerable extent upon world prices for these goods. Much of the export growth which took place in the early twentieth century can be explained by European recovery from the 'Great Depression' between the 1870s and 1890s. Demand for vegetable oils increased because of their new use for margarine and tinplating in the canning of food, while the rising incomes of a growing population of European and American wage-earners increased the consumption of such 'colonial goods' as chocolate and coffee.[43]

Cotton again remains the great problem here because the cost of its production for Africans was not matched by any great increase in its price. British, French, German and Portuguese regimes promoted African cotton for strategic rather than market reasons. They perceived the textile industry as vital to their domestic economies and did not want to rely entirely upon the United States for supplies. However the American South, despite the crisis caused by boll-weevil infestation at the turn of the century, continued to produce cotton far more efficiently than Africa. Moreover the growth of European industrial demand slackened in the course of the twentieth century. European governments and even associations of textile manufacturers recognized that colonial cotton production required subsidies of some kind, but these mainly took the form of funding research efforts and guaranteeing minimum profits to expatriate operators of purchasing and ginning stations in the cotton-growing areas. The African cultivators realized little of such premiums in the form of direct cash payments, especially when it is remembered that the savanna growing regions were generally far from the coast and thus burdened – even after railways were built – with heavy transport costs.

Cotton was a moderate export success in German and British East Africa, where it found an unanticipated market in the newly expanding textile industries of India and Japan. In Northern Nigeria peasants at first refused to expand cotton growing (and local Hausa merchants to finance it) preferring the far more profitable and secure cultivation of peanuts. Eventually Northern Nigerian cotton production did increase but most of the crop was consumed by the indigenous handloom textile industry, which grew despite British threats to suppress it. However, throughout colonial Africa cotton was the cash crop least popular with peasants and thus most revealing of the role of coercion in promoting commercial cultivation.[44]

Coercion in one form or another was necessary in the development of virtually all colonial export agriculture. Its degree depended, as suggested by the discussion of cotton, upon the strength of market incentives for initiating or continuing various cash crops. Another important factor was the institutional environment faced by colonial regimes. Optimally they could rely on established African authorities to impose desired agricultural efforts upon their subordinates; in other circumstances, it was necessary to create new instruments of coercion.

Although colonial peasant agriculture was perceived as the ideal 'legitimate' antithesis to an economic order of plantations and slave trade, African slavery was, in fact, one of the key institutions employed in the creation of the modern export system. For the most part this contradiction resulted from the continuity in specific regions between colonial crops and the agricultural exports developed during the nineteenth century. Slaves or ex-slaves thus continued to function as an important part of the labour force for cash-crop farming in the Ghana cocoa belt, and the peanut zones of Senegambia.[45] The development of cocoa production by displaced coastal merchant groups among the coastal Yoruba of Nigeria and the Duala of Cameroon depended upon the purchase of new slaves and their development in medium-sized plantations.[46] In the two areas with the largest pre-colonial slave plantation systems, the Swahili coast of East Africa and the Sokoto Caliphate of Northern Nigeria, colonial officials hesitated to abolish slavery for fear that agricultural productivity might decline. Eventually a compromise was devised in each region. In East Africa, land and labour legislation kept the Zanzibar and Kenya coastal plantations intact, forcing local peasants into the position of tenants or squatters. In Sokoto, with more open agricultural frontiers, slaves were allowed to move off plantations on to their own holdings, but forced to pay heavy monetary taxes on the principle that the newly occupied land belonged to the community, which was represented by the colonial state.[47]

Where a base of African rural entrepreneurship did not exist, colonial governments often felt compelled to introduce European rural capitalism, even at the inevitable cost of supporting or at least condoning coerced recruitment of labour. Apart from the brutal gathering of wild export products by concession companies, discussed earlier in the chapter, many regions of what were to become mainly peasant colonies (such as Uganda or the Ivory Coast) were dotted, during their early decades, with small European plantations.[48]

Finally, colonial governments often used their own instruments of administrative pressure and taxation to 'encourage' Africans to undertake cash-crop production. A major role was filled in this process by African chiefs, whether 'traditional' or newly created. The chief (particularly in French and German colonies) was often given the task (sometimes a very lucrative opportunity) of establishing his own export plantation with tributary labour from his subjects.[49]

Except in relatively remote regions growing crops for which there was no great market incentive, coercive devices of this kind gave way in most of West Africa, West-Central Africa, and even much of British East Africa to more voluntary, small-scale peasant production. The anti-slavery impulses behind colonialism were important here in several ways. Colonial governments were directly constrained first to cut off slave supplies from the interior to the coast and then to abolish slavery itself. More generally, pressure from missionaries and liberal-to-socialist groups in the metropole could create political scandals out of any appearance of abusive coercion in African territories under direct colonial ministry control. Moreover merchant groups in both West and East Africa joined in such campaigns partly out of genuine moral/ideological conviction, and partly to protect their own trading interests against direct links between producers and overseas industrial consumers of African commodities.[50]

In strictly market terms it appears that small-scale producers, once their inhibitions against investing in new crops had been overcome, were more efficient in producing the major tropical export crops than plantations of any kind. The new transport systems had eliminated the cost advantages of areas nearer the coast which had formerly imported labour from distant regions. Moreover the agricultural processes involved in most African commercial farming involved few economies of scale (but see pp. 145ff. below). There were some advantages to close integration of farming, processing and transporting of certain bulky or perishable commodities, which helps explain the dominance of Europeans in timber-cutting and banana-growing. However, investment in palm-oil milling, even by major firms like Unilever, almost always led to financial losses unless it was combined directly with tree planting.[51] The greater efficiency of mechanical oil presses was of limited economic value to African households, where women simply felt threatened by separation from a task which they performed at very low opportunity costs. Moreover, the higher oil yields of central mills did not compensate for the combination of their own overhead costs and the added peasant labour involved in transporting whole, rather than processed, fruit from its point of harvesting.

Peasant agriculture: the limitations of development

The role of coercion – transitional as it may have been – provides a clue to the central contradiction of étatist-peasant economic regimes: a persistent gap, measured in technology, social organization and revenue, between the 'commanding heights' of state-merchant sectors and the agricultural producer 'base'. The full meaning of this contradiction, however, only became apparent after peasant systems had taken on a spontaneous momentum as the major source of export commodities and yet ceased to undergo any further internal transformations.

The chronology of this process varied from colony to colony and even among districts within each territory. For regions near the West African coast already producing palm oil or peanuts, the major change brought by colonialism was the abolition of the formal status of slavery, accomplished without major disturbances soon after the turn of the century.[52] In the most important British tropical colonies without settlers, the Gold Coast, Nigeria, Tanganyika and Uganda, new or radically expanded export systems based on cocoa, coffee, peanuts, and cotton were essentially established by the early 1920s.[53] In several of the French colonies such as Cameroon, Chad, Ivory Coast and Ubangi-Shari (present-day Central African Republic) it was not until the last half of the 1930s that concession companies or plantations run by Europeans and local chiefs gave way to independent smallholder commercial farming.[54] Other areas on the fringe of the oceanic-oriented transport systems, or unsuited for the efficient production of export crops, specialized at a very early stage in providing agricultural goods and livestock for the growing local food markets. Finally there were remote inland regions – particularly the sahelian belt of French West and Equatorial Africa – which entered the colonial economy essentially as suppliers of migrant labour to more favoured areas.[55]

Measured in simple quantitative terms, almost all of these peasant economies continued to grow up to the time of independence, as transport facilities improved, populations expanded and found it safe to occupy land accessible to markets, and overseas demand for African commodities increased. What did not change was the systems of production at the individual farm level.

The question raised by this apparent stagnation touches the central issues which have preoccupied earlier chapters of this study and will recur in discussions of late colonial and post-colonial efforts to bring about transformations of African agriculture. The present chapter will briefly relate these issues to the debate over market and structuralist interpretations of colonial economic history and then examine some of the relationships between colonial state policy and rural African entrepreneurship.

All students of the African étatist-peasant regimes have called attention to the high degree of colonial government intervention in economic affairs. For liberals, however, the motive behind this effort is perceived as an economically irrational paternalism and its immediate effects are seen in the exchange and processing sectors rather than in agricultural production.[56] Radical structuralists, on the other hand, have insisted that the interventionist policies of the colonial state were designed to serve the interests of European economic domination over Africans and that the ultimate goal was to preserve traditional modes of production in agriculture. The riposte among liberal scholars concerned with agriculture has been to note that traditional African production systems persisted not because of support or inhibition from outside but because they proved their efficiency against the competition of European private enterprise and allegedly 'expert' public technical advice.[57]

The structuralist case rests on the belief that despite – or even because of – the failures of direct European competition in the agricultural sectors, the colonial state did represent interests in direct conflict with the development of African rural entrepreneurship. These interests included the state itself, which appropriated agricultural revenue for strategic-political projects; the local European merchant community, which profited from control over trade with fragmented African producers; and the metropole, which received tropical goods at low cost from small-scale producers, while paying for them in the convenient currency of manufactured consumer exports.

This case is difficult to defend at the level of conscious intent since colonial regimes in tropical Africa were never as clear about their goals as those in settler regions, where not only European, but also African capitalism took on (as will be seen below) a highly visible political profile. Instead it is necessary to examine the specific linkages between various government policies and the accessibility of factors of production for rural African entrepreneurs and then evaluate the allocations made by African farmers of those resources available to them.

The factor most easily measured and most directly linked to government policy is capital. It is easy to demonstrate that tax exactions accounted for a considerable proportion of the potentially disposable income of African commercial cultivators throughout the colonial system, and at specific times and places limited very severely any fund that might have been used for local investments.[58] Even in situations of relative prosperity, such as the period immediately after the Second World War, marketing boards in British West and East Africa reduced considerably the peasant share of monetary benefits. Nonetheless, there remain significant periods and places where peasants did enjoy some degree of wealth: the 1920s, the late 1930s and (despite marketing boards) the late 1940s to mid-1950s; the forest cocoa-growing and coffee-growing areas rather than the savanna peanut and cotton regions or palm-oil zones. Moreover in the Gold Coast and southern Nigeria up to the late 1930s taxation was largely indirect, via import duties, thus allowing farmers a certain degree of discretion between consumer-public revenue expenditures and the purchase of producer goods and services. Some portion of the money appropriated by the colonial state even flowed back into African hands through the creation of employment opportunities in the various branches of government, in transport, service occupations, etc. These positions were, of course located in the urban rather than rural areas but much of the income they generated reached the countryside in the form of marriage payments (constantly rising everywhere throughout the colonial period), remittances to relations and even direct investments in farms. In short, while it is quite possible to imagine an export system which left more disposable cash in the hands of indigenous rural entrepreneurs, étatist colonial regimes clearly allowed significant opportunities for Africans to make capital investments of their own choice.[59]

It is also sometimes argued by contemporary structuralist critics as it was by reformist policy-makers of the colonial era that rural enterprise was systematically inhibited by government policies limiting the commercial transfer of land. Such restrictions did exist in many areas, either as outright prohibitions or insistence on keeping land allocation under the control of traditional African authorities. Moreover, the aims of such policies were often quite explicitly conservative, i.e. to prevent capitalist class differentiation in the countryside. Undoubtedly, policies of this kind complicated the process of acquiring freehold title to land, even making it impossible in some cases. However, it must be kept in mind that throughout the colonial period there were no great scarcities of land in even the most desirable commercial cultivation zones. Moreover, in many of these areas (particularly the rich forest areas of West Africa) some individuals, whether through purchase or the manipulation of political authority and kinship, did manage to acquire large landholdings. However, the organization of production on these estates proved to be little different – indeed, sometimes even less intensive – than on the farms of smallholders.[60]

The scarcity of labour in relationship to land has also been presented as an explanation of low intensity in colonial African agriculture. Here the colonial governments' role lay in the enforced abolition of slavery, the one classical method of concentrating labour under conditions of 'open resources'. Such an observation does help us to understand the distinction between pre-colonial African slavery (although, as noted above, this seldom involved radical alterations in production organization) and colonial migrant labour. The latter was usually employed for wages on a short-term basis, which inhibited possibilities for new organization. For longer-term labour, the major inducement was the eventual receipt of rights to autonomous landholdings along with sufficient liquid capital to carry over the early, unproductive years of tree crops such as cocoa or coffee.[61] But again, if the colonial regime took away one form of entrepreneurial coercive power over labour, it ultimately provided the basis for another: indebtedness, a frequent and often crushing factor under the volatile price conditions of most African export commodities. Yet those African merchants and richer farmers who thus gained control over the labour of their less fortunate peasant neighbours again did not use this power to effect any different form of agriculture than could be found on fully independent small farms.[62]

If, despite some inhibiting effects of state policy, the factors of production for more intensive agriculture became available to rural African entrepreneurs, why were they not combined in a manner more congruent with the dominant European industrial capitalist system? The answer given by market theorists has been that such a choice would have been irrational, since European technology offered no effective efficiency gains to African farming. This argument about economies of scale, like those about the state, is both important and ultimately insufficient to explain the reluctance to change.

The experience of various European plantation companies and even processing firms which entered the African countryside provided ample negative demonstration effects of modern technology. First of all, the devices they used (especially ploughs and also some fertilizers) proved unsuitable to the savanna and forest conditions of virtually all of West and West-Central Africa and much of East Africa. Secondly, they were costly to adopt. The problems of integrating cattle into agricultural systems have already been discussed (Chapter 1) and the modern form of non-human energy, tractors, required prohibitive cash outlays for purchase, maintenance, and fuel.

Nonetheless, some forms of inexpensive new technology were accessible to African peasant farmers by the late 1920s, particularly light ploughs, small hulling devices, hand-operated oil presses and pesticide sprayers, often specifically designed for African conditions. Moreover, colonial governments themselves invested a good deal in diffusing such implements to African farmers along with instructions on how to 'improve' local agriculture generally. Yet even these innovations met a consistent and widespread resistance which cannot be accounted for adequately through material cost-benefit calculations.[63]

Precisely because technological change in agriculture was promoted by colonial authorities, it is not surprising that it should have induced a generally negative reaction from peasants who had good reason to mistrust the state as a generally alien and often oppressive force. Moreover cost calculations of alterations in basic methods of production also had to take into account the impact of the related social changes. Colonial administrators were explicitly told how ploughing would upset the sexual division of labour in rural households. Palm-oil pressing, as we have already seen, was continued in its traditional form partly because it was a female task whose costs were considered quite low.[64] The reluctance – or inability – of wealthy individuals to impose new labour disciplines upon males over whom they had some economic advantages must also be ascribed to contradictions between existing social relations and the demands for labour under conditions of enlarged scale and mechanized (or even animal-powered) agriculture. The circumstances under which such new forms of production could be effectively adopted will be seen in Chapter 7 which deals with settler-dominated African societies.

However, for the more successful and ambitious rural entrepreneurs under étatist-peasant regimes, the failure to take up more intensive farming must be seen in relationship to opportunities outside the farming sector. In the first place, it is clear that surplus rural wealth was invested in such a direction: more specifically, into commerce, transport, and the education of children for white-collar occupations. On the surface, such enterprises might appear more hazardous than investment in farming, since they put Africans in potential competition with Europeans, Asians and Levantines who enjoyed various advantages in the commercial and urban sectors. However, African failure in these new endeavours risked nothing but the surplus capital specifically invested for such a purpose while experimentation with agriculture threatened the material and social base upon which rural communities depended for their ultimate survival.

This need for a cushion against setbacks in, or at least retirement from, the urban sectors accounts both for the need to reinvest some urban wealth in farming and the tendency to do so along conservative lines, as insurance policies rather than profit-maximizing ventures. Investments in other kinds of rural relationships or distinctions – marriages, honorific titles, the building of conspicuous private houses or contributions to churches and mosques – was itself a reward for success in areas of higher profit than farming. Finally, to antagonize rural dependents by exploiting them in new forms of agriculture was to risk losing their support in the political endeavours of the urban sphere (even the 'office' and commercial politics of the era preceding decolonization).[65]

The economic opportunities of the colonial regime were thus used by the most successful Africans to forge new forms of patron–client networks. But, unlike comparable relationships in the Asian and Levantine communities, these endeavours led away from intensive concentration on specialized enterprises and towards a diffusion of both risk and ambition.

Conclusion: étatist-peasant regimes and the contradictions of colonialism

The initial paradox of European colonial partition – the expansion of political commitment at a moment of declining African significance in the world economy – appeared to have been resolved by the étatist-peasant regimes. Export production reached levels which could cover the costs of even somewhat redundant infrastructures. At the same time the survival of traditional technology and social organization in the countryside assured a minimum of tension between poorly paid farmers and a bureaucratic-commercial elite enjoying Western middle class standards of income.

But inevitably this system could not escape the pressures for change generated by even its own conservative pattern of growth. From an internal African perspective, the expansion of population and commercial production would eventually strain the ecological capacities of the continent. And, from the outside, European powers soon proved willing to risk the security of stable colonial arrangements in order to act out more energetically the compulsions which had brought them into Africa in the first place.

The effect of peasant cash-crop expansion on the African environment is ultimately the most serious of these pressures but it was not felt very strongly during the colonial period. A major reason for this delay is that up until the 1920s colonial rule probably caused a decline rather than an increase in African population. Military campaigns against primary and even second-stage African resistance, forced labour, the spread of diseases through accelerated inter-regional contacts and environmental changes, famines induced by combinations of drought and precipitous commitment to commercial agriculture – all contributed to high death rates in these early decades, counterbalanced by few effective public health or food distribution programmes.[66] Given the existence of much open land in tropical Africa, peasants could, even in times of recovered population growth, increase their agricultural efforts without any need to alter the systems of production.

The breakdown of colonial rule was thus initiated by factors external to its economic base, as will be seen in Chapter 9 and Chapter 10. Late colonial regimes viewed the intensified development of Africa as a solution to metropolitan rather than overseas crises of political economy. European governments in Africa were succeeded by Westernized nationalists with even greater ambitions for promoting social change. To the proponents of these new visions, étatist-peasant regimes were the very embodiment of contradiction, since they had done so little to bring the African economy into step with the forces which determined its relationship to the outside world. But none of the efforts initiated in the mid-twentieth century have yet provided a successful alternative to this limited form of modern development.

In the final chapter of this book we will have to ask whether the contradictions of étatist-peasant regimes are a phenomenon of specific colonial conditions or derive from the fundamental structures of African economic history. The next chapter will examine a form of colonialism which stimulated more dynamic economic change, but at a social and political cost which represents, in its most developed form, a truly unbearable degree of contradiction.

Notes

1. Wilks (1975) pp. 640–65; also Chapters 2 and 4 above, passim. For the one indigenous African state, Ethiopia, which actually attempted infrastructural modernization, but with only limited success, see Marcus (1975) p. 199f.
2. Hargreaves (1974) p. 35f.
3. Flint (1960); Galbraith (1972); Iliffe (1979) pp. 91–8; Müller (1959); Pearson (1971); on Rhodes's British South Africa Company, see Chapter 7 below.
4. Slade (1962) pp. 171–203; Harms (1975); Walz (1917).
5. Hammond (1966) pp. 147–91; Vail (1976).
6. Ballhaus (1968); Coquery-Vidrovitch (1972); Rudin (1938) pp. 290–6.
7. Crowder (1971); Headrick (1981) pp. 83–126.
8. On the general political economy of railways in the Third (and Second) World: Coatsworth (1981); White (1976). There is no general analytic study of the African cases but see Austen and Headrick (1983); Baltzer (1916); Dumett (1975); Iliffe (1969) pp. 77–8; Huybrechts (1970); Katzenellenbogen (1975); O'Connor (1965); Pfeffer (1976); Sautter (1967); Vail (1975).
9. E.A.J. Johnson (1970); Lovejoy (1970).
10. Hazlewood (1964) pp. 38–57, 197–8; Kay (1972) p. 21f.; Njoku (1978); Pfeffer (1976).
11. Meredith (1976).
12. Mason (1978); Sautter (1967).
13. Austen (1970); Cookey (1966); Coquery–Vidrovitch (1972) pp. 233–43; Gertzel (1959) p. 438f.; Suret–Canale (1964) p. 28f.
14. Bauer (1954); Davies (1973) p. 103f.; Hopkins (1973) pp. 198–203; Hopkins (1976); Munro (1976) pp. 130–1f.
15. Hopkins (1966b) vs. Holmes (1972) pp. 103–34.
16. Austen (1983); Hopkins (1966a, 1980); Porter (1963) pp. 109–18.
17. There is no satisfactory historical study of the rise of either of these well-known groups but see Dongmo (1981); Isichei (1983) pp. 435–6; Tardits (1960).
18. Cruise O'Brien (1975); Mangat (1969); Merioni and Van der Laan (1979); Van der Laan (1975) (the best work on non-European immigrant economics); Zarwan (1975).

19. Amselle (1977); Cohen (1969); Kitching (1980) pp. 212–17; Lovejoy (1970); Sudarska (1979).
20. Kay (1975); Kitching (1980) p. 413f.
21. Hopkins (1976); Kilby (1975) p. 495f.
22. Brett (1973) p. 266f.; Johnson (1974); Suret–Canale (1950).
23. Fieldhouse (1979) p. 339f.
24. Elkan (1958); Johnson (1978); Stout (1966) pp. 5–16.
25. Callaway (1965); King (1977); see Chapter 9, below, for further discussion of the informal sector.
26. Marion Johnson (1970, n.d.); Jones (1958); see also Chapter 1, above.
27. Gervais (1982); Hopkins (1966c).
28. Fieldhouse (1971) pp. 606–12; Gervais (1982); Hopkins (1970); Hopkins (1973) pp. 149–51, 206–9; Tetzlaff (1970) pp. 164–6.
29. Baier (1980) pp. 105–10; Coquery–Vidrovitch (1972) pp. 156–64; McCarthy (1976); Ofanagoro (1979).
30. Munro (1976) pp. 160–2. For more detail on colonial external trade policies, see Chapter 8 below.
31. Austen (1977b); Guyer (1980c); Koerner (1965) pp. 105, 126, 154–83; Poquin (1957) p. 140f.; Thompson and Adloff (1958) pp. 355–62.
32. Ehrlich (1970); Helleiner (1966) p. 153f.; Hopkins (1973) pp. 286–8; McCarthy (1982) pp. 24–63.
33. For theoretical debates on African peasantries, see Bernstein (1978, 1979); Cooper (1981); also Chapter 9 below.
34. Grier (1981); Howard (1980).
35. Hogendorn (1975).
36. Guyer (1980b); Kaniki (1980).
37. Ingham (1979); Smith (1979).
38. Hogendorn (1978); Usoro (1974).
39. Simmons (1976); Wrigley (1959).
40. Stuerzinger (1980); Tosh (1980).
41. On rubber see: Egboh (1979); Munro (1976) pp. 99–100; on kola see: Agiri (1972).
42. Austen (1968) pp. 95–6.
43. Stover (1970).
44. Austen and Headrick (1983) pp. 59–61; Gregory (1971) pp. 500–3; Iliffe (1969) pp. 23, 77–8, 99–100; Johnson (1974); Marseille (1975); Tosh (1978); Vail and White (1980) pp. 272–9.
45. Klein (1981); Reynolds (forthcoming).
46. Austen (1977a); Hopkins (1978).
47. Cooper (1980); Lennihan (1983); Watts (1983) pp. 156–71.
48. Chauveau (1980); Mutibwa (1976).
49. Austen (1968) pp. 96–7; Austen and Headrick (1983) pp. 58–60; Guyer (1980a); Richards et al. (1973) pp. 14–20.
50. Hopkins (1973) p. 213; Nworah (1971); Suret–Canale (1964) p. 28f.
51. Austen (1977b); Fieldhouse (1979) p. 494f.; Kaniki (1980); Kilby (1969) pp. 146–68.
52. Lovejoy (1983) pp. 248–55. See also notes 45, 46 above.
53. Berry (1975) pp. 126–57; Iliffe (1979) p. 273f.; Szereszewski (1965); Wrigley (1959).
54. Austen and Headrick (1983) pp. 58–60; Chauveau (1980).
55. Amin (1974); Cordell and Gregory (1982).
56. Ehrlich (1973); Rimmer (1983).
57. Brett (1973) p. 297; Grier (1981); Howard (1980); Suret–Canale (1964) pp. 367–84. For the liberal view, Hopkins (1973) p. 209f.
58. The best documented study is Vanhaeverbeke (1970).
59. Berry (1985) passim (perhaps the best available analysis of African peasant capitalism); Dunn and Robertson (1973) pp. 41–67; Gastellu and Yapi (1982) (see more on Ivory Coast peasants in Chapter 9 below).

60. Clarke (1980); Dunn and Robertson (1973) pp. 50–67.
61. Berry (1975) p. 126f.; Chauveau (1980).
62. Morgan and Pugh (1969) pp. 527–8; Southall (1978).
63. Hart (1982) pp. 73–5; Kilby (1969) pp. 147–9, 159–65.
64. Austen (1968) p. 97; Kaniki (1980).
65. Berry (1985) especially pp. 78–83; Garlick (1971) pp. 110–16; Gastellu and Yapi (1982).
66. Coquery–Vidrovitch (1985) pp. 49–61.

Bibliography

Agiri, Babatunde Aremu (1972), 'Kola in western Nigeria, 1850–1930: a history of the cultivation of *Cola nitida* in Egba-Owade, Ijebu Remo, Iwo, and Ota areas' (Unpublished PhD dissertation, University of Wisconsin)

Amin, Samir (ed.) (1974), *Modern Migrations in West Africa* (London: Oxford University Press)

Amselle, Jean-Loup (1977), *Les négociants de la savanne: histoire et organisation sociale des Kooroko (Mali)* (Paris: Anthropos)

Austen, Ralph A. (1968), *Northwest Tanzania under German and British Rule* (New Haven: Yale University Press)

Austen, Ralph A. (1970), 'The abolition of the overseas slave trade: a distorted theme in West African history', *Journal of the Historical Society of Nigeria*, vol. 5, no. 2, pp. 257–74

Austen, Ralph A. 1977(a), 'Slavery among coastal middlemen: the Duala of Cameroon', in Suzanne Meiers and Igor Kopytoff (eds), *Slavery in Africa* (Madison: University of Wisconsin Press), pp. 305–33

Austen, Ralph A. 1977(b), 'Duala versus Germans in Cameroon: economic dimensions of a political conflict', *Revue Française d'Histoire d'Outre-Mer*, vol. 64, no. 4, pp. 477–97

Austen, Ralph A. (1983), 'Metamorphoses of middlemen: the Duala, Europeans, and the Cameroon hinterland, ca. 1800–ca. 1960', *International Journal of African Historical Studies*, vol. 16, no. 1, pp. 1–24

Austen, Ralph A. and Rita Headrick (1983), 'Equatorial Africa under colonial rule', in David Birmingham and Phyllis M. Martin (eds), *History of Central Africa*, Vol. 2, (London: Longman), pp. 27–94

Baier, Stephen (1980), *An Economic History of Central Niger* (Oxford: Clarendon Press)

Ballhaus, Jolanda (1968), 'Die Landkonzessionsgesellschaften', in Helmuth Stoecker (ed.), *Kamerun unter deutscher Kolonialherrschaft*, Vol. 2 (E. Berlin: Akademie), pp. 99–179

Baltzer, F. (1916), *Die Kolonialbahnen mit besonderen Berücksichtigung Afrikas* (Berlin: G.J. Goeschen)

Bauer, P.T. (1954), *West African Trade: A Study of Competition, Oligopoly, and Monopoly* (Cambridge: Cambridge University Press)

Bernstein, Henry (1978), 'Notes on capital and peasantry', *Review of African Political Economy*, no. 10, pp. 60–73

Bernstein, Henry (1979), 'African peasantries: a theoretical framework', *Journal of Peasant Studies*, vol. 6, pp. 421–43

Berry, Sara S. (1975), *Cocoa, Custom, and Socio-Economic Change in Rural Western Nigeria* (Oxford: Clarendon Press)

Berry, Sara S. (1985), *Fathers Work for their Sons: Accumulation, Mobility, and Class Formation in an Extended Yoruba Community* (Berkeley: University of California Press)

Brett, E.A. (1973), *Colonialism and Underdevelopment in East Africa: The Pattern of Economic Change, 1919–1939* (London: Heinemann)

Callaway, Archibald (1965), 'From traditional crafts to modern industries', *Odu*, vol. 2, no. 1, pp. 28–51

Chauveau, Jean-Pierre (1980), 'Agricultural production and social formation: the Baule region of Toumodi–Kokumbo in historical perspective', in Klein (ed.), pp. 142–74

Clarke, Julian (1980), 'Peasantization and landholding: a Nigerian case study', in Klein (ed.), pp. 176–219

Coatsworth, John (1981), *Growth against Development: The Economic Impact of Railroads in Porfirian Mexico* (De Kalb: Northern Illinois University Press)

Cohen, Abner (1969), *Custom and Politics in Urban Africa: A Study of Hausa Migrants in Yoruba Towns* (Berkeley: University of California Press)

Cookey, S.J.S. (1966), 'The concession policy in the French Congo and the British reaction, 1898–1906', *Journal of African History*, vol. 7, no. 2, pp. 263–78

Cooper, Frederick (1980), *From Slaves to Squatters: Plantation Labor and Agriculture in Zanzibar and Coastal Kenya, 1890–1925* (New Haven: Yale University Press)

Cooper, Frederick (1981), 'Peasants, capitalists and historians: a review article', *Journal of Southern African Studies*, vol. 7, no. 1, pp. 284–314

Coquery-Vidrovitch, Catherine (1972), *Le Congo au temps des grands compagnies concessionaires, 1898–1930* (Paris: Mouton)

Coquery-Vidrovitch, Catherine (1985), *Afrique noire: permanences et ruptures* (Paris: Payot)

Cordell, Dennis D. and Joel W. Gregory (1982), 'Labour reservoirs and population: French colonial strategies in Koudougou, Upper Volta, 1914 to 1939', *Journal of African History*, vol. 23, no. 2, pp. 205–24

Crowder, Michael (ed.) (1971), *West African Resistance: The Military Response to Colonial Occupation* (New York: Africana Publishers)

Cruise O'Brien, Rita (1975), 'Lebanese entrepreneurs in Senegal: economic integration and the politics of protection', *Cahiers d'Etudes Africaines*, vol. 15, no. 1, pp. 95–115

Davies, P.N. (1973), *The Trade Makers: Elder Dempster in West Africa, 1852–1972* (London: Allen & Unwin)

Dewey, Clive and A.G. Hopkins (eds) (1978), *The Imperial Impact: Studies in the Economic History of Africa and India* (London: Athlone Press)

Dongmo, Jean-Louis (1981), *Le dynamisme Bamiléké* (Yaoundé: University de Yaoundé)

Duignan, Peter and L.H. Gann (eds) (1975), *Colonialism in Africa, 1870–1960*, Vol. 4, *The Economics of Colonialism* (Cambridge: Cambridge University Press)

Dumett, Raymond E. (1975), 'Joseph Chamberlain, metropolitan finance, and railway policy in British West Africa in the late nineteenth century', *English Historical Review* vol. 90, no. 355, pp. 287–321

Dunn, John and A.F. Robertson (1973), *Dependence and Opportunity: Political Change in Ahafo* (Cambridge: Cambridge University Press)

Egboh, E.O. (1979), 'The Nigerian rubber industry, 1939–1945', *Nigerian Field*, vol. 44 pp. 2–13

Ehrlich, Cyril (1970), 'Marketing boards in retrospective – myths and reality', in *African Public Sector Economics* (Edinburgh: Centre of African Studies, Edinburgh University)

Ehrlich, Cyril (1973), 'Building and caretaking: economic policy in British tropical Africa 1890–1960', *Economic History Review*, vol. 26, no. 4, pp. 649–67

Elkan, Walter (1958), 'The East African trade in wood carvings', *Africa*, vol. 28, no. 4 pp. 314–23

Fieldhouse, David K. (1971), 'The economic exploitation of Africa: some British and French comparisons', in Prosser Gifford and Wm Roger Louis (eds), *France and Britain in Africa* (New Haven: Yale University Press), pp. 593–662

Fieldhouse, David K. (1979), *Unilever Overseas: The Anatomy of a Multinational* (London: Croom Helm)

Flint, John E. (1960), *Sir George Goldie and the Making of Nigeria* (London: Oxford University Press)

Galbraith, John S. (1972), *Mackinnon and East Africa, 1878-1895* (Cambridge: Cambridge University Press)

Garlick, Peter C. (1971), *African Traders and Economic Development in Ghana* (Oxford: Clarendon Press)

Gastellu, J.M. and S. Affou Yapi (1982), 'Un mythe à décomposer: la "bourgeoisie" des planteurs', in Y.A. Fauré and J.F. Médard (eds), *Etat et bourgeoisie en Côte d'Ivoire* (Paris: Karthala), pp. 149-79

Gertzel, Cherry J. (1959), 'John Holt: a British merchant in West Africa in the era of imperialism' (Unpublished D. Phil dissertation, Oxford University)

Gervais, Raymond (1982), 'La plus riche des colonies pauvres: le politique monétaire et fiscal de la France au Tchad', *Canadian Journal of African Studies*, vol. 16, no. 1, pp. 93-112

Gregory, Robert G. (1971), *India and East Africa* (Oxford: Clarendon Press)

Grier, Beverly (1981), 'Underdevelopment, modes of production, and the state in colonial Ghana', *African Studies Review*, vol. 24, no. 1, pp. 21-47

Guyer, Jane I. 1980(a), 'Head-tax, social structure, and rural income in Cameroon, 1922-1937', *Cahiers d'Etudes Africaines*, vol. 20, pp. 305-29

Guyer, Jane I. 1980(b), 'Food, cocoa and the division of labor by sex in two West African societies', *Comparative Studies in Society and History*, vol. 22, no. 3, pp. 355-73

Guyer, Jane I. 1980(c), *The Provident Societies in the Rural Economy of Cameroon, 1945-1960* (Boston: Boston University Press)

Hammond, R.J. (1966), *Portugal and Africa, 1815-1910: A Study in Uneconomic Imperialism* (Stanford: Stanford University Press)

Hargreaves, John (1974), *West Africa Partitioned*, Vol. 1, *The Loaded Pause, 1885-1889* (Madison: University of Wisconsin Press)

Harms, Robert (1975), 'The end of red rubber: a reassessment', *Journal of African History*, vol. 16, no. 1, pp. 73-88

Hart, Keith (1982), *The Political Economy of West African Agriculture* (Cambridge: Cambridge University Press)

Hazlewood, A.D.H. (1964), *Rail and Road in East Africa: Transport Co-ordination in Underdeveloped Countries* (Oxford: Clarendon Press)

Headrick, Daniel (1981), *The Tools of Empire* (New York: Oxford University Press)

Helleiner, Gerald K. (1966), *Peasant Agriculture, Government and Economic Growth in Nigeria* (Homewood, Ill.: Irvine)

Hogendorn, Jan S. (1975), 'Economic initiative and African cash farming: pre-colonial origins and early colonial developments', in Duignan and Gann (eds), pp. 283-328

Hogendorn, Jan S. (1978), *Nigerian Groundnut Exports: Organization and Early Development* (Zaria: Ahmadu Bello University Press)

Holmes, III, Alexander Baron (1972), 'Economic and political organization on the Gold Coast, 1920-1940' (Unpublished PhD dissertation, University of Chicago)

Hopkins, A.G. 1966(a), 'Richard Beale Blaize, 1854-1904: merchant prince of West Africa, *Tarikh*, vol. 1, no. 2, pp. 70-9

Hopkins, A.G. 1966(b), 'Economic aspects of political movements in Nigeria and the Gold Coast, 1918-1939', *Journal of African History*, vol. 7, no. 2, pp. 133-52

Hopkins, A.G. 1966(c), 'The currency revolution in southwestern Nigeria in the late nineteenth century', *Journal of the Historical Society of Nigeria*, vol. 3, no. 3, pp. 471-83

Hopkins, A.G. (1970), 'The creation of a colonial monetary system: the origins of the West African Currency Board', *African Historical Studies*, vol. 3, pp. 101-32

Hopkins, A.G. (1973), *An Economic History of West Africa* (New York: Columbia University Press)

Hopkins, A.G. (1976), 'Imperial business in Africa. Part II: interpretations,' *Journal of African History*, vol. 17, no. 2, pp. 267-90

Hopkins, A.G. (1978), 'Innovation in a colonial context: African origins of the Nigerian cocoa-farming industry, 1880-1920', in Dewey and Hopkins (eds), pp. 83-96

Hopkins, A.G. (1980), 'Property rights and empire building: Britain's annexation of Lagos,

1861', *Journal of Economic History*, vol. 40, no. 4, pp. 777–98

Howard, Rhoda (1980), 'Formation and stratification of the peasantry in colonial Ghana', *Journal of Peasant Studies*, vol. 8, no. 1, pp. 61–80

Huybrechts, André (1970), *Transports et structures de développement au Congo* (Paris: Mouton)

Iliffe, John (1969), *Tanganyika under German Rule, 1905–1912* (Cambridge: Cambridge University Press)

Iliffe, John (1979), *A Modern History of Tanganyika* (Cambridge: Cambridge University Press)

Ingham, Barbara (1979), 'Vent for surplus reconsidered with Ghanaian evidence', *Journal of Development Studies*, vol. 15, no. 3, pp. 19–37

Isichei, Elizabeth (1983), *History of Nigeria* (London: Longman)

Johnson, E.A.J. (1970), *The Organization of Space in Developing Countries* (Cambridge: Harvard University Press)

Johnson, Marion (1970), 'The cowrie currencies of West Africa', *Journal of African History*, vol. 11, no. 1, pp. 17–50, vol. 11, no. 2, pp. 331–50

Johnson, Marion (1974), 'Cotton imperialism in West Africa', *African Affairs*, vol. 73, no. 291, pp. 178–87

Johnson, Marion (1978), 'Technology, competition, and African crafts', in Dewey and Hopkins (eds), pp. 259–69

Johnson, Marion (n.d.), 'Cloth-strip currencies' (Unpublished paper)

Jones, G.I. (1958), 'Native and trade currencies in southern Nigeria during the eighteenth and nineteenth centuries', *Africa*, vol. 28, no. 1, pp. 43–53

Kaniki, Martin (1980), 'Economical technology against technological efficiency in the palm oil industries of West Africa', *Development and Change*, vol. 11, pp. 273–84

Katzenellenbogen, Simon E. (1975), 'The miner's frontier: transport and general economic development', in Duignan and Gann (eds), pp. 360–426

Kay, G.B. (ed.) (1972), *The Political Economy of Colonialism in Ghana* (Cambridge: Cambridge University Press)

Kay, Geoffrey (1975), *Development and Underdevelopment* (London: Macmillan)

Kilby, Peter (1969), *Industrialization in an Open Economy: Nigeria, 1945–1960* (Cambridge: Cambridge University Press)

Kilby, Peter (1975), 'Manufacturing in colonial Africa', in Duignan and Gann (eds), pp. 470–520

King, Kenneth J. (1977), *The African Artisan: Education and the Informal Sector in Kenya* (London: Heinemann)

Kitching, Gavin (1980), *Class and Economic Change in Kenya: The Making of an African Petite-Bourgeoisie* (New Haven: Yale University Press)

Klein, Martin A. (ed.) (1980), *Peasants in Africa: Historical and Contemporary Perspectives* (Beverly Hills: Sage)

Klein, Martin A. (1981), 'The transition from slave labor to free labor: the case of Senegambia' (Canadian Historical Association Meetings, Papers)

Koerner, Heiko (1965), *Kolonialpolitik und Wirtschaftsentwicklung: der Beispiel französisch Westafrikas* (Stuttgart: Fischer)

Lennihan, Louise D. (1983), 'Rights in men and rights in land: slavery, labor and small holder agriculture in northern Nigeria', *Slavery and Abolition*, vol. 2, no. 3, pp. 111–39

Lovejoy, Paul (1970), 'The wholesale kola trade of Kano', *African Urban Notes*, vol. 5 no. 2, pp. 129–42

Lovejoy, Paul (1983), *Transformations in Slavery: A History of Slavery in Africa* (Cambridge: Cambridge University Press)

McCarthy, Dennis M.P. (1976), 'Media as ends: money and the underdevelopment of Tanganyika to 1940', *Journal of Economic History*, vol. 36, no. 3, pp. 645–62

McCarthy, D.M.P. (1982), *Colonial Bureaucracy and Creating Underdevelopment Tanganyika, 1919–1940* (Ames: Iowa State University Press)

Mangat, J.S. (1969), *A History of the Asians in East Africa, c. 1886 to 1945* (Oxford: Clarendon Press)

Marcus, Harold G. (1975), *The Life and Times of Menelik II: Ethiopia 1844–1913* (Oxford: Clarendon Press)

Marseille, Jacques (1975), 'L'industrie cotonnière française et l'impérialisme coloniale', *Revue d'Histoire Economique et Sociale*, vol. 53, nos. 2/3, pp. 386–412

Martin, Anne (1956), *The Oil Palm Economy of the Ibibio Farmer* (Ibadan: Ibadan University)

Mason, Michael (1978), 'Working on the railway: forced labor in Northern Nigeria, 1907–1912', in Peter C.W. Gutkind, Robin Cohen and Jean Copans (eds), *African Labor History* (Beverly Hills: Sage), pp. 56–79

Meredith, David (1976), 'The construction of Takoradi harbour in the Gold Coast 1919 to 1930: a case study in colonial development and administration', *Transafrican Journal of History*, vol. 5, no. 1, pp. 134–49

Merioni, H.V. and L.H. Van der Laan (1979), 'The Indian traders in Sierra Leone', *African Affairs*, vol. 78, no. 34, pp. 240–50

Morgan, W.B. and J.C. Pugh (1969), *West Africa* (London: Methuen)

Müller, Franz-Ferdinand (1959), *Deutschland-Zanzibar-Ostafrika: Geschichte einer deutschen Kolonialeroberung* (East Berlin: Rütter & Loening)

Munro, J. Forbes (1976), *Africa and the International Economy, 1800–1960* (London: Dent)

Mutibwa, P.M. (1976), 'White settlers in Uganda: the era of hopes and disillusionment 1905–1923', *Transafrican Journal of History*, vol. 5, no. 2, pp. 112–22

Njoku, O.N. (1978), 'The development of roads and road transportation in Southern Nigeria, 1903–1939', *Journal of African Studies*, vol. 5, no. 4, pp. 471–97

Nworah, Kenneth Dike (1971), 'The Liverpool "Sect" and British West African policy', *African Affairs*, vol. 70, no. 4, pp. 349–64

O'Connor, A.M. (1965), *Railways and Development in Uganda* (Nairobi: Oxford University Press)

Ofanagoro, Walter I. (1979), 'From traditional to British currency in southern Nigeria: analysis of a currency revolution, 1880–1946', *Journal of Economic History*, vol. 39, no. 3, pp. 623–54

Pearson, Scott R. (1971), 'The economic imperialism of the Royal Niger Company', *Food Research Institute Studies*, vol. 10, pp. 69–88

Pfeffer, Paul E. (1976), 'Political and economic strategies for French colonial railroads in West Africa: the Senegal–Sudan rail axis', *Proceedings of the French Colonial Historical Society*, vol. 2, pp. 60–71

Poquin, Jean-Jacques (1957), *Les relations économiques extérieures des pays d'Afrique Noire de l'Union Française, 1925–1955* (Paris: Colin)

Porter, Arthur (1963), *Creoledom: A Study of the Development of Freetown Society* (London: Oxford University Press)

Reynolds, Edward (forthcoming), *Chiefs, Farmers and Preachers: Tradition and Modernization in Akuapem*

Richards, Audrey I. et al. (1973), *From Subsistence to Commercial Farming in Present-Day Buganda* (Cambridge: Cambridge University Press)

Rimmer, Douglas (1983), 'The economic imprint of colonialism and domestic food supplies in British tropical Africa', in Robert I. Rotberg (ed.), *Imperialism, Colonialism, and Hunger in East and Central Africa* (Lexington: D.C. Heath), pp. 141–65

Rudin, Harry (1938), *Germans in the Cameroons, 1884–1914* (New Haven: Yale University Press)

Sautter, Giles (1967), 'Notes sur la construction du chemin de fer Congo–Océan, (1921–1934)', *Cahiers d'Etudes Africaines*, vol. 7, no. 2, pp. 219–99

Simmons, John (ed.) (1976), *Cocoa Production: Economic and Botanical Perspectives* (New York: Praeger)

Slade, Ruth (1962), *King Leopold's Congo* (New York: Oxford University Press)

Smith, Sheila (1979), 'Colonialism in economic theory: the experience of Nigeria', *Journal of Development Studies*, vol. 15, no. 3, pp. 38–59

Southall, Roger J. (1978), 'Farmers, traders, and brokers in the Gold Coast economy', *Canadian Journal of African Studies*, vol. 12, no. 2, pp. 185–211

Stout, J. Anthony (1966), *Modern Makonde Sculpture* (Nairobi: Kibo Art Gallery)

Stover, Charles C. (1970), 'Tropical exports', in W. Arthur Lewis (ed.), *Tropical Development, 1880–1913* (London: Allen & Unwin), pp. 46–63

Stuerzinger, Ulrich (1980), *Baumwollbau im Tschad* (Zurich: Atlantis)

Sudarska, Niara (1979), 'From stranger to alien: the socio-political history of the Nigerian Yoruba in Ghana, 1900–1970', in William A. Shack and Elliott P. Skinner (eds), *Strangers in African Society* (Berkeley: University of California Press), pp. 141–67

Suret-Canale, Jean (1950), 'L'industrie des oléagineux en AOF', *Cahiers d'Outre Mer*, vol. 3, pp. 280–8

Suret-Canale, Jean (1964), *Afrique noire: occidentale et centrale*, Vol. 2, *L'ère coloniale (1900–1945)* (Paris: Editions Sociales)

Szereszewski, R. (1965), *Structural Change in the Economy of Ghana, 1891–1911* (London: Weidenfeld & Nicolson)

Tardits, Claude (1960), *Contribution à l'étude des populations Bamiléké de l'Ouest Cameroun* (Paris: Berger-Levrault)

Tetzlaff, Rainer (1970), *Koloniale Entwicklung und Ausbeutung: Wirtschafts- und Sozialgeschichte Deutsch-Ostafrikas, 1885–1914* (Berlin: Duncker u. Humblot)

Thompson, Virginia and Richard Adloff (1958), *French West Africa* (Stanford: Stanford University Press)

Tosh, John (1978), 'Lango agriculture during the early colonial period: land and labour in a cash-crop economy', *Journal of African History*, vol. 19, no. 3, pp. 415–39

Tosh, John (1980), 'The cash-crop revolution in tropical Africa: an agricultural reappraisal', *African Affairs*, vol. 79, no. 314, pp. 79–94

Usoro, Eno J. (1974), *The Nigerian Palm Oil Industry* (Ibadan: Ibadan University Press)

Vail, Leroy (1975), 'The making of an imperial slum: Nyasaland and its railways, 1895–1935', *Journal of African History*, vol. 16, no. 1, pp. 89–112

Vail, Leroy (1976), 'Mozambique's chartered companies: the role of the feeble', *Journal of African History*, vol. 17, no. 3, pp. 389–416

Vail, Leroy and Landeg White (1980), *Capitalism and Colonialism in Mozambique* (Manchester: Manchester University Press)

Van der Laan, H.L. (1975), *Lebanese Traders of Sierra Leone* (The Hague: Mouton)

Vanhaeverbeke, André (1970), *Rémunération de travail et commerce extérieur: essor d'une économie paysanne exportatrice et termes de l'échange des producteurs d'arachides au Sénégal* (Louvain: Université Catholique)

Walz, Heinrich (1917), *Das Konzessionswesen in belgischen Kongo* (Jena: G. Fisher)

Watts, Michael (1983), *Silent Violence: Food, Famine and Peasantry in Northern Nigeria* (Berkeley: University of California Press)

White, Colin M. (1976), 'The concept of social savings in theory and practice', *Economic History Review*, vol. 29, no. 1, pp. 82–100

Wilks, Ivor (1975), *Asante in the Nineteenth Century* (Cambridge: Cambridge University Press)

Wrigley, C.C. (1959), *Crops and Wealth in Uganda* (Kampala: East African Institute of Social Research)

Zarwan, John (1975), 'The social and economic network of an Indian family business in Kenya, 1920–1970', *Kroniek van Afrika*, vol. 6, no. 3, pp. 219–36

 *7*

The Colonial Economies: II
Regimes of Competitive Exploitation

The regions of Southern, Central, and East Africa where Europeans sought direct control of land, mineral resources, and labour experienced patterns of twentieth-century economic development very different from those discussed in Chapter 6. Here Africans could not simply adapt their existing forms of production to complement new European structures of administration, transport, and commerce. Instead, indigenous cultivators were forced either to compete with Europeans by taking on new systems of technology and labour organization, or submit to the terms of employment offered by European farms, mines, and factories. The degree and variety of expatriate penetration into the African economic base also brought about competition among Europeans with differing interests in both local production systems and the external world economy.

Colonial economic change in this portion of Africa was not only more intensive but also closely bound to political conflicts. This chapter will therefore have to consider the issues and outcomes of struggles for control over government – first between various European powers, and then between established metropolitan authorities, local white settlers, and African entrepreneurs – more formidable than those discussed in Chapter 6. The European private sector here took much greater responsibility for infrastructural development, although the assignment of such roles also put the government in danger of becoming the instrument of local investors. At the same time the majority of local white settlers could, at least in British-ruled territories, demand control over the state for the purpose of pursuing their own interests. Finally, local governments were compelled by various pressures to give some consideration to the protection of African interests against the total white minority. The present discussion will only consider the varying responses to this last imperative during the period of European rule; the degree to which economic structures changed after African governments took over in the majority of these territories will be dealt with in Chapter 9.

Much of this chapter focuses upon the one major African country which still remains under European control: the Republic of South Africa. South Africa is, in many respects, a unique case of both large-scale metropolitan capital investment and effective local economic nationalism among Europeans. Nonetheless, it has also served as a model and even a source of material support for parallel European development farther to the north. The pages which follow will thus give some attention to settler agricultural and/or major mining enterprise in the Portuguese possessions of Angola and Mozambique, Kenya, the Rhodesias (Zambia and Zimbabwe), and the Belgian Congo (Zaire). There were also lesser direct-exploitation enclaves in a number of other colonial territories (e.g. Cameroon, French Equatorial Africa, Gold Coast, Guinea, Ivory Coast, Liberia, Nigeria, Sierra

Leone, Tanganyika, Uganda), but in the interests of stressing analytic coherence rather than descriptive comprehension, these will be either ignored or treated only very briefly here. What set apart the territories which are the focus of this chapter is not only the scale of European productive activities but also their impact on overall development both in the structure of class formation and the movement towards industrialization.

South Africa before the mineral revolution: the weak frontier

The area presently occupied by the Republic of South Africa and the several questionably independent African states which it surrounds and adjoins represents the extreme end of a subcontinent whose history has always diverged somewhat from that of the rest of Africa. By the period of contact with extra-African economies, the region was still experiencing the establishment of domesticated food-production systems and was thus poorly integrated into internal exchange networks. When it first entered the system of international trade, South Africa functioned essentially as a supplier of victuals for merchants whose ultimate goal was the carriage of higher-value goods between Europe and Asia. Paradoxically, such a secondary role led, from its earliest stages, to a deeper penetration by foreigners than on other, more attractive, African commercial frontiers. The African experience of this process up until the major mineral discoveries of the late nineteenth century involved drastic social and demographic shifts for those groups in direct contact (meaning both trade and warfare) with Europeans but no major adaptation of local economies to meet new market opportunities.

THE INDIGENOUS DOMESTIC ECONOMY
The basic shift from foraging to domesticated modes of food production came relatively late and incompletely to South Africa. At the time of European contact in the sixteenth century, significant hunter-gatherer populations of Bushmen/San still existed in the open lands of the present-day Cape Province as well as the mountains and desert regions of the interior. More significantly, the group which had displaced the Bushmen/San in most of the Cape region, the Khoikhoi (known to local Europeans as 'Hottentots'), had adopted domesticated animals but not agriculture. The Khoikhoi were thus vulnerable both to dependency upon foraging when ecological disasters reduced their cattle herds, and to the loss of autonomy and/or territory when confronted by populations with a more stable base of domesticated subsistence.[1]

The first peoples to offer such a challenge to the Khoikhoi were Bantu-speakers who had reached the northern edge of the Cape Province by as early as the eighth century AD. Up until the seventeenth century the ratio between Bantu demographic growth and available land seems to have allowed the Khoikhoi to escape any serious pressure. However, by the early seventeenth century the Xhosa Bantu peoples at the north-eastern frontier of the Cape had begun to penetrate Khoikhoi pastures, eventually taking over the land and assimilating the much smaller Khoikhoi populations.

The coexistence of such varied populations in South Africa encouraged the growth of commercial networks for the exchange of specialized goods – products of the hunt from the Bushmen/San, cattle and cattle products from the Khoikhoi, iron and copper from the interior to the Cape, and *dagga* (a local form of narcotic hemp) throughout the region. Such trade does not, however, appear to have been as significant a factor in local development as the competition for territory among groups with economies which duplicated, or overlapped, rather than complemented one another.[2]

The most dramatic recorded change in South African Bantu history is the *mfecane*, a movement of political organization and conflict which, in the late eighteenth and early nineteenth century, formed a series of powerful new states and sent other groups upon long and violent migrations throughout the subcontinent and as far north as Lake Victoria. The *mfecane* occurred well after the first European contacts with South Africa but it originated among a people and in a region – the northern Nguni (centred around the present-day Zulu) of Natal – which had not yet been much affected by that contact. Rather than a response to trade opportunities, which were only marginally present in Natal, the *mfecane* seems to have been a result of cyclical shifts in local ecology, first allowing the northern Nguni to increase considerably their livestock herds and then forcing them into a major struggle over the pasturage necessary to maintain such prosperity.[3] The *mfecane*, as will be seen, facilitated European expansion into the Southern African interior, but was not significantly caused by Europeans, nor did it involve adaptation of European technology to meet either military or agricultural needs. Instead of guns and ploughs, Dingiswayo, Shaka and the other *mfecane* leaders manipulated existing institutions of age organization and warfare to reallocate control over land and population. Thus it was precisely on the frontier where European economic expansion presented its most threatening aspect that Southern African societies proved – until it was too late – least willing to shift to more intensive systems of production.[4]

EARLY EUROPEAN COMMERCE AND AGRICULTURE

The first four centuries of European presence in South Africa – from the Portuguese explorations of the late fifteenth century to the discoveries of precious minerals in the late nineteenth century – may be seen, in economic terms, as a single period. During this time the political position of Europeans went through a series of major changes from relations between passing ships and independent African societies in the sixteenth century, to the establishment of a Dutch Colony at the Cape of Good Hope in 1652, to the replacement of the Netherlands by Britain in the early nineteenth century, followed by further European sovereignty in Natal on the east coast and the Orange Free State and Transvaal in the interior. In all this time, however, the Europeans did not introduce any major change in the local systems of production. Rather, they extended and modified the existing livestock economies so as to participate more fully – but never very profitably – in international markets. The major change in the period was the constant expansion of the frontier of European settlement, always at the expense of indigenous Africans. Attempts by the Dutch and British governments to control this process so as to fit the colonial economy into the broader structure of the respective empires met with little success and inevitably exacerbated the violent movement across the frontier.

From the moment when the Portuguese established a direct sea route to the Indies, all European powers with Asian imperial ambitions felt compelled to establish strategic way stations somewhere in Africa. In purely navigational terms, the site of Cape Town seems like the ideal point for such a post. But because its hinterland offered no opportunities for immediate trade in items of international value, the Portuguese bypassed the Cape of Good Hope in favour of Mozambique, which lay closer to south-east African goldfields. The Dutch, in their assault upon Portuguese maritime hegemony, originally sought to take over Mozambique but when this plan failed they finally established the first permanent European settlement on the Cape.[5]

Two internal features of the Cape Town area and its immediate environment made it attractive as a provisioning base for ships travelling between Europe and the Indies. First, the local Khoikhoi herdsmen appeared willing to provide beef supplies at a very low cost. Secondly, the temperate local climate and plentiful rainfall would allow a small number of European farmers (*boers*) to produce fruits, vegetables, wine and mutton for passing ships as well as grain for their own sustenance.

The Cape Town colony was a success insofar as it survived for almost two centuries and did provide the Dutch East Indies fleet and other merchant vessels with victuals necessary for the long trans-oceanic voyages. The costs of maintaining this station, however, always exceeded the immediate returns from sales of foodstuffs or the few wild export goods, such as ivory, ostrich feathers and skins which arrived from the interior. The Khoikhoi soon refused to sell cattle in sufficient quantities to meet Cape Town's needs and efforts to put pressure upon them (see pp. 159–60 below) led to expensive conflicts. Farms with a wide range of crops as well as sheep and cattle were established within the immediate vicinity of Cape Town by Europeans, but it proved impossible to maintain them at a level sufficient to assure regular supplies without also providing some form of subsidy to compensate for the limited size of the market they could reach.

During the first decades of British rule the South African economy continued much as it had before, although the scale of European enterprise was increased by the immigration of about 10 000 new settlers to the Cape (increasing the existing white population by almost half) and another 5 000 to the newly founded colony of Natal. By the 1830s farmers in the hinterland of the Cape had begun to develop a product for which there was a major demand in Europe: wool from imported Merino sheep. Although the methods of grazing (mainly carried on by African servants in any case) did not involve a major change from previous agricultural practices, the revenues brought in created an unprecedented level of local prosperity. However, South Africa was never able to control as significant a share of the British wool market as Australia, so that in world terms the colony still remained relatively poor and highly vulnerable to downturns in metropolitan prices, such as occurred in the late 1860s. Natal, meanwhile, was beginning to develop plantation sugar production although this, too, was minor by world, and even South African, standards.[6]

EUROPEAN COMPETITION WITH AFRICANS AT THE CAPE

The most important change in the South African economy between the fifteenth century and the late nineteenth century was ultimately not the increasing level of production for the world market but rather the expanding control by Europeans over all resources on the subcontinent. To a considerable extent this European expansion was, like the African movements which preceded and competed with it, motivated more by concerns for maintaining growing populations at comfortable levels of subsistence (mainly by grazing large herds of cattle) than by efforts to supply commodities to external consumers. However, the living standards of even the most remotely settled and illiterate Dutch farmers required some form of contact with markets. The outward movement of the white settler frontier in South Africa thus represents at one and the same time both the Africanization of a European population and the direct integration, on however weak a basis, of a vast area into the European economy.

Even in its market aspects, the South African frontier was always different from the other meeting points of continental and international trade. The difference on the African side was most extreme in the case of the first set of partners encountered at the Cape, the Khoikhoi.[7] As a purely pastoral and relatively uncentralized society, the Khoikhoi had limited initial need for European commodities. They could not invest any of these goods in production; even the initially much-sought metals were valuable only for making weapons. Likewise, there appears to have been little possibility for controlling the flow of non-utilitarian trade items to the benefit of any dominant groups within Khoikhoi society. Some of the imports were passed on to other groups, both Khoikhoi and Bantu; but again there were limitations, partly derived from fear that these secondary recipients would become militarily stronger than the primary traders. More significantly the Dutch demands for return goods could not easily be met by any Africans.

In contrast to foreign traders on other African frontiers, the Dutch did not seek products foraged or cultivated outside the basic African subsistence economy but rather demanded a commodity which was at once the symbol and substance of indigenous wealth: cattle. The Khoikhoi and Bantu were always willing to sell off a certain proportion of the increase or marginal population of their herds, but they could not regularly provide the Dutch with the number and quality of animals the latter required. In fact the goal of African trading was ultimately to increase their herds by selling low-value cattle and exchanging part of the return for more valuable stock from neighbours. The Dutch, even in their first limited settlements, were also involved in this same strategy since they hoped to build up their own local herds as a surer source of beef and dairy products. The entire trading system therefore threatened to remove cattle from the Khoikhoi without giving them anything of comparably enduring value in return.

The inevitable Khoikhoi resistance to the presence of competitive pastoralists in their territory led very quickly to violent conflicts which the Dutch, with their superior weaponry, inevitably won. Various Khoikhoi who lost cattle either through over-commitment to trade, unsuccessful warfare, or natural disaster then began to take service among the Dutch as servants, labourers, and herders. This had always been an established tactic among unfortunate Khoikhoi, who would become clients of wealthier individuals with the hope of eventually receiving the basis for creating a new herd. In the case of the Dutch, however, Khoikhoi clients never received the means for regaining an independent existence. Instead European *trekboers* (farmers on the frontiers of settlement) would move out from the initial Cape Town perimeter to take over the pasturage which had once belonged to the Khoi. The process was exacerbated in 1713 when a smallpox epidemic cut the Khoikhoi population from about 100 000 to about 50 000. By the late eighteenth century, the 26 000 Europeans living at the Cape constituted a significant proportion of the total local population.

The number of Europeans settled at the Cape at this time represented the midpoint of an extremely rapid growth process. In 1713 there were only 2 000 whites in the region, by 1865 there were a quarter of a million. While immigration contributed to some of this rise, the most important factor was natural increase. Demographic expansion thus accounts for the constant pressure of the Dutch population on first the Khoi and then the Bantu frontier. Economic logic dictated that the form of this expansion would be extensive cattle grazing. Most Dutch families lacked the capital to go into more intensive farming, for which there was a limited market in any case. Herds could be built up relatively easily by participating in the incursions upon the Khoikhoi and land was virtually free in the interior. The costs of the munitions, sugar, tobacco and other minimal goods needed to maintain a European life style and the loyalty of a few Khoikhoi or San retainers could always be met by the sale of beef to Cape Town as well as other urban settlements developing along the coasts and the near interior from the early nineteenth century. By the 1830s wool-farming offered a more lucrative alternative to cattle-grazing for interior farmers but it was taken up mainly by new English immigrants, as well as by some autonomous 'Coloured' communities. Many of the British were settled on land vacated by Dutch-speaking Boers, who had trekked to even more remote pastures in quest of both a livelihood and the preservation of what had by then become an established social order.[8]

EUROPEAN-BANTU COMPETITION

From the 1770s on, the continuation of Dutch pastoralist migration clashed with the movement southward of Bantu-speaking peoples. The first major area of conflict was the western frontier of the Cape, where Xhosa groups were undergoing both internal demographic expansion and pressures from the *mfecane* occuring to their north. The Xhosa and Dutch engaged in patterns of trade and violent conflict similar to those which had characterized the earlier Khoikhoi contacts. But while the political organization and agricultural base of the Xhosa made them better trading partners (supplying ivory as well as cattle), it also allowed them to compete more vigorously with the Dutch for control of territory and cattle herds (among other things, by obtaining guns in trade). From 1779 to 1853 the Xhosa and neighbouring Europeans fought between six and nine 'Kaffir wars' along their mutual frontier. Despite the often formidable Xhosa resistance, the Europeans eventually won and confined the Xhosa to what have today become the Ciskei and Transkei 'Homelands' or 'Bantustans'. Throughout this process, most Xhosa retained their herds and their economic autonomy. However in 1857, despairing at their inability to push back the Europeans, tens of thousands of Xhosa engaged in ritual killing of their cattle and destruction of their grain, in the hope that this action would bring spiritual forces to their aid. Instead, the result was widespread death from starvation (although the population losses were subsequently regained) and the reduction of large numbers of the Xhosa to dependent status as employees of Europeans.[9]

Despite their suffering, the very survival of the Xhosa had blocked Dutch expansion to the west. In 1837 some 5 000 Dutch pastoralists crossed the northern borders of the Cape Colony on their famous 'Great Trek' into interior territories where no European communities had been established before. The trekkers' motives for leaving the Cape included bitter resentment at British government policies (see below pp. 161–2) and a conviction that large tracts of unoccupied pasturage were available in the interior. The latter belief arose from observations by Dutch explorers of the areas in the central veld and the coastal plains of Natal cleared temporarily of their Bantu populations by the unrest of the *mfecane*. Once arrived in these regions, the white *voortrekkers* had to fight extended wars with the highly militarized African states they encountered: most prominently the Zulu, the Ndebele, and the Sotho. Although Natal was eventually abandoned (mainly because of British rather than African pressures) the Dutch pastoralists did succeed in establishing two major two centres of settlement in the Transvaal and the Orange Free State. This migration is both the central motif of contemporary Afrikaner (white, Dutch-speaking South African) nationalist ideology and an immediate expression of frontier development in the nineteenth century. The spread of the *voortrekkers* to such a remote area cut them off almost entirely from contemporary European culture and its economy. But, to maintain their hegemony, these settlers had to assert their European-Christian identity in the most extreme terms and make sure that minimal contacts with the external market were maintained.[10]

ECONOMY AND THE STATE IN THE CAPE COLONY

Before examining how this marginal frontier of European agriculture became the main centre of South African economic growth it is necessary to look briefly at the efforts of Cape Colony governments to control local development in the interests of their respective metropolitan economies. For all but the last few years of Dutch rule, the Cape was administered by representatives of a commercial organization – the Dutch East India Company (DEIC) – whose major goal, as its name implied, was to maintain profitable control over Indonesia.[11] In political terms, the DEIC was highly autocratic, allowing local settlers no say in their own affairs. Translated into economic policy, this approach meant that the DEIC sought control over land distribution and all links to the oceanic market. When Cape agriculture began to suffer from labour shortages, the DEIC chose to import slaves from elsewhere in Africa and from Asia rather than more settlers, who would only make additional demands upon the government. The result of all these policies was external success: the Cape fulfilled its function as a victualling station at relatively low cost; but internal failure: settlers were continuously dissatisfied to the point of periodic rebellion, DEIC trade regulations were thwarted whenever possible by smuggling, and the hinterland frontier, upon which the DEIC placed strict limits, was regularly violated by white hunters, traders, and ultimately *trekboers* whose way of life represented an institutionalized rebellion.

Britain, in the first two-thirds of the nineteenth century, was no more interested than the DEIC had been in expending large sums on the hinterland of what amounted essentially to a naval base.[12] Rather than maintaining mercantilism and autocracy, however, the British sought to solve South Africa's problem through a policy of economic and political liberalism. Additional white settlers were thus brought to the Cape and Natal as a spur to spontaneous economic growth; by 1871 the Cape Colony had also achieved full self-governing status for its internal affairs. However liberal policies towards settlers also implied concern for the rights of non-whites. The British abolished slave trading to the Cape at the moment of their arrival, outlawed local slavery in 1833, and in 1828 granted the Cape Coloured population (descendents of Khoikhoi, ex-slaves, and mixed unions) equal economic status to that of whites. Moreover, in the aftermath of its various military interventions on the eastern Cape frontier, the British government attempted to guarantee at least limited safeguards for Xhosa land rights. These 'negrophile' aspects of British liberalism – inspired in large part by local missionaries representing the same movement which brought about abolition of the Atlantic slave trade – antagonized the *trekboer* element of Cape society even more than had the autocracy of the DEIC. The new independent republics established in the Transvaal and Orange Free State by the Great Trek thus sought to safeguard a very different set of labour and property relations between whites and blacks than those being promoted at the Cape.

The mineral revolution in Southern and Central Africa

Between 1865 and 1900 South Africa was transformed from a marginal outpost of European commerce and agriculture to the world's leading supplier of diamonds and gold. These mining enterprises were revolutionary not simply in the increments of wealth and importance they brought to the sub-continent, but also because their operation required large-scale and sophisticated capital investment. South Africa was able to draw together local and international capital for the creation of its own mining industry and in turn became a major base for the pursuit of new mineral wealth further to the north. During the imperialist partition of the 1880s and 1890s, private capital played a role in Southern and South-Central Africa which was not possible for the merely commercial enterprises established on other African frontiers. Finally, and most critically, the intensive mining centres throughout this larger region created new sets of labour relations and provided at least a potential foundation for the development of wider industrial economies.

The major sequence of mineral development in Southern and Central Africa began with the discovery of diamonds on the Cape Colony frontier in 1867, surged even higher with the exploitation of the Transvaal goldfields from 1886, and in the early twentieth century proceeded less spectacularly or steadily but with ultimate success to the gold of Southern Rhodesia (Zimbabwe) and the copper of Northern Rhodesia (Zambia) and the Katanga (Shaba) province of the Belgian Congo (Zaire). The discussion which follows will concentrate on these four sectors of the South and Central African mining industry because they remained major factors in their respective territorial economies and have also been studied in a manner which allows us to use them as representatives of the internal development of a much wider range of mining enterprises in this region as well as in West Africa.[13]

The link between virtually all significant production and marketing of high-value African minerals is a group of international corporations with overlapping interests that connect in important ways with South Africa. The development of these corporations can be traced directly to the first modern mining complex in Africa, the Kimberley diamond fields to the north of the Cape Colony. In its initial stages Kimberley was only a spectacular version of the kind of alluvial mining which Africans in many parts of the continent had been carrying on for over a millennium. However, by the mid-1870s surface diamond deposits had been exhausted and the exploitation of deeper and richer sources required a shift from the anarchy of individual prospectors' claims to sophisticated technological investments by large-scale capitalists. Within two decades of their opening, the Kimberley mines were dominated by a single firm, De Beers Consolidated Mines. The formation of this corporation, like other such ventures throughout the region, was initiated and directed by locally based English speaking entrepreneurs – in this case none other than Cecil Rhodes – but made possible only through support from major English financiers. De Beers, in turn, was eventually able to control the marketing of diamonds throughout the Western world and to maintain important shares in corporations producing diamonds in other parts of Africa, including Angola, the Belgian Congo, Sierra Leone, and South West Africa (Namibia).

The opening of the Witwatersrand goldfields in the Transvaal required sizeable investments from the very beginning, since little of the precious metal lay near the surface or in particularly rich deposits. Means for mobilizing the necessary capital lay readily at hand in the Kimberley diamond fields, although in the case of the Rand, the extent of workable seams was sufficiently great to allow several corporations to establish themselves. Despite early competition, relations between these gold-mining firms soon developed many of the characteristics of a monopoly: nothing any single mine did could change the world price of gold – fixed largely by governments and currency markets in individual countries – and mine-owners as a whole shared an interest in lowering production costs. By the 1920s a single firm, the misleadingly named Anglo American Corporation of South Africa (an essentially British and South African conglomerate controlled by Sir Ernest Oppenheimer and later his son, Harry) came to dominate the finances of the South African gold industry and also acquired, with the takeover of De Beers, control of diamond mining.

The modern exploitation of gold mines in Rhodesia – in earlier centuries the source of indigenous East African gold exports – began as a personal venture of Cecil Rhodes, financed out of the liquid capital and reputation of the De Beers and Rand undertakings. Rhodes's British South Africa Company (BSAC) was initially both monopoly landowner and political sovereign of lands claimed from the indigenous inhabitants of Southern and Northern Rhodesia. But the gold available in these territories never repaid the sums invested in direct production by the BSAC and other highly capitalized firms which it initially licensed. Only after 1903, when the BSAC began leasing ore-bearing sites to smaller, lower-cost, operations in return for more modest royalties on their winnings was Rhodesian gold able to become a profitable proposition. Once such a guarantee of returns was established, large investors from the Rand re-entered Rhodesia on a limited but locally very significant basis.

Copper had also been an object of Rhodes's northward ambitions as early as the 1890s. Katanga in the Belgian Congo was known to be a still very active indigenous source of this metal, whose world market value was rising with the increasing role of electricity in industrial societies. After several false starts Katangan copper was finally brought into production in 1912 by a corporation, Union Minière du Haut-Katanga, which was jointly financed through Belgian sources and a British-controlled offshoot of the BSAC, Tanganyika Concessions Ltd.

Northern Rhodesian copper deposits, on the other hand, could not be worked profitably by either the BSAC or any of its collaborating firms. Ironically, the greatest source of revenue for the BSAC was to come from the royalties paid by copper producers after the Company had given up political control of Northern Rhodesia in 1923. By this time new technology and increasing market demand allowed two very large investors – Anglo American and the truly American Rhodesia (later Roan) Selection Trusts (a subsidiary of American Metals Climax) – to make Northern Rhodesia one of the world's prime sources of copper.

MINING CAPITAL AND IMPERIALIST EXPANSION

The spread of international mining enterprise beyond South Africa obviously depended upon the expansion of European political control. Yet the subjugation of various territories in Southern and Central Africa to colonial rule formed part of a wider imperialist partition process which did not depend upon the influence of major economic interest groups. Thus the connection between imperialism and mining capital in this region requires some explanation, and yet cannot be reduced to any simple or even clear formula.

Contemporary observers of events in South Africa at the end of the nineteenth century found it easy to believe that British political actions here resulted from a conspiracy on the part of mine-owners and financiers. In 1895 Cecil Rhodes actually launched an unsuccessful plot – the Jameson Raid – to overthrow the independent Afrikaner government of the Transvaal. Four years later Britain was engaged in a major war against both the Transvaal and the Orange Free State which were then incorporated into the British empire as part of the Union of South Africa. It was difficult not to assume some congruence between Rhodes's position as a mine-owner, Cape Colony politician (he was prime minister in 1895), and advocate of expansion to the north. Moreover, other mining magnates were also involved in the Jameson plot, continued to quarrel with the Transvaal government after 1895, and supported Britain during the 1899–1902 South African War.

Liberal revisions of this early interpretation have stressed the continued primacy of strategic rather than economic motivations in British South African policies. According to this view, Rhodes used his mining wealth to act out a personal vision of British political and cultural goals. He was in turn used by British officials as an apparently inexpensive instrument for preventing the Afrikaner republics from employing their new mineral wealth to dominate the subcontinent. The evidence to support such an argument is the failure of most mine-owners to support either the Jameson plot or the aggressive British diplomacy which preceded the outbreak of war.[14]

Recent research into the economic issues of the Anglo–Boer conflict indicates that the tensions over Transvaal gold may have involved more than threats to the route to India. With their high capital investment and relatively low yields, the Witswatersrand mines were more vulnerable to pressures from hostile governments than most overseas mineral operations. In particular, the control of labour supplies – a major factor in determining profitability – required close co-operation with local political authorities. Finally, Britain itself was undergoing a serious gold reserve crisis at the time of the South African conflict.[15]

However, none of this new scholarship reveals a conscious effort by miners or bankers to solve their problems by instigating a British takeover of the Transvaal. Moreover, the regime established by Britain after its military victory simultaneously provided a more hospitable climate for mining enterprise and re-enfranchised Afrikaner nationalists. The latter would use their political power within a more modern state to impose upon mining capital a pattern of development derived from the local imperatives of inter-racial economic and social patterns.

Rhodesia is a clearer case of economic imperialism than South Africa because here British strategic concerns simply provided a license for Rhodes to establish a regime which was at once an imperial outpost and a mining operation.[16] The difficulty with this area, however, was that it always remained a minor producer of minerals, thus deriving its greatest regional significance from its geographical relationship to other mining areas and an internal development based to a far greater extent upon agriculture.

The division of the copperbelt between separate Northern Rhodesian and Congo territorial jurisdictions was the result of conscious efforts by first King Leopold II and then the Belgian government to assure Katanga's autonomy from the British South African sphere of influence.[17] Such political concerns could never fully counteract the imperatives of international finance and regional transport logistics which linked Katanga to the rest of the Southern African mining complex.

Nevertheless, the colonial boundaries are one factor explaining the variations among territories in the relationship between mines and the surrounding society.

CAPITAL AND LABOUR IN THE MINING ECONOMIES

Large-scale mines provided much greater profits and incentives to private fixed-capital investments than other forms of African export production. However, their impact upon the surrounding economies could vary considerably and depended very heavily upon labour policies.[18]

Although the major mines of Southern and Central Africa provided, as did peasant exporter cultivators, primary goods which were sent overseas for advanced stages of processing, the forms of production in the mines were clearly industrial; that is, they incorported large numbers of workers into labour processes organized around centralized machinery. The needs of this system were met by differing mixes of three basic types of labour: Europeans, occupying skilled positions and receiving the highest wages; unskilled Africans, migrating on a temporary basis as single males from rural areas and receiving the lowest wages; and skilled Africans, 'stabilized' with their families in urban areas and paid intermediate wages.

During the early phases of all mining enterprises, the labour force was composed mainly of skilled Europeans and unskilled African migrants. At this point few skilled Africans were available and, in any case, there was a preponderant need for unskilled labour in constructing the facilities for mechanized extraction, processing, and transportation of ores. Moreover, migration initially provided both capital and labour with a low-risk means of accommodating to the needs of a mining economy. From the employers' viewpoint, migrants were relatively inefficient workers and incurred recurrent costs of recruitment and transportation; but they more than made up for this by their limited wage demands, resulting from the fact that social costs of family maintenance and worker insurance and retirement were borne by the rural areas of origin. The migrants themselves, while undergoing considerable physical and psychological strain, at least did not have to give up the security of a rural subsistence base. Indeed, as low as wages were, they often provided critical capital for investment in land, cattle, and marriage while local political authorities received recruitment bonuses which strengthened their political and social position.[19]

Within each mining system, however, a point was eventually reached when economic considerations dictated a shift towards a skilled, stabilized African work force. Part of this pressure came from the side of labour supply where, for reasons to be discussed below, opportunities for new entrants into peasant agriculture decreased. For mine-owners, once mechanization had been achieved, it simply became cheaper to substitute Africans for higher-paid Europeans in skilled jobs. It was also rational to encourage long-term urban residence despite the absorption of traditional social costs as well as modern health and educational services, because these were now balanced by the higher return on investments in job-training.

Yet the degree of transition from a racially defined, migration-based labour system differed considerably from one sector of the Southern and Central African mining system to the other. The variations were determined partly by conditions of ore extraction and labour supply but most significantly by political factors.

South Africa represents one extreme on the continuum of change: its labour structures remained essentially the same throughout a century of intensive mining experience.[20] The Kimberley diamond mines found it fairly easy to recruit a migrant African labour force both from the displaced populations around the Cape region and from more distant Bantu-speaking groups who appreciated the political advantages of obtaining firearms, a major currency of payment in this system. Because of anxieties about diamond thefts, but also the need to control labour in the more capital-intensive situation of deep-level mining, the Kimberley mine-owners developed a system for housing African workers in closed compounds during the entire duration of their labour contracts. Even in areas without the smuggling problems of the diamond industry, such compounds proved an effective means of meeting the maintenance costs of migrant labour and limiting desertion, absenteeism, or the impingement of large numbers of single black males upon nearby European urban communities.[21]

The compound system worked particularly well in the gold mines of the Rand where African workers had to be sought from such distant points as Mozambique and were even replaced, during a severe labour shortage immediately after the 1899–1902 South African War, by indentured Chinese recruits. The continued use of low-paid migrants met with opposition from the white community, especially poor Afrikaners who after the South African War were losing access to land and migrating into cities looking for unskilled work.

This tension between mining needs and white labour reached a climax in the early 1920s when mine-owners, faced with declining profit rates, attempted to replace some of the existing skilled European labour force with Africans. White workers responded to these measures with a strike so severe that in 1922 the Rand became the scene of a virtual civil war. Although the incumbent moderate nationalist government of Jan Christiaan Smuts supported the mine-owners, it is not clear whether there was really a movement at this time towards a stabilized African labour force. In the first place, the success of the compound system and the difficulty of replacing men with machines in narrow underground shafts led to the adoption by mine-owners of an official policy (formalized under the name of its principal proponent as 'Stallardism') in favour of continuing the migrancy system. Perhaps more important was the defeat of Smuts in the 1924 South African election by a 'Pact' coalition of white workers and rural-based hardline South African nationalists, who imposed new restrictions on the mobility of black labour.[22] As a result, African mine employees remained confined to low-paid positions and temporary compound sojourns while their white counterparts were assured privileged access to skilled jobs at a level of pay which allowed them to enjoy living standards comparable to those of the most advanced Western economies.

At the extreme opposite pole of South-Central African mining organization was the stabilized labour system developed during the 1920s in Katanga by Union Minière and imitated by other mining enterprises in the Belgian Congo as well as the Diamang diamond complex of Angola.[23] By comparison (and in competition) with South Africa, the Katanga mines experienced great difficulties recruiting and maintaining migrant labour during their early years of operation. At the same time white labour was more expensive in the Congo since it had to be recruited from South African or overseas rather than drawn from an established local European community.

It was particularly attractive for Union Minière to shift from large-scale unskilled labour to a smaller and better-paid skilled force since the Katanga copper was removed from open pits with space for the introduction of labour-saving machinery, as opposed to the restricted underground conditions of the Rand gold mines and Northern Rhodesian copperbelt. Moreover the Katanga management had little difficulty in suppressing the demands of its white employees for a colour-bar since the workers (many of whom were South Africans up to the early 1920s) had no means of mobilizing the authoritarian colonial government of the Congo on their side. On the contrary, Belgian administrators placed pressure on Union Minière to undertake stabilization in order to reduce the disruptive effects of perpetual recruitment upon the welfare and agricultural productivity of a some-what thinly populated countryside.

The result of the shift to stabilized labour was that an African community around the mines enjoyed modest wages but relatively high standards of housing, health, and educational opportunities for children. In effect the miners of Katanga became a black labour aristocracy but one very much under the control of Union Minière and lacking political, social or, as will be seen, economic influence comparable to the position of white South African workers.

The Rhodesias occupied a middle ground, both geographically and organiza-tionally, between the South African and Katangan patterns of labour. By the time of their consolidation just before the First World War the Southern Rhodesian gold mines were sufficiently organized to resist demands for a privileged posi-tion by white workers but too poor to offer blacks any major wage or welfare benefits.[24] The compound system was used here to control newly recruited workers, but with longevity in employment black miners could look forward to increased freedom of movement, some rise in wages, and the possibility of living in quarters large enough to contain a family. However medical services in these compounds were minimal and the only education offered was in the form of night schools run by mission societies and partially financed by mineworkers themselves.

The Northern Rhodesian copper mines seriously considered adopting the labour stabilization policies of neighbouring Katanga but ultimately remained on a system of official contract migrancy, modified by the reality that most labourers had settled in urban areas with their families.[25] Mine-owners themselves faced some economic obstacles to stabilization which did not occur in Katanga – diffi-culty in mechanization and the skimming of profits for potential reinvestment by the BSAC royalty holders – but on the whole favoured such a move. The major obstacles came from well-entrenched white labour unions, who upheld a colour-bar wage system, and the British colonial administration. The latter, in contrast to the Belgian Congo authorities, felt that rural social stability was more threatened by the permanent loss of workers than by their migratory movement between village and city. Northern Rhodesian mines did offer workers relatively good wages, housing, food and medical care and exerted control over compounds through a system of elected 'tribal elders' usually related to hereditary rural chiefs. However up to the eve of independence relatively little was spent on African education or any forms of welfare which would induce families to stay in urban areas beyond the period of active employment.

The significance of these distinctions in mining labour policy is most easily interpreted in terms of the immediate well-being of miners and the degree to which their work situation mobilized them into more active pursuit of their own inter-ests. This last point will be pursued in Chapter 9 but here the impact of mining complexes will be examined mainly in relation to other forms of economic produc-tion. The advanced technology of the mines was initially surrounded by economies still based on classical African forms of agricultural and handicraft production. It was quite possible for the mines to function as enclaves, providing benefits to their owners, the overseas consumers of ores, and even African workers without transforming the broader local economies. The ultimate measure of such transformation is the introduction of industrial manufacturing into these production systems. But the link between mining and manufacturing, where it even developed, cannot be understood without first considering changes in Southern and Central African agriculture.

Varieties of agricultural transformation

Within the geographical region and time period covered by this chapter, general economic development was always uneven. At one extreme South Africa began, by the 1930s, to move into an advanced stage of industrialization. Less impressive, but nonetheless significant, sectors of secondary industry also appeared in Southern Rhodesia and Kenya, which were able to dominate surrounding markets, and in the Belgian Congo, which remained more self-contained. At the opposite pole were such countries as Bechuanaland (Botswana), Basutoland (Lesotho), Mozambique, and Nyasaland (Malawi), and Ruanda-Urundi (Rwanda and Burundi) which depended for cash incomes largely on the export of labour. Among the importers of this labour were not only the industrializing territories but also countries such as Northern Rhodesia, Tanganyika and Uganda which, like the étatist-peasant colonies, produced only primary goods for export and internal consumption.

The critical explanation for this variation is not geography – unlike comparable states in West Africa, the poorer partners in this system are not all landlocked and/or poorly endowed with farmland – nor the distribution of major mining sectors, which fails to account for Kenya and Northern Rhodesia and does so only weakly for Southern Rhodesia and the Belgian Congo. Rather, the most important single feature deciding which territories would become regional development centres was the existence of capitalist agricultural sectors with the ability to influence government policy.

The most striking feature distinguishing agriculture in these territories from the tropical colonies discussed in Chapter 6 is the competition for land between European and African farmers. This competition had the effect of reducing many Africans to a proletarian status, but it is also linked (along with ecological factors) to the emergence of more concentrated entrepreneurship among a minority of successful African landowners. In the period covered in this chapter it was only European rural capitalists who were able to influence industrialization through their articulation with metropolitan and local governments as well as with other economic interest groups in commerce and mining. However this model of local European capitalism has relevance, as Chapter 9 will show, for post-colonial development under black African rule.

THE SPREAD OF EUROPEAN LANDHOLDING
The establishment of white farmers in the Cape Colony in the period before European mineral exploitation had depended upon three factors unique to this frontier of the continent: the strategic imperative of servicing trade routes connecting Europe and Asia; climate and soil conditions which allowed European-style agriculture; and a local African economy not developed in such a way as to meet external market demands. As the colonial frontier advanced northward from the Cape these factors of strategy, sub-tropical ecology, and discontinuity with

indigenous commerce continued to influence the new development patterns, but in a complex and ambiguous form which reproduced neither temperate-zone white-settler colonial patterns nor (at least in much of the region) the peasant-based export economies of the previously discussed tropical African dependencies.

Strategic concerns in South and Central Africa are not directly linked to agriculture but it is necessary to review them briefly in order to understand the state structures which were to have a major influence on the allocation of rural resources. The critical actors here are the Afrikaners of South Africa, the Portuguese rulers of Angola and Mozambique, and Britain whose response to the other two is the most important force of all.

Afrikaner *trekboer* migration from the Cape was not limited to the boundaries of the present-day Republic of South Africa.[26] By the 1860s Afrikaner traders and prospectors were already moving into what later became Southern Rhodesia (Zimbabwe). British statesmen feared that such expansion would undermine their efforts to maintain hegemony over the subcontinent and its critical position on the route to Asia. The foundation of Southern Rhodesia was thus motivated by a desire to contain the Afrikaners although the latter, somewhat ironically, became an important force in the European farming and mining community of Northern Rhodesia (Zambia).

Portugal, following its establishment of inland trading links from coastal positions in both Angola and Mozambique, initially claimed hegemony over all of South Central Africa.[27] Because metropolitan Portugal had failed to keep pace with the political and economic development of advanced industrial states, these colonial claims had several types of local consequences. Most immediately, by the late nineteenth century they were subject to challenge by other European powers, prompting the complex diplomacy which eventually awarded the Congo (Zaire) to Belgium and spurred Britain to extend its formal hegemony into the Rhodesias and Nyasaland (Malawi). Within the considerable territories which Portugal retained, economic policy was dictated by the immediate mercantilist needs of the metropole, uninhibited (as was also the case in South Africa) by threats to the regime in power from liberal or humanitarian criticism.

The position of Britain in this region was the most complicated of all. After 1910 it effectively gave up all control over South Africa; after 1923 it retained only tenuous sanctions over the internally self-governing settler regime of Southern Rhodesia; Basutoland (Lesotho), Bechuanaland (Botswana), and Swaziland were under direct British political control but economic hostages to South Africa; Northern Rhodesia, Nyasaland, Kenya, Tanganyika, and Uganda were Crown Colonies which could theoretically be operated (as Tanganyika and Uganda largely were) along the étatist-peasant lines of West Africa. Whatever may have been the direct interest of Britain in these territories, it was heavily influenced by the broader concern for protecting maritime access to Asia via the Cape of Good Hope and Egypt.[28]

The instrument used by the British in expanding north of South Africa was the chartered company: the Imperial British East Africa Company (IBEAC) for Kenya and Uganda; Cecil Rhodes's British South Africa Company (BSAC) for South Central Africa. The IBEAC quickly collapsed (see Chapter 6) although its great project, the railway from the Indian Ocean in Kenya to the Nile headwaters in Uganda, left a distinctive mark on Kenya's development.

The BSAC survived as the governing power of Southern and Northern Rhodesia until 1923 and was even able to build railways through these territories linking them to South Africa, to the copper mines of Katanga in Belgian territory and to the Indian Ocean across Mozambique.[29] The BSAC could do this because it had the backing of South African mining capital but it never succeeded in developing Rhodesian mining in a form which could pay off its investments. Instead the BSAC was forced to cut its costs by parcelling out small mining concessions and large agricultural zones to white settlers in Southern Rhodesia and to develop Northern Rhodesia as little more than a supplier of food and labour for the mining regions at either end of its line of rail. Even when Northern Rhodesia became a Crown Colony and the possessor of a formidable copper-mining sector of its own, this legacy proved difficult to overcome.

The strategic imperatives of European penetration of Southern and Central Africa thus ensured that the colonial state would be tied to the interests of European agricultural producers as well as to the trading firms which dominated the expatriate sectors of the West African colonial economy. This tendency was reinforced and complicated by an ecological endowment, as well as the demographic and commercial history of the region, which encouraged European entry into agriculture but also spurred African competition.

While Southern and Central Africa does contain some tropical forest areas along with dry savannas and even deserts, its major productive zones are rather different from the typical agricultural regions of West Africa. They are relatively well-watered areas of grassland and light forest suitable for a combination of cereal agriculture and cattle husbandry, which was the principal basis for the food-production systems of most of the local Bantu-speaking populations.[30]

Not all portions of the region were attractive to European farming; many contained sandy soils and received sparse rainfall so that only limited herds and the West African types of cereal – sorghum and millet – could thrive; commercial farming here was restricted to cotton, peanuts, or – in a few places – tobacco. However the heavier red soils in choice portions of South Africa, the Rhodesias, Kenya and Mozambique were adaptable to new forms of development: commercial maize cultivation above all else but also intensified beef and dairy pastoralism. Furthermore oxen could be used effectively under these conditions to shift from hoe to plough preparation of fields and for the transport of produce to markets.

While these new forms of cultivation were introduced to the region by European settlers (maize was already present but as a minor crop and without the hybrid seeds eventually utilized) there was no reason why they could not be taken up by Africans, as, in fact, they eventually were. However Europeans first assumed that only they could carry out any degree of efficient farming; in effect, that the encounters with the Khoikhoi at the Cape and the Zulu *mfecane* further north would repeat themselves. The reasons for this perception help explain not only why European agriculture established itself so strongly in the first place but also how the eventual competition with Africans was to be pursued.

Much of the insistence on African incompetence in agriculture has nothing to do with economic evaluations but is simply an outgrowth of racial prejudice combined with political competition. Ironically the Afrikaners, who express this bias most strongly, themselves first practised virtually the same extensive mixed farming as the Bantu-speaking peoples whom they encountered on the Cape frontier. Even the later Afrikaner shift to more intensive maize cultivation provided considerable opportunity for autonomous enterprise by African squatters. Nonetheless it was the demands of such white farmers for favoured treatment over Africans which gave the territories they dominated a direction of development very different from the paternalist emphasis on African peasant production in the tropical colonies. Indeed considerable credit for the African agricultural development which did take place must be given to the influence and direct efforts of missionaries, the one paternalistic link between the two forms of colonial economy.

Apart from any feelings they may have had concerning Africans whom they did encounter, the creators of these new territories saw some evidence that indigenous populations simply lacked the density necessary to establish commercial agriculture. Even the leaders of the Afrikaner Great Trek, it should be remembered, were inspired to settle Natal and the central Veld by the depopulation they witnessed in the aftermath of the *mfecane* wars. The lands alongside the Kenya–Uganda rail line appeared empty at the turn of the century because they were shared by Kikuyu cultivators and thinner populations of Masai pastoralists, all of whom had suffered recent losses of stock and human populations because of rinderpest, smallpox and cholera epidemics. Likewise the railway in Zambia seemed to run through a rather underpopulated zone although an ancillary motive for giving farm land here to Europeans (as in some of the early Rhodesian agricultural policies) was to pressure Africans into wage labour on surrounding mines.[31]

Finally, those parts of the South and Central African interior connected to the Indian Ocean by nineteenth-century trade routes produced mainly slaves and ivory, commodities which could not, as did the vegetable oils of West Africa, provide a basis for colonial peasant exports. Moreover much of this commerce was controlled by South Asians who were unable to emulate the major European trading houses of West Africa by lobbying colonial governments for the maintenance of a system serving their interests.

COMPLEMENTARITY AND COMPETITION IN COMMERCIAL FARMING

The conditions under which colonial agriculture developed in these territories therefore guaranteed a far more complicated array of production systems than in West Africa, ranging from classic peasant export crops, through enterprises clearly dominated by Europeans, to a major area of overlap and competition. The more northern parts of the region – northern Mozambique, Nyasaland, Kenya, Tanganyika, and Uganda – produced many of the same export crops as West Africa, particularly coffee, cotton, and peanuts. For the most part these commodities were cultivated on small landholdings with traditional hand-hoeing methods.

European preponderance was unchallenged in those areas of agriculture which enjoyed obvious economies of scale through the applicability of some degree of mechanization, control over massed labour, and close integration of cultivation with processing. It is perhaps surprising that most such situations occurred again in the northern territories which were least under settler or mining control: sisal in Tanganyika; tea in Kenya and Nyasaland; sugar, first in South Africa's Natal Province but later in Uganda (where Asians supplanted Europeans as the main planters).[32]

Ecological factors and the sympathy for settlers among even British Crown Colony governments in this region help to explain the wider scope of European farming compared with West Africa. But it is important to note that, despite easier access to land and labour and the model of mining operations, Southern and East Africa did not become a significant site for major modern plantations: that is, very large-scale, highly mechanized undertakings, operated in the tropics by salaried managers and owned by metropolitan corporations who also produced and distributed the final industrial product. In general, such plantations are more characteristic of Latin America and the Caribbean or South-East Asia than colonial Africa, and their few African manifestations were as likely to be found in tropical, forest regions as in the more temperate situations favouring settler agriculture.

Thus the one case of an African economy totally dominated by a corporate plantation system is Liberia in West Africa which, in 1926, ceded over 400 000 ha of land along with labour recruitment rights to the American Firestone Rubber Company.[33] Liberia, however, was not a colony in any of the senses used here but rather a nominally independent state, ruled by urban-based black American immigrants. The agreement with Firestone was designed to rescue the country from overwhelming international debts. Rather than typifying colonial Africa, therefore, Liberia represents a classic Central American/Caribbean situation, transplanted across the Atlantic.

The one major plantation success in a formally colonial context is western Cameroon, a forest and volcanic highland region within a territory which straddles the boundaries between West and Central Africa.[34] European landholdings, established here around the turn of the century, were large and highly capitalized but the investors were German trading firms and bankers rather than manufacturers. The development pattern did not, therefore, differ radically from smaller settler farms and the plantations shifted their production first from coffee to temporarily successful cocoa, and finally to crops where they enjoyed a lasting advantage: palm products, rubber, and bananas.

Large-scale plantations in African colonies dominated by settler and mining interests enjoyed, at best, a mixed success. Early attempts at mechanized cotton-growing in German Tanganyika and in Nyasaland proved a failure and the massive, government-sponsored Tanganyika Groundnut (peanut) Scheme of the late 1940s represents one of the greatest fiascos of European enterprise in all of colonial Africa.[35] In 1911 the government of the Belgian Congo granted a land concession of almost 800 000 ha to Lever Brothers, a major soap and margarine conglomerate which had previously been refused similar rights, on grounds of social policy, by the peasant-oriented British regimes in the Gold Coast and Nigeria. While Lever's (later Unilever's) Huileries du Congo Belge did survive until independence and is customarily cited alongside Union Minière and Forminière (the Kasai diamond concession) as one of the pillars of the colonial Congo economy, it was not, in fact, a profitable undertaking. Unlike the more modest and diversified Cameroon plantation firms, Huileries du Congo Belge committed itself to a scale of infrastructure, processing and, rather belatedly, cultivating investments which extended well beyond any gains in efficiency, especially from the viewpoint of the parent firm, which could have purchased all the palm oil and palm kernals it needed more cheaply on the open market.[36]

The most important case of successful major metropolitan corporate penetration of agricultural production in the settler regions of colonial Africa is the tea industry of Kenya.[37] Here, during the interwar period, two of the largest British tea concerns, Brooke Bond and James Finlay purchased estates totalling slightly over 4000 ha, which constituted about 80 per cent of the entire area devoted to tea in the territory. However most European agriculture in Kenya was controlled by locally based settlers, often with rather limited finances.

Most European farming throughout Southern and East Africa concentrated on crops which required cultivation methods and levels of capital outlay which were also within the reach of Africans. The overlap did not always generate controversy although in retrospect it appears that Africans generally suffered disadvantages. In Southern Rhodesia, from the 1920s onward, light Virginia-leaf tobacco which requires fairly elaborate processing became the major settler export crop.[38] Shona farmers had earlier been engaged in commercial production of less-delicate Turkish-leaf varieties but, given lack of encouragement by the government in a generally unstable tobacco market, the indigenous industry died out by the 1930s. In Malawi, on the other hand, it was European Virginia-leaf cultivation which stagnated in the late 1920s while African tenant farmers and independent smallholders expanded their production of more-easily cured dark-leaf American tobaccos.[39]

In East Africa coffee-growing is the most notorious case of economically unwarranted discrimination against African producers. Africans dominated the growing of indigenous, lower-priced *robusta* beans in north-western Tanzania and southern Uganda but settlers in the Kenya highlands claimed a monopoly over the higher-priced *arabica* varieties. Actually *arabica*, which requires dryer, more elevated environments than *robusta* but involves few economies of scale, did quite well among African smallholders in suitable areas such as Mount Kilimanjaro, the southern highlands, and the western escarpment of Tanganyika as well as Mount Elgon in Uganda.[40] Restrictions on *arabica*-growing in Kenya were therefore much resented by African farmers.

The greatest competition between Africans and Europeans occurred in the cultivation of maize and the often closely linked breeding of beef and dairy cattle. As already indicated, this kind of rural enterprise was easily adapted to the indigenous African domestic economy although Europeans introduced important new varieties of seed, new animal strains, and new husbandry methods. African farmers were attracted to the commercialized maize-growing and cattle-rearing because they were easy fields to enter, offered little threat to food supplies, and profited from relatively secure urban-mining markets within the region as well as the more volatile overseas demand. Although Europeans insisted that their own farms were always more efficient than those of Africans, data on the most easily measurable result, maize yields per planted acre, suggest no significant differences when comparable capital inputs were available (see Table 7:1). In South Africa, the Rhodesias and Kenya, maize (and to a lesser extent, cattle) became the focus of rural economic competition between Europeans and Africans.

The major weapon employed by Europeans in this context was therefore not their superior access to various forms of producer capital but rather their influence over the state. The former advantage could often lead to disastrous over-investment in large-scale agriculture and, in any case, was eventually offset by the ability of Africans to learn new techniques and their lower labour costs. The state, however, could be used to manipulate the distribution of all factors of production. Land, in the settler-dominated territories, was thus divided into European zones, enjoying the best farming conditions, and African 'reserves' of inevitably inferior quality and often inadequate extent. Labour was channelled to European farms by both restricting African access to autonomous commercial agriculture and levying taxes requiring a cash income. Public capital investments in the form of transportation, irrigation, agricultural extension, market regulations, or price subsidies regularly favoured European over African farmers. The degree and form of this state intervention varied with the differing levels of commitment to local political goals in each regime, with South Africa, as might be expected, representing the extreme of suppression.

Table 7.1   *African and European maize yields*

	Yield (tons per acre)			
	African	European	Date	Technology
1. Kenya				
	0.3		1931	hand hoe(hh)
	1.2		1941	hh[1]
	0.9		1952	hh/ox-plough(op)[2]
	0.77		1942–61	(total Highlands)
	1.25		1942–61	(choice areas) tractor(tr), fertilizer(fe)[3]
	1.75		1972	tr, fe, hybrid seed(hy)[4]
2. N. Rhodesia (Zambia)				
	0.98		1951	op, fe
	0.88		1951	op, fe (less of both)
	0.44		1951	op
		1.07	1951	tr, fe
		2.23	1951	tr, fe, hy[5]
	0.61		1971	op, fe
	1.42		1971	op, fe, hy
	1.72		1971	tr, fe, hy[6]
3. S. Rhodesia (Zimbabwe)				
	0.93		1965–6	op, some fe
	0.39		1965–6	some op
	0.57		1965–6	op, some fe
	0.27		1965–6	op[7]
		0.54	1915–40	op, fe
		1.11	1955–65	tr, fe, hy[8]
	3.33		1968–9	op, fe, irrigation scheme(ir)
	1.21		1968–9	hh/op, fe, ir[9]
4. South Africa				
	0.37		1960	(Lesotho) op[10]
	0.39		1959–60	(Swaziland) op[11]
	0.25		1959–60	(tenants) op
		0.38	1959–60	tr, fe[12]

[1]Kitching (1980) pp. 149–50.   [2]Fearn (1961) p. 198.   [3]Odingo (1971) p. 84.
[4]Ströbel (1973) pp. 59–63.   [5]Hellen (1968) p. 130.   [6]Schultz (1976) p. 117.
[7]Weinrich (1975) pp. 309 *et passim*. This table does not do justice to the complex variables of education, labour relations, and motivation incorporated into Weinrich's analysis of these farmers.
[8]Palmer (1977) p. 92; M. Yudelman (1964) p. 88.   [9]Weinrich (1975).
[10]Lipton (1977) pp. 73–4. The Lesotho, Swaziland and tenant figures are used because Lipton insists that the few calculations available for black farmers in the then 'reserves' (now 'homelands') are unreliable.
[11]Daniel (1964) p. 215.   [12]South Africa (1963).

The South African state most directly served the interests of ambitious white farmers who represented, in the late nineteenth and early twentieth century, a middle group between urban capitalism and the impoverished majority of the European rural population.[41] At the time when a growing mining sector and post-South African War reconstruction efforts vastly expanded the local market for agricultural goods, whites had already appropriated most of the valuable farmland in South Africa but were in no position to exploit it themselves. The richer landlords were often absentee urban entrepreneurs who welcomed African tenants both as efficient farmers and as a pool of recruits for industrial labour needs. The Afrikaner farmers who remained on their own holdings made informal arrangements with African 'squatters' since there was neither the cash nor the institutional basis among the descendants of *trekboers* to maintain a supervised demesne wage-labour system. This era was the heyday of black South African 'peasant' enterprise (see below pp. 178–9): that is farming (and also transport ventures) undertaken by men with their own family labour, oxen, and ploughs on land either allocated as 'native reserves', purchased in white areas, or occupied there in return for rent and occasional work services.

The decline of autonomous African farming in South Africa can be partly attributed to economic factors: population and livestock increases weakened the mobility of black tenants and thus their bargaining power in relation to white landowners; rail and motor transport eliminated the need for African oxen transport; finally, the general prosperity of the country released capital for investment in mechanized and wage-labour production on the larger European farms. Yet all these processes moved at a very uneven pace and semi-autonomous African squatters continued to produce a significant proportion of marketed produce, particularly maize, until the 1940s. Historically, it was not the logic of economic change but rather the action of the state which destroyed the black peasantry.

The specific measures directly attacking the autonomy of blacks in the South African countryside were a series of anti-squatting measures, centring around the 1913 Native Land Act and the 1936 Native Lands and Trust Act, followed by the influx and pass laws which constituted the formal core of post-1948 apartheid policies. The Europeans responsible for this legislation included both mining companies, now anxious to concentrate their labour supply in reserves, and Afrikaner capitalist farmers, who wanted to establish themselves on a more modern basis. At another level, the laws were inspired by general fears of independent African cultivators competing or coalescing with the poorer rural whites (often themselves tenants) and thus threatening the racial hierarchy at the base of South African society.

By the 1950s the black work force in South African agriculture had effectively been reduced to a low-wage proletariat thoroughly under the control of whites. The economic impact of this change is as ambiguous as its sponsorship. In strictly market terms, it is probable that medium-sized black farmers could have achieved the same levels of output as the triumphant large-scale white estates, and done so at a lower cost.[42] From a structural perspective, however, the system which was established offered two advantages to South African development; it assured a supply of cheap black labour and encouraged a capital-intensive form of agriculture with backward linkages to heavy industry.

The first benefit may not have been very important in the long run, given black population growth within South Africa and the ready availability of migrant labour from surrounding countries. However, the relationship to manufacturing is significant, as will be seen in the final sections of this chapter. In any case, these agricultural policies proved very costly to rural blacks, now restricted to residence in reserves which did not provide the means for full subsistence, to say nothing of profitable commercial farming.

In colonial Southern Rhodesia the state served the needs of white farmers in a much more straightforward but less devastating manner.[43] When Rhodes's BSAC failed to develop the territory as a mining domain, it recouped its investments by selling off not only mineral concessions but also land concessions (legally claimed by right of conquest following the Ndebele and Shona uprisings) to individual white immigrants. Once these settlers had achieved direct control over internal government, they were able to expand the areas under their ownership continuously, and push Africans into ever narrower and less productive reserves. The 1930 Land Apportionment Act provided the critical legal basis for this policy and included, as in the previously discussed South African laws, measures to remove African tenants from newly designated white areas.

The Southern Rhodesian settlers were never able, however, to introduce comprehensive Europeanization of farming on South African lines, mainly because the European population was not large or affluent enough to take over all commercial agriculture. Segregation policies always incorporated some efforts to develop more effective market agriculture in the African sectors and at times (particularly in the 1950s) there was a somewhat complementary division of enterprise, with Europeans concentrating on tobacco and Africans on maize. In fact the European stifling of African competition reached its peak only in the 1960s and 1970s as part of the reaction against external liberal pressures, expressed in the Unilateral Declaration of Independence by local whites. But these measures also culminated in the undermining of the regime by rural-based African guerrilla warfare. Southern Rhodesia thus illustrates the limited efficacy of even a settler-ruled colonial state in imposing direct exploitation upon the African countryside.

In Kenya and Northern Rhodesia settler populations held less political power, because of their smaller numbers and the status of both territories as British Crown Colonies. Nevertheless white farmers here succeeded in exercising considerable influence over agricultural policy through formal representation on legislative councils, advisory bodies, and marketing boards as well as the less official channels of contact with compatriots in bureaucratic positions. Moreover the distribution of land suitable for intensive cultivation is uneven in both countries so that white control over the most fertile and best-connected areas seriously inhibited African commercial farming.

The most effective check on settler interests in Kenya and Northern Rhodesia came from other European interests which were able to pressure the regime. In Northern Rhodesia from the 1920s copper mining began to overshadow agriculture entirely.[44] For a long time this situation worked in favour of European farmers even though it became increasingly obvious that whites could not fully meet urban food needs and that migrant mine labour was no longer in short supply from the African countryside. Beginning in the 1930s, but especially after the Second World War, the government began supporting more efficient African market cultivation. The agriculture problem, inherited by the post-colonial Zambian regime, shifted from competition between Europeans and Africans to balancing the attraction of the mining enclave and its immediate hinterland along the railway line with the larger rural sectors of the country.

The colonial state in Kenya found itself almost completely dependent on agriculture as a revenue base and thus forced to arbitrate between the demands of settlers and the necessity for indigenous cash cultivation.[45] Without links to the

Southern African mining system, the Kenyan authorities also remained more sensitive to the pressures of paternalist ideology, favouring peasant farming. This position was articulated most strongly in East Africa and the metropole by missionaries, but was also taken up by some district administrators and local European merchants. A further complication was the frustration of well-established South Asian merchants, who wished to buy farms in the Kenyan 'White Highlands'. In order to maintain segregation while neutralizing protests from nationalists within British India – who had the ear of imperial policy-makers – the Colonial Office announced in 1923 that its true goal in Kenya was 'African paramountcy' as opposed to the interests of any 'immigrant races'.

In the period between the two world wars the Kenyan dilemma was met by maintaining a 'dual policy'. European settlers still received protection but autonomous African agriculture was also promoted and even extended, during the financial strains of the 1930s, to the previously exclusively white realm of *arabica* coffee cultivation. The 1940s and early 1950s, however, produced a new crisis when settler numbers increased at the same time as a growing African population put new pressures on land. African squatters, who had previously fared reasonably well on European estates, were now expelled and joined other landless groups to provide the base for the Mau Mau uprising.[46] Unlike Rhodesia two decades later, the colonial government was able to suppress violent resistance in the Kenyan countryside. But Britain also saw this event as a signal to place the territory in the mainstream of tropical African territories which would be turned over to rule by representatives of their African majorities. Kenya is thus the best example of a settler-dominated colonial system whose most lasting impact can be seen in the degree of capitalist relations developed within the African sectors.

CLASS DIFFERENTIATION AMONG AFRICAN CULTIVATORS

In contrast to peasant-dominated African economies, indigenous rural populations experienced the effects of incorporation into the Southern African and Kenyan economies in a very uneven fashion. Within the same territories and even the same districts the size of landholdings and, more important, the modes of cultivation, differed sharply. At one extreme it is possible to identify here a genuine rural bourgeoisie and at the other a class so dependent on wage labour that even if its members owned small amounts of land they could justifiably be labelled a proletariat. The two major factors creating this situation were, first, relative scarcity of land because of European appropriations and variable natural endowments and, second, the possibility of realizing economies of scale on enlarged landholdings through plough cultivation.

Rich and poor populations existed in all the rural areas of this region but the distinctions in wealth were not always based directly on agriculture. In what may be called the impoverished reserve model of Southern African rural society there were no possibilities of efficient African production. In the more generously apportioned African farm areas the dependency of the majority population was an immediate condition for the prosperity of a significant minority.

The improverished reserve model was characteristic of all of South Africa, much of Southern Rhodesia, and portions of Northern Rhodesia by the 1940s.[47] In some cases the areas set off for African ownership were reasonably fertile (as in the South African Ciskei and Transkei) but after a period of prosperity and then precarious stability, became rapidly overcrowded. Others (like Belingwe in Rhodesia) had limited fertility and thus moved from low-level self sufficiency to more gradual overcrowding. The ultimate effect has been increasing dependence on outmigration for cash incomes, which in turn deprives local farms of male labour, particularly needed for plough cultivation. The income saved from generally low wages has been invested in cattle which represent, at the individual level, the most secure available store of wealth and the means for negotiating marriage payments. Collectively, however, under conditions of increasing land shortage such herds tended to overgraze the southern African reserves, thus producing soil erosion and animals too undernourished to provide commercially viable beef or dairy products.

Although economic inequalities existed within the restricted reserves, they were not based on agricultural success. The South African and Rhodesian governments prohibited spontaneous land consolidation in these areas, insisting instead that the distribution of farming plots be controlled by traditional chiefs with the goal of retaining existing communal structures. As a result it is chiefs themselves or others in positions of authority or wage employment directly linked to the white (or more recently in South Africa, Bantustan) governments, who have formed the local elite. The reserve agricultural system thus combines the worst economic features both of settler regimes (inadequate resources for peasant cultivation) and bureaucratic tropical colonies (limited entrepreneurship among the rural elite).

But there have been times and places in the history of Southern and Central Africa where settler penetration of the countryside produced a new class of African rural entrepreneurs who have been labelled by analysts from various perspectives as 'progressive', 'modernizing', or 'capitalist' farmers. The critical characteristics of these cultivators has been their combination of new technology with new property and social relations. They invested in new equipment and land improvements; they sought individual title to enlarged landholdings; and they employed as permanent wage labourers other men who could not be considered as either kin, communal work parties, or eventual holders of their own commercial farms.

Plough cultivation was a necessary but not sufficient condition for such a change. In portions of Tanganyika and Zambia ploughing was adopted in commercial farming without changes in landholding patterns or social organization of production. In all the areas which have large African estates alongside communal or tenant peasant farms, the latter have been able to produce plough-cultivated crops at comparable (sometimes even higher) levels of efficiency.[48] The explanation of why a new type of farmer arose in this region and how such a class would affect the rest of the African economy depends as much upon structural factors as upon market calculations.

The circumstances necessary for the emergence of African rural capitalism included the disruption of African communal organization (usually by a combination of endogenous forces and settler incursions), availability of land, some protective force within the European establishment, and opportunities for generating capital in off-farm employment. The classical, although ultimately abortive, instance of such development is South Africa from the middle to the end of the nineteenth century.[49]

During this period the Bantu-speaking peoples of the eastern Cape, Natal and the central High Veld were faced with two crises, the internally generated Zulu *mfecane* and the accelerated expansion of the white settler frontier. Of the many Africans thus displaced from their homes and social moorings, most became politically dependent upon Europeans and struggled to rebuild the kind of rural society they had known before. However others seized the opportunity of movement into new areas and a breakdown of traditional sanctions to imitate European patterns of farming, in particular the incorporation of male labour and cattle into agriculture through the use of the plough.[50] The most extensive exemplars of this change were the Mfengu ('Fingos'), an ethnic entity formed in the Cape and Transkei out of several thousand Nguni refugees from Natal and noted, in their new homeland, for their close attachment to missionary patrons. In Natal itself smaller and more fragmented groups of displaced peoples settled around the very numerous rural mission stations to form a distinct social group known as 'Kholwa' ('believers', that is African Christians). Under mission protection the Mfengu and Kholwa took up the goals of establishing capitalist agriculture. The transition was not simple, however, requiring extensive periods of wage employment to accumulate capital and also a secondary specialization in ox-drawn 'transport riding' a lucrative undertaking at this point in South Africa's development because of the widely dispersed centres of commerce, agricultural, and mining enterprise and the absence of inland waterways, railways, or motor transport. This rural bourgeoisie proved far more vulnerable than the tenant peasantry to the onslaught of the white South African state and the overcrowding of reserves but its potential role in the national economy can be compared with the one actually played by white capitalist farmers in the industrialization process discussed below.

In Southern Rhodesia, African capitalist farmers emerged less dramatically and as far as the limited available research reveals) more narrowly at the margins of the segregrated land system.[51] While, by the end of the 1930s, European settlers had successfully removed a small but substantial number of African freeholders from the areas designated for white habitation, a simultaneous programme was established by a combination of government and missionary forces for encouraging 'progressive' farming within the reserves. The two pillars of this effort were the teaching of new farming methods through agricultural extension services and the re-establishment of qualified indigenous freeholders in 'Native Purchase Areas' (NPAs) at the boundaries of the reserves. Most researchers have stressed the limited effectiveness of the programmes because of the meagre resources given to the agencies responsible for carrying them out, the difficulty of any development within the reserves due to overcrowding as well as political decisions to maintain control over land by chiefs, and the poor quality of many of the NPAs. Nonetheless, Weinrich has provided us with a profile of a significant minority of 'master farmers' (formally trained modern cultivators in both the reserves and NPAs) which matches the pattern of European and African rural capitalism elsewhere in the region. Moreover the growing number of requests for NPA plots through the 1960s and evidence of rural African aspirations even during and immediately after the guerrilla war against the white Rhodesian regime suggests that capitalist farmers may be a major force in the future Zimbabwean economy.[52]

Kenya provides the best-documented case of an African bourgeoisie rising from agriculture and also an opportunity (see Chapter 9) to examine some of the consequences of its presence in the post-colonial situation.[53] The disruption of rural African society by European settlers was far less horrendous here than in South Africa or Southern Rhodesia because the land appropriated for what became the White Highlands' was immediately inhabited mainly by pastoral populations, particularly the Masai. However by this action the settlers broke into the patterns of expansion and land-sharing of the main agricultural group in Kenya, the Kikuyu, who were thus forced to come to terms with European conceptions of rural property rights. Moreover the labour demands of European enterprise affected all sections of the Central (Kikuyu) and Western (Nyanza) Provinces of Kenya, the main population centres of an otherwise rather sparsely inhabited and inhospitable country. At the same time government and missionary policy, as described above, ensured that Africans would retain some resources for autonomous development in rural areas.

Differentiation of Kenyan African success in this linkage to the European economy involved a complex mixture of agricultural and off-farm undertakings. The earliest and most obvious variance derived from employment within the European sectors. Africans with the requisite ambition, ability and education (and mission patronage was again important here) could gain good salaries from European private employers as well as positions of influence within local administrative bodies (for the Kikuyu especially, traditional chiefdom was not used as an instrument to inhibit enterprising individuals). For the less fortunate majority of rural dwellers, migratory labour on much less favourable terms became a necessity, first under coercion from recruitment agents and taxation, later as a function of population pressure upon limited land resources.

Throughout the Central Province and in some portions of Nyanza, inequalities of access to European opportunities were translated into differential divisions of landholding. The more successful used their accumulated capital and influence to acquire land along with the ploughs and other equipment needed for cultivation on an enlarged scale. Many poorer farmers, or those who did not recognize quickly enough the shift in value between cattle herds and cultivatable land, found themselves without plots large enough even to maintain self-sufficiency in food and thus became ever more dependent upon low-level wage employment including labour on the farms of their more fortunate neighbours. For the Kenya African elite farming never became an exclusive enterprise; it was always combined with continuing wage employment (especially when wives could be left at home to supervise rural enterprises) and investments in such related activities as transport, rural trade, and the processing of agriculture goods. But farms were always among the major assets sought and developed by this group. They were particularly well-positioned to take advantage of the dismantling of the settler regime from the mid-1950s, a process which was accelerated by the Mau Mau revolt of those impoverished peasant workers whom the rural African elite, along with the Europeans, had previously exploited.[54]

Because of its obvious exploitative characteristics, the emergence of a rural African capitalist class has been deplored by most of the scholars responsible for revealing its historical existence. As indicated earlier in this discussion, the activities of such groups throughout Southern and Central Africa cannot be justified on the basis of greater productivity; the rationale for acquiring large landholdings is not to farm each more efficiently but rather to acquire a higher level of individual income and thus emulate the consumption rather than the production model proffered by Europeans. For the adoption of more intensive methods by smallholders some such model was obviously necessary although it can be argued, from Tanzanian and Zambian examples, that a few Europeans may accomplish this with much less disruption of the African social order than was the case in South Africa, Southern Rhodesia, or Kenya. But as the comparison of Kenyan capitalism and Tanzanian socialism in Chapter 9 will indicate, an indigenous entrepreneurial elite may be preferable to an unchallenged state-party apparatus in moving from commercial agriculture to higher levels of industria development. The rest of this chapter will examine such movement (to the degree that it occurred) within the colonial-settler regimes of this region and its relationship to the multiple class interests of the European community.

From primary production to industrialization

The topic of industrialization was given little attention in Chapter 6 in which étatist-bureaucratic colonial economies were discussed because its occurrence under such regimes was, until the eve of their disintegration, extremely limited. Only in African territories whose primary production was at last in part under direct European control – specifically Belgian Congo, Kenya, Southern Rhodesia, and South Africa – did colonialism produce any significant levels of industrial development. The explanation for this distinction lies partly in technological and market factors: immediate linkages between more intensive primary production and secondary industry as well as investment capital generated by the greater revenue of European-run export enterprises. However the translation of these conditions into a sustained industrialization process depended upon social and political relations between the groups controlling various sectors of the economy, as will be seen in the variations of outcome among the territories being discussed here.

INTERNATIONAL VS. NATIONAL ECONOMIC ACTORS
The analysis of the factors involved in industrialization may be clarified – although with some danger of over-schematization – by drawing a distinction between international and national orientations among the most influential groups within the economy.[55] The international actors are, broadly, those whose interests are focused on export production and import trade at the lowest possible local cost; the national actors are those who are willing to tax exports and imports for the sake of more advanced and autonomous local development. The major over-simplifications here are to assume that economic interests can always be classified within one of these two categories and that they are necessarily opposed to one another on critical issues of industrialization. The discussion which follows will use the international–national dichotomy as a base, but attempt to suggest some of the contradictory nuances in specific historical situations.

The international actors in territories of direct exploitation include those elements shared with étatist-peasant regimes – African peasant producers, the metropolitan-based bureaucracy, and large export-import merchants – as well as one of the major forces unique to this system – mines and corporate-run plantations. The national actors are almost all unique and therefore critical; middle-range merchants, settler-farmers and politically enfranchised labour aristocracies.

The international orientation of elements common to the two forms of colonial regime has been explained to some extent in Chapter 6. Peasants had a limited ability to influence policy in areas with a major settler and/or mining presence, but their simple existence as a real or potential alternative to capitalist agriculture strengthened the hand of groups seeking to maintain a minimal-cost export economy. Colonial governments, especially British but also Belgian, never pursued a vigorous industrialization policy in this region. Such a goal conflicted with their alleged primary mission of providing their respective metropoles with markets for manufactured goods and cheap raw material supplies. Even the immediate needs of bureaucratic regimes for maintaining a secure local revenue base were not served by the economic risks (including a loss of valuable import tariffs) and potential social and political disruption of industrialism. Major merchants were also committed to a flow of goods through international channels, where their own greatest competitive advantages lay, and were hesitant to shift their investments from export-import inventories to the risky fixed-capital demands of manufacturing.

Properly run mines and plantations appeared to many colonial economists to be the model form of European enterprise in Africa precisely because they introduced modern modes of production rather than feeding off the marginal output of traditional rural structures.[56] They were also able to finance their own infrastructural needs, thus relieving the state of the costs of major transport investments and presumably ensuring that these would be oriented toward economic rather than strategic goals. Most of the mines and plantations suffered in their early stages from problems of labour recruitment, leading to some of the difficulties already described for gold and copper production and extending to serious abuses in the plantations of West Cameroon and even the Congo concessions of the self-consciously progressive Unilever.[57] However, once labour was stabilized on these various enterprises, the relatively high wages and social benefits accruing to African employees was considered one of their major selling points. Finally, the profits from these undertakings were available for investment in other activities both directly, through the needs of mines and plantations for supplies and inputs into production, and indirectly, as a tax base for the government.

All these positive features of mines and plantations indicate a potential for contributing to the growth of surrounding territories; but, without the pressure of effectively competitive national sectors, such capital-intensive forms of primary production had a tendency to develop as enclaves which contributed little to broader development. Like railways in peasant-centred economies, mines and plantations operated with equipment which could only be supplied by metropolitan industries so that their backward linkages were largely external, as were the forward linkages of the raw materials produced. The railways built for mines in Southern and Central Africa ran along routes which took little account of local market needs, often leaving the indigenous population (e.g. in Mozambique and, until its copperbelt was developed, Northern Rhodesia) as impoverished as they would have been without such transport assets.

The stabilized labour forces actually employed in the most benevolent of these enterprises represented only a tiny proportion of the working population of their respective territories. Indeed, the counterpart to increased employer investment in machinery and individual personnel costs was a reduction in labour force size.[58] Resulting consumer demands upon agriculture and manufacturing did not provide a major stimulus to wider development. Finally, mining (but not plantation) interests had some incentives to invest in other industrialized activities which provided inputs for metal extraction and processing, but such coal mines, or sulphur and arsenic plants, operated in a relatively closed circuit of primary-goods production. It was not in the interests of mine or plantation owners to invest in forms of local manufacturing directed towards wider markets, since African industries were not likely to add significantly to the demand for primary goods nor could the profits available from African factories compete with opportunities elsewhere in the world market. Instead the prospect of nearby secondary industry presented major disadvantages to export producers: rising wage bills because of competition on the relevant labour market; rising taxes and external costs because of subsidies and protective market regulation which governments would have to provide for the new undertakings.

Among the economic actors classified here as national, smaller-scale merchants might be expected to invest in the local manufacture of inexpensive, high-bulk, consumer goods, as also noted in Chapter 6. Such easy import-substitution was feasible at particularly early stages in settler colonies. Settler-farmers also looked favourably on local manufacturing as an outlet for their production which might be more secure than the fluctuating external market. Here a national perspective clashed very directly with the policies of metropolitan-oriented colonial governments, which tended to react to declines in export prices by cutting local risks still further and increasing the quantity of goods shipped outward.

Finally, European wage labourers generally favoured any expansion of job opportunities. Again, moments of crisis such as the Great Depression of the 1930s accentuated this need whereas an international firm such as Union Minière in the Belgian Congo would attempt, during the same period, to reduce its stabilized African labour force by sending workers back to their villages.

The case studies which follow will display a number of variations on the scheme of sectoral economic relations. However the key points to be kept in mind are that sustained industrialization depended upon the existence of effectively articulated local economic interests and that a relative advance by one territory in the development of non-durable, import-substitution industries could provide an important impetus towards domination of surrounding, less 'nationalist' colonial and post-colonial economies.

CASE STUDIES OF COLONIAL INDUSTRIALIZATION

The Belgian Congo represents an apparent exception to the formula stated above since it experienced an exceptional level of industrialization carried out entirely by the international sector of the economy.[59] The critical element here was the colonial government, which represented a metropolitan economy too small and too advanced to benefit from any control over the primary exports and consumer imports of its African dependency. Belgium did, however, specialize in the export of manufacturing equipment which, by the early 1920s was used to set up a whole range of import-substitution industries in the Congo. The mining and plantation enclaves which dominated Congo exports played a supportive role here in three ways: by supplying the state with tax revenues independent of imports; by undercutting the position of large merchant firms; and by creating concentrated markets for local light industries in their relatively well-paid stabilized labour forces. The weakness in this system was its limited linkage to the smaller agriculturalists of the countryside; instead of participating in the market economy as either peasant or settler-capitalist entrepreneurs, the producers in this sector were forced to deliver food supplies and a small percentage of exports at officially fixed low prices.[60]

The consumer industries of the Congo were thus, like the heavier mine-related chemical and metallurgical undertakings, merely adjuncts to export enclaves, not even effectively integrated with one another, let alone the majority rural sector of the economy. While these economic factors are not sufficient to explain the chaotic state of the Congo/Zaire after independence, they do indicate why its quantitative growth under colonial rule did not provide the basis for a dynamic national development and regional role.

Kenya was part of a British colonial system which did little to encourage industrial growth in its African colonies and even actively discouraged several manufacturing enterprises in neighbouring peasant-dominated territories.[61] Merchant enterprise in this part of Africa remained highly competitive between European and South Asian firms, many of whom did, therefore, seek to improve their position by industrial investments, at least in export-processing. It was the white settler-farmers, however, who demanded import-substitution industries as early as the 1920s and succeeded, through their formal and informal influence on the local government, in obtaining tariffs to protect such development. The world economic crisis of the 1930s spurred renewed efforts by settlers to establish local manufacturing, this time supported also by the threat to the entire colonial order of unemployed, landless Africans. The successful establishment of even relatively light industries in Kenya required investments by metropolitan manufacturers, so that to call such enterprises 'national' is obviously misleading. Nonetheless, many firms did have participation by locally-based settlers and merchants (both European and Asian). Even when, after independence, Europeans would be replaced by Africans, the position of Kenya as a growth pole for East Africa remained firmly established and presents, as will be seen in Chapter 9, a major case for the evaluation of capitalistic paths to African development.

Southern Rhodesia was never, from its beginnings as a dependency, under direct metropolitan control.[62] Even the BSAC, which ruled the territory until 1923, did not exercise any constraint upon local enterprise and, with the subsequent attainment of local self-government, the settlers were free to take whatever measures appeared necessary for their own economic interests. The major role of mining in the export system did not inhibit the growth of manufacturing, since the mines were relatively uninfluential in politics and also provided a concentrated, if poorly paid and only partially stabilized, African consumer market for manufactured goods.

Despite rail links to South Africa, merchants and manufacturers from that already-industrialized state quickly found it advantageous to set up import-substitution enterprises in Southern Rhodesia without any of the protectionist barriers established in Kenya. The Southern Rhodesian government only began to take an active interest in industrialization from the 1930s, to a large extent under the pressure of not only farmers and already-established manufacturers, but also of highly vocal white workers. Protectionism, as opposed to subsidies and direct state investment in heavier enterprises did not play a significant role until the late 1950s when Southern Rhodesia entered the ill-fated Central African Federation with Northern Rhodesia and Nyasaland. With the collapse of this joint endeavour and the failure of African purchasing power within Southern Rhodesia to expand significantly, economic growth faltered.[63] But the advantages of an industrial base were again demonstrated by the vigorous response of the local economy to the trade boycott placed on Rhodesia as a result of the 1965 Unilateral Declaration of Independence from Britain. With the advent of internationally recognized independence under a black regime in 1980, these economic assets have served as an incentive to moderation in carrying out major social transformations.

The failure of the good guys to win at least the short-term race to African industrial development is most vividly illustrated by the spectacular growth of South Africa under a system of harsh, racist apartheid.[64] The Cape Colony had received self-government as early as 1872 and, given the small scale of local merchant enterprise and the predominance of white settler-farmers in the electorate, light protection was used almost immediately to foster a wide range of import-substitution industries. These enterprises grew considerably during the crises of the South African War and the First World War although no significant further help was given by the governments of either the individual colonies or the Union regime formed in 1910.

Local manufacturers had been lobbying for additional aid from the beginning of the twentieth century, but their efforts were opposed by the large Cape merchants and the mine interests of the Transvaal, who represented the major economic forces of the time. The relationship of these groups to the majority farmers among voters was complicated by the fact that the bulk of the latter were Afrikaners who regarded all urban sectors as dangerously alien. However, on a more practical level the Afrikaner leadership had learned to profit from political control of the mining sectors. Before the South African War the Transvaal government had encouraged one major South African industry by granting Alfred Nobel a local monopoly of dynamite manufacture and forbidding the gold mines to import any explosives. After the restoration of Afrikaner power, the early Union government of Botha and Smuts avoided large-scale protectionism but taxed the mines to provide subsidies for the support of increasingly consolidated capitalist farming among rural Afrikaner notables.

The shift to heavy industrial capitalism came about mainly after 1922, when Smuts's support of the mine-owners' efforts to lower costs by increasing the employment of black labour created major opposition to him in the white working class. By this time a large part of this class was Afrikaner, since demography, war damage, and the development of rural capitalism had pushed much of the white population off the land and into the cities. In 1924 the Smuts government was defeated by a coalition of Afrikaner nationalists – based on poorer agriculturalists – and the urban South African Labour Party. It was this new 'Pact' government which finally made industrial growth a central goal, designed both to create jobs for European workers outside the mines and to strengthen the national economy against what were perceived to be generally suspect international forces. The means to this end were increased measures of protectionism for both agriculture and industry and direct state capitalism in the form of a major parastatal iron and steel complex, ISCOR.

Nationalism and racism thus played a critical role in moving South Africa along the road to full industrialization. Not only did the direct intervention of Afrikaner governments provide immediate support for local manufacturing, but the privileged position of several million white workers and farmers assured the new enterprises of a sufficiently large and affluent market to sustain not only the production of the usual import substitutes, but also of consumer durables and farm machinery with a high linkage to such heavy basic industries as iron and steel and chemicals complexes.

At the same time the coercively enforced low pay scales of African workers (black mine wages did not rise in real terms between 1900 and 1965) ensured that consumerism would not lead – as it did in comparable populist new industrial economies of Latin America and Israel – to uncontrollable inflation. Even the constant fear of losing control over black workers has been a spur to labour-saving investments such as massive electrification, which provided the basis for still further industrialization.[65]

It must be recognized, however, that outside the parastatal sectors, the key base for South African industry has remained the gold mines. Whatever the cost they may have incurred from interference with their labour markets and from protectionism, the Witwatersrand mines continued to prosper through the 1920s and especially the 1930s world depression (the real period of South African industrial takeoff). During the 1940s a new set of very productive goldfields was opened in the Orange Free State. In a less nationalist environment mining firms might have earned somewhat higher profits and exported more of their capital out of South Africa. But circumstances being what they were, South Africa offered attractive manufacturing investment opportunities, even for international economic sectors. Large European firms, especially in engineering and chemicals, vied competitively for service and equipment contracts in South Africa. Mining capitalists in the country not only contributed to facilities needed for their own primary operations but also benefited from insider knowledge of other local undertakings and even began to develop (especially when joined by a new class of large-scale Afrikaner entrepreneurs) a degree of national sentiment.[66]

The strength of the South African economy has thus been its ability to domesticate mining wealth and build a strong local industrial base. Its major weaknesses are a continuing dependence on mineral exports (see Appendix, Figure A5) and capital imports and, most seriously, the tensions engendered by the repressive and exclusionary character of the apartheid system.

Conclusion: South Africa as an African model

Alone on the African continent, South Africa appears to have overcome the limitations of internal growth and external dependency which burden other local economies. It has achieved a level of industrialization comparable to the most advanced economies in Europe, Asia, and America. Its role in the world economy as a source of minerals, an attraction to international investment, and even a source of such investment can hardly be described as marginal (see Appendix, Table A4).

The obvious cost of this economic achievement has been the political and social repression of the non-white majority within the South African population (75 per cent and more of the whole) which lives at a far lower level of welfare than the white minority. It is universally recognized that such a system cannot be sustained in perpetuity, but analysts differ in predicting the direction of change. One argument perceives South Africa as potentially recapitulating the history of Western industrial economies, whose working classes were also forced for a time to endure the stage of 'polarized accumulation' so that savings and investments could be concentrated in areas where they would produce maximum growth. At various moments (during the Second World War and in some of the reform efforts of the early 1980s) Afrikaner politicians who identified with capitalist interests have made gestures in the direction of incorporating at least a part of the black work force into the centre of the economy. It is argued that only such liberalization can generate the consumer demand needed for increased production and reduce the heavy costs of repression.[67]

However, the critical aspects of South Africa's situation make such an analogy with the core Atlantic economies implausible. First, it is difficult to separate the ideology of racial competition from the class interests in South Africa. The less affluent sectors of white society – wage labourers and small-to-medium-sized farmers – feel threatened by concessions even to a minority black middle class. At the same time the impact of capital intensification in South African industry has been to render a large part of the black population economically redundant. Even under a democratic political regime, there is no place for this underclass in the core industrial sectors. The presently designated alternative, absorption in self-governing black homelands, is also unrealistic given the land and capital resources available in these areas. The industrial economy of South Africa may thus have been built upon foundations of apartheid (as opposed to the liberal view of a constant contradiction between racism and economic logic) but it must ultimately succumb to its failure to incorporate the very group it has exploited (as opposed to the Marxist view of racism as simply the local form of capitalist class exploitation).[68] In short, the economy of South Africa is neither European nor African, thus neither drawing upon nor providing a model for development anywhere else.

The moment when South Africa suggested what may be a more constructive solution to future development in other colonies of competitive exploitation was in the late nineteenth and early twentieth centuries, when an African capitalist class emerged in the countryside. Within South Africa, this class was overwhelmed by the resources and internal competition of European mining capital and politically powerful agricultural communities. But in other, less extreme colonial regimes of the same type (notably Kenya and Zimbabwe) comparable black social formations offer a more modest but possibly more enduring basis for transcending the dilemmas of modern economic transformation.

Notes

1. Elphick (1977) pp. 1–68; Ross (1978). On the Bushmen/San, see Chapter 1 above.
2. Harinck (1969); Sansom (1974). For Bantu penetration of South Africa, see Chapter 1 above.
3. Guy (1980). For arguments (based on very limited evidence) that external trade did play a major role in the *mfecane* see Smith (1969) and Hedges (1978).
4. Ballard (1980); it should be noted that the author of this article would probably not agree with the conclusions which have been drawn here from his data.
5. Axelson (1973) pp. 34–5. On the entire development of the Cape Colony up to the early nineteenth century see Elphick and Giliomee (1979); Katzen (1969); Wilson (1969); Davenport (1969).
6. Neumark (1957) pp. 165–8 (on Cape sheep farming). There is no good economic history of Natal in this period but De Kiewiet (1957) pp. 68–9 measures the relative paucity of sugar output by the inability of Natal to finance railway construction.
7. Elphick (1977) p. 69f.
8. Guelke (1966, 1979); Neumark (1957). On the tragic fate of the Coloured farmers on the Cape frontier see Ross (1976).
9. Giliomee (1979); Keller (1978).
10. I know of no thorough economic analysis of the trekker republics, but for a general account see Thompson (1969a, 1969b) pp. 364–73, 405–66; for land-labour relations, Trapido (1978).
11. Katzen (1969); Schutte (1979).
12. Davenport (1969); Trapido (1980).
13. Katzenellenbogen (1975) pp. 362–80 for a general overview; Flint (1974) p. 42f; Hocking (1973) and Innes (1984) for the critical De Beers/Oppenheimer/Anglo American enterprises; for more intensive comparative studies, see the sections on imperialist expansion, mining labour and industrialization below.
14. The classic 'miners'/financiers' conspiracy' view is Hobson (1900); for recent liberal refutations: Jeeves (1973); Kubicek (1979); Mawby (1974); for radical counter-attacks,

188   *The Colonial Economies: II*

Blainey (1965), Denoon (1968), Mendelsohn (1980); for the difficulty of determining (or denying) the existence of key mining-interest beneficiaries of British imperialism, Jeeves (1975); Richardson and Van-Helten (1984).

15. Marks and Trapido (1974); Van-Helten (1982) (for severe qualification of the gold crisis argument); for the labour supply issue, see below.
16. Phimister (1974); Robinson and Gallagher (1961) pp. 234–53.
17. Fetter (1976) pp. 18–32, 58–68; Katzenellenbogen (1973).
18. Kantor and Kenny (1976); Perrings (1977) for the general arguments in this section.
19. Beinart (1980); Harries (1982); Kimble (1982).
20. Wilson (1972).
21. Van Onselen (1976) p. 128f.; Turrel (1982).
22. Davies (1979); Lacey (1981).
23. Fetter (1976) pp. 80–118; Perrings (1979); Vellut (1983); Egerton (1957) pp. 227–37 (a useful, if apologetic, account of Diamang).
24. Phimister (1977); Van Onselen (1976).
25. Berger (1974); Parpart (1983); Perrings (1979).
26. Gann (1965) pp. 45–51, 71–4.
27. Clarence-Smith (1983); Hammond (1966).
28. Brett (1973); Robinson and Gallagher (1961) pp. 53–4, 234–53, 427–61.
29. Katzenellenbogen (1975) p. 380f.; Phimister (1976); Roberts (1976) p. 125f.
30. Allan (1965) pp. 17–18, 176–218; the volcanic soils and high altitude of the Mt Kenya region are particularly hospitable to intensive temperate-zone agriculture.
31. Arrighi (1970); Omer-Cooper (1966) pp. 176–9; Sorrenson (1968) pp. 27–9.
32. Ehrlich (1965); Iliffe (1979) pp. 146–7; Pachai (1973) pp. 158–60; Swainson (1980) pp. 78–92.
33. Brown (1941); Liebenow (1969); Sundiata (1980).
34. Michel (1969); Bederman (1968).
35. Iliffe (1979) pp. 145–6; Pachai (1973) p. 163f.; Tetzlaff (1970) pp. 136–54; on the Groundnut Scheme, see Chapter 8 below.
36. Fieldhouse (1978) p. 494f.
37. Swainson (1980) pp. 78–92.
38. Kosmin (1977); Palmer (1977) pp. 93, 210–11, 242–3.
39. McCracken (1983); Pachai (1973) pp. 153–63.
40. Iliffe (1979) pp. 154–5, 274–81; Kitching (1980) pp. 79–80; Wrigley (1959) pp. 40–2.
41. Bundy (1979); Keegan (1979); Morris (1976); Trapido (1978).
42. Lipton (1977).
43. Palmer (1977); but see qualifications in Ranger (1978). Mosley (1982, 1983) presents an elaborately quantified effort to defend settler farming against charges of inefficiency and the 'underdevelopment' of African peasants; the data base, however, is questionable (Choate 1984; Mosley, 1984) and the analysis of Kenyan and Southern Rhodesian African rural entrepreneurship is better executed in other, earlier, studies cited below.
44. Baylies (1978); Hellen (1968); Long (1968); Muntemba (1980); Palmer (1983).
45. Lonsdale and Berman (1979); Stichter (1982).
46. Furedi (1974).
47. Beinart (1982); Mafeje (1981); Simkins (1981); Stultz (1979) p. 31f.; for Zimbabwe: Hodder-Williams (1983) pp. 138–9; Zachrisson (1978); for a Zambian case: Vail (1977).
48. Comaroff (1981); Knight (1974); Wright (1983).
49. Bundy (1979); Etherington (1978a); Lewis (1984); Matsetela (1982).
50. Beinart (1982) describes the exceptional case of the Pondo, who made the transition to plough agriculture while retaining their traditional political structure; for the more common pattern of cultural resistance to ploughing, see Peires (1981) pp. 107–8.
51. Palmer (1977) pp. 163–87, 213–25; Weinrich (1973, 1975); for a first-hand example, Muzorewa (1978) pp. 9–24.
52. Ranger (1985).

53. Cowen (1973); Kitching (1980); Stichter (1982) p. 69f.
54. Leo (1984) pp. 57–62.
55. Ehrensaft (1976); Davies, Innes, and O'Meara (1976); for a critique of this model in its classic South African context, Yudelman (1983).
56. Hancock (1942) pp. 188–200, 269f. (this work is mainly a critique of the peasant bias in British West African economic policy).
57. DeLancey (1978); Fieldhouse (1978) pp. 513–17.
58. Vellut (1983) pp. 136–8.
59. Lacroix (1967) p. 20f.
60. Jewsiewicki (1983) pp. 115–18; Vellut (1977).
61. Brett (1973) pp. 278–81; Swainson (1980) pp. 25–7, 40–3.
62. Murray (1970) p. 175f.
63. Phimister (1983) pp. 284–6.
64. Christie (1984); Ehrensaft (1976); Nattrass (1981) pp. 152–89.
65. Christie (1984); the conclusion drawn here is only implicit in Christie's account of what he sees as a paradoxical conjuncture of cheap labour and capital-intensification policies.
66. Bozzoli (1975); Christie (1984) pp. 31–8, 93–5; Innes (1984) pp. 123–30; Yudelman (1983) for the strongest, somewhat overstated, argument that 1922–4 was not a critical turning point in South African socio-economic history.
67. O'Dowd (1974); Nattrass (1981) p. 304f.
68. Southall (1980) describes the very limited modern African entrepreneurial sector; for the Marxist view of apartheid as an instrument of capitalism Wolpe (1972); for a radical pessimist refutation of both liberal and Marxist positions, Clarke (1978).

Bibliography

Abshire, David (1979), *Portuguese Africa: A Handbook* (New York: Praeger)

Allan, William (1965), *The African Husbandman* (New York: Barnes and Noble)

Arrighi, Giovanni (1970), 'Labour supplies in historical perspective: a study of the proletarianization of the African peasantry in Rhodesia', *Journal of Development Studies*, vol. 6, no. 3, pp. 197–236

Axelson, Eric (1973), *Portuguese in South-east Africa, 1488–1600* (Johannesburg: Struik)

Ballard, Charles (1980), 'John Dunn and Cetshwayo: the material foundations of political power in the Zulu kingdom, 1857–1878', *Journal of African History*, vol. 21, no. 1, pp. 75–91

Baylies, Carolyn (1978), 'The emergence of indigenous capitalist agriculture: the case of the Southern Province, Zambia', *Rural Africana*, vol. 5, pp. 65–81

Bederman, Sanford (1968), *The Cameroons Development Corporation* (Bota: CDC)

Beinart, William (1980), 'Production and the material basis of chieftainship: Pondoland c. 1830–1880', in Marks and Atmore (eds), pp. 148–70.

Beinart, William (1982), *The Political Economy of Pondoland, 1860-1930* (Cambridge: Cambridge University Press)

Berger, Elena L. (1974), *Labour, Race and Colonial Rule: The Copperbelt from 1924 to Independence* (Oxford: Clarendon Press)

Birmingham, David and Phyllis M. Martin (eds) (1983), *History of Central Africa*, Vol. 2 (London: Longman)

Blainey, G. (1965), 'Lost causes of the Jameson Raid', *Economic History Review*, vol. 18, pp. 350–66

Bozzoli, Belinda (1975), 'Ideology and the manufacturing class in South Africa: 1907–1926', *Journal of Southern African Studies*, vol. 1, no. 2, pp. 194–214

Brett, E.A. (1973), *Colonialism and Underdevelopment in East Africa: The Politics of Economic Change, 1919-1939* (New York: Nok)

Brown, George W. (1941), *The Economic History of Liberia* (Washington, DC: Associated Publishers)

Bundy, Colin (1972), 'The emergence and decline of a South African peasantry', *African Affairs*, vol. 71, no. 285, pp. 369-87

Bundy, Colin (1979), *The Rise and Fall of the South African Peasantry* (Berkeley: University of California Press)

Choate, Stephen (1984), 'Agricultural policy in settler economies: a comment', *Economic History Review*, vol. 37, no. 3, pp. 409-13.

Christie, Renfrew (1984), *Electricity, Industry and Class in South Africa* (Albany: State University of New York Press)

Clarence-Smith, W. Gervase (1983), 'Capital accumulation and class formation in Angola', in Birmingham and Martin (eds), pp. 163-99

Clarke, Simon (1978), 'Capital, fractions of capital, and the state: "neo-Marxist" analysis of the South African state', *Capital and Class*, vol. 5, pp. 32-77

Comaroff, John L. (1981), 'Class and culture in a peasant economy: the transformation of land tenure in Barolong', in Richard P. Werbner (ed.), *Land Reform in the Making: Tradition, Public Policy and Ideology in Botswana* (London: Rex Collings), pp. 85-113

Cooper, Frederick (1981), 'Peasants, capitalists, and historians: a review article', *Journal of Southern African Studies* vol. 7, no. 1, pp. 284-314

Cowen, M.P. (1973), 'Notes on agricultural wage labour in a Kenya location', in Christopher Allen and Kenneth King (eds), *Developmental Trends in Kenya* (Edinburgh: University of Edinburgh, Centre of African Studies)

Daniel, J.B. M. (1964), 'The Swazi rural economy', in J.F. Holleman (ed.), *Experiment in Swaziland* (Oxford: Oxford University Press)

Davenport, T.R.H. (1969), 'The consolidation of a new society: the Cape Colony', in Wilson and Thompson (eds), pp. 272-333

Davies, Robert H. (1979), *Capital, State, and White Labor in South Africa, 1900-1960* (Atlantic Highlands: Humanities)

Davies, Robert H., Duncan Innes, and Dan O'Meara (1976), 'Class struggle and the periodization of the state in South Africa', *Review of African Politcal Economy*, no. 7, pp. 4-30

De Kiewet, C.W. (1957), *A History of South Africa: Social and Economic* (London: Oxford University Press)

DeLancey, Mark W. (1978), 'Health and disease on the plantations of Cameroon, 1884-1939', in Gerald Hartwig and K. David Patterson (eds), *Disease in African History* (Durham: Duke University Press), pp. 153-79

Denoon, D.J. (1968), ' "Capitalist influence" and the Transvaal government during the Crown Colony period, 1900-1906', *Historical Journal*, vol. 11, no. 2, pp. 301-21

Egerton, F. Clement C. (1957), *Angola in Perspective* (London: Routledge & Kegan Paul)

Ehrensaft, Philip (1976), 'Polarized accumulation and the theory of economic dependence: the implications of South African semi-industrial capitalism', in Peter C.W. Gutkind and Immanuel Wallerstein (eds), *The Political Economy of Contemporary Africa* (Beverly Hills: Sage), pp. 58-89

Ehrlich, Cyril (1965), 'The Uganda economy, 1903-1945', in Vincent Harlow and E.M. Chilver (eds), *History of East Africa*, Vol. 2 (Oxford: Clarendon Press), pp. 395-475.

Elphick, Richard (1977), *Kraal and Castle: Khoikhoi and the Founding of White South Africa* (New Haven: Yale University Press)

Elphick, Richard and Herman Giliomee (eds) (1979), *The Shaping of South African Society, 1652-1820* (Cape Town: Longman)

Etherington, Norman (1978a), *Preachers, Peasants, and Politics in Southeast Africa, 1835-1880: African Christian Communities in Natal, Pondoland, and Zululand* (London: Royal Historical Society)

Etherington, Norman (1978b), 'African economic experiments in colonial Natal, 1845–1880', *African Economic History*, vol. 5, pp. 1–15

Fearn, Hugh (1961), *An African Economy: A Study of Economic Development in the Nyanza Province of Kenya, 1903–1953* (Nairobi: Oxford University Press)

Fetter, Bruce (1976), *The Creation of Elizabethville, 1910–1940* (Stanford: Hoover Institution Press)

Fieldhouse, David K. (1978), *Unilever Overseas: The Anatomy of a Multinational, 1895–1965* (London: Croom Helm)

Flint, John (1974), *Cecil Rhodes* (Boston: Little, Brown)

Furedi, Frank (1974), 'The social composition of the Mau Mau movement in the White Highlands', *Journal of Peasant Studies*, vol. 1, no. 4, pp. 486–505

Gann, Louis H. (1965), *A History of Southern Rhodesia: Early Days to 1934* (London: Chatto & Windus)

Giliomee, Herman (1979), 'The eastern frontier, 1770–1812', in Elphick and Giliomee (eds), pp. 291–337

Guelke, Leonard (1966), 'Frontier settlement in early South Africa', *Annals of the Association of American Geographers*, vol. 66, no. 1, pp. 25–42

Guelke, Leonard (1979), 'The white settlers, 1652–1780', in Elphick and Giliomee (eds), 41–74

Guy, Jeff (1979), *The Destruction of the Zulu Kingdom* (London: Longman)

Guy, Jeff (1980), 'Ecological factors in the rise of Shaka and the Zulu Kingdom', in Marks and Atmore (eds), pp. 102–19

Hammond, R.J. (1966), *Portugal and Africa, 1815–1910: A Study in Uneconomic Imperialism* (Stanford: Stanford University Press)

Hancock, William Keith (1942), *Survey of British Commonwealth Affairs*, Vol. 2, *Problems of Economic Policy, 1918–1939*, Part 2 (London: Oxford University Press)

Harinck, Gerrit (1969), 'Interaction between Xhosa and Khoi: emphasis on the period 1620–1750', in Thompson (ed.), pp. 145–70

Harries, Patrick (1982), 'Kinship, ideology and the nature of pre-colonial labour migration: labour migration from the Delagoa Bay hinterland to South Africa, up to 1895', in Marks and Rathbone (eds), pp. 142–66

Hedges, David W. (1978), 'Trade and politics in southern Mozambique and Zululand in the eighteenth and early nineteenth centuries' (Unpublished PhD dissertation, University of London)

Hellen, John A. (1968), *Rural Economic Development in Zambia, 1890–1964* (Munich: Weltforum)

Hobson, John A. (1900), *The War in South Africa: Its Causes and Effects* (London: Nisbet)

Hocking, Anthony (1973), *Oppenheimer and Son* (New York: McGraw Hill)

Hodder-Williams, Richard (1983), *White Farmers in Rhodesia, 1890–1965. A History of the Marandellas District* (London: Macmillan)

Houghton, D. Hobart (1967), *The South African Economy* (Cape Town: Oxford University Press)

Iliffe, John (1979), *A Modern History of Tanganyika* (Cambridge: Cambridge University Press)

Innes, Duncan (1984), *Anglo American and the Rise of Modern South Africa* (New York: Monthly Review Press)

Jeeves, Alan (1973), 'Rand capitalists and the coming of the South African War, 1896–1899', *Canadian Historical Association, Historical Papers*

Jeeves, Alan (1975), 'The control of migratory labour in the South African gold mines in the era of Kruger and Milner', *Journal of Southern African Studies*. vol. 2, no. 1, pp. 3–29

Jewsiewicki, Bogumil (1983), 'Rural society and the Belgian colonial economy', in Birmingham and Martin (eds), pp. 95–125

Johnstone, Frederick (1976), *Class, Race, and Gold* (London: Routledge, Kegan Paul)

Kantor, B.S. and H.F. Kenny (1976), 'The poverty of neo-Marxism: the case of South Africa', *Journal of Southern African Studies*, vol. 3, no. 1, pp. 20–40

192 The Colonial Economies: II

Kaplan, David E. (1976), 'The politics of industrial protection in South Africa, 1910–1939', *Journal of Southern African Studies*, vol. 3, no. 1, pp. 70–91

Katzen, M.F. (1969), 'White settlers and the origin of a new society, 1652–1778', in Wilson and Thompson (eds), pp. 183–232

Katzenellenbogen, Simon (1973), *Railways and the Copper Mines of Katanga* (Oxford: Clarendon Press)

Katzenellenbogen, Simon (1975), 'The miner's frontier: transport and general economic development', in Peter Duignan and L.H. Gann (eds). *Colonialism in Africa, 1870–1960*, Vol. 4, *The Economics of Colonialism* (Cambridge: Cambridge University Press), pp. 360–426

Keegan, Tim (1979), 'The restructuring of agrarian class relations in a colonial economy: the Orange River Colony, 1902–1910', *Journal of Southern African Studies*, vol. 5, no. 2, pp. 234–54

Keller, Bonnie B. (1978), 'Millenarianism and resistance: the Xhosa cattle killing', *Journal of Asian and African Studies*, vol. 13, nos. 1–2, pp. 95–111

Kimble, Judy (1982), 'Labour migration in Basutoland, c. 1870–1885', in Marks and Rathbone (eds), pp. 119–41

Kitching, Gavin (1980), *Class and Economic Change in Kenya: The Making of an African Petite-Bourgeoisie* (New Haven: Yale University Press)

Knight, C. Gregory (1974), *Ecology and Change: Rural Modernization in an African Community* (New York: Academic Press)

Kosmin, Barry A. (1977), 'The Inyoka tobacco industry of the Shangwe people: the displacement of a pre-colonial economy in Southern Rhodesia, 1898–1938', in Palmer and Parsons (eds), pp. 268–88

Kubicek, Robert V. (1979), *Economic Imperialism in Theory and Practice: The Case of South African Gold Mining Finance, 1886–1914* (Durham: Duke University Press)

Lacey, Marian (1981), *Working for Boroko: The Origins of a Coercive Labour System in South Africa* (Johannesburg: Ravan)

Lacroix, Jean-Louis (1967), *Industrialisation au Congo: la transformation des structures économiques* (The Hague: Mouton)

Leftwich, Adrian (ed.) (1974), *South Africa: Economic Growth and Political Change* (London: Allison & Busby)

Leo, Christopher (1984), *Land and Class in Kenya* (Toronto: Toronto University Press)

Lewis, Jack (1984), 'The rise and fall of the South African peasantry: a critique and reassessment', *Journal of Southern African Studies*, vol. 11, no. 1, pp. 1–24

Liebenow, J. Gus (1969), *Liberia: The Evolution of Privilege* (Ithaca: Cornell University Press)

Lipton, Merle (1977), 'South Africa: two agricultures', in F. Wilson, A. Kooy and D. Hendrie (eds), *Farm Labour in South Africa* (Cape Town: Philip), pp. 72–85

Long, Norman (1968), *Social Change and the Individual: A Study of the Social and Religious Response to Innovation in a Zambian Rural Community* (Manchester: Manchester University Press)

Lonsdale, John and Bruce Berman (1979), 'Coping with the contradictions; the development of the colonial state in Kenya, 1895-1914', *Journal of African History*, vol. 20, no. 4, pp. 587–605

McCracken, John (1983), 'Planters, peasants, and the colonial state; the impact of the Native Tobacco Board in the Central Province of Malawi', *Journal of Southern African Studies*, vol. 9, no. 2, pp. 172–92

Mafeje, Archie (1981), 'On the articulation of modes of production: review article', *Journal of Southern African Studies*, vol. 8, no. 1, pp. 123–38

Marks, Shula and Anthony Atmore (eds) (1980), *Economy and Society in Pre-Industrial South Africa* (London: Longman)

Marks, Shula and Richard Rathbone (eds) (1982), *Industrialisation and Social Change in South Africa* (London: Longman)

Marks, Shula and Stanley Trapido (1974), 'Lord Milner and the South African state', *History Workshop*, vol. 8, pp. 50–80

Matsetela, Ted (1982), 'The life story of Nkgona Mma-Pooe: aspects of sharecropping and proletarianisation in the northern Orange Free State, 1890–1930', in Marks and Rathbone (eds), pp. 212–37

Mawby, A.A. (1974), 'Capital, government, and politics in the Transvaal, 1900–1907: a revision and a reversion', *Historical Journal*, vol. 17, no. 2, pp. 387–415

Mendelsohn, Richard (1980), 'Blainey and the Jameson Raid: the debate revived', *Journal of Southern African Studies*, vol. 6, no. 2, pp. 157–70

Michel, Marc (1969), 'Les plantations allemandes du Mount Cameroun, 1885–1914', *Revue Française d'Histoire d'Outre-Mer*, vol. 57, no. 2, pp. 183–213

Morris, M.L. (1976), 'The development of capitalism in South African agriculture: class struggle in the countryside', *Economy and Society*, vol. 5, no. 3, pp. 292–343

Mosley, Paul (1982), 'Agricultural development and government policy in settler economies: the case of Kenya and Southern Rhodesia, 1900–1960', *Economic History Review*, vol. 35, no. 3, pp. 390–408

Mosley, Paul (1983), *The Settler Economies: Studies in the Economic History of Kenya and Southern Rhodesia, 1900–1963* (Cambridge: Cambridge University Press)

Mosley, Paul (1984), 'A reply to Choate', *Economic History Review*, vol. 37, no. 3, pp. 414–16

Muntemba, Maude Shimwaayi (1980), 'Regional and social differentiation in Broken Hill Rural District, Northern Rhodesia, 1930–1964', in Martin A. Klein (ed.), *Peasants in Africa: Historical and Contemporary Perspectives* (Beverly Hills: Sage), pp. 243–69

Murray, D.J. (1970), *The Governmental System in Southern Rhodesia* (Oxford: Clarendon Press)

Muzorewa, Abel Tendekai (1978), *Rise Up and Walk: An Autobiography* (London: Evans)

Nattrass, Jill (1981), *The South African Economy* (Cape Town: Oxford University Press)

Neumark, S. Daniel (1957), *Economic Influences on the South African Frontier, 1652–1836* (Stanford: Stanford University Press)

Odingo, Richard S. (1971), *The Kenya Highlands: Land Use and Agricultural Development* (Nairobi: EAPH)

O'Dowd, Michael (1974), 'South Africa in the light of the stages of economic growth', in Adrian Leftwich (ed.), *South Africa: Economic Growth and Political Change* (London: Allison & Busby), pp. 29–43

O'Meara, Dan (1983), *Volkcapitalisme: Class, Capital, and Ideology in the Development of Afrikaner Nationalism, 1934–1948* (Cambridge: Cambridge University Press)

Omer-Cooper, J.D. (1966), *The Zulu Aftermath: A Nineteenth Century Revolution in Bantu Africa* (London: Longman)

Pachai, B. (1973), *Malawi: The History of a Nation* (London: Longman)

Palmer, Robin (1977), *Land and Racial Domination in Rhodesia* (London: Oxford University Press)

Palmer, Robin (1983), 'Land alienation and agricultural conflict in colonial Zambia', in Robert I. Rotberg (ed.), *Imperialism, Colonialism, and Hunger in East and Central Africa* (Lexington: D.C. Heath), pp. 89–112

Palmer, Robin and Neil Parsons (eds) (1977), *The Roots of Rural Poverty in Central and Southern Africa* (Berkeley: University of California Press)

Parpart, Jane (1983), *Labour and Capital on the African Copperbelt* (Philadelphia: Temple University Press)

Peires, J.B. (1981), *The House of Phalo: A History of the Xhosa People in the Days of their Independence* (Berkeley: University of California Press)

Perrings, Charles (1977), 'The production process, industrial labour strategies, and worker responses in the Southern African gold mining industry', *Journal of African History*, vol. 18, no. 1, pp. 129–35

Perrings, Charles (1979), *Black Mineworkers in Central Africa: Industrial Strategies and the Evolution of a Black Proletariat in the Copperbelt, 1911–1941* (New York: Africana Press)

Phimister, I.R. (1974), 'Rhodes, Rhodesia, and the Rand', *Journal of Southern African Studies*, vol. 1, no. 1, pp. 24–90

Phimister, I.R. (1976), 'The reconstruction of the Southern Rhodesian gold mining industry, 1903–1910', *Economic History Review*, vol. 29, no. 3, pp. 465–81

Phimister, I.R. (1977), 'White miners in historical perspective: Southern Rhodesia, 1890–1953', *Journal of Southern African Studies*, vol. 3, no. 2, pp. 187–206

Phimister, I.R. (1983), 'Zimbabwe: the path of capitalist development', in Birmingham and Martin (eds), pp. 251–90

Ranger, Terence O. (1978), 'Growing from the roots: reflections on peasant research in Central and Southern Africa', *Journal of Southern African Studies*, vol. 5 no. 1, pp. 99–133

Ranger, Terence O. (1985), *Peasant Consciousness and Guerrilla War in Zimbabwe* (London: Currey)

Richardson, Peter (1983), *Chinese Mine Labour in the Transvaal* (Manchester: Manchester University Press)

Richardson, Peter and Jacques Van-Helten (1984), 'The development of the South African gold mining industry, 1895–1918', *Economic History Review*, vol. 37, no. 2, pp. 319–40

Roberts, Andrew (1976), *A History of Zambia* (New York: Africana Press)

Robinson, Ronald and John Gallagher (1961), *Africa and the Victorians: The Official Mind of Imperialism* (London: Macmillan)

Ross, Robert (1976), *Adam Kok's Griquas: A Study in the Development of Stratification in South Africa* (Cambridge: Cambridge University Press)

Ross, Robert (1978), 'The Khoikhoi of South Africa' [review of Elphick, 1977], *Journal of African History*, vol. 19, no. 2, pp. 282–3

Sansom, Basil (1974), 'Traditional economic systems', in W.D. Hammond-Tooke (ed.), *The Bantu-Speaking Peoples of Southern Africa* (London: Routledge & Kegan Paul), pp. 135–76

Schultz, Jürgen (1976), *Land Use in Zambia: Part 1* (Munich: Weltforum)

Schumann, C.G.W. (1938), *Structural Change and Business Cycles in South Africa, 1806–1936* (London: P.S. King)

Schutte, Gerrit (1979), 'Company and colonists at the Cape', in Elphick and Giliomee (eds), pp. 173–210

Simkins, Charles (1981), 'Agricultural production in the African reserves of South Africa, 1918–1969', *Journal of Southern African Studies*, vol. 7, pp. 256–83

Smith, Alan (1969), 'The trade of Delagoa Bay as a factor in Nguni politics 1750–1835', in Thomson (ed.), pp. 171–89

Sorrenson, M.P.K. (1967), *Land Reform in the Kikuyu Country* (Nairobi: Oxford University Press)

Sorrenson, M.P.K. (1968), *The Origins of European Settlement in Kenya* (Nairobi: Oxford University Press)

South Africa (1963), *Agricultural Census No. 34. Report on Agricultural and Pastoral Production, 1959–60* (Department of Statistics)

Southall, Roger (1980), 'African capitalism in contemporary South Africa', *Journal of Southern African Studies*, vol. 6, no. 1, pp. 38–70

Stichter, Sharon (1982), *Migrant Labour in Kenya: Capitalism and African Responses, 1895–1975* (London: Longman)

Stokes, Randall and Anthony Harris (1978), 'South African development and the paradox of racial particularism: towards a theory of modernization from the center', *Economic Development and Cultural Change*, vol. 26, no. 2, pp. 245–69

Ströbel, Herbert (ed.) (1973), *An Economic Analysis of Smallholder Agriculture in the Kericho District (Kenya)* (Berlin: Technische Universität)

Stultz, Newell (1979), *Transkei's Half Loaf: Race Separatism in South Africa* (New Haven: Yale University Press)

Sundiata, I.K. (1980), *Black Scandal: America and the Liberian Labor Crisis, 1929–1936* (Philadelphia: ISHI)

Swainson, Nicola (1980), *The Rise of Corporate Capitalism in Kenya, 1918–1977* (Berkeley: University of California Press)

Tetzlaff, Rainer (1970), *Koloniale Entwicklung und Ausbeutung: Wirtschafts- und Sozialgeschichte Deutsch-Ostafrikas, 1885–1914* (Berlin: Duncker u. Humblot)

Thompson, Leonard (1969a), 'Co-operation and conflict: the Zulu Kingdom and Natal', in Wilson and Thompson (eds), pp. 334–90

Thompson, Leonard (1969b), 'Co-operation and conflict: the high veld', in Wilson and Thompson (eds), pp. 391–446

Thompson, Leonard (ed.) (1969c), *African Societies in Southern Africa* (London: Heinemann)

Trapido, Stanley (1971), 'South Africa as a comparative study of industrialization', *Journal of Development Studies*, vol. 7, no. 3, pp. 309–20

Trapido, Stanley (1978), 'Landlord and peasant in a colonial economy: the Transvaal, 1880–1910', *Journal of Southern African Studies*, vol. 5, no. 1, pp. 26–57

Trapido, Stanley (1980), ' "The friends of the natives": merchants, peasants, and the political and ideological structure of liberalism in the Cape 1854–1910,' in Marks and Atmore (eds), pp. 247–74

Turrel, Rob (1982), 'Kimberley: labour and compounds, 1871–1888', in Marks and Rathbone (eds), pp. 45–76

Vail, Leroy (1977), 'Ecology and history: the example of eastern Zambia', *Journal of Southern African Studies*, vol. 3, no. 2, pp. 129–55.

Vail, Leroy and Landeg White (1980), *Capitalism and Labor in Mozambique: A Study of Quelimane District* (Minneapolis: University of Minnesota Press)

Van-Helten, Jean Jacques (1982), 'Empire and high finance: South Africa and the international gold standard, 1890–1914', *Journal of African History*, vol. 23, no. 4, pp. 529–48

Van Onselen, Charles (1976), *Chibaro: African Mine Labour in Southern Rhodesia, 1900–1935* (London: Pluto)

Vellut, Jean-Luc (1977), 'Rural poverty in western Shaba, c. 1890–1930', in Palmer and Parsons (eds), pp. 294–316

Vellut, Jean-Luc (1983), 'Mining in the Belgian Congo', in Birmingham and Martin (eds), pp. 126–62

Weinrich, A.K. (1973), *Black and White Elites in Rural Rhodesia* (Manchester: Manchester University Press)

Weinrich, A.K. (1975), *African Farmers in Rhodesia: Old and New Peasant Communities in Karangaland* (London: Oxford University Press)

Wilson, Francis (1972), *Labour in the South African Gold Mines, 1911–1969* (Cambridge: Cambridge University Press)

Wilson, Monica (1969), 'Co-operation and conflict: the Eastern Cape frontier', in Wilson and Thompson (eds), pp. 233–71

Wilson, Monica and Leonard Thompson (eds) (1969), *The Oxford History of South Africa*, Vol. 1 (Oxford: Clarendon Press)

Wolpe, Harold (1972), 'Capitalism and cheap labour-power in South Africa: from separation to apartheid', *Economy and Society*, vol. 1, pp. 425–56

Wolpe, Harold (1978), 'A comment on "The poverty of neo-Marxism" ', *Journal of Southern African Studies*, vol. 4, no. 2, pp. 240–56

Wright, Marcia (1983), 'Technology, marriage, and women's work in the history of maize growers in Mazabuka, Zambia: a reconnaissance', *Journal of Southern African Studies*, vol. 10, no. 1, pp. 71–85

Wrigley, C.C. (1959), *Crops and Wealth in Uganda* (Kampala: East African Institute of Social Research)

Yudelman, David (1983), *The Emergence of Modern South Africa: State, Capital, and the*

Incorporation of Organized Labor on the South African Gold Fields (Westport, Conn: Greenwood)

Yudelman, Montague (1964), *Africans on the Land: Economic Problems . . . with Special Reference to Southern Rhodesia* (Cambridge: Harvard University Press)

Zachrisson, Per (1978), *An African Area in Change: Belingwe, 1894–1946* (Gothenburg: Gothenburg University)

 *8*

From Neo-Mercantilism to Decolonization
Africa in the Mid-Twentieth-Century World Economy

Little more than half a century after the creation of modern colonial regimes in Africa, the continent went through another set of rapid and dramatic political changes. The economic significance of decolonization is not as obvious as that of imperial partition. The first transformation destroyed the indigenous institutions which had controlled access to internal markets and resources, replacing them with structures linked directly to industrial Europe. Decolonization removed Europeans from formal control of these new structures, but did not dismantle the structures themselves. It is even possible to write an economic history of Africa without designating the shift to independence as a major turning point.[1]

Decolonization is therefore treated here less as an event creating a new economic situation than as a chronological marker for long-term changes in the relationship between African economies and the international system. The historical problem in understanding this relationship lies in sorting out the linkages between its various dimensions: the market forces determining demand for the export goods so vital to colonial African prosperity; the public policy deliberations by European rulers which determined African responses to the market; and the political and economic actions of European private-sector enterprises with direct interests in Africa.

As with the previous discussions of the economics of pre-colonial Africa and the imperialist partition, the account presented in this chapter will take issue with the liberal and structuralist historiography which perceives a purposeful pattern in the movement away from formal colonial rule. The argument in most of this literature has been that colonialism provided the institutional basis for overcoming certain barriers between Africa and the international economy and that by the period of the 1950s and 1960s this apparatus could be safely left in the hands of indigenous successors who would use it to serve the needs of either – depending upon the perspective – African development or external exploitation.[2]

The contention of the present account is that Africa had arrived at a new and stable position within the international economy well before the changes of the 1930s and 1950s that led to decolonization. These changes resulted from public-sector visions of using African colonies to resolve major economic dilemmas of the European metropoles. They did not, however, correspond either to the long-term market position of Africa or to the imperatives of critical elements in the European private sector.

The resulting historical process thus illustrates in particularly dramatic form the paradoxes which have constituted a central theme of this entire book. The period is one of both unprecedented African economic growth and disastrous indications of the problems involved in such growth. During these decades Africa was more closely integrated into the economies of Europe than at any time in the past, yet they conclude with Europe voluntarily abandoning the political instruments which reinforced such integration. From an international perspective, the movement is from a peak of delusions about Africa's economic significance to a new and much clearer recognition of the continent's marginality. From an African perspective – to be explored more directly in Chapter 9 – the movement is from very clearly defined dependency to a very ambiguous form of freedom.

The chronology of change: markets and public policy

Because of the disparities between what was happening to the African economies and the economic uses to which European rulers wished to put Africa, a periodization of the stages leading from a 'classic' system of colonial rule to decolonization is difficult to establish.[3] Historians have generally agreed that Africa was seriously affected by the major fluctuations in demand for tropical goods connected with the relative prosperity of the 1920s, the Great Depression of the 1930s, the shortages of the Second World War and its immediate aftermath, and the oversupply of the mid-1950s and 1960s. These market movements were accompanied by general shifts in colonial economic policy, affecting such matters as intervention in internal African distribution and production systems, incorporation of Africa into protectionist trade structures, and the allocation of metropolitan funds for major African development programmes.

Broadly speaking there is a degree of correlation between market cycles and policy orientations: laisser-faire liberalism during the 1920s; neo-mercantilist interventionism during the 1930s and 1940s; and neo-liberal disengagement from the mid-1950s on. However, even this schematization suggests serious contradictions; why, for instance, neo-mercantilism in periods of both declining and rising prices? Looked at more closely, the logic behind the chronology becomes even less clear. Instead of a fully coherent progression, what we must understand in the changes of this entire period are the often confused dialectics of a highly asymmetrical world economic system.

THE 1920s: COLONIAL STABILITY AND IMPERIAL VISIONS
As indicated in the previous two chapters, within a few years after the First World War most African colonial economies had overcome the early dilemmas of abortive experimentation and violent imposition to establish reasonably workable systems for producing export goods through various combinations of peasant agriculture, settler farming, and mining. After a series of severe fluctuations at the beginning of the 1920s, prices for these goods became secure and export production grew steadily almost everywhere for the rest of the decade (see Appendix, Table A4, Figures A2, A4). The resulting revenues were able to finance the recurrent costs of most colonial administration and also provided the assurance necessary to raise modest development capital from private lenders in the metropoles.

With all this relative local prosperity, African colonial exports did not generally command any decisive share of world markets. Gold was the most critical product, but it came mainly from the effectively independent settler state of South Africa. The African cocoa farmers of the Gold Coast (present-day Ghana) and Nigeria (with lesser contributions from Cameroon and the Ivory Coast) had achieved dominance of world production, but this crop would prove particularly sensitive to both ceilings on demand elasticity and downward fluctuations in overseas purchasing power.[4]

At the local level European policy orientation during this period corresponded fairly closely to the market situation. Colonial governments generally supported those production systems which had proved most efficient (despite some concessions to settler interests in East and Central Africa), pursued new transport and other infrastructure investments with prudent optimism, and were permitted to encourage trade and investment from whatever quarters might provide sustenance. This last point was somewhat qualified by long-term metropolitan policies: British and Belgian colonies simply remained committed to free-trade during this period, but France retained its basically protectionist tariff system, despite some movement toward colonial fiscal autonomy in 1928. Portugal, on the other hand, shifted in the 1920s towards a new 'British-style' open-door regime in its African colonies.[5]

While this stable interlude of the colonial economies coincided with a period of general growth in the world economy, within the European metropoles recovery from the First World War did not come so easily. Throughout the decade Britain experienced unprecedented and apparently irreducible levels of unemployment; France, up until at least 1926, saw its national currency suffer from constant devaluation. These persistent problems gave new life to the economic views of the political groups which had previously advocated imperialists partition. In Britain the Chamberlain-Milner wing of the Conservative Party, whose mantle had now fallen upon Leopold Amery, argued that British consumer and capital goods industries could only be brought back to life through an imperial customs union and substantial public investments in the colonies. The centre-left *Groupe coloniale* in the French parliament of the 1920s was led by Albert Sarraut, who advocated a major programme of investments in Africa and Indo-China which would alleviate France's dependency on imports from outside the franc zone.

Neither Amery nor Sarraut was able to influence his respective government to risk much public capital on colonial ventures. However, by the end of the decade some movement towards greater intervention was initiated by opposing political groups, in the form of major colonial loan programmes. Thus the British Labour cabinet of 1929 passed the Colonial Development Act and in the same year the conservative Tardieu government of France drew up the programme for its 'Great Colonial Loan Acts'. Both these schemes were based upon the assumption that enough resources were now available in the metropoles to finance African development (particularly in France, which had finally stabilized the franc) and that such development would provide the basis for further metropolitan growth.[6] With the almost immediate advent of the Great Depression, these concepts would be severely questioned, although eventually reformulated in broader terms.

THE 1930s: DEPRESSION AND NEW VISIONS

The bulk of the loans and grants offered to African colonies in the first years of new British and French programmes were designed to improve infrastructure (particularly transport) and thus to increase production of exports (see Table 8.1). Such an effort made little sense during the Depression, when the problems of the home economies far exceeded any relief which could come from contracts for colonial projects and the world demand for all African commodities (except gold) plummeted sharply. The British and French had the additional misfortune of

Table 8.1   *Colonial development aid*

1. Britain

		Allocated		*Disbursed*
		£ current (millions)	$US 1960[1] (millions)	$US 1960 (millions)
1880–1914	Colonial Office grants[2]	3.198	64.638	56.9
1896–1914	East African loans[3]	8.503	42.513	42.513(?)
1919–39	Guaranteed Loan Act loans[4]	25.383	264.416	264.416(?)
1921–40	Colonial Office aid[5]	4.653	49.508	49.508
1929–39	Colonial Development Act[6]	3.779	46.909	33.868
Sub-total pre-Second World War		45.527	593.164	572.385
1946–60	Colonial Development and Welfare Act[7]	145.070	559.305	460.308
1948–60	Colonial Development Corporation[8]	75.402	277.339	151.594
1945–60	Colonial Service Votes[9]	89.949	391.510	391.510
1947–55	Overseas Food Corporation[10]	41.300	191.950	191.950
Sub-total 1945–60		351.361	1 420.104	1 245.852
Grand total		396.888	2 013.268	1 825.975

	Infra-structure	*Deployment* (percentages) Production	Social development	*Terms* (percentages) Loans	Grants
1880–1914	75 +			72.7	27.3
Colonial Office aid		unknown		mostly loans	
Guaranteed Loan Act		unknown		100.0	
Colonial Development Act	56.0	23.0	16.0	34.0	66.0
1919–1940 (rough estimate)				90.5	9.5
Colonial Development and Welfare Act	40.7	20.3	39.1	0.9	99.1
Colonial Development Corporation	52.5	47.5		100.0	
Aggregate, 1946–60[11]				26.5	73.5
Overseas Food Corporation				100.0 (none repaid)	

2. France

		current francs (millions)	$US 1960 (millions)
to 1914	guaranteed loans	276	176.640
1919–30	guaranteed loans	493	65.733
1931–9	Great Colonial Loan Acts	5 527[12]	736.933
Subtotal pre-Second World War (allocated)		6 296	979.307
(disbursed)		4 344.24[13]	675.722

		CFA francs[14] (millions)	$US 1960 (millions)
1946–60	French state	66 430	587.247
1947–60	FIDES	286 757.8	2 332.733

Table 8.1   *continued*

	CFA francs[14] (millions)		
1947–60 CCE/CCFOM	63 776.9		417.016
1959–60 FAC[15]	27 261		111.061
Subtotal 1946–60	444 225.7		3 448.057
Grand total	888 647.96	(metro-politan francs)	4 123.779

	Infrastructure	Deployment (percentages) Production	Social development	Terms (percentages) Loans	Grants
1907–19	87.5	0.1	12.3	100.0	
1920–38	86.6	0.4	13.1[16]	100.0	
CCE/CCFOM				100.0	
FIDES I (1946–56)	64.0	18.0	18.0		100.0
FIDES II (1956–60)	49.0	30.0	21.0[17]		100.0
French state, FAC					100.0
1946–60	aggregate			14.4	85.6

[1]Transformations into constant 1960 dollars are based on various combinations of calculations already incorporated into the secondary sources consulted (Bloch-Lainé, 1956, for pre-Second World War French data) and use of cost-of-living tables in *La grande encyclopédie* (Paris: Larousse, 1973), Vol. 8, p. 5057; International Monetary Fund, *International Financial Statistics*; Mitchell and Dean (1962) pp. 344–5, 378. Transformations from sterling and francs into dollars is based on official rates.

[2]Kesner (1981) pp. 34–43. Almost 99 per cent of this money went to a single project, the Uganda Railway.

[3]Constantine (1984) p. 12. Again the Uganda Railway took up a large majority of this allocation (65 per cent); it is not even clear whether the entire remaining sum was actually disbursed. I have omitted from both this figure and the interwar British aid accounts loans raised by African territories under various forms of special legislation which were supposed to provide colonies with favourable interest rates but generally functioned much like the rest of the private capital market.

[4]Constantine (1984) pp. 295–7. These are all nominal loan figures which do not indicate whether the sums were ultimately disbursed; however, since the requests were initiated by the recipient governments without any prompting from metropolitan development planners, probably the disbursement level is very close to the allocations. It should also be noted that slightly more than half of these loans went to the Sudan, a territory which has generally been omitted from the analysis in the rest of this volume.

[5]Constantine (1984) pp. 273–4, *et passim*.

[6]Meredith (1975) p. 491; Wicker (1958) p. 176.

[7]*Colonial Development and Welfare Acts, Report . . .*, Parliamentary Papers, 1960–61, vol. 27.

[8]Colonial Development Corporation, *Annual Report and Statement of Accounts . . . 1960* (London: HMSO).

[9]No specific account of this source is available; its relationship to the other forms of British aid is explained in OEEC (1961) pp. 100–1. The present figure was arrived at by subtracting

Colonial Development and Welfare and Colonial Development Corporation aid from the total British official aid to Africa reported in Great Britain, *Statistical Abstracts*, 1961, pp. 234–5. The amounts assigned in this source to East Africa make it clear that the Overseas Food Corporation Groundnut Scheme (see next note) is not included.

[10]Cmd 8125, *The Future of the Overseas Food Corporation*, Parliamentary Papers, 1950/51, vol. 27; Overseas Food Corporation, *Annual Report and Statement of Accounts . . . 1955*, Parliamentary Papers, 1955/56, vol. 26.

[11]Based on Great Britain, *Statistical Abstracts*, 1961, pp. 232–3.

[12]Bloch-Lainé (1956) p. 109.

[13]Calculated from Poquin (1957) p. 188. The totals, as in the case of pre-Second World War Britain, are probably somewhat underestimated, due in this case to the absence of any information on metropolitan government expenditure on development other than the guarantee of loans. In the French case, there were no formal grant programmes but it is known that extensive deficits in the budgets of African colonial governments had to be made good from Paris; however, apart from the problems of calculation, it is difficult to know which of these outlays were for development (and whether this meant anything other than paying off railway loan arrears) rather than basic administration or military costs and how much of the funds expended would have to be charged against levies on the few colonies which did run in the black (on the latter point, see Austen and Headrick (1983) and Manning (1982) pp. 171–4.

[14]From 1946 to 1948, 1 CFA franc = 1.7 metropolitan francs; for 1949–60, 1 CFA franc = 2 metropolitan francs.

[15]Younes (1964) *passim*; FIDES = Fonds d'investissement pour le développement économique et sociale; CCE/CCFOM = Caisse centrale de coopération économique/Caisse centrale de la France d'Outre-Mer; FAC = Fonds d'aide et du coopération.

[16]Ngango (1973) p. 87; these percentages are based upon projected, rather than realized, undertakings.

[17]Hayter (1966) p. 38; these figures are also based upon planning rather than implementation.

making their largest single sets of African investments of the early 1930s in three efforts which would not have been justified under any circumstances: a bridge across the Zambezi River allowing an under-used Mozambique rail line to enter impoverished Nyasaland (present-day Malawi); the final stages of the notorious Congo–Océan railway, which duplicated Cameroonian and Belgian Congo lines already serving French Equatorial Africa; and the Office du Niger irrigated agriculture scheme in what is now Mali.

Given the low prices of their exports, the administrations of African territories were experiencing difficulty paying off debts contracted during the 1920s and thus did not welcome the new loans with great enthusiasm. In the end only about three-quarters of the capital issue envisaged in the legislation of 1929 was ever authorized and not even all of this was taken up in actual loans.[7]

The idea of African territories as a device to overcome metropolitan economic difficulties was nevertheless given new life in the 1930s by the shift of all colonial powers towards more protectionist trade policies. In the 1932 Ottowa Agreements, Britain, once the bastion of free trade, adopted a general system of imperial preference. In 1936 France abrogated its reciprocal treaty with Britain guaranteeing free trade in West Africa. Portugal, under the Salazar dictatorship, shifted from free trade to protectionism in 1930 and even Belgium began to encourage imports of tropical goods from its own colonies. The material impact of these changes in Africa was limited by the unshakeable open-door stipulations of the 1885 Berlin Congo treaty (covering British East Africa, the Belgian Congo, and much of the Sudan, Mozambique and French Equatorial Africa), and the League of Nations Mandates regulations. Moreover Britain took only limited advantage of opportunities to impose protectionist regimes on its other African colonies after 1932. At a minimum, however, all the colonial powers now granted preferential quotas on trade between their domestic markets and African dependencies.[8]

Nonetheless, colonial protectionism, in the earliest and most severe phase of the Depression of the 1930s, could do little for European recovery since the African economies were themselves going through great difficulties. The initial reaction of local administrators and investors was to cut back on expenditures. Government employment and public-works projects thus had to be reduced, and many mines and planatations closed down or at least laid off a high proportion of their European and African staff. At the same time remaining resources were deployed to increase efforts by African peasants – both in territories where they already dominated export production and those where they did not – to increase their commercial cultivation efforts.

This last policy is, of course, the classic response of a 'small nation' producer to falling prices in a world market over which it has no control. However, the very advantage of turning to African smallholders – their low production costs – also meant that the Africans were themselves less directly dependent on remaining in the market than their colonial masters. Thus in order to keep up or increase production in the face of falling prices, extra-market coercion, ranging from taxation, to verbal harangues, to occasional use of direct force, needed to be exerted.[9]

The combination of protectionism and coercive production helped African colonial economies survive the Depression, but in a manner which called into question all existing policies. Without these measures, it is conceivable that the administrative and transport infrastructure of many of the colonies might have suffered severe damage. Moreover, France, Belgium and Portugal (but not Britain) substantially increased their share of trade with African dependencies and African colonial shares of metropolitan trade during the early 1930s.[10] At the same time African peasant producers responded to the role being assigned to them in this system by various forms of protest, including cocoa hold-ups, riots, and several minor rebellions.[11]

Within metropolitan policy-making circles, the experiences of the early 1930s at once discredited the earlier forms of neo-mercantilism and gave birth to more ambitious visions of joint economic development. With the dissolution of the Empire Marketing Board in 1933 Amery and his circle lost their grip over British African policy; at about the same time, the Groupe coloniale disappeared from the French parliament.[12] But, partly because of the disturbances in the classical equilibrium which had been stirred up by the efforts of the previous years, African and colonial issues retained their newly acquired prominence in European public life. Given the continued economic insecurity within Europe along with rising international political tensions, no major influential political groups – including the Socialists and Communists forming the French Popular Front government of 1936–8 – were willing to countenance the total abandonment of colonies. Instead dissatisfaction with existing arrangements took the form of seeking reforms which would at once overcome the immediate abuses of the present situation and provide a sounder basis for long-term African contributions to European prosperity.

The formulation of these new policies emerged from a continuation of the research which had been one of the positive contributions of the earlier imperialist establishment as well as a new level of contact between politicians now responsible for African affairs and professional colonial administrators, many of whom were particularly sensitive to the costs of recent policies. What emerged from this process was a demand for public investment which would place less emphasis on production and distribution and more on social development, particularly in the areas of health and education. The most explicit and far-reaching schemes emerged from consultations between colonial governors and the Popular Front ministers in France in 1936, but the only concrete legislation enacted in this period was the more modest British Colonial Development and Welfare Act of 1940.[13]

Thus the Depression gave African colonies a greater role in European markets and economic policy deliberations. However, the realization of this new conjuncture awaited the changed world conditions of the 1940s and 1950s.

WORLD WAR AND RECONSTRUCTION: THE APOGEE OF NEO-MERCANTILISM

The crises experienced by the European colonial powers during and immediately after the Second World War are conventionally represented as factors contributing directly to the process of decolonization.[14] In political terms, this assumption is quite valid: the war and its aftermath marked the definitive ascendancy of the superpowers, the United States and the Soviet Union, who pressured Britain, France, Belgium, and even Portugal to grant self-government to their overseas possessions. The examples of decolonization in South East Asia, South Asia, and the Middle East had a significant impact upon sub-Saharan Africa and the promulgation of limited constitutional reforms within African territories created an arena for nationalist political mobilization which rapidly produced demands for still greater concessions.

In the economic sphere, however, the importance of Africa for Europe during this period was growing and policies were formulated with the aim of tightening rather than loosening the bonds between colonies and metropoles. This contradiction between political and economic momentum did not result in any severe conflicts because, by the mid-1950s, both the substance and perception of Africa's position in the European economy had again shifted in a direction more consistent with the termination of formal colonial rule. However the intervening phase of what may be termed 'welfare neo-mercantilism' unleashed the main forces of economic change in this period and revealed problems which would continue well beyond the colonial era.

The most directly economic basis for accelerated neo-mercantilism in the 1940s was the sharp rise during this period in world demand for African commodities. The war itself disrupted markets for many of the goods exported from Africa, especially the mainstay of the West African colonies, cocoa. But the combination of suddenly expanded military needs and the cutoff, through Japanese conquest, of competing South East Asian supply areas meant that markets for rubber, sisal and even coffee and cocoa recovered dramatically from their Depression lows. Moreover the mobilization of Africans for military service and the use of African territories as military bases created demands for manpower and food supplies which might otherwise not have entered the market at all.[15]

This rise in demand, reflected in African commodity prices, continued in the post-war era when normal European markets were reopened and, unlike the years immediately following the First World War, did not experience any subsequent crisis. The percentage of French and British trade taken up by African colonies also reached its peak in this period, partly as a result of preferential policies to be discussed below. Similarly, the development investments of the metropoles (see Table 8.1) raised the level of African imports from Europe and also heated up the internal African demand for labour, services, and supplies.

The eclipse of the Western European powers by the United States and the Soviet Union during the Second World War represented the realization of the very nightmare which had spurred on imperialist partition of Africa in the late nineteenth century. In the mid-twentieth century two solutions offered themselves to this dilemma: either to develop the neglected 'colonial estates' as large-scale extensions of separate European national economies, or to integrate Western Europe into a single equivalent of the external superpowers. During the 1930s and 1940s the latter strategy was identified with a dangerous tradition of continental expansion, represented in its latest and most radical form by Adolf Hitler. Overseas colonialism, on the other hand, appeared even in Nazi Germany as the more moderate and rational path to national economic security.[16] After the Second World War, therefore, Britain, France and (to a lesser extent) Belgium chose to recover as much as possible of their previous international status by turning to the colonies. Given the unavoidable loss of control over Asian territories, this meant essentially strengthening economic ties with what looked like the more promising dependencies in Africa.

European neo-mercantilist policies initially ran into serious opposition from American statesmen, whose own goals for the post-war world included an open-door commerical system followed by the speediest possible dissolution of all colonial empires. Once the joint effort against Germany and Japan gave way to Cold War competition with the Soviet Union, however, the United States was easily convinced that the strengthening of its Western European allies took precedence over any economic or political concerns for Africa. If Britain and France needed closer links with their colonies in order to maintain economic stability and as long as such efforts included measures which could also be presented as benefiting Africans, the United States was willing not only to accept them but even to provide major subsidies through Marshall Plan aid.[17] Here we have yet another fold in the convoluted and paradoxical process of Africa's changing position in the new world system. America's concern for European recovery provided the basis for both neo-mercantilism and the economic recovery and integration within Europe which ultimately rendered African colonies economically irrelevant.

The objectives of European colonial policies undertaken during the 1940s revived the visions of earlier empire advocates such as Sarraut and Amery. The African territories were to provide critical raw materials for France and Britain within the zones covered, respectively, by the franc and sterling currencies, both of which were under great pressure from the American dollar. Secondly, metropolitan export industries for both consumer and capital goods might now find a secure market in a sheltered and economically expanding colonial sphere.[18]

To meet these goals, the colonial powers built upon the commercial controls fashioned during the Depression and added both new forms of market intervention and unprecedented levels of development aid. As might be expected from their previous histories, British efforts at pursuing neo-mercantilism in this era were somewhat less elaborate than those of France, although each of the major African colonial systems outdid the other in some areas of innovative economic policy.

The most significant single device for regulating commerce, sterling and franc currency controls, essentially dated back to the earliest stages of colonial rule (see

Chapter 6). Under the foreign exchange crisis conditions of the post-Second World War period, however, Britain and France no longer allowed free conversion of their monies into other currencies, a restriction hitting particularly hard at the African economies which imported so many of their marketed goods. For British territories the need to cover sterling issues by 100 per cent reserve deposits in London also meant that a proportion of the large African export earnings of this era were contributing to the stabilization of the British monetary system as a whole rather than being made available in Africa for local expenditures or investment. France was more liberal, creating during the Second World War a new monetary unit, the CFA (Colonies françaises d'Afrique) franc, which was valid throughout the federations of French West and Equatorial Africa, and also freely exchangeable with the differently valued metropolitan franc. France thus gained no use of financial reserves (few of her African territories ran trading surpluses in any case). However, by exercising control over the central agency which issued CFA francs, the metropole retained immense power over monetary allocations within the entire French African economy.[19]

The tariff structure of Britain and France in relation to their colonies did not change greatly during the 1940s. However a variety of existing and new practices were used to guide the flow of commodities between African territories and the respective metropoles. The great innovation of Britain in this period was 'bulk buying', the purchase by the metropolitan government of the entire output of specific export commodities from various colonies. Bulk purchase had been introduced during the Second World War, partly to provide some income for producers of commodities temporarily cut off from their normal markets (especially West African cocoa), but more commonly to assure Britain a supply of strategic military and food goods. The practice was continued on a selective but very broad basis up to the mid-1950s, mainly to alleviate Britain's continuing difficulty in obtaining tropical goods. The policies were also supposed to provide security for African exports, but the world prices for bulk-purchased goods in this period generally ran well above the amounts paid by the British government, which even made some profits by re-exports outside the sterling zone.[20]

French arrangements for buying from and selling to the African colonies during this period were less obviously novel but far more complex. Some domestic industrial users did enter into bulk-purchasing arrangements for African goods such as vegetable oil and cotton but this was not the most significant form of control. Instead the flow of French colonial goods into the metropole was assured by reinforcement and elaboration of existing tariff preferences, quotas (all foreign purchases had to be 'paired' with equivalent purchases within the franc zone), and legislated *surprix* (above market prices) added on to African goods entering France and French consumer goods entering the colonies. Unlike the British case, costs here were thus shared by African and French consumers, but the effect was to maintain a privileged position for exporters at each end within the imperial marketing system.[21]

The most striking innovation of the post-Second World War colonial economies was the vast increase in public expenditure on African development (see Table 8.1). Not only did Britain and France allot immensely larger sums than metropolitan governments had ever made available under previous legislation, but now the largest part of this funding took the form of outright grants rather than loans. The new policy began officially with the British Colonial Development and Welfare (CDW) Act of 1940, although little money was actually allocated to Africa until after the war, when the amounts allowed were increased farther by the CDW Acts of 1945, 1950, 1955, and 1959. France channelled its major public investments in Africa through the Fonds d'investissement pour le développement économique et social (FIDES), whose first ten-year plan was enacted in 1946 to be followed by a second in 1956. Funds flowing through both these programmes were matched by metropolitan loans and contributions from colonial government revenues.[22]

The titles of CDW and FIDES both indicate an intention to realize the new visions of the later 1930s, in which governmental efforts would be directed towards social as well as economic development. Investments in health, education urban amenities and other aspects of social welfare did have a great impact on Africa during this period, but the breakdown of expenditures in Table 8.1 reveals (more clearly for the French, whose programme was more centralized) that the bulk of the resources continued to go into more traditional projects for improving infrastructure and enhancing productive capacities.

Infrastructure in the post-Second World War context denoted a base for broader developments than the earlier colonial emphasis on railways and harbours. Considerable investment went into motor roads, which allowed more flexible movements of goods within territories and provided opportunities for numerous indigenous transport entrepreneurs. The most ambitious infrastructural projects of this period were dams for generating hydroelectric power.[23] Such ventures were very expensive but fulfilled a longstanding vision of compensating for Africa's lack of easily accessible coal and petroleum by harnessing what appeared like another handicap: the rivers which descended with unnavigable rapidity over the shelf separating the interior of the continent from the coast. Hydroelectric power was also supposed to provide the basis for transcending agriculturally based economies by supplying a major component of industrialization.

As things turned out in the 1950s (and after independence) hydroelectric plants did little to change the structure of African economies. The more successful schemes, as at Edea in Cameroon or Samou in Guinea, sold their energy to aluminium smelters which essentially served external manufacturing economies. Local manufacturing benefited only when it had already been initiated on some previous basis, as exemplified in the cases of the major Owens Falls dam in Uganda and the lesser Djoue project in Congo-Brazzaville, which could only remain profitable by selling large proportions of their generating capacity to the established industrial centres of respectively neighbouring Kenya and the Belgian Congo. The largest of all the dam projects initiated during this period, Kariba on the Zambezi River, was deliberately designed to strengthen existing patterns of growth since its customers were the copper mines of Northern Rhodesia (present-day Zambia) and the relatively well-developed industries of Southern Rhodesia (present-day Zimbabwe).

The public investments of the 1940s and 1950s devoted directly to production enterprises were also more generous in scale and design than their pre-war predecessors. In 1948 Britain funded two special agencies, the Overseas Food Corporation (OFC) and the Colonial Development Corporation (CDC), to initiate and finance productive efforts in Africa while France gave high priority to such projects within both the FIDES plans. The great majority of these efforts involved primary production rather than manufacturing, but some effort was made to encourage the production of minerals, forest and agricultural goods which could be used locally rather than being exported. Nonetheless, the largest individual production undertakings, which absorbed a major proportion of available funds, did concentrate on commodities of strategic concern to the metropoles.

The very large budget of the OFC (see Table 8.1) was expended entirely on a single project, the East African [Tanganyika] Groundnut [peanut] Scheme.[24] The unambiguous goal here was to provide Britain with a secure and inexpensive source of vegetable fats, a vital food item which had to be imported from what looked like an undersupplied world market. FIDES and CDC funds were invested at about the same period in similar, if less massive, mechanized peanut-growing schemes in Senegal and Nigeria. The French also put considerable resources into efforts at increasing African cotton exports through mechanization and large-scale irrigation efforts in what is now Mali (where the pre-war Office du Niger was vastly expanded) and in south-eastern Chad. Unlike the East African scheme, however, these West African projects all included major components of local food production, particularly rice in the two French cotton efforts. The second largest productive enterprise of FIDES, the Richard-Toll irrigation and mechanization project in Senegal, concentrated entirely on growing rice to replace the large imports into this region from Indo-China, which was rapidly moving out of French control.[25]

No element of the entire British and French colonial policy of the immediate post-Second World War era aroused more controversy than the various production schemes. In part, particularly in Britain, the debates centred around the contradictions between neo-mercantilist goals of securing favourable import conditions for primary goods and the claims that development was supposed to give priority to African needs.[26] Metropolitan governments, however, had little problem defending themselves against charges of excessive attention to domestic concerns and African nationalist discontent, as will be seen in Chapter 9, did not focus on this dimension of colonial economics. Instead, what made the production projects so damaging to the whole enterprise of neo-mercantilist policy was their stupendous and unambiguous failure.

In retrospect, the reasons for these failures seem so obvious that it is difficult to understand how such large sums could have been spent in such foolish ways. Much of the explanation must lie in the psychological effect of the Second World War, which at once created a desperation concerning the need to solve the problems of metropolitan decline and colonial stagnation as well as a confidence that efforts of the scale and type used in fighting a highly mechanized war (also paid for, on the Allied side, out of apparently boundless United States resources) could be applied to constructive development efforts.[27]

The projects were based on an assumption that earlier colonialism had opened African land and labour resources to the world market, but that the critical factor now necessary for their efficient utilization was an injection of capital allowing large-scale technological innovation. The primary error in these calculations was an underestimation of the barriers to more intensive exploitation of African land. Lack of reliable rainfall (even in irrigation schemes), soil difficulties, and the attacks of various parasites on crop and livestock products were the most immediate source of difficulties. Secondly, the costs of installing and maintaining mechanized farming equipment in Africa turned out to be far higher than any of the project planners had estimated. Finally, for undertakings such as the Office du Niger and the Mokwa peanut growing area in Nigeria, which depended upon extensive African resettlement, the necessary manpower proved unavailable. The unwillingness of African farmers to take the risk of moving into these areas is easily understood. The major projects were located in savanna regions where colonial

agricultural demands had always involved higher costs to traditional food production systems than the cash crops of African forest and highland zones. Moreover,
the promised material benefits of the new farming settlements were undercut not
only by the declining prices and unexpectedly low outputs of planned crops but
also by the charges which project administrators imposed for production services
and marketing. Existing systems of peasant agriculture were still viable at this time
and, for rural Africans seeking new opportunities, the booming post-war economy
offered other attractions (particularly in the cities) far more appealing than
authoritarian settlement schemes.

DISILLUSIONMENT, PROSPERITY, AND DECOLONIZATION

By themselves, the failures of the massive agricultural development schemes might
not have brought about any decisive change in colonial economic policy towards
Africa. In fact, the European and American sponsors of the projects were more
than capable of absorbing their financial losses and continued, for reasons to be
discussed below, to fund comparable projects in later years. However, the
realization that such efforts would not be likely to bring great benefits to Europe
occurred at a conjuncture in the history of the international economy when
Africa's general position shifted back again to the peripheries of European concern. Metropolitan interests now focused upon relations among European
economies themselves. The institutionalized expression of this shift, the Common
Market/European Economic Community (EEC), in turn became the basis of a
differently structured economic relationship beween the former colonial powers
and Africa.

The most obvious indicator of the changing role for Africa in the larger economic world was the steady decline in the prices of the continent's major export
commodities in the mid-1950s (see Appendix, Figure A4). Despite the growing
demand for such goods in an increasingly prosperous industrial world, supplies
from various tropical areas were now more than sufficient, a condition which was
only temporarily masked by the flurry of panic stockpiling which followed the
outbreak of the Korean War in 1950. At the same time, as indicated in Table A4 of
the Appendix, European trade with Africa began a relative decline compared to
commerce with other industrialized countries, particularly within Europe itself. In
short, European economies had recovered from the trade deficits and commodity
shortage of the 1940s without any significant help from, or perceivable future need
for, their African colonies.[28]

The actual decisions to surrender European sovereignty in Africa, like the
unrolling of the original scramble for colonies, largely followed political rather
than economic lines. The drafting of constitutional reforms, conflicts and negotiations between European officials and African leaders, and considerations of
international status versus the avoidance of overseas warfare occupied far more
debate than questions of commerce and investment.[29] Nonetheless, the heavy-
handed and costly efforts at post-war neo-mercantilist development necessarily
attracted more serious attention within this process than had the largely speculative European stake in nineteenth-century Africa during the colonial partition. It is
worth briefly examining this economic corollary to the politics of decolonization.
The political position of its main protagonists – consistently to the right of
centre – reveals how decisive was the disillusionment with neo-mercantilism; its
substance suggests some of the directions which would be taken by subsequent
relations of economic dependency between Europe and Africa.

The British articulation of disillusionment is easier to trace for several reasons: a greater tradition of public concern with colonial affairs, a greater break between previous economic policies and post-war neo-mercantilism, and the isolation of the more dramatically unsuccessful investment efforts in the OFC and the CDC.

The OFC, whose East African Groundnut Scheme ultimately cost over $190 million, became the target of parliamentary attacks by Conservative MPs as early as 1949 against the Labour government responsible for its initiation; two years later similar assaults were launched against the CDC for the relatively minor costs of the abortive Gambian Poultry Scheme, whose loss turned out to be one item in an ultimate write-off of about $40 million on loans throughout Africa, the West Indies, and South East Asia.[30] The market aspects of neo-mercantilism were attacked in the leading orthodox economic literature of the mid-1950s, especially the very influential *West African Trade* of Peter Bauer, and Charlotte Leubuscher's study of bulk-buying. The epitaph for this entire phase of policy came in a confidential study commissioned by the Conservative government of Harold Macmillian in 1957 which determined that there were no serious economic costs involved in giving way to the political momentum of decolonization.[31]

France's commitment to post-war African development represented a significantly larger share of national income than did that of Britain, but French debates on the economic rationality of such investments surfaced much later and more abruptly. This hesitancy reflected a less central public establishment concerned with colonialism, a greater continuity between the new neo-mercantilism and pre-war policies, and the camouflage of specific projects such as the Office du Niger (ultimately costing about $175 million) in the general structure of FIDES. Indeed, the French carried out most of the investments in their own large Senegal peanut project, the Compagnie générale des oléagineux tropicaux, after the failure of the British East African Groundnut Scheme was already well known.[32]

The major attack on the prevailing policies was finally launched in the mid-1950s, not by parliamentarians or academics but by a popular right-liberal journalist, Raymond Cartier of *Paris Match*. *Cartierisme* quickly became shorthand for a belief that public investments in Africa represented wasteful use of resources that were needed for economic and social development in metropolitan France. This position was subsequently adopted by economists and politicians and attacked by French and African figures both to the right and left of centre. However, its direct influence on government policy is difficult to trace, since the decisive political steps regarding sub-Saharan Africa depended immediately upon the crisis in Algeria and the replacement of the Fourth Republic with the new regime of Charles de Gaulle.[33]

The positive side of European economic disillusionment with African colonies was the accompanying recognition of great potentialities for metropolitan growth through closer ties with other industrial powers. Such a shift in orientation required changes in both domestic investment patterns and foreign trade policies but it also provided potential assistance in what now seemed like the onerous burden of public investment in tropical dependencies.

France, which was slower to recognize the costs of the post-war colonial endeavours, was quicker to confront the alternatives, due to its founding role in the formation of the EEC. During the early stages of negotiations leading to the 1957 Treaty of Rome, which formally established the EEC, French colonial interests were defended against the pressures of other powers. But by 1956 both France and Belgium were urging the other participants to share responsibility for aid to

Africa. The result was the inclusion of the French and Belgian dependencies in the new organization as 'associates' with the former metropoles still playing a major patron role but trade and aid relations open to the entire EEC.[34]

Britain's unsuccessful first attempt to enter the EEC in 1961–2 required the dissolution of the Commonwealth Preference system established in 1933, but this structure had never directly affected most African colonies. At the time when France was already entering the EEC the British government was indicating a similar desire to rid itself of aid burdens by ruling that the somewhat discredited CDC should cease making loans to newly independent territories, which were now required to turn for such assistance to the private-sector-based Commonwealth Financial Development Corporation or the multilateral World Bank and International Monetary Fund. The shifting locus of initiatives in maintaining such relations is indicated by the pressure put upon Britain by tropical ex-colonies to continue this aid programme, which survived as the Commonwealth Development Corporation.[35]

Soon after their independence the former French and Belgian African territories (together with Somalia) negotiated a new form of preferential trade association with the EEC through the 1963 Yaoundé Convention. Nationalist leaders in other parts of Africa initially rejected this arrangement as neo-colonial, but in subsequent years participated in a new set of conventions linking them to the EEC on similar terms (Arusha 1968, 1969; Lomé 1975, 1980). Out of these arrangements emerged a formal grouping of fifty-four 'developing countries', the ACP (Africa, Caribbean, and Pacific Countries; forty-four of the countries and an overwhelming proportion of the population and territory are African). The self-professed African motivation for joining the ACP was fear that outsiders would lose access to European markets and EEC aid. In fact, despite the conventions, the trading position of Africa in all portions of the EEC (including, finally, France) declined significantly in the first decades after independence. The ACP–EEC relationship thus embodies the continuity of both the market shifts leading to decolonization and the dependency ties inherited from colonialism.[36] Before examining the external motivations for maintaining these ties it is necessary to consider some other economic dimensions of the the neo-mercantile/decolonization process.

Costs and benefits of change: European private sectors

The currents of broad world market trends and European public policy deliberations do not tell us everything we need to know about the links between African colonial development and the world economy. A wide range of private European entrepreneurs had stakes in African colonialism as merchants, producers of export commodities within Africa, and providers of metropolitan goods and services to Africa. All of these undertakings were affected by the same market factors which influenced public policy decisions and had to come to terms with the impact of policy changes. While colonialism was essential for the development of most of these private interests, it is surprising to note how little impact they made upon the politics of decolonization. The reasons for this weak defence of empire vary from case to case, but we can broadly divide the interests involved into those whose changed position made them indifferent to the political regimes ruling Africa and those whose vulnerability to decolonization was matched by their insignificance for the metropolitan economies.[37]

The clearest example of a successful transition from a classical colonial situation to the neo-mercantilist and post-colonial eras is offered by the large trading firms of West Africa. It will be remembered that by the 1920s the export-import commerce of this region had come under the domination of a small group of enterprises (see Chapter 6). The Great Depression of the 1930s had further strengthened the position of these firms by eliminating still more of the intermediate trading organizations which could compete with them. However, the obvious nature of the oligopoly which subsequently developed made the firms vulnerable to criticism from frustrated African merchants (see Chapter 9) and to restriction or competition from government intervention in the purchase of export goods.

After the Second World War the firms themselves recognized that even without external pressures, the profits to be made from sprawling, low-capital marketing networks were less attractive than alternative investment of their now considerable assets. One response to this situation was to withdraw capital from Africa, as is evident in the cases of the two largest French firms, CFAO and SCOA. However the expanded scale of market production and public development investment in Africa also offered the firms opportunities to exploit their established colonial position by moving into new areas of engineering contracting, the import and servicing of consumer durables (e.g. automobiles and refrigerators), and the more sophisticated distribution of general consumer goods through urban supermarkets (also a popular investment for these companies in Europe). While thus profiting from the new affluence at the centres of the colonial economy, the trading firms turned over rural produce-buying and petty retailing to African entrepreneurs, whether in the private or the state sector. In effect, the trading companies now concentrated on activities where they created no competitive tension with Africans and were not even dependent on Africa for the entire continuity of their operations. The low-risk commercial operations of the colonial era were successfully transformed into more capital-intensive but also more diversified operations suitable for the age of decolonization.[38]

European enterprises directly engaged in export production through mining and agriculture, on the other hand, would appear to have been severely threatened by decolonization, which could potentially deprive them of their control over African land and labour. In reality the transition did not necessarily damage the larger operations with an enclave character although it was resisted by settler farmers who depended upon the colonial state in their competition with African commercial cultivators. In the large-scale operations the post-Second World War period accelerated the process of 'labour stabilization' which at once reduced tension between European owners and their black labour force (see Chapter 9) and insulated the enterprises from changes in the territory as a whole. The major fear of such firms was that African nationalism might take a radical form which would disrupt orderly links to external markets and seek to nationalize large private property.

In the two cases which are well documented, those of the copper mining firms Union Minière in the Belgian Congo (Zaire) and Anglo American and Roan Selection Trusts in Northern Rhodesia (Zambia), it is quite clear that little attempt was made to persuade the metropolitan governments to resist African demands for self-government. In both areas the mining corporations found themselves drawn into financing conservative alternatives to the main nationalist programme: in the Congo, Union Minière supported the secession of Katanga (now Shaba) province the site of their operations; and in the neighbouring British areas Anglo American and Roan Selection Trust backed attempts to hold Northern Rhodesia in the Central African Federation which was dominated by Southern Rhodesian whites. But in neither case did the mining interests initiate or significantly control such manoeuvres or restrict their financial contributions to conservative parties; when the nationalists ultimately won control, no punitive action was taken. Ultimately, and for quite different reasons, both Zaire and Zambia did nationalize their copper mines. But basically the same European firms had to be kept in place as the operators of the mines and market intermediaries abroad on terms which did not severely damage their economic position.[39]

The European economic losers in decolonization (and the main forces behind such efforts as Katanga secession and the Central African Federation) were smaller-scale entrepreneurs in commerce and, especially, agriculture as well as privileged white workers in the mining sectors. While some measures were taken by European governments to see that such groups did not suffer unduly when Africans replaced them (particularly in the case of the Kenya settlers, generously compensated for giving up landholdings) the process of change revealed how insignificant – even burdensome – they were to long-term European interests in the continent.[40] Another group to suffer were the Levantines and South Asian merchants, manufacturers, and planters who had taken up intermediate-scale positions between the European and African populations. These communities played no very significant role in decolonization politics but after independence were left in a highly ambiguous situation of expanded economic opportunity combined with threats to their property and political rights. These included confiscation and expulsion as well as pressures, at least in East Africa, to declare themselves local citizens, thus abandoning any protection from the governments of the former colonial power or their countries of origin.[41] The critical problem, from an African perspective, was how such a cadre of locally based entrepreneurs would be replaced.

In metropolitan Europe, industrial exporters, taken as a whole had never found the African colonies to be a significant proportion of their market. However, certain sectors of manufacturing, mainly the British and French cotton goods industry, did depend heavily upon colonial protectionism to mitigate their general decline on the world market, especially against competition from Japan and India. Here the preferential quotas of the 1930s mark the high point of neo-mercantilism. After the Second World War metropolitan economic planners developed enough confidence in more sophisticated industries to leave African textile markets not only to Asians but also to the Africans themselves. Expansion of such primary industrialization in the Third World – like politically supported late colonial development projects – increased the demand for European capital goods as well as specialized consumer products so that the more dynamic manufacturing sectors of the home economy had little to fear and something to gain from the dismantling of the earlier colonial structures.[42]

Given the positive effect of both late colonial and post-colonial development programmes upon sectors of the Western economy which had scarcely been involved in Africa before, a final set of issues has to be explored concerning the influence of such interests upon the policies leading to decolonization. Radical critics of this process have raised two such questions. First, given the fact that a considerable number of the more sophisticated firms in the post-Second World War international economy were multinational corporations based in the United States, did United States anti-colonialism in this era, like British liberalism in the mid-nineteenth century, function as a device for preventing weaker competitors from protecting their markets against the major industrial power of the time?[43] Second, can it be argued, from a more general Western perspective, that the development and aid expenditures of the late colonial and post-colonial periods were designed primarily to subsidize not Africans but the metropolitan contractors, technicians and capital goods suppliers who were the immediate recipients of most of the funds allocated?[44] There is important empirical evidence to support both these contentions, but ultimately it appears that they misrepresent Africa's position in the contemporary world economy.

During and immediately after the Second World War the United States government was subject to some pressure from domestic private firms and their collective representatives, including the National Association of Manufacturers and the US Chamber of Commerce, to eliminate protectionist trade restrictions in Africa and other portions of the then colonial world. The leaders of the United States economy were still haunted at this time by the trauma of the 1930s Depression and encouraged to seek trade outlets in Africa by their ability to penetrate the continent's markets through wartime Lend-Lease supply programmes. Official American responses to these urgings included demands not only for political reforms in the colonies but also a new international commercial system, under the rubric of the International Trading Organization, which would eliminate all vestiges of earlier protectionism.[45]

As already demonstrated at some length, however, the economic regime governing Africa during the subsequent decades took the form not of liberalization but rather of intensified neo-mercantilism. Furthermore, there is little evidence of United States objections to these arrangements after the mid-1940s. The major grounds for retreating from earlier open-door demands were undoubtedly political: the strengthening of Western Europe against perceived Communist threats vastly outweighed any interest in African markets. The role of tropical Africa in US trade did decline during this period from a wartime peak of 3.6 per cent to an average of below 2 per cent between 1948 and 1960. However the simultaneous boom in the American domestic economy as well as the large increase of trade with other areas of the world made this African shift (including the rise to 2.6 per cent in the post-independence decades) quite unimportant. As for the United States firms most concerned with retaining their new African foothold of the mid-1940s, the manufacturers of automotive and farm equipment, they had little to worry about since their overall exports climbed dramatically in the post-war period.[46] There are no easily available statistics about the proportion of this trade going to Africa, but it is known that Britain was unable to supply enough tractors from its home industries to support the East African Groundnut Scheme and thus had to contract for new equipment from the Canadian firm of Massey-Ferguson, which produced the requisite machines in United States factories.[47]

The most controversial American postures concerning African decolonization emerged after the first wave of independence in the early 1960s when political attention focused on those regions of Southern Africa still under the rule of Portugal (Angola and Mozambique) or local white settlers (Rhodesia and South Africa). Although the United States had more significant economic stakes in this region than in the tropical areas which earlier came under black rule, it does not appear that these gave any clear direction to what was always a rather equivocal policy.

The Portuguese case was particularly difficult since, unlike the core West

European advanced industrial societies, Portugal depended heavily upon supplies of raw cotton from Mozambique and profits from Angolan diamond and coffee exports to sustain its metropolitan economy. Portugal also belonged to the North Atlantic Treaty Organization, occupying a strategic position at the entry to the Mediterranean Sea, and was thus supplied by the United States with weapons, which it used in African anti-colonial wars. Nonetheless, Portuguese colonial authorities considered the United States sufficiently unreliable to exclude American firms from their major African development project in Africa, the huge Cabora Bassa dam in Mozambique.[48]

United States corporations which were operating in Angola and Rhodesia maintained a very apolitical position during the independence crises of these territories. Gulf Oil in the Cabinda enclave adjoining Angola received military protection from the Portuguese regime in return for important revenues but after independence continued the same co-operation with a Marxist government which was not even recognized by the United States.[49] During the period of autonomous but also unrecognized white rule in Rhodesia, right-wing American groups lobbied for the removal of sanctions on trade between Rhodesia and the United States; but there is no evidence that the supposed major corporate beneficiaries of such a change, the domestic manufacturers of ferrochrome metals, played an important role in this agitation. In the case of fully industrialized South Africa, replacement of white by black rule will obviously require much more radical political changes than even in the rest of Southern Africa and foreign corporate investments here are no longer an autonomous factor but rather an immediate target of those who wish to undermine the present regime. The response of American corporations has been to seek a 'middle ground' by promising to counter apartheid through egalitarian race relations within the bounds of their own enterprises.[50]

In both tropical and Southern Africa the political role of the United States has expanded dramatically since the 1960s. However everywhere but in South Africa the economic pattern remains essentially that which was set in the period of neo-mercantilism: marginal trade and investments linked through Europe to the complex world of multinational corporations rather than specific national interests. Immediate African commercial and capital ties thus remain focused on Europe. But how has the vast increase in the scale of these ties benefited the advanced sectors of the Western economy as a whole?

While the major goal of neo-mercantilist public policies in the post-Second World War era had been to secure vital raw materials supplies and shelters against dollar outflows, a subsidiary theme was the shift from consumer to capital-goods exports. Superficially, therefore, this last phase of colonialism resembles a belated affirmation of the Hobson-Lenin thesis, which envisioned capital surpluses as the taproot of imperialism'. Indeed there is evidence from statements by the architects of this new colonial policy that their aim was to provide outlets for the expansion of their own advanced technology which could thus remain competitive with industries developed within the larger domestic market of the United States.[51]

The difficulty with pursuing such an interpretation of development efforts in the Africa of the 1940s and 1950s is that Western capital markets during this entire period were in a deficit rather than a surplus situation. Europe had to borrow – and accept outright grants – from the United States in order to reconstruct its own war-damaged economy, although demands for capital in the expanding United States were by no means slack. The *cartieriste* critique of continued investment in the African colonies rested precisely upon the contention that capital thus expended could otherwise be used to improve social conditions in Europe or to build a metropolitan industrial base better geared to trading with other advanced Western countries. This is not merely a theoretical argument, as illustrated in the case of France by the competition for public support between large textile firms which had shifted part of their manufacturing bases to Africa and corporations of comparable size but working with more advanced technology, for whom Africa remained an entirely insignificant market. It is the latter firms which have gained a dominant influence in French government industrial policies.[52]

Postscript: the contemporary world economy and Africa

The end of neo-mercantilist policies and colonial regimes has not brought about an absolute decline in either external investment in Africa or African economic development. It has meant, however, that the flow of outside capital into Africa is no longer governed by the imperatives of creating a critical adjunct to the metropolitan economy or assuming direct responsibility for the outcome of such ventures within Africa.

It is the continuing decline of Africa's role in the world market which most immediately explains this economic indifference of Europeans and Americans. African agriculture, far from being the source of scarce export goods, now attracts attention principally because of its diminishing capacity for providing Africans themselves with sufficient food.[53] Mineral exports have at times attained high prices, particularly petroleum from Nigeria and Gabon from the mid-1970s, but this lever on the international economy proved short-lived (see Appendix, Figure A5). Publicists on the right and left occasionally point to the diamond and metal resources of Central and Southern Africa as a 'Persian Gulf of minerals' vital to the industrialized portions of the world. But prices for these commodities over the last decades, which reflect the wide range of stockpiles, alternative sources, and substitutes, suggest only the negative dimensions of the analogy with petroleum.[54] Some attempt has been made to bring a few African states into the family of 'newly industrializing countries' by using them as a base for the manufacture of low-cost export articles and components but so far (for reasons to be discussed in Chapter 9) this effort has also proved unprofitable.

If tropical Africa is really so marginal to the post-colonial world economy, what has kept investments flowing into the region? In general, the explanation for this phenomenon closely resembles those for Africa's growing involvement in the international system during the nineteenth-century interlude between the end of the slave trade and the onset of imperialist partition. A major factor here is the simple growth of the world economy as a whole, which simultaneously reduces Africa's relative position while increasing its absolute access to markets and capital. Secondly, there is a direct link, via colonial ventures and colonial guilt, between the ideologies of anti-slavery and development aid. Both these belief systems are linked in complex ways to the internal tensions of metropolitan industrial societies and (in the post-colonial world) the institutional role of such international organizations as the United Nations, the International Labour Organization, and the World Bank. Thus, it is not always necessary to seek out any immediate economic return as the explanation for a particular set of African investment decisions.

Perhaps the most compelling theme in all these efforts echoes the immediate motivations of the colonial partition: a concern for maintaining key strategic positions in a highly competitive (and for the United States, essentially polarized) world political order. Even a good deal of private-sector investment in Africa can be seen in these terms, as multinational corporations place marginal percentages of their capital in marginal markets so as to avoid losing what may at some distant horizon turn out to be critical increments of advantage to competitors.[55]

In the public sphere, American and West European investment, which accounts for the major share of both bilateral and multilateral aid to Africa, is motivated to a considerable extent by fear of losing influence on the continent to the Soviet bloc. Africanists regularly denounce such attitudes as both selfish and unrealistic, since they subsume the internal needs of African development to an elaborate set of donor-defined political, ideological, and even military considerations.[56] However, as in the paradoxical relationship between America, Europe, and Africa during the neo-mercantilist period, these Cold War concerns may have become the main basis for directing material resources of some kind to Africa.

The most serious cost to Africa of foreign investments not guided by any realistic concern for the continent's own needs is an increasing polarization between the base and the superstructure of the African economy. The former has not changed radically from the peasant agriculture of the 1920s, punctuated by enclaves of more intensive production. The infrastructure, as represented by technology and social organization dedicated to government, transport, communications, secondary industry and high-level consumption, has grown immensely over the last forty years but remains concentrated in the cities and heavily dependent upon external support. Because of this support, African post-colonial regimes have been able to continue the projects of transformation initiated during the neo-mercantilist era. The course of some of these efforts and their results will be assessed in the next chapter.

Notes

1. Wallerstein (1976).
2. Hopkins (1973); Wallerstein (1976); Robinson (1972) (for both perspectives). See Flint (1983) for an essentially political argument consistent with the present account.
3. Coquery-Vidrovitch (1976c); Gallagher (1982); Marseille (1984) are closer to the argument used here than the 'open–closed economy' thesis of Hopkins (1973). I will return to the latter in Chapter 9.
4. Yeung and Singh (1976).
5. Fieldhouse (1971); Smith (1974).
6. Drummond (1972) is good on British policy during this period; Andrew and Kanya-Forstner (1981) pp. 209–48 and Sauvy (1965) Vol. 1, pp. 107–8 are less satisfactory for France; Marseille (1984) is an insightful account of French colonial economics which became available too late to be taken fully into account in this chapter.
7. Meredith (1975) is the main source; see also Munro (1976); Coquery-Vidrovitch (1976b); Austen and Headrick (1983); Vail (1975).
8. Fieldhouse (1971) pp. 602–5; Munro (1976) pp. 157–61; Smith (1974).
9. Coquery-Vidrovitch (1976a); Guyer (1980, 1981); Jewsiewicki (1977); Milewski (1975).
10. Fieldhouse (1971).

11. See references in note 9; McCarthy (1982) pp. 65–78; Ehrler (1977).
12. Drummond (1972) pp. 66–7; Andrew and Kanya-Forstner (1981), pp. 247–8.
13. Abbot (1970); Coquery-Vidrovitch (1976b); Marseille (1977); Morgan (1980).
14. Albertini (1971); Louis (1977); Gifford and Louis (1982) (the chapters by Fieldhouse and Suret-Canale on economic issues in this last volume are useful but not tied well into the more general issues of decolonization).
15. We do not have a really good account of the Second World War and Africa; *faute de mieux* see Leubuscher (1956); Olusanya (1973).
16. Hildebrand (1969, 1970); Michalka (1983).
17. Gardner (1956); Gardner (1964); the American retreat from earlier open-door aims has received less attention than the original statements of intentions, leading to such skewed interpretations of international relations in this period as Wallerstein (1980). For details on Marshall Plan contributions to colonial development funds, see Price (1955), espec. pp. 384–5.
18. Suret-Canale (1972) (summarized in his contribution Gifford and Louis, 1982) gives a good account of French neo-mercantilism but the British version is covered only briefly in Fieldhouse (1982); Pearce (1982) pp. 94–7; more to the point is Cowen (1982).
19. Fieldhouse (1971) pp. 606–13.
20. Leubuscher (1956).
21. Suret-Canale (1972) pp. 136–49.
22. Morgan (1980); Rendell (1976) (on CDW); Coquery-Vidrovitch (1976b); Hayter (1966); Suret-Canale (1972) pp. 103–11, 116–22.
23. Rubin and Warren (1968); Suret-Canale (1972) pp. 67–77.
24. Hogendorn (1981); Morgan (1980) Vol. 2, p. 295.
25. Baldwin (1957); Beusekom (1984); De Wilde et al. (1967); Suret-Canale (1972) pp. 122–6, 130–2; Stuerzinger (1980).
26. Morgan (1980); Cowen (1982).
27. Wood (1950).
28. Cairncross (1981); Girault (1982) (both these works indicate very dramatically the shift of British and French trade out of the respective currency zones).
29. Goldsworthy (1971) (it is significant that there is no French equivalent for this book; cf. citations in notes 32, 33 below).
30. Goldsworthy (1971) pp. 200–2; Morgan (1980); Rendell (1976).
31. Bauer (1954); Leubuscher (1956); Morgan (1980).
32. Suret-Canale (1972) pp. 202–4.
33. Albertini (1971); Sorum (1977); Ehrhard (1957) is a rather weak scholarly statement of the *cartieriste* position; Marseille (1984) begins his book with a citation from Cartier, but discusses *cartierisme* under the heading *complexe hollandais* (pp. 357–65).
34. Burgelin (1964); Zartman (1971) pp. 6–18.
35. Rendell (1976).
36. Mytelka and Dolon (1980); Zartman (1971).
37. Kahler (1984) p. 274f. gives the best general treatment of this theme.
38. Coquery-Vidrovitch (1975); Hopkins (1976).
39. Sklar (1978); Peemans (1980).
40. Chanock (1977); Kahler (1981); Wasserman (1976).
41. Ghai and Ghai (1970); Van der Laan (1975).
42. Drummond (1972) pp. 121–37; Marseille (1975); Mytelka (1982).
43. Wallerstein (1980).
44. Suret-Canale (1972) pp. 156–64; Hayter (1971).
45. Dougherty (1975); Gardner (1964); Maier (1977).
46. US Department of Commerce (1953, 1965, 1979).
47. Morgan (1980) Vol. 2, pp. 253–4.
48. Middlemas (1975) p. 49f.
49. Maxwell (1982); Minter (1972).
50. Lake (1976); Meyers (1981).

51. Morgan (1980) p. 21f. (good documentation of the simultaneity of concerns for developing capital goods markets and the shortage of capital); for France, see the discussion of colonial industrialization in Marseille (1984) p. 332f.
52. Mytelka (1982).
53. Berry (1984).
54. Jackson (1982).
55. Hymer (1977).
56. Jackson (1982).

Bibliography

Abbot, George (1970), 'British colonial aid policy during the 1930s', *Canadian Journal of History*, vol. 5, pp. 73–89

Albertini, Rudolph von (1971), *Decolonization: The Administration and Future of the Colonies, 1919–1960* (New York: Doubleday)

Andrew, Christopher M. and A.S. Kanya-Forstner (1981), *France Overseas: The Great War and the Climax of French Imperialism* (London: Thames & Hudson)

Austen, Ralph A. and Rita Headrick (1983), 'Equatorial Africa under colonial rule', in Birmingham and Martin (eds), pp. 27–94

Baldwin, K.D.S. (1957), *The Niger Agricultural Project* (Cambridge: Harvard University Press)

Bauer, P.T. (1954), *West African Trade: A Study of Competition, Oligopoly, and Monopoly* (Cambridge: Cambridge University Press)

Berry, Sara A. (1984), 'Agrarian crisis in Africa? a review and an interpretation', *African Studies Review*, vol. 27, pp. 59–112

Beusekom, Monica van (1984), 'Problems surrounding rice cultivation at the Office du Niger' (Unpublished workshop paper, Johns Hopkins University)

Birmingham, David and Phyllis M. Martin (eds) (1983), *History of Central Africa*, Vol. 2 (London: Longman)

Bloch-Lainé, François (1956), *La zone franc* (Paris: PUF)

Bouvier, Jean *et al.* (eds) (1982), *Histoire économique et sociale de la France* (Paris: PUF)

Burgelin, Henri (1964), 'La décolonisation et les relations entre puissances occidentales', in J.-B. Duroselle and Jean Meyriat (eds), *La communauté internationale face aux jeunes états* (Paris: Colin), pp. 61–97

Cairncross, Alec (1981), 'The postwar years, 1945–77', in Roderick Floud and Donald McCloskey (eds), *The Economic History of Britain since 1700*, Vol. 2 (Cambridge: Cambridge University Press), pp. 370–416

Chanock, Martin (1977), *Unconsummated Union: Rhodesia and South Africa, 1900–1945* (Manchester: Manchester University Press)

Clarence-Smith, Gervase (1983), 'Capital accumulation and class formation in Angola', in Birmingham and Martin (eds), pp. 163–99

Constantine, Stephen (1984), *The Making of British Colonial Development Policy, 1914–1940* (London: Frank Cass)

Coquery-Vidrovitch, Catherine (1975), 'L'impact des intérêts coloniaux: SCOA et CFAO dans l'ouest africain, 1910–1965', *Journal of African History*, vol. 16, no. 4, pp. 595–624

Coquery-Vidrovitch, Catherine (ed.) (1976a), *L'Afrique et la crise de 1930 (1924–1938)* Special Number of Revue Française d'Histoire d'Outre-Mer, vol. 63, nos. 232/233

Coquery-Vidrovitch, Catherine (1976b), 'L'impérialisme français en Afrique noire: idéologie impériale et politique d'équipement, 1924–1975', *Relations Internationale*, vol. 7, pp. 261–82

Coquery-Vidrovitch, Catherine (1976c), 'Le mise en dépendance de l'Afrique noire: essai de periodisation, 1800–1970', *Cahiers d'Etudes Africaines*, vol. 16, no. 1, pp. 7–58

Coquery-Vidrovitch, Catherine (1978), 'Economie de traite et misère des investissements en Afrique noire', *Herodote*, vol. 11, pp. 68–96

Coquery-Vidrovitch, Catherine (1979), 'Colonisation ou impérialisme: la politique africaine de la France entre les deux guerres', *Mouvement Sociale*, vol. 107, pp. 51–76

Cowen, Michael (1982), 'The British state and agrarian accumulation in Kenya', in Martin Fransman (ed.), *Industry and Accumulation in Africa* (London: Heinemann), pp. 142–69

De Wilde, John C. et al. (1967), *Experiences with Agricultural Development in Tropical Africa*, Vol. 2, *Case Studies* (Baltimore: Johns Hopkins University Press)

Dougherty, James J. (1975), 'Lend-lease and the opening of French North and West Africa to private trade', *Cahiers d'Etudes Africaines*, vol. 15, no. 3, pp. 481–500

Dougherty, James J. (1978), *The Politics of Wartime Aid: American Assistance to France and French Northwest Africa, 1940–1946* (Westport: Greenwood Press)

Drummond, Ian M. (1972), *British Economic Policy and the Empire, 1919–1939* (London: Allen & Unwin)

Ehrhard, Jean (1957), *Le destin du colonialisme* (Paris: Eyrolles)

Ehrler, Franz (1977), *Handelskonflikte zwischen europaeischen Firmen und einheimischen Produzenten in Britisch Westafrika: die 'Cocoa Holdups' in der Zwischenkrieqzeit* (Zurich: Atlantis)

Fieldhouse, David K. (1971), 'The economic exploitation of Africa: some British and French comparisons', in Prosser Gifford and Wm Roger Louis (eds), *France and Britain in Africa* (New Haven: Yale University Press), pp. 593–662

Fieldhouse, David K. (1982), 'Decolonization, development, and dependence: a survey of changing attitudes', in Gifford and Louis (eds), pp. 483–514

Flint, John (1983), 'Planned decolonization and its failure in British Africa', *African Affairs*, vol. 82, no. 328, pp. 389–411

Gallagher, John (1982), *The Decline, Renewal, and Fall of the British Empire* (London: Oxford University Press)

Gardner, Lloyd C. (1964), *Economic Aspects of New Deal Diplomacy* (Madison: University of Wisconsin Press)

Gardner, Richard N. (1956), *Sterling–Dollar Diplomacy* (Oxford: Clarendon Press)

Ghai, D.P. and Y.D. Ghai (eds) (1970), *Portrait of a Minority: The Indians of Uganda* (Nairobi: Oxford University Press)

Gifford, Prosser and Wm Roger Louis (eds) (1982), *The Transfer of Power in Africa: Decolonization, 1940–1960* (New Haven: Yale University Press)

Girault, René (1982), 'Les relations économiques avec l'extérieur (1945–1975)', in Bouvier et al. (eds), pp. 1379–1423

Goldsworthy, David (1971), *Colonial Issues in British Politics, 1945–1961* (Oxford: Clarendon Press)

Guyer, Jane (1980), 'Head-tax, social structure, and rural income in Cameroon, 1922–1937', *Cahiers d'Etudes Africaines*, vol. 20, pp. 305–29

Guyer, Jane (1981), 'The Depression and the administration in South Central Cameroon', *African Economic History*, no. 10, pp. 67–79

Hayter, Theresa (1966), *French Aid* (London: Overseas Development Institute)

Hayter, Theresa (1971), *Aid as Imperialism* (Harmondsworth: Penguin)

Hildebrand, Klaus (1969), *Vom Reich zum Weltreich: Hitler, NSDAP und Kolonialfrage, 1919–1945* (Berlin: Wilhelm Funk)

Hildebrand, Klaus (1970), *The Foreign Policy of the Third Reich* (Berkeley: University of California Press)

Hogendorn, Jan (1981), 'The East African Groundnut Scheme: lessons of a large-scale agricultural failure', *African Economic History*, no. 10, pp. 81–115

Hopkins, A.G. (1973), *An Economic History of West Africa* (New York: Columbia University Press)

Hopkins, A.G., (1976), 'Imperial business in Africa. Part II: interpretations', *Journal of African History*, vol. 17, no. 2, pp. 267–90

Hymer, Stephen (1977), *The Multinational Corporation: A Radical Approach* (Cambridge: Cambridge University Press)

Jackson, Henry F. (1982), *From the Congo to Soweto: United States Foreign Policy toward Africa since 1960* (New York: Morrow)

Jewsiewicki, Bogumil (1977), 'The Great Depression and the making of the colonial economic system in the Belgian Congo', *African Economic History*, no. 4, pp. 153–76

Kahler, Miles (1981), 'Political regimes and economic actors: the response of firms to the end of the colonial era', *World Politics*, vol. 33, no. 3, pp. 383–412

Kahler, Miles (1984), *Decolonization in Britain and France: The Domestic Consequences of International Relations* (Princeton: Princeton University Press)

Kesner, Richard M. (1981), *Economic Control and Colonial Development: Crown Colony Financial Management in the Age of Joseph Chamberlain* (Westport, Conn.: Greenwood Press)

Killingray, David (1982), 'The Empire Resources Development Committee and West Africa, 1916–1920', *Journal of Imperial and Commonwealth History*, vol. 10, pp. 194–210

Kirkpatrick, Colin and Frederick Nixson (1981), 'Transnational corporations and economic development', *Journal of Modern African Studies*, vol. 19, no. 3, pp. 367–99

Kolko, Joyce and Gabriel Kolko (1972), *The Limitations of Power: The World and United States Foreign Policy, 1945–1954* (New York: Harper & Row)

Lake, Anthony (1976), *The 'Tarbaby' Option: American Foreign Policy toward Southern Rhodesia* (New York: Columbia University Press)

Lee, J.M. (1967), *Colonial Development and Good Government: An Examination of the Ideas Expressed by the British Official Classes in Planning Decolonization, 1939-1964* (Oxford: Clarendon Press)

Leubuscher, Charlotte (1956), *Bulk Buying from the Colonies* (London: Oxford University Press)

Louis, Wm Roger (1977), *Imperialism at Bay, 1941–1945: The United States and the Decolonization of the British Empire* (Oxford: Clarendon Press)

McCarthy, D.M.P. (1982), *Colonial Bureaucracy and Creating Underdevelopment: Tanganyika, 1919–1940* (Ames: Iowa State University Press)

McGhee, George (1983), *Envoy to the Middle World: Adventures in Diplomacy* (New York: Harper & Row)

Maier, Charles (1977), 'The politics of productivity: foundations of American economic policy after World War II', *International Organization*, vol. 31, pp. 607–33

Manning, Patrick (1982), *Slavery, Colonialism and Economic Growth in Dahomey, 1640–1960* (Cambridge: Cambridge University Press)

Marseille, Jacques (1975), 'L'industrie cotonnière française et l'impérialisme coloniale'. *Revue d'Histoire Economique et Sociale*, vol. 53, no. 213, pp. 386–412

Marseille, Jacques (1977), 'Le conférence des gouverneurs généraux des colonies (novembre 1936)', *Mouvement Sociale*, vol. 101, pp. 61–84

Marseille, Jacques (1984), *Empire colonial et capitalisme français: histoire d'un divorce* (Paris: Albin Michel)

Maxwell, Kenneth (1982), 'Portugal and Africa: the last empire', in Gifford and Louis (eds), pp. 337–85

Meredith, David (1975), 'The British government and colonial economic policy, 1919–1939', *Economic History Review*, vol. 28, no. 3, pp. 484–98

Meyers, III, Desaix (1981), 'U.S. domestic controversy over American business in South Africa', in Alfred O. Hero Jr and John Barnett (eds), *The American People and South Africa* (Lexington: D.C. Heath), pp. 67–82

Michalka, Wolfgang (1983), 'Conflict within the German leadership on objectives and tactics of foreign policy, 1933–9', in Wolfgang Mommsen and Lothar Kettenacker (eds), *The Fascist Challenge and the Policy of Appeasement* (London: Allen & Unwin), pp. 48–60

Middlemas, Keith (1975), *Cabora Bassa: Engineering and Politics in Southern Africa* (London: Weidenfeld & Nicholson)

Milewski, Jan (1975), 'The Great Depression of the early 1930s in a colonial country: a case study of Nigeria', *Africana Bulletin*, vol. 23, pp. 7–45

Minter, William (1972), *Portuguese Africa and the West* (New York: Monthly Review Press)

Mitchell, B.R. and Phyllis Dean (1962), *Abstract of British Historical Statistics* (Cambridge: Cambridge University Press)

Morgan, D.J. (1980), *The Official History of Colonial Development* (5 Vols, London: Macmillan)

Munro, J. Forbes (1976), *Africa and the International Economy, 1800-1960* (London: Dent)

Mytelka, Lynn Krieger (1982), 'The French textile industry: crisis and adjustment', in Harold K. Jacobson and Dusan Sidjanski (eds), *The Emerging International Order* (Beverley Hills: Sage), pp. 129–166

Mytelka, Lynn and Michael Dolon (1980), 'The EEC and the APC countries', in Dudley Seers and Constantine Vaitsos (eds), *Integration and Unequal Development: the Experience of the EEC* (New York: St Martin's Press), pp. 237–60

Ngango, Georges (1973), *Les investissements d'origine extérieure en Afrique Noire francophone* (Paris: Présence Africaine)

OEEC (Organization for European Economic Co-Operation) (1961), *The Flow of Financial Resources to Countries in the Course of Economic Development, 1956-1959* (Paris: OEEC)

Olusanya, G.O. (1973), *The Second World War and Politics in Nigeria, 1939-1953* (London: Evans)

Pearce, R.D. (1982), *The Turning Point in Africa: British Colonial Policy, 1938-1948* (London: Cass)

Peemans, Jean-Philippe (1980), 'Imperial hangovers: Belgium – the economics of decolonization', *Journal of Contemporary History*, vol. 15, no. 2, pp. 257–86

Poquin, Jean-Jacques (1957), *Les relations extérieures des pays d'Afrique Noire de l'Union Française, 1925-1955* (Paris: A. Colin)

Price, Harry Bayard (1955), *The Marshall Plan and its Meaning* (Ithaca: Cornell University Press)

Rendell, William (1976), *History of the Commonwealth Development Corporation, 1948-1972* (London: Heinemann)

Robinson, Ronald (1972), 'Non-European foundations of European imperialism: sketch for a theory of collaboration', in Roger Owen and Bob Sutcliffe (eds), *Studies in the Theory of Imperialism* (London: Longman), pp. 117–40

Rood, Leslie L. (1975), 'Foreign investment in African manufacturing', *Journal of Modern African Studies*, vol. 13, no. 1, pp. 19–34

Rubin, Newell and William M. Warren (1968), *Dams in Africa* (New York: Augustus Kelly)

Sarraut, Albert (1923), *Le mise en valeur des colonies françaises* (Paris: Payot)

Sauvy, Alfred (1965), *Histoire économique de la France entre les deux guerres* (Paris: Fayard)

Sklar, Richard (1978), *Corporate Power in an African State: The Political Impact of Multinational Mining Corporations in Zambia* (Berkeley: University of California Press)

Smith, Allan K. (1974), 'António Salazar and the reversal of Portuguese colonial policy', *Journal of African History*, vol. 15, no. 4, pp. 653–67

Sorum, Paul (1977), *Intellectuals and Decolonization in France* (Chapel Hill: University of North Carolina Press)

Stuerzinger, Ulrich (1980), *Der Baumwollbau im Tschad* (Zurich: Atlantis)

Suret-Canale, Jean (1972), *Afrique noire occidentale et centrale*, Vol. 3, *De la colonisation aux indépendances (1945-1960)* (Paris: Éditions Sociales)

Twaddle, Michael (1975), *The Expulsion of a Minority: Essays on Uganda Asians* (London: Athlone Press)

US Department of Commerce (1953, 1965, 1979), *Survey of Current Business* (Washington, DC: US Government Printing Office)

Vail, Leroy (1975), 'The making of an imperial slum: Nyasaland and its railways, 1895-1935', *Journal of African History*, vol. 16, no. 1, pp. 89–112

Van der Laan, H.L. (1975), *Lebanese Traders in Sierra Leone* (The Hague: Mouton)

Vellut, Jean-Luc (1982), 'Hégémonie en construction: articulation entre état et entreprises dans le bloc colonial Belge (1908–1960)', *Canadian Journal of African Studies*, vol. 16, no. 2, pp. 313–30

Wallerstein, Immanuel (1976), 'The three stages of African involvement in the world-economy', in Peter C.W. Gutkind and Immanuel Wallerstein (eds), *The Political Economy of Contemporary Africa* (Beverley Hills: Sage), pp. 30–57

Wallerstein, Immanuel (1980), 'Imperialism and development', in Albert Bergesen (ed.), *Studies of the Modern World-System* (New York: Academic Press), pp. 13–23

Wasserman, Gary (1976), *The Politics of Decolonization: Kenya Europeans and the Land Issue* (Cambridge: Cambridge University Press)

Wicker, E.R. (1958), 'Colonial Development and Welfare, 1929–1957; the evolution of a policy', *Social and Economic Studies*. vol. 7, no. 4, pp. 170–92

Wood, Alan (1950), *The Groundnut Affair* (London: Bodley Head)

Yeung, Patrick and Shamsher Singh (1976), 'Global supply and demand for cocoa', in John Simmons (ed.), *Cocoa Production: Economic and Botanical Perspectives* (New York: Praeger), pp. 341–72

Younes, M. (1964), *Les investissements publics d'origine locale et d'origine extérieure dans les pays francophones d'Afrique tropicale* (Paris: Institut d'Étude du Développement Économique et Social)

Young, Crawford (1970), 'Decolonization in Africa', in L.H. Gann and Peter Duignan (eds.), *Colonialism in Africa, 1870-1960*, Vol. 2, *The History and Politics of Colonialism, 1914-1960* (Cambridge: Cambridge University Press), pp. 450–502

Zartman, I. William (1971), *The Politics of Trade Negotiation between Africa and the European Economic Community: The Weak Confront the Strong* (Princeton: Princeton University Press)

9

From Decolonization to
Post-colonial Regimes
Efforts at Internal Transformation

The aim of this chapter is to examine the economic base and economic consequences of the African state systems which have succeeded European colonial regimes everywhere but in South Africa. The period covered is brief, concentrating heavily upon the two decades since independence, but the quantity of data and secondary literature available vastly exceeds that for any previous era of African history. The analysis cannot, therefore, deal adequately with all the relevant issues of political economy. What I hope to contribute here to both the preceding arguments in this book and the wider discussion of contemporary African development is some sense of the historical process linking the colonial and even pre-colonial past with the most recent situation.

The general conditions of mid-twentieth-century continuity and change have already been suggested in earlier chapters and can be summed up by the inversion of a frequently evoked motto: *plus ça reste la même chose, plus ça change*. What has remained the same are some of the key features of the colonial economies: a dominant position for the state; a weak role for indigenous entrepreneurs and organized labour; and a heavy dependence upon external markets and capital sources.

Yet this inherited position of the state allowed post-colonial African regimes an opportunity for much wider economic innovation than their colonial predecessors. The new elites had taken over the local authoritarian power of the colonial rulers without any inhibiting responsibility to a metropolitan constituency. Moreover, as already noted, the sources of external capital had now become so varied, mutually competitive, and detached from economic outcomes within Africa that the recipient regimes enjoyed considerable latitude, at least for the short run, in their choice of policies.

The real question to be asked here, however, is whether the ability to initiate new policies under conditions of structural continuity could bring about lasting change. In order to pursue this question it is necessary, first of all, to examine the class formations of the new African regimes as they took shape during the terminal phases of colonial rule. The second, and longest, portion of this chapter will analyse specific efforts at economic change undertaken by four post-colonial African regimes representing variations in both ideology and colonial background.

The internal economics of decolonization

It was contended in Chapter 8 that changes in colonial economic policy from the 1930s to the 1950s resulted largely from external factors: fluctuations in market demand for African commodities and, above all, efforts at using Africa to solve the problems of the European colonial metropoles. Decolonization, according to this argument, drew its positive dynamic from political forces and made economic sense only when Europeans again recognized Africa's marginality to their own market and investment concerns.

During this same period, however, the African economies did not remain stagnant. On the contrary, as the data already presented indicate, from the 1930s to the 1960s Africa experienced both serious crises and unprecedented levels of growth. A major source of these changes was again external: the effects of world markets and neo-mercantilist policy initiatives. However, it is possible to argue, as A.G. Hopkins has done, that equal attention ought to be given to 'the internal dynamics of the open economy', i.e. to a rise of forces within the African commercial, labour, and agricultural sectors which demanded a greater role for themselves than allowed by the colonial economic system.[1]

Hopkins is undoubtedly right in identifying the internal dynamics of African economies with the relationship between private sectors and the state. However, the prominence he accords to these sectors in the politics of decolonization implies that, once independence was achieved, there should have been major changes in this relationship. The present chapter began, however, with an assertion that no such change has taken place. In the discussion of African economic interests and decolonization which follows, therefore, the problems of transformation will be discussed without any assumption that the desired goals were actually reached. It has, in fact, been just as possible for post-colonial African regimes to maintain the model of an 'open economy' as to replace it with some form of economic nationalism. This choice determined the character of the new regimes but not necessarily the outcome of their economic efforts. In either case, the alignment of the critical internal forces first revealed itself in the era of neo-mercantilism and decolonization.

THE POLITICAL ELITE

Whatever may have been its effect on various private sectors, the terminal colonial period gave renewed prominence to the state, which served as the main instrument of neo-mercantilist policies and the vehicle for the emergence of the dominant class in the new African economy.

The two decades following the Great Depresssion of the 1930s marked the abandonment by the colonial state of its established posture as a risk avoider and (in areas of direct European exploitation) neutral mediator between competing groups. Instead, the public sector now began to intervene strongly and directly into all areas of the economy. The entry into marketing through elaborate regulations and direct government commodity purchasing followed, as has been seen, a tradition of étatist economic policy which had been present even in more cautious periods. Concerns with intensified infrastructural development and, particularly, agricultural production represented more radical departures as they flooded the African countryside with whole new sets of officials and private contractors, all connected ultimately to the state. The resulting consciousness of the public sector as a force entering previously untouched areas of African economic life contributed, as will be seen, to wide popular involvement in decolonization politics.

But the most immediate effect of the expansion of state activities and the willingness of Europeans to abandon political control over this entire apparatus was
the enfranchisement of a new African ruling class. The analysis of this dominant
group within post-colonial economies has formed a major concern of recent Africanist scholarship and produced a number of provocative concepts under such
labels as 'neo-colonialist', 'bureaucratic bourgeoisie', 'over-developed state',
'comprador elite', 'neo-absolutism', etc.[2] The nuances of this regime analysis will
be pursued most fully in the section devoted to case studies. But a few general
points have to be made about the relationship of this politically defined class
to its colonial predecessors, its broader external constituency, and its domestic
constituency.

Despite – or because of – the direct opposition between indigenous nationalists
and colonial administrators, it was these Europeans who provided the major
model for the new African rulers. The critical resource for entry into this class was
formal education. It was the insistence that the possession of such education
qualified them for replacing Europeans which allowed African nationalists to
claim political enfranchisement, both directly from colonial governments, and
indirectly through the support of various liberal and leftist sectors in the
metropoles. The assumption of European governments in turning over political
office to this most 'Westernized' group of Africans was that they would maintain
the structures which had nurtured them. In strictly political terms, the definition of
these systems is somewhat confused by the introduction of constitutionalism and
multi-party elections into the process of decolonization. However soon after independence, most African governments shifted permanently to more authoritarian
forms of rule. While the latter are certainly influenced by the liberal politics which
first brought them to power (and the case studies to be examined below all have
civilian rather than military governments) they bear less resemblance to the metropolitan models upon which the democratic experiments of the 1950s and 1960s
were based than to the classic colonial regimes which prevailed before the Second
World War.

In economic terms the continuity with colonial étatism is even more pronounced. It has been argued that the most serious concern of the departing European rulers was to defend 'the structures and requisites of the colonial political
economy'.[3] However, as Chapter 8 suggested, it was not clear by the late 1950s
what specific European requisites should be served by economic ties to Africa.
Whatever the intentions of metropolitan policy-makers, the new African regimes
were constrained to preserve some aspects of the open economy, and thus dependence upon the West, by their insistence upon maintaining a modern apparatus of
rule and the concomitant consumption styles. The means for such an existence
could only be imported from already-industrialized economies, forcing African
governments to earn foreign exchange through exports in at least partly the same
way as their colonial predecessors.

In presenting themselves to their domestic constituencies, African nationalists
leaders never placed great emphasis on the details of economic issues. Much of the
nitty-gritty of early party organization and later patronage distribution followed
regional or ethnic rather than class lines. The motif of this era is summed up in the
exhortation engraved upon the statue of the first of the new indigenous rulers,
Ghana's Kwame Nkrumah: 'Seek ye first the political kingdom and all things will
be added unto you.'

Belief in such messianic economics was sustained by the all-encompassing

opposition between European colonizers and African subjects. The frequent introduction of socialism into this discourse served similar purposes, since capitalism
was identified with foreign domination rather than any specific economic system.[4]

The possibilities of breaking with the colonial order were thus approached very
ambiguously. Much as they depended upon external markets for their sustenance,
the new African rulers could also combine the interventionist power of the late
colonial state with the substance of their socialist rhetoric to essay a major departure from the open economy model. The paths chosen depended a great deal on
personal choice but also upon the relative influence of private-sector interest
groups.

THE ENTREPRENEURIAL ELITE

The complement of the self-defined prominence of political elites in the modern
African social order is the absence of any competitive group within the indigenous
private sector. The earlier chapters on the colonial economy have pointed out
some of the factors weakening indigenous entrepreneurs: merchants and manufacturers unable to compete effectively with better-capitalized and politically connected foreign firms; planters unable or unwilling to control labour, manage
economies of scale, or stand up to discriminatory policies in favour of European
settlers. Again, it was the logic of the colonial order which induced Africans to
divert such surplus capital as they could accumulate from investment in commercial or agricultural enterprises to the formal education of children for entrance into
bureaucratic careers (see Chapter 6).

But these weaknesses were neither so uniform nor so extreme that private-sector
entrepreneurs could not play an important role in the process of decolonization
and the economy which succeeded it. Generally, this role was more significant in
the early stages of nationalism, when private entrepreneurs had the greatest and
most easily articulated grievances against the colonial regimes, and diminished
later as these sectors were co-opted, outflanked, and partially subjugated by the
changes accompanying the last stages of European rule.

The militant leadership stage of African entrepreneurial politics can be traced
back as far as the early twentieth century in British West Africa, although it
reached its climax there in the Ghana cocoa hold-ups of the 1930s and the formation of that country's first modern political party, the United Gold Coast Convention (UGCC) in 1947. Rural landowners among the Kikuyu of Kenya formed
political associations as early as the 1920s to promote their various commercial
interests. In the Ivory Coast, the Syndicat Agricole Africain, an organization of
relatively prosperous planters, was formed in 1944 to combat privileged European
farmers and subsequently became the basis of a general nationalist political party.[5]

By the early 1950s, however, the edge had come off the grievances of most of
these entrepreneurial groups as many of their demands were met, directly or
indirectly, by the reforms and development projects of the late colonial era.
Throughout British and French West Africa, as noted above, the oligopolistic
European trading firms had pulled out of local retail trade, leaving a vastly
expanded field for African merchants. Produce purchasing had, in many areas,
been taken over by government boards but a parallel policy of encouraging co-
operative marketing societies provided a base for a new set of semi-private African
entrepreneurs. The infrastructural improvements and construction projects of this
period as well as the generally eased access to motor vehicles vastly increased the
opportunities for Africans to enter the fields of transport and contracting. During

the 1950s a number of African merchants in West Africa (notably in Senegal, Ghana, and Nigeria) expanded into light industrial enterprises such as food- and export-processing and textile manufacturing, sometimes with government assistance.[6] Finally, in both the Ivory Coast and Kenya the spectre of violent conflict between European settlers and local populations brought about a major change in colonial agricultural policies, which now encouraged the growth of what it was hoped would be a 'moderate' rural African bourgeoisie.[7]

Within the politics of decolonization entrepreneurial elites did tend to play a moderate role. There is virtually no evidence of their sensitivity to the long-term disadvantages inherent in the neo-mercantilist aspects of concurrent colonial policy. They generally opposed such radical nationalist movements as Nkrumah's Convention People's Party in Ghana, the Mau Mau rebellion in Kenya, or the Union des Populations du Cameroun. But, while colonial governments often took measures to suppress radical nationalists, they also gave in to pressure for extending the electoral franchise, thus making it difficult for local propertied classes to attain political power on their own terms. Where European authorities countered undesired nationalist parties by sponsoring more acceptable alternatives, these tended to be based on regional or ethnic loyalties, often with traditional rulers rather than merchants or planters at their head. Entrepreneurial elites were thus put in the position of supporting rather than leading nationalist movements. Their money and often their networks of connections were important in such political efforts and they were no more likely to identify with the regionalist conservative parties than with the more centralizing movements, even when the latter, like Nkrumah or the French West African Rassemblement Démocratique Africain, claimed adherence to socialism.[8]

For successful nationalist leaders, the support of local entrepreneurial elites was ultimately less important than the direct appeal for the votes of a mass electorate (whose class base will be discussed below) and the political and financial patronage of external forces. Local entrepreneurs were ultimately dependent upon these same external sources of capital, which came increasingly to be mediated through the indigenous political establishment. The movement towards African independence thus strengthened the indigenous private sector as a possible base for further economic development but also placed it at the mercy of policy choices by the new post-colonial state.

ORGANIZED WAGE LABOUR

In most of colonial Africa, with the notable exception of the Portuguese territories and Zimbabwe, the political struggle for independence was far briefer and less violent than in the former European possessions in Asia. Nevertheless, if these movements had been confined to the educated and entrepreneurial elites, even liberal colonial governments would have found it possible to maintain themselves in power for much longer periods than was actually the case. The success of African nationalist leadership thus depended upon the mobilization of a mass base in both the urban and rural sectors of society.

At the time of independence, the urban populations of all African countries still represented a small minority within the population as a whole. However, cities and the occupations connected with them were growing rapidly and represented – as they still do – the most immediate popular constituency of new political movements. In economic terms, the urban work force must again be divided into two major sub-sectors: the wage labourers in the formal sectors, widely organized after the Second World War into trade unions; and more rapidly growing congeries of individuals either irregularly attached to the formal sector, employed or self-employed by various arrangements in the informal sector, and to a considerable extent underemployed or unemployed. These latter groups were usually organized along kin and ethnic lines not directly related to economic roles.

The issue of how relevant and representative organized labour was for the attainment of African independence is a very controversial one among analysts of recent African socio-economic change. One school of radical historians has placed great emphasis on the formal working class as a key factor in bringing about both political independence and eventual transformation of the economy. Another group of both liberal and radical scholars has argued that the organized sector of the work force is essentially a 'labour aristocracy' which was even more dependent than indigenous entrepreneurial classes on the patronage of governments and foreign firms for the gains it could make, often at the expense of the urban and rural African majority. In the short run it appears that the latter position is, in qualified form, more tenable.[9]

Within the colonial economy, even in its late stages, the areas within which African workers could possibly organize remained rather circumscribed and privileged. Already by the 1930s labour was a surplus factor in almost all African territories so that workers enjoyed a strong bargaining position only in occupations requiring some degree of learned skill and/or functioning under a management which was sensitive to pressure from liberal forces in Europe or nationalist politics in Africa. The only employers falling into these latter categories were the government (always the largest single enterprise in any case) and major European (as opposed to both indigenous and Asian/Levantine) firms. The specific occupations of organized labourers were therefore the bureaucracy, the major public technical services (particularly railways and harbours), and European mines, commercial establishments, and factories.

Within these situations, African workers were able, particularly after the Second World War, to form unions and carry out often lengthy strikes in pursuit of demands for higher wages and other benefits. These actions often required great courage and extended sacrifice on the part of participants. Nonetheless, their success derived to a considerable extent from autonomous decisions in Europe to recognize trade unions as a stable, and even potentially conservative, alternative to radical nationalist movements. In connection with these policies, the British and French governments encouraged representatives of their metropolitan labour organizations to come to Africa and tutor local workers in 'legitimate' union organization. European firms also favoured the unionization of their workers (on a company rather than an industry-wide or national basis) as a device for replacing European skilled labour with 'stabilized' African workers and co-opting these workers into a shared concern for preserving the existing economic system.

These tactics did not always work, and in colonial territories with a strong sense of racial antagonism (and sometimes because of overly effective suppression of broadly based African political parties) labour unions did support radical nationalist movements, as in Cameroon, Guinea, and Kenya. (In the last case, African unions were radicalized by their association with Indian labour leaders, reacting to the very harsh conditions in Asian-owned private enterprises.)[10]

In most cases, however, African labour unions developed in very clear separation from (usually a few years ahead of) nationalist political parties. The unions were important to political leaders both as a model for mass organization and, at the moments of strikes, as a dramatic focus for nationalist sentiment. However, while nationalist organizations sometimes helped strikers (particularly during the great French West African railway strike of 1947–8), unions would seldom allow strikes to be used as a political weapon. Moreover, despite the enrolment of their members in the nationalist movements, unions could not offer political parties much financial support since they were not able to collect dues on any major scale and, in fact, depended for their own operations on overseas subsidies.[11]

African labour unions made their greatest gains during the late 1940s and early 1950s when reformist colonial governments were most sympathetic to their concerns and positive terms of trade for African commodities allowed real wages to rise. In the period just before and after independence the African political parties began to take control over the unions in most countries, and declining export commodity prices as well as rising government expenditures created inflationary conditions which reduced the real gains even from rises in wages.

The argument against a view of organized African workers as a labour aristocracy rests upon evidence that the gap between their standard of living and that of unorganized African workers and peasants (with whom organized workers most often share much of their income in any case) is now not nearly as great as that between themselves and the African and expatriate state and entrepreneurial elite. On the other hand the continued expansion of multinational firms in Africa with capital-intensive operations demanding relatively smaller numbers of more highly skilled workers and paying relatively high wages pulls in the opposite direction. Moreover, organized workers still appear to identify their economic interests in ways which dampen anything resembling a proletarian class consciousness. Thus individual workers have been shown to aspire towards saving their wages as investment capital for entry into small, independent businesses.[12] Collectively, even closely controlled unions are in a position to put some pressure on governments with regard to such issues as food-pricing policies which, as will be seen, generally discriminate against rural producers throughout post-colonial Africa.

THE INFORMAL URBAN SECTORS

The decade immediately following the Second World War witnessed a major acceleration of African migration from the countryside to cities. In principle, this movement could be explained as an outcome of forces internal to the colonial African economy, particularly population pressures upon rural resources, lowered costs of movement to urban regions, and a shift from agriculture to industry as the most dynamic form of African production. But these factors played, at best, only a partial role in stimulating urbanization. By the 1940s only a few regions of Africa were experiencing shortages of land for cultivation. The new transport improvements had a far less significant impact on costs of movement than the early introduction of mechanized carriage on rails and road. And the 'take off' to industrial manufacturing can hardly be said to have begun in most of the continent by this time.

Instead we must look again at the external effect of neo-mercantilist colonial policies as the key to the pace of urbanization. Africans were encouraged to leave rural areas because marketing controls now limited the immediate returns to cultivators of crops for export or local consumption. Expansion of education and health services, on the other hand, favoured the cities where more such amenities were available along with opportunities to make use of school-learned skills. Finally, the development programmes of the period largely failed to transform farming, but gave the urban centres a new set of functions in managing and servicing these efforts.[13]

The result of this situation was that urban employment paid far higher direct and indirect returns than rural enterprise. Large numbers of migrants came looking for these opportunities, although relatively few would obtain positions in the formal sector. Instead most of those who stayed in cities found work only in casual manual labour, service occupations, petty trade, the various types of small-scale, semi-modern artisanal manufacturing described in Chapter 6, and an increasing number of criminal activities.[14]

Articulation of group interests in this sector was thus a complicated matter. Certain categories of petty entrepreneurs such as market women or taxi drivers and truck drivers could form loose 'guilds' which sometimes acted to make demands upon public authorities or control market conditions. Labour organizations from the formal sector also tried to incorporate other categories of workers, thus swelling union numbers but weakening their cohesion, since conditions in the informal sector did not lend themselves to collective confrontation between employers and employees.

Nonetheless, the labour force in the informal sector did not form an inchoate urban mass. Usually the very entry of migrants into the city was based upon the support of kin and ethnic ties to areas of rural origin. These were further expressed through ethnic and sometimes neighbourhood associations which often cut across incipient 'class' lines to form the basis of patron–client networks. The political elite in particular made use of these structures to mobilize electoral support, organize mass demonstrations, and recruit full-time party cadres from unemployed young elementary school graduates (Nkrumah's notorious 'verandah boys' and the 'youth wingers' of countless other African nationalist parties).[15]

With less clear ties than the regular labour unions to economic structures outside the political arena, the informal urban sector was the urban interest group which most closely linked anti-colonial nationalism to the problems of neo-mercantilism. The urban unrest of this period directly expressed dissatisfaction with the material rewards distributed to Africans from the new development programmes: not enough jobs for those who had left the countryside (represented most dramatically by Senegalese and Ghanaian war veterans) and not enough consumer goods in return for extended exports delivered to the protected markets of struggling European metropoles.

But if nationalist politics provided an outlet for aspirations inconsonant with limited economic reality, it did not necessarily offer substantive solutions to the problems being addressed. Unlike formal labour unions, workers in the informal sector could not easily be controlled or bought off with enclave employment. Instead they required large-scale public expenditures to improve urban life combined with some accommodation to the self-help methods by which the urban poor met their immediate needs for incomes, housing, and links to the elite sectors. These demands at once stretched public resources and threatened the self-image of sparkling modernity and pristine tradition which African political leaders sought to project.

THE PEASANTRIES

The ultimate test of African nationalist movements rested upon their ability to mobilize mass support outside the cities among the majority rural populations. In most tropical African colonies, even including some of those with settler agriculture sectors, peasants were assumed to be a conservative force, concerned with defending their relatively undisturbed agricultural base and identified with local rather than territorial/national political units. Compared to urban groups, colonial African peasants certainly did live in a stable, parochial situation. However the developments of the last three decades of European rule disturbed rural life in ways which made peasants highly susceptible to the appeals of nationalism.

Despite important elements of coercion, the first phases of the colonial export economy can reasonably be understood as low-cost expansion of opportunities for small farmers to produce goods for attractive external markets. But from the 1930s onward, export markets and rural production were managed in ways which frustrated or contradicted the self-perceived interests of peasants. The shift began during the Depression, with its combination of falling export prices and pressures from colonial governments to increase the quantities of exports (see Chapter 8). When export demand recovered during and after the Second World War, peasants received only a limited share of the rewards as marketing boards and various forms of neo-mercantilist control over foreign trade limited the share of rising prices and consumer goods which went to primary producers.

The main beneficiary of the new redistribution of agricultural income was the late colonial state. Public authorities did dedicate some of their enhanced tax and aid revenue to rural development, but in a manner which won little favour with peasants. Already during the 1930s, European regimes had begun what has sometimes been called 'the second colonial occupation', a movement of technical experts into the countryside to intervene directly in African cultivation systems.[16] The first and most consistent theme of this intervention was the prevention of soil erosion. Colonial administrators correctly observed that new cash crops, accelerated food production, and expanded cattle populations were destructive of ecological systems previously based upon less-intensive exploitation. However, the solutions proposed, such as tie ridging and other forms of conservationist farming practice, or the culling of herds with minimal compensation for surrendered animals, were neither popular with peasants nor, it now appears, well-grounded in agricultural science. Cocoa farmers in West Africa also disliked the destruction of diseased trees by government agents, although this measure was probably unavoidable.

An equally negative response was evoked by those features of new rural policies directed more immediately at increased production. The general unpopularity of large-scale settlement schemes combining irrigation and mechanized agriculture has already been discussed (see Chapter 8). Even more threatening to African farmers was the encouragement given after the Second World War to white settler cultivation, not only in the expected areas of British and Portuguese East and South Central Africa but also in the French western African territories of Ivory Coast, Cameroon, Congo and Ubangi-Shari (Central African Republic).[17]

Peasant reactions to these policies took the form of both direct protest and exit from agriculture. The former option was initially quite localized, ranging from riots to individual passive resistance. The growing opportunities in rural distributive occupations and urban employment of all kinds also drew large portions of the African population away from farming although often, as seen in the above discussion of the informal sector, on terms which preserved close ties to rural communities. The secret of nationalist political penetration of the African countryside was that it gave a focus to all these spontaneous local responses. Nationalist leaders used the networks of migrants, trader-transporters, co-operatives and

ethnic associations to make contact with rural constituencies and presented themselves as the potential solution to a whole series of problems which peasants
perceived as emanating from central rather than local sources.[18]

The mobilization of peasants in nationalist causes is easy to explain; the direction
of this movement, once independence was attained, presents greater difficulties.
The political leaders had promised an end to threats against peasant security and
better access to urban advantages for emigrants from rural life, but it was not at all
clear what positive plans they had for agriculture itself. The issues of controlling
producer prices, ecological deterioration, and intensification of farm production
remained very much alive and subject, as will be seen, to greatly varied policy
directions.

Post-colonial economic regimes

However much the search for the 'political kingdom' may have obscured economic
issues in the rhetoric of African nationalist movements, once independence was
attained important economic policy decisions had to be made by the new African
rulers. Despite all the constraints of external dependency and internal weakness,
this capacity put considerable power in the hands of the African political elite.
When the resulting choices were made in a coherent manner we can identify
variations in policy which follow two major ideological orientations. The shorthand terms to be used here for these ideologies and the regimes which developed
from them are 'socialist' and 'capitalist'.

REGIME CATEGORIES: SOCIALISM AND CAPITALISM

Before explaining what is meant by such terms it is necessary to indicate briefly
what they do not cover. The cataloguing of states according to regime types is a
necessary although also a dangerous occupational obsession among Africanists.
There are too many political units within Africa to deal with them all in their own
terms and the categories previously employed in this book, geographical regions
and forms of colonialism, are inadequate for the post-colonial era. But the lists of
regime types threaten at once to reduce African historical realities to a set of
abstract equations, and at the same time have usually proved to be far too superficial to provide any enduring framework for analysis of continental development.[19]
The justification for using such categories here is that they will be applied to a
relatively small number of cases which can thus be examined in some degree of
detail while still maintaining a general and comparative focus.

The cases chosen and those with which they will be compared represent only
those African economies where serious post-colonial development efforts have
taken place. Omitted, therefore, are the less fortunate but equally representative
states whose resource endowments and/or political history since independence
have rendered positive economic change impossible. The first condition applies to
the landlocked, mineral- and rainfall-deficient French-speaking states of West and
Equatorial Africa as well as several micro-states along and off the coasts of the
continent. Political disasters, in the form of rampant military despotisms, have
struck some of these states as well as the otherwise more viable economies of
Uganda and Zaire, which are likewise omitted from the present categories. But it
should not be forgotten that the conditions making for these economic catastrophes
– general poverty, ecological crises, and destructive use of state power – are not
entirely foreign to the more successful African economies. As with all the other

regime lists, even this one may reflect little more than the narrow perspective of two short decades since independence.

For better or worse, the present analysis will concentrate on four cases. Socialist regimes are represented by Ghana under Nkrumah (from about 1960 to 1966) and Tanzania since about 1967; capitalist regimes by the Ivory Coast and Kenya throughout the post-independence period. A much wider range of post-colonial regimes have seriously professed socialism, including Congo, Guinea, and Mali among the first generation of independent states and, since the 1970s, Benin (formerly Dahomey), Ethiopia, Madagascar, Somalia, and the former Portuguese territories of Angola, Guinea-Bissau, and Mozambique.[20] Ghana and Tanzania have been chosen because they are exceptionally well-documented, have completed a certain cycle of socialist experimentation and, despite their general failure, did so on a more solid economic basis than any of the other African socialist regimes for which we have a comparable record.

Few African states have explicitly declared themselves to be following a 'capitalist' pattern of development although, given the continuing preponderance of West European and American influence in the continent, capitalism may be considered the residual pattern for those states which have not consciously chosen any alternative. Undoubtedly the most important capitalist regime in Africa (and the most important of the post-colonial states in general) is Nigeria, to which some reference will be made in the following discussion.[21] But to place Nigeria at the centre of a comparative analysis would inevitably cause problems of imbalance, not only because of the scale of Nigerian development (including the factor of major oil wealth) but also because it would be impossible to ignore the complex political transition of post-colonial regimes from the First Republic, through civil war and military regimes, to the Second Republic and its military successors. Other cases which might be considered as examples of African capitalism are Cameroon, Malawi, Senegal, and (at a future date) probably Zimbabwe. Ivory Coast and Kenya have been chosen because they too are well-documented examples of a sustained effort at development within a capitalist system. While of comparable scale, they also represent the contrast between East and West Africa, British and French colonial experiences, and a peasant-dominated versus settler-dominated colonial economic regime.

The cases to be discussed here are defined in terms of ideology. However, the object of inquiry is not ideologies themselves but rather the policy choices they imply and the economic consequences of these policies. There is, in fact, no close correlation between the character of ideological statements by African leaders and the degree to which they pursue the logic of either socialist or capitalist development strategies. Socialist regimes have generally produced far clearer and more elaborate rationales for their actions than have their counterparts (the key document outlining Kenyan capitalist policies is entitled *African Socialism and its Application to Planning in Kenya*[!]). The intellectual distinctions among African socialists between orthodox Marxist/Leninist positions (as with much of Nkrumah's writing in Ghana) and the more populist *ujamaa* doctrine of Tanzania's Julius Nyerere tells us little about the economic practice of these regimes.[22] More attention to the nuances of ideology would be necessary if the issue here were the comparison of regimes in their broadest sense, as in the important recent literature dealing with the class basis of authoritarianism in developing countries throughout the world; but this kind of analysis has not produced very significant results when applied to Africa, largely because of the limitations of the very economic development which is at issue here.[23]

Only one point about the intellectual content of African development ideologies needs to be pursued in the present context: their relationship to the academic analytic perspectives which inform the effort throughout this book to understand African economic history. The socialist position, whether it draws upon Marxism or some understanding of the distinction between Western and African cultural patterns, clearly falls into the structuralist camp. Its efforts at immediate socio-economic transformation are thus both radical, and at the same time in conformity with much of previous colonial experience and later Western modernization theory. The capitalist regimes generally accept a market theory of spontaneous and piecemeal change. They are conservative in regard to the degree of transformation necessary in internal and external relationships but radical in their belief that Africans can function within this open economic system as effectively as the foreigners who created and still dominate it. In effect, therefore, both ideological stances draw on certain aspects of the colonial heritage and reject others; as will be seen this ambiguity of change and continuity also characterizes their practical approaches to economic development.

The comparison of socialist and capitalist regimes will focus on three sets of issues: the relationship between state and private sectors; the relationship of the domestic to the world economy; and class relationships within the domestic economy. Briefly outlined the socialist position on these issues is as follows: the state should have a dominant role in the economy by planning radical changes, controlling distribution, and managing major productive enterprises; external capital is necessary for development but should be accepted only under carefully controlled conditions so as to attain as rapidly as possible a position of economic autonomy ('socialism and self-reliance' is the central slogan of Tanzania's key ideological manifesto, the 1967 Arusha Declaration); entrepreneurial classes are to be discouraged or even repressed in order to ensure that the benefits of development are distributed equitably to the worker and peasant masses.

The capitalist position differs, although even at an ideological level certain common elements of the post-colonial African situation emerge: the private sector and market factors are to be given free play, although the state will also inevitably exercise a major economic role (the official terms for the economic policy of Ivory Coast is 'state capitalism', a term also used for such regimes by many outside analysts); foreign investment and trade are actively encouraged on terms which insist only on a maximal participation of indigenous managers or entrepreneurs; the success of enterprising individuals is perceived as the best means of assuring a process of economic growth which will ultimately benefit all groups (the term 'class' is generally avoided) within society.

When we turn from the articulation of goals to the implementation of economic policy, the distinction between socialist and capitalist African regimes becomes more subtle. Nevertheless, there are important differences which indicate, among other things, the range of choice available to the architects of post-colonial African economic development.

One very obvious distinction is that the socialist regimes to be considered here have all been economic failures, while the capitalist regimes have enjoyed relative success in sustaining stable economic growth. These results are based on very short-run performances and have by no means closed the debate concerning the ultimate outcomes and needs of African development. The discussion of state activities which follows immediately will deal with the narrowest distinction between socialism and capitalism and the measurable economic outcome of the two orientations. The subsequent sections will discuss the structural issues confronted by such policies and their implications for longer-term economic change.[24]

Table 9.1   *Profiles of case study countries*[1]

	Ghana	*Ivory Coast*	*Kenya*	*Tanzania*
Population (1980)				
(thousands)	11 679	7 973	16 402	17 934
Area (sq km)	238 540	322 460	582 640	945 090
Population density				
(per sq km)	49	25	28	19
Gross Domestic Product (1960)				
(current US$ millions)	1 092	610	632	518
Per capita GDP (1960)				
(current US$)	161	176	77	51
Gross Domestic Product (1980)				
(current US$ millions)	4 118	10 488	6 992	4 993
Per capita GDP (1980)				
(current US$)	353	1 315	426	275

[1]UNCTAD (1969, 1983) Tables 6.1, 6.2.

THE STATE AND ECONOMIC PERFORMANCE

If development patterns were defined by the prominence of the state in economic affairs, all African regimes would have to be considered socialist. If the definition rested upon the capacity of public authorities to control the economy, all would be labelled capitalist. The strong position of the state in contemporary African economies is derived from the étatist colonial tradition, the weakness of indigenous entrepreneurial classes, and the shift, shortly after independence, from parliamentary democracy to one-party authoritarian regimes. The economic weakness of these states results from their limited administrative capacity, their dependence upon external sources of capital, and the difficulty of the developmental tasks which they have taken on. The effect of this paradoxical balance has been that capitalist regimes have given less freedom to the private sector than they claim and that socialists regimes have attempted to do far more with the public sector than they are capable of.

As in the colonial period, the state loomed largest in the economies of all independent African states because of the continued expansion of administrative and infrastructural activities at a pace which easily matched – and sometimes outstripped – growth in the sectors dealing with the production, distribution and processing of material commodities. To the expansion of existing bureaucracies was added new military formations (not of overwhelming size in any of the countries discussed here), and separate establishments for political parties. Social services (particularly education) were vastly augmented and large new infrastructural projects undertaken (major dams in Ghana and Ivory Coast, an entire harbour complex in Ivory Coast, a new trans-territorial rail line in Tanzania).

The colonial precedent of extensive intervention in the distributive sector was also followed by all regimes. Variations here often had less to do with ideological orientation than the specific institutions bequeathed by Europeans. Thus capitalist Kenya and Nigeria as well as socialist Ghana retained some version of the British-founded government marketing boards for purchasing and retailing such commodities as maize, beef, cocoa or palm oil. Capitalist Ivory Coast left marketing in private hands but controlled producer prices through the French-established *caisses de stabilisation*. All regimes also subsidized their newly founded manufacturing industries by heavy protective tariffs. The socialist regimes distinguished themselves here only by the degree to which produce-buying came under direct central control (at the expense of local co-operative societies rather than private firms) and the establishment of public control over importation and, in the case of Tanzania, banking, insurance and (for a brief period) rented housing and local retailing.

The more critical distinctions between socialist and capitalist development options emerge from the choices between state and private enterprise in agricultural and industrial production. Even here there is a major residual factor of institutions inherited from the colonial, and even pre-colonial, past. Thus in all four countries the majority of farm goods are cultivated by peasant smallholders. The largest numbers of manufacturing firms (although not the major shares of production) fall under the category of small-scale semi-artisanal African enterprises. Even within the modern, formal industrial sector, most manufacturing capacity in both socialist regimes at their high point and in capitalist economies was mainly owned by private expatriate corporations. Moreover both socialist and capitalist regimes have made considerable use of public capital for financing production and controlling it directly through parastatal corporations.

The difference in the degree of control over production between the two types of regimes is, however, quite considerable. The major investments made by Nkrumah's Ghana in agriculture went to the State Farms Corporation and Workers' Brigade camps which were to grow food and hitherto neglected export crops on large tracts of government land, using centrally managed labour and mechanized production methods. In Tanzania after 1967 the state took over about half of the large sisal estates which had once been the leading agricultural export earners; but its more ambitious rural efforts came between 1969 and 1975 when several million peasants throughout the country were regrouped into 'ujamaa villages' where they would share modern production facilities, urban amenities, and part-time labour on collective fields.[25]

The industrial policies of both Ghana and Tanzania dealt with manufacturing either through nationalization of existing firms, the formation of government-majority partnerships with foreign owners, or the creation of entirely new industrial parastatals. As indicated in Table 9.2 these efforts still left a considerable proportion of the manufacturing capacity in private hands. However, the publicly owned firms were more important than their share in output would indicate since they absorbed an extremely large proportion of government revenue and credit, they pervaded all forms of manufacturing, and they achieved a dominant or even monopoly position in several of the most capital-intensive sectors, such as textiles, metallurgy, tyres and (for Tanzania) the production of key intermediate goods like cement and fertilizer.

Under capitalist African regimes, the major role of the state in agricultural production has been to provide credit and technical assistance to private cultivators, ranging from peasants to medium- and large-sized landholders. However both Ivory Coast and Kenya have created large-scale public enterprises for the production of crops which lend themselves to close integration between growing and centralized processing (palm, fruits, vegetables, rice and sugar in the Ivory

Coast, sugar, vegetables and tea in Kenya). Ivory Coast's massive sugar plantations operate on an 'industrial' basis with direct control over labour. The other
projects in both countries are mainly organized around 'contract farming' in which
peasant outgrowers on their own land enter into obligations to deliver produce to
publicly owned factories in return for guaranteed payments and extensive technical assistance.[26]

Table 9.2   *Public and private sector enterprise*[1]

	Public sector	Private sector
	(percentage shares)	
Ghana		
1966	56	44
1968–70	48	52
Ivory Coast		
1968–75	35	65
1973	50	50
Kenya		
1964–84	24	76
1977	37	63
Tanzania		
1962–72	63	37
1972	74	26

[1]Ghana (1961–9); Tuinder (1978), pp. 326–7, 354; Kenya (1965–85); Clark (1978), p. 268.
The figures for Ghana are based on shares of wage employment; the other figures represent
proportions of entrepreneurial capital formation.

Capitalist regimes have been far more cautious than African socialist governments about taking direct responsibility for manufacturing enterprises outside the
public service and agro-industry sector. Both Ivory Coast and Kenya have entered
urban manufacturing mainly by way of minority shareholdings in expatriate
firms. The holding companies making these investments represent an important
parastatal element within the industrial capital market, particularly in Kenya, but
their major policy goal has been to make this sector more indigenous rather than
less capitalist.[27]

If we compare the economic performances of the socialist and capitalist regimes
in this sample by the simple criteria of production growth (see Figure 9.1) it seems
apparent that the capitalists have done a good deal better. Obviously world
market conditions (and particularly rising fuel costs) set the parameters of such
growth, so that all these countries were worse off in the late 1970s and early 1980s
than they were previously (see Appendix, Figure A5). However in good or bad
years the capitalist countries made greater gains than the socialists.

There is a direct correlation between these disparities in performance and the
differing role of the state in the productive sectors of the two economic systems.
Generally, parastatal enterprises in all parts of Africa have had a poor record in
farming and manufacturing, i.e. they operated at high costs, with low utilization of
capacities, and turned out goods at higher prices than competing producers either
on the continent or overseas.[28] The economies of Ghana and Tanzania suffered the
most from investments in parastatal production but in Ivory Coast also the decline
in growth at the end of the 1970s can be attributed in significant part to large
expenditures on publicly run agricultural projects, particularly the sugar estates.

Figure 9.1   *Growth of Gross Domestic Product*[1]

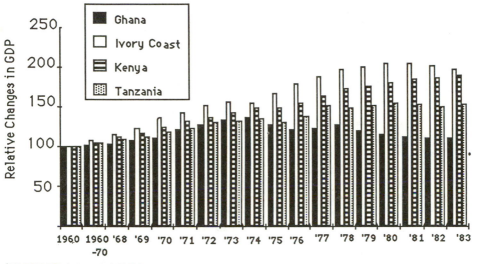

[1]UNCTAD (1972–85) Table 6.2.

Contract farming, although not always successful (especially in the Ivory Coast) cost governments a good deal less and thus did not represent as great an economic risk.

These negative outcomes result to a large extent from the inadequacy of the contemporary African state as an instrument for the planning or management of large-scale economic ventures. The planning failures are squarely in the tradition of the late colonial period, with its belief that the transfer of high-level technology to Africa would automatically solve the problems of 'backwardness'. Persistence in pursuing such schemes and the flagrant mismanagement of many of them must also be attributed to the corruption of African officials, who were subject to little public scrutiny and considerable pressures and temptations to maximize their immediate incomes.[29] On the other hand, this factor cannot explain too much since the known levels of public corruption are highest in Ghana, Kenya, and Nigeria, which experienced quite varied economic success, while both Tanzania and Ivory Coast are equally divergent, although neither is noted for extreme malfeasance of this kind. More important, perhaps, is the simple lack of manpower trained to exercise the kind of administrative control demanded by ambitious state economic projects, even in Ghana, which entered independence with the highest level of education in sub-Saharan Africa.

The narrow criteria of productivity within a period of less than two decades and the efficiency of public-sector versus private-sector enterprise is certainly an inadequate basis upon which to judge broad-ranging approaches to economic development. Nevertheless, it is one of the major grounds upon which both Nkrumah of Ghana and Nyerere of Tanzania chose a socialist policy. Both were dissatisfied with the rate of growth and particularly the rate of industrialisation achieved under the economic system inherited from the colonial era. Socialism was thus, among other things, a 'big push' approach to rapid development under state direction, and in this sense it was a very obvious failure.[30]

At the same time, it was the capitalist-oriented leaders (particularly Ivory

Coast's Houphouët-Boigny in his celebrated 1957 'wager' with Nkrumah about the results of their policies ten years later)[31] who stressed immediate, measurable economic results as a test of national achievement. African socialist ideology, in its most developed forms, sought other kinds of transformation in the relations between African and external economies and the distribution of wealth within Africa. It is to these structural issues, which are not only significant in themselves but also have consequences for longer-term economic growth, that we must now turn.

AFRICAN ECONOMIES AND FOREIGN CAPITAL
Since the goal of all contemporary African regimes is to transform their economies into some variant of the systems prevalent in the fully industrialized outside world, by definition none of them yet possesses the capital resources needed for such development. The acquisition of this capital thus requires one form or another of asymmetrical relationship with those who do control it.

Several avenues for acquiring foreign capital are available to African countries: its purchase with hard currency earned through raw material exports; the invitation of multinational corporations to set up subsidiary operations at their own expense; private loans for the establishment of indigenous modern enterprises; public loans and aid from foreign governments or international agencies. All these types of capital transfer have been used by various African regimes in differing forms and combinations (see Figures 9.2 A–C). Before examining the foreign ties characteristic of socialist and capitalist economies, it is necessary to consider some of the general problems engendered by each form.

Figure 9.2 A   *Net Western capital flows*[1]

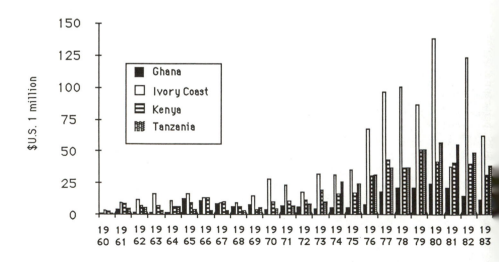

[1]OEEC/OECD (1961–84); UNCTAD (1972–85) Tables 5.5, 5.7.

Figure 9.2 B *Net private sector capital flows*[1]

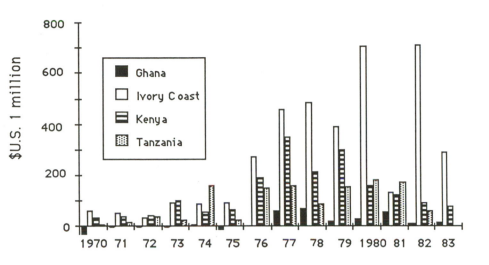

[1]UNCTAD (1972–85) Tables 5.5, 5.7.
Tanzania 1983 = $US5.6 million.

Figure 9.2 C *Western development aid*[1]

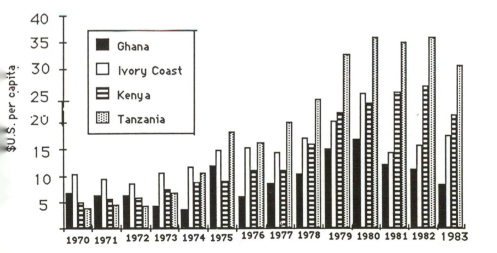

[1]UNCTAD (1972–85) Tables 5.5, 5.7, 6.1.

Export earnings provided Africans with critical capital in both the colonial and pre-colonial period, and their shortcomings are quite obvious. The levels of revenue are unpredictable and, with the exception of oil and strategic mineral products, never very high. The classic base for this type of accumulation, peasant agriculture, has limited growth possibilities and few linkages with the rest of the economy. In more intensive forms, export production initially absorbs capital and thus requires support from some other source.

Multinational corporations offer the most direct method for bringing modern industry to Africa. However, their interests in doing so inevitably conflict in part with African development goals, and, given the marginality of Africa to their global operations, corporations are in a position to drive a fairly hard bargain. Thus the corporations are usually allowed to export a considerable proportion of their profits by explicit agreements to this effect as well as through tax concessions. Further leakage often occurs by means of book-keeping manipulations (particularly in the pricing of transfers between the subsidiary and its parent company) which are difficult for African officials (often the target of bribe offers) to regulate. Finally, the corporations operate with sophisticated technology, marketing methods, and organizations which maximize linkages with their metropolitan bases, often at the expense of locally abundant (but less compatible) factors of production.[32]

Private financing, especially through banks, is less prominent as a medium of capital transfers to Africa than to Latin America, the Middle East, and Asia. As in the nineteenth century, when tropical Africa remained even further outside the 'financier's frontier', the risks are too high and the expected returns (with the instructively disastrous exception of mineral and oil countries like Zaire) are too low[33] (see Table 9.3). One form of private lending which has played a significant role in several countries being considered here is 'supplier credit' transactions: advances of equipment made without banking intermediaries at usually very high interest rates with short terms for repayment. Here the risk is placed almost entirely upon the borrower, with potentially damaging financial effects upon African states particularly when (as was often the case) the equipment never earns its costs.[34]

Table 9.3   *Foreign debt obligations*[1]

	Total obligations (US$ millions)			Debt service as percentage of export earnings		
	1975	1980	1983	1975	1980	1983
Sub-Saharan Africa	14 187	40 335	57 884	6.8	9.4	19.0
Ghana	743	1 231	1 415	5.9	6.7	19.1
Ivory Coast	957	4 608	4 957	9.1	24.6	31.3
Kenya	672	2 171	2 854	9.2	15.6	23.9
Tanzania	836	1 734	2 343	8.1	16.2	26.3
Nigeria	1 399	5 248	11 954	4.4	4.3	19.6
Zaire	897	4 218	4 108	18.4	20.7	9.2
Latin America	65 268	177 594	282 615	8.8	11.2	16.7
Argentina	4 314	16 002	31 283	25.7	34.5	41.9
Brazil	22 755	57 042	80 265	27.7	25.1	40.1
Mexico	16 562	43 519	79 252	39.0	38.8	47.7

[1]UNCTAD (1985) Table 5.14.

Public loans and aid from a variety of western and East European/Asian countries as well as international agencies play a critical role in virtually all African countries. Large amounts of such capital are available for use in African development projects either under favourable borrowing conditions or sometimes as outright grants. Whether these capital transfers are bilateral or multilateral (mainly via the World Bank) they do, however, come largely from Western, capitalist countries (especially the former colonial powers and the United States) and are thus tied (sometimes literally through capital goods contracts) to the economic interests of these countries. Among other things, Western public donors have favoured infrastructural and export agriculture projects over manufacturing and (until the mid-1970s) food cultivation. When African countries encounter foreign exchange problems, they must turn for relief to the sister agency of the World Bank, the International Monetary Fund, which demands in return internal economic policy changes which are often distasteful to African governments, such as currency devaluations, reduction of public expenditures, and higher food prices.[35]

Foreign indebtedness thus makes African economies vulnerable to loss of control over their own assets. This is an issue of particular difficulty for socialist regimes, because of both their commitments to self-reliance and their poor economic performance records. They have suffered more immediately from the 'debt trap' than their more solvent capitalist neighbours. However, the efforts by Ghana and Tanzania to escape dependency on foreign capital illustrate some of the intricacies of this relationship while the more literally 'open economies' of Ivory Coast and Kenya test the effects of such capital when it is accepted more or less on its own terms.

The paradox of socialist resistance

As indicated by the levels of indebtedness in Table 9.3, socialist African regimes have by no means bypassed the need for foreign capital. The strategies employed to overcome some of the effects of such external dependence are close control over the uses to which the borrowed capital is put and diversification of the sources of support so as to include Eastern Europe and China.

Export agriculture has remained a major source of capital accumulation for Ghana and Tanzania, but the policy of these regimes in their socialist phase was to de-emphasize the crops which had been the traditional mainstays of foreign exchange earnings. In both cases, the move towards socialism was partly a response to the falling prices of key exports immediately after independence: cocoa in the Ghanaian case, sisal in Tanzania. The new policies thus invested little in these areas (or, for Tanzania, the other major established cash crops, coffee and cotton). Instead attempts were made to develop new exports but, above all, to alter the entire organization of agriculture through the state intervention described above and a stress on local processing of commodities such as cocoa and (in Tanzania) coffee and cashew nuts. The fact that production of the established crops ultimately stagnated or declined while the new undertakings (with the partial exception of rather traditional tea- and tobacco-growing in Tanzania) failed to generate gains in export earnings, contributed to the economic difficulties of both regimes (see Figure 9.3).

Socialist regimes were more directly hostile to the establishment of foreign-owned plantations and factories than to peasant cash-cropping. Again, part of this attitude derived from the disappointing level of private manufacturing investment

Figure 9.3   *Growth of exports*[1]

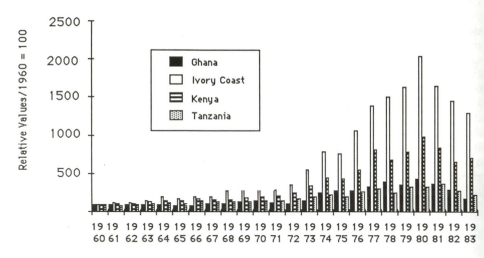

[1]UNCTAD (1980, 1985) Table 7.2.

immediately after independence, particularly for Tanzania, which had to compete with the more favourable industrial environment of neighbouring Kenya. Once socialist policies had been announced, both Ghana and Tanzania severely limited further direct foreign private investment in the economy and Tanzania quickly proceeded to nationalize (with mutually agreed compensation) the more significant expatriate enterprises already in existence.

However, the emphasis on the state sector did not eliminate the need for foreign capital, most of which came from the multinational corporate sector. Neither banks nor, as already indicated, public lending and aid agencies were attracted to these kinds of investments and, in any case, much of whatever liquid capital was raised would eventually have to be paid to corporations for the equipment and technical managerial skills needed to operate industrial undertakings. In Ghana, it was the state enterprises which accounted for most of the huge supplier-credit indebtedness accumulated by the Nkrumah regime. For Tanzania, the more common practice was a management contract or partnership between a parastatal industry and a foreign firm.[36]

With these arrangements the socialist states seem to have experienced the worst of both worlds. The enterprises themselves were extremely inefficient because of both the inadequacies of the responsible government agencies and the lack of incentives for foreign participants to act prudently (in fact they often provided unrealistically optimistic feasibility studies) since they risked few or no losses or equity. At the same time these operations overcame none of the flaws of direct multinational investments: large profits went to the foreign partners through both contractual agreements and transfer-pricing leakage; the operations were usually *more* capital-intensive and thus more technologically incompatible with 'the African factor environment than previous, foreign-owned, subsidiary operations

As indicated in Figure 9.2B, the private capital market other than supplier credit accounted for no significant share of Ghana's or Tanzania's external support Public grants and loans, on the other hand, were extremely important to both countries, despite the lack of sympathy for socialism among Western donors. The use of Eastern Europe and China as alternate sources of capital accounts for some, but not the major part, of this inflow. Ghana owed 17 per cent of its supplier credit debts to Soviet and East European state firms, which may be considered a form of public loan, but did not come on less onerous terms than similar arrangements with private contractors from the West. Of the long-term public credit received by Nkrumah's regime (mainly from the World Bank and USAID), well over half went to a single project, the Volta River hydroelectric scheme, in which a private firm, Kaiser Aluminium, was also a major partner. In purely technical terms, this undertaking was the one great success of the Nkrumah era but, as an economic asset, it did little for Ghana. Kaiser's aluminum smelter imported the ore which it processed, and exported the intermediate alumina for further processing to aluminium elsewhere. What Ghana gained was an electric power capacity, which proved to be neither cheap nor critical enough to spur major industrial development.[37]

Tanzania did far better than Ghana in attracting public foreign support for its development efforts. By the mid-1970s it led all Africa in its per capita receipt of foreign aid (see Figure 9.2c). Eastern Europe contributed very little but China (which also provided about 11 per cent of Ghana's much smaller sum of long-term loans) proved very generous and efficient in financing and constructing the railway from Dar es Salaam to the Zambian border, a project which the Western dominated World Bank had declared unfeasible. Unfortunately the 'Great Uhuru' line now appears to be another technologically marvellous white elephant. Tanzania has found it very difficult to maintain its equipment and the traffic load once Zambia was able to reopen transport links with independent Zimbabwe) no longer covers operating costs. Again, the unrealized hope was that the line would provide a transport base for a major industrial complex, in Tanzania's case to be located near the untapped coal and iron resources of the Southern Highlands region.[38]

Tanzania also received help from the World Bank (it is the major African beneficiary from this source) and from a variety of Western donors (Sweden playing a particularly prominent role). Much of this capital went to agricultural programmes, both those promoting the usual export crops (particularly tea) and the 'villagization' connected with rural ujamaa.[39]

Western hostility to socialism may thus account for some of the unfavourable terms under which Ghana had to import capital but it inhibited neither the Volta River scheme nor the major projects of Nyerere's Tanzania. It was only after the failure of both regimes to keep up with the debt burden resulting from these ventures that the West used the leverage of the International Monetary Fund to impose austerity and liberalization upon their economies. For Ghana this occurred after the coup that overthrew Nkrumah, an event that does not appear to have significant connections with the influence of Western creditors; in Tanzania, Nyerere has managed for a considerable time to resist the full prescription of 'IMF medicine'. In any case, indebtedness clearly hampered the ability of both nations to continue socialist experiments. The question which remains to be answered is whether the comparable experience of capitalist regimes and the internal dynamics of socialist economic efforts provide any grounds for seeking such a continuation.

The capitalist embrace and its costs

Under the open investment regimes of the Ivory Coast and Kenya there has been relatively little difficulty in either raising development capital or fitting the imperatives of donors into local policies. Nonetheless, African capitalist economies have also experienced some difficulties in controlling foreign entrepreneurs and avoiding large commitments to unprofitable projects.

A key contrast with the socialist regimes is the concern of both Ivory Coast and Kenya with continued expansion of the staple export crops, coffee in both countries, cocoa in Ivory Coast, and tea in Kenya (see Figure 9.3). It should be noted that not all African capitalist countries have followed this experience: the output and earnings of both export and domestically oriented agricultural sectors in Nigeria have declined drastically since 1967, a result which can be explained as much by the oil boom as by any active government policy.[40]

Even for Ivory Coast and Kenya, the foreign exchange earned by export commodities has never equalled the cost of imports. These imports consist mainly of capital goods (some for abortive efforts at industrialization and agricultural diversification) that consequently have to be financed from other sources of liquid capital and credit. Moreover, the income from export commodities has fluctuated as much during the last two decades as during any period in the modern history of the world economy, thus making it difficult for governments to plan around this item in their budgets. Finally there are serious questions about the availability of suitable land for the continued expansion of such agriculture, especially in overcrowded Kenya. Nonetheless, export earnings have provided Ivory Coast and Kenya with a basic 'floor' in their capital accounts which is important in explaining their ability to avoid severe debt crises.

The major position of multinational corporation subsidiaries in Ivory Coast and Kenya is perhaps the most critical indicator of their open economies.[41] Both countries have consistently encouraged such investments with the result that foreign-owned firms occupy a dominant role in their manufacturing sectors. The historical basis for this pattern differs, however, between the two cases. Thanks to the economic nationalism of its white settlers (see Chapter 7) as well as its central role in the wider East African market (integrated until 1977 under a regional economic organization), Kenya had attracted multinational corporate investment and Colonial Development Corporation loans for industrialization well before independence. Ivory Coast, on the other hand, only began to flourish as a major agricultural (as well as timber) exporter in the last decades of colonial rule and such limited industrial development as took place in the French West African Federation was concentrated in Senegal, the colonial administrative capital.

In both countries, however, the continued expansion of modern industry has been linked to the establishment of investment codes which both provide incentives for multinational firms to locate in their borders and some stipulations to guarantee that the investments will provide local benefits. The concessions to the firms include: the right to repatriate a certain percentage of their profits; exemption from some local taxes; commissions on sales or a monopoly position in the production of certain categories of goods; protective tariffs against competition from imports; and duty-free entry of manufacturing inputs. In return governments have specified that firms should bring in their capital from outside, allow a minority local public participation for purposes of access to management decision-making, locate outside the established metropolitan areas in at least some cases, and attempt to Africanize their executive ranks whenever possible.

By comparison with socialist regimes, these 'open' investment policies have enjoyed a considerable degree of success, or at least fewer blatant failures. Ivory

Coast and Kenya attained higher levels of industrialization than their neighbours, both in absolute terms and as a percentage of their (considerably higher) Gross National Products. The state was not paying for any major underutilized plants, as was the case in Ghana and Tanzania, although in the 1970s both capitalist regimes lost considerable sums on public investment in unsuccessful expatriate-managed textile export operations.[42]

Precisely what Ivory Coast and Kenya have gained from the presence of these industries is not so easy to calculate. The heavy capital inflows of the early years of import-substitution manufacturing have declined and there is now a threat of net outflows by means of profit exports, salaries of expatriate management, payments for imported inputs, and the ever-present transfer pricing between parent firms and local subsidiaries. Moreover the tariff protection of these firms imposes costs upon African consumers, who could often buy imported finished goods more cheaply.

Some of this cost is again counterbalanced by the export of manufactured goods to less-developed neighbouring countries in Africa and to Europe, but neither of these strategies has produced very large pay-offs except, again, by comparison with Ghana and Tanzania (see Table 9.4).

Table 9.4 *Manufactures as share of exports (values in millions of current $U.S.)*

	Total exports	Manufactured exports		Other exports	
Ghana					
1960–69	286.40	2.86	1%	283.54	99%
1970–79	724.90	10.81	1%	714.09	99%
Ivory Coast					
1960–70	302.45	10.49	3%	291.97	97%
1971–82	1 733.42	138.29	8%	1,595.12	92%
Kenya					
1961–70	231.00	14.55	6%	216.45	94%
1971–80	799.20	94.63	12%	704.57	88%
Tanzania					
1962–70	227.78	28.05	12%	199.72	88%
1971–81	438.82	50.92	12%	387.90	88%

UN, *Trade Statistics*, 1961–1980; UNCTAD, (198), Table 4.1. The data here is very problematic because the definitions of 'industrial' exports in the UN sources vary from year to year. The measurement of industrial shares in production rather than exports might also be more revealing, but this presents even greater difficulties due to the internal pricing policies of African states, which tend to over-value industrial goods at the expense of agricultural products.

In the long run, however, the value of such expatriate capital to a developing country is not measurable by the share of profits between importer and exporter but rather by the stimulus it gives to wider internal economic growth. The measurable linkages between foreign-owned manufacturing enterprises and the local economy appear to be somewhat higher for Ivory Coast and especially Kenya than for Ghana and Tanzania, but it is not clear how significant this difference is. Multinational firms in both Ivory Coast and Kenya have been criticized for their high capital intensity (with concomitant low employment of local labour), their imposition of consumer tastes oriented towards import-dependent final products, and a general lack of interest in developing local linkages. A greater degree of linkage and location outside established urban centres has been achieved in some industries which process local raw materials for export. But insofar as these firms seek to meet the standards of a competitive world market, they are under even greater pressure than that of import-substitution industries to use imported, capital-intensive technology.

If we accept these critiques of multinational operations in Africa, it seems difficult for local governments, whether capitalist or socialist, to improve any aspect of their positions other than the share of immediate profits. However, capitalist regimes have attempted to attack one of the structural problems of dependency upon imported producer capital by insisting upon Africanization of managerial positions within the private sector. The effectiveness of these efforts will be examined in the next section of this chapter.

Along with their openness to direct foreign investment through multinational subsidiaries, Ivory Coast and Kenya have absorbed large amounts of finance capital, both through private loans and arrangements with various bilateral and multilateral public agencies. The most obvious distinction from socialist regimes is the major role of the private capital market (see Figure 9.3B). Kenya's involvement with this form of finance is relatively recent and still fairly cautious. Ivory Coast, on the other hand, was always more heavily committed to private capital-borrowing than other non-oil/mineral African states and, following somewhat uncontrolled bank arrangements made by agricultural parastatals during the 1970s, has become quite heavily leveraged, with a higher ratio of debt to export earnings than even Zaire (see Figure 9.3).

In addition to their private borrowing, Ivory Coast and Kenya have been the recipients of large amounts of public aid and loans from their respective former metropoles, and from the United States, West Germany, the European Development Fund of the EEC (for Ivory Coast) and the World Bank (for Kenya). These loans have not been concentrated in any particular projects comparable to the Volta River dam and the Great Uhuru railway but they made possible the large number of public development initiatives by both capitalist regimes.

The combination of heavy borrowing, high oil import prices, unfavourable terms of trade for exports, and poor weather conditions forced both Ivory Coast and Kenya to apply for assistance to the IMF in the late 1970s. The medicine has produced some unpleasant side effects in both cases; quarrels over monetary versus structural restraints in the case of Kenya, general and far-reaching austerity measures (including a major reduction of parastatals) in Ivory Coast.[43]

However, unlike either Nkrumah's Ghana, Tanzania or an apparently less exposed capitalist state like Zaire, Ivory Coast and Kenya have been able to stand up to this pressure without any major internal upheavals or loss of external credibility. Their major visible assets were their agricultural exports, less vulnerable to long-term or dramatic reversal than copper or oil, and a system of political authority which seems able to retain its legitimacy. The latter factor also works in favour of Tanzania despite the apparently grave economic miscalculations of Nyerere who publicly admitted in 1977 – ten years after the Arusha Declaration – that his country 'is neither socialist nor self-reliant . . . we have not reached our goal; it is not even in sight.'[44]

Obviously Nyerere was encouraged to go on by a vision of socialist transformation which went beyond even the structure of relations with external capital. Th ultimate test of this effort at change and its capitalist counterpart must thus be sought in the class relations fostered by the variant post-colonial economies.

REGIMES AND CLASSES

This chapter began with an attempt to understand the internal dynamics of decolonization by examining the economic and political roles of African social groups. The analysis of post-colonial economies will conclude with a discussion of their relationship to these same groups; state elites, entrepreneurial elites, organized labour, the informal urban sectors, and peasantries. As suggested in the earlier section on these groups, it is their situation, rather than the more easily measurable factors of public as against private enterprise and the presence of foreign capital, which defines the economic path of various African regimes.

As with the dependence on external investment, the heritage of internal economic structures presented all these regimes with a common set of problems. The difficulties of using the state apparatus for direct control of new economic enterprises has already been discussed. The indigenous entrepreneurial elite provided only a weak alternatve to the public sector, especially for efforts to move beyond agriculture and commerce to modern industry. Formally employed labour still remained a small proportion of the national work force in all African countries, but was often in a position to demand a greater share of influence and material resources than the state was willing to grant. The informal urban sectors challenged official development policies from another direction with their pressure both for the amelioration of slums and acceptance of their unauthorized modes of economic enterprise. Finally, the peasantries remained as a basis for continuity with colonial agricultural policies but a potential obstacle to the transformation of rural production. In their postures towards class relations all the regimes were also forced to choose between maximizing production by favouring groups who could make the greatest contribution towards economic growth, or stressing more equitable distribution of economic rewards.

Socialism: whom does the state represent?

The accusations by liberals and conservatives that African socialist regimes are inherently inefficient have been more than matched by critiques from the left, claiming that these regimes serve nothing more than the hegemony of a new exploitative class, the 'bureaucratic' or 'petty' bourgeoisie.[45] In the case of Ghana, as will be seen, this argument can be developed further to represent the state as the vehicle of particular sectors of the entrepreneurial elite seeking monopoly privileges in commerce and access to public development funds for their private consumption, i.e. a betrayal of socialism by non-competitive and unproductive capitalists. Tanzania exemplifies a purer type of a state apparatus apparently driven by a compulsion to control all sectors of the economy whether out of belief by its leaders that their vision of change was correct or by a simple instinct for authority in a potentially unstable situation. In both instances the state elites failed to win the economic allegiance of any other classes although in Tanzania, as already indicated, political legitimacy seems to have survived. It is not proposed here to pursue the contradictions between a vision of more genuine socialism (presumably growing out of class relationships within the production sectors) and this form of state dominance, but rather to examine how various classes came to terms with such regimes.

The immediate local enemy of socialist regimes in both Ghana and Tanzania was the emerging indigenous entrepreneurial elite, although it was only in Ghana that such a group existed in any significant strength.[46] Indeed, local merchants and wealthy farmers (often the same people in rural cocoa markets) here played a leading role in pre-Second World War anti-colonial protest movements and some were early adherents of Nkrumah's Convention People's Party (CPP) despite its populist character. In the first phase of his tenure of power (from 1951 to 1960) Nkrumah established programmes to support local businessmen by granting them credit, privileged access to government contracts, and other benefits. In substance, however, little was accomplished by the indigenous bourgeoisie in their more traditional areas of endeavour and the entire Nkrumah period witnessed an expansion of the role of foreign entrepreneurs, both European and Levantine.

Once Nkrumah had committed himself to socialism, however, those party members with business backgrounds found new opportunities to pursue their interests. Nkrumah established the Ghana National Trading Corporation to compete with private import firms. However, a considerable share of this market was left to independent merchants who managed to survive socialism without major decline, if also without major gain. It was the cruelly misnamed United Ghana Farmers' Council (UGFC) which provided the key opportunity for CPP-affiliated merchants, since this organization achieved a total monopoly of cocoa exports. The immediate victims of this shift were foreign firms, already on the way out of such activities (see Chapter 8), and the local brokers and co-operative societies, who more directly represented farmers, if mainly the wealthier ones. In contrast to more purely 'state elite' nationalized enterprises in Tanzania, the UGFC did get the cocoa crop effectively marketed but with an element of personal and institutional corruption which seriously compromised the entire notion of socialism in Ghana.[47]

Indeed, a tradition of illegitimate collusion between government and business interests may have been the most lasting heritage of the Nkrumah era, as reflected in the widespread corruption of subsequent military and civilian regimes and the present regression to what may be a despotism of the type associated with far less-developed African countries.[48]

In Tanzania indigenous entrepreneurial classes had developed to only a very limited extent during the colonial period. The nationalist regime thus had some success in imposing a leadership code upon government and party cadres so as to prevent them from using their public positions to promote private-sector careers. Local mercantile and industrial enterprises were largely in the hands of immigrant South Asians rather than Africans. It is interesting that this community was never subject to economic restrictions on ethnic grounds, as occurred in more capitalist neighbouring Kenya and Uganda. But the Asians of Tanzania ultimately emigrated in large numbers as a result of the far-reaching incursions upon the commercial activities with which they were most identified, i.e. the 1970 State Trading Corporation takeover of over 4000 import and wholesale firms, the 1971 appropriation of all urban buildings not occupied by their owners, and the 1976 attack on private retailing. Given the inefficiency of its public-sector operations as well as the need to come to terms with foreign lenders in a period of desperate financial need, the Tanzania government eventually rescinded the latter two of these measures and decentralized the State Trading Corporation, but the possibility of strong and legitimate private-sector capitalism had suffered possibly irreparable damage.[49]

Early in their nationalist struggles both Nkrumah's CPP and the Tanganyika

African National Union (TANU) led by Nyerere had been strongly identified with militant labour unions. The problem for both regimes once they came into power was not only that the unions represented a potential source of authority independent of the state but that the greatest militancy took place in what had always been state enterprises: the railways and docks. Union organization in private-sector firms, which might presumably have been the common targets of organized workers and a socialist regime, was more paternalistic or, in the Tanganyika sisal estates, simply ineffectual.

Nkrumah and Nyerere thus moved very quickly after independence to place national labour unions under new central organizations, headed by loyal party figures. All wage employees now had to join but strikes were forbidden and little room was left for autonomous expressions of worker interests. In response to these efforts to control them, the unions did, in fact, become instruments for protest of a class which felt most immediately the shortcomings of the new socialist efforts. In 1961, when Nkrumah introduced new taxes, import restrictions, and compulsory savings schemes to make the people aware of 'false standards and illusory ideas of wealth . . .' the unions, led by militant railway workers, went out on a major general strike. The strike was eventually suppressed and its leaders imprisoned, but the unions subsequently remained enemies of Nkrumah and enthusiastically welcomed his fall five years later.[50]

In Tanzania the situation was more ambiguous. The publication of official *Mwongozo* guidelines for labour relationships in 1971 became the occasion for a series of strikes and later takeovers of factories by workers, who complained about the incompetence and unjustified material privileges of management as well as the official union leadership. The government first suppressed the strikes, then gave some encouragement to reform of unions and to worker participation in managing parastatal firms, and finally shifted back to a more repressive policy. It has been argued that, in this final reversal, the Tanzania authorities acted in response to pressures (actual or anticipated) from foreign investors in the parastatal industrial sector.[51] In any case, neither Ghanaian nor Tanzanian socialism succeeded in winning over the organized-labour sector, whether out of failings in the regimes themselves or out of an inherent contradiction between the relatively privileged position of formal-sector workers and broader needs (to complete the quotation from Nkrumah begun above) 'in an economy which has not yet got off to a real start on the road to reconstruction and development.'[52]

The Ghanaian and Tanzanian leadership were no more effective in coming to terms with the large proportion of urban populations who could not find any place in the formal sectors of the economy. Both socialist regimes first sought solutions to the presence of such groups within their main cities by attempting to return them to more useful occupations in the countryside. Nkrumah's device for achieving this goal was to recruit the urban unemployed into the rural-based Workers' Brigade which distributed them to various camps where they were paid salaries to engage in modern intensive agriculture as well as the transport and marketing of foodstuffs. Like the State Farms Corporation, with which it was closely linked, the Workers' Brigade proved to be a very costly failure. Tanzania, in the years between independence and the Arusha Declaration on Socialism, attempted a less centralized 'villagization' programme, in which the TANU Youth League employed city dwellers in settlement schemes, which also failed to produce goods equal in value to their capitalization costs.[53]

Despite these efforts the informal sectors actually flourished under socialist regimes. Nkrumah's Ghana is the setting for Keith Hart's classic study of this form of economic endeavour. On both sides of the continent socialist policies created new demands and opportunities for 'underground' enterprise such as the smuggling of export commodities (particularly Ghanaian cocoa) into neighbouring countries offering better market opportunities and petty brokerage between otherwise employed consumers and the state agencies which were supposed to deliver various goods and services to the internal market.[54]

In the late 1970s Tanzania, with World Bank support, did attempt a 'model' solution to informal-sector housing problems by initiating an extensive 'site and services' programme, i.e. provision of roads, water, sewerage, electricity, etc. to poor neighbourhoods where local entrepreneurs would be allowed to construct houses according to the modest standards already prevailing in these areas. Unfortunately this effort became so entangled in the procedures for obtaining state approval of construction projects that it led to the building of very few houses and all of these at a far higher cost than most slum residents could afford.[55]

Peasant farmers had been the other mainstay of nationalist mass support in the decolonization period but, as already indicated, neither of the socialist regimes under discussion here was committed either to the maintenance of traditional smallholder cultivation or to the emergence from it of a rural bourgeoisie. The efforts to create a new agricultural system varied greatly between Ghana and Tanzania but the result of both was very similar: an 'exit' of the peasantry from the national system with damaging effects on productivity.

The Ghanaian case is simpler because Nkrumah's state farms projects simply paralleled the existing smallholder cultivation system, which continued to account for the major export earning through cocoa production. Resentment of the lack of government support for peasant enterprise and more direct exploitation by the officially sanctioned UGFC marketing monopoly initially took the form of refusals to increase cocoa production. Peasants also failed to undertake seriously the cultivation of alternative cash crops, which Nkrumah was trying to link with a series of raw-material processing plants. Given the life cycle of cocoa trees, exports of this key cash crop actually declined only after Nkrumah's removal but the first stage of peasant economic withdrawal can be traced back to the experience of socialism.[56]

Tanzanian socialism envisaged the peasantry as the base for a new economic order but only if peasants would regroup themselves into 'ujamaa villages' with their collective cultivation and access to more modern equipment. Critics of ujamaa have pointed to two sets of flaws: its corruption, as 'kulaks' (wealthy peasants as perceived in Marxist terms) formed alliances with local government staff representatives; and the inevitable and successful resistance of the mass rural population to programmes imposed upon them (often through the use of force) by an alien state apparatus.[57] The latter argument is probably more central, since the ujamaa programme did generally undermine the position of wealthier farmers both by diverting resources to other sectors (through price controls and taxation as well as direct actions) and by destroying the locally based co-operatives which had allowed some members of the rural elite to enter large-scale merchandizing.

There were no wider-scale political reactions against ujamaa but by the mid-1970s food shortages and declining commercial exports seemed to indicate that Tanzanian peasants were exercising their 'exit' option at considerable cost to the rest of the economy. There is some dispute among scholars as to how much of this decline can be attributed to disaffection with ujamaa villagization policies as opposed to drought, low producer prices (subsequently raised), and increased costs of imported inputs (due to rising oil prices).[58]

At best the Tanzanian regime may be said to have reached a truce with its peasantry: rural populations remained in their new villages and enjoyed access to increased social facilities (particularly schools; less so water supplies and medicine) but collective cultivation has been abandoned and the technology, social organization and productivity of agriculture remained what it was before the massive ujamaa 'operations'.

Capitalism: is there a national bourgeoisie?

The critique of dominant classes in African capitalist systems focuses on two questions, again about representativeness, but in different terms to those asked of socialists. First, given the major role of foreign private firms as well as the local state in these economies, how autonomous and effective is the indigenous entrepreneurial elite? Second, to what degree do the rewards of economic success benefit groups outside the elite?

While such questions are equally appropriate to Ivory Coast and Kenya, the resulting answers differ considerably. One factor which has to be considered is the far greater level of information about the social basis of certain economic sectors available for Kenya. This situation may simply reflect the disparity in resources between English-speaking and French-speaking researchers although it also suggests that in Ivory Coast there is greater domination even of data relating to these sectors by foreign entrepreneurs and the state. One very clear substantive difference lies in the relationship between political power and rural entrepreneurship. Despite a widely conveyed view that the relatively successful capitalist orientation of Ivory Coast and Kenya derives from the common base of both regimes in an indigenous plantocracy, the distinctions between the two regimes in this area are critical to the general divergence in their experiences of capitalist development.

Both promoters and critics of Ivory Coast capitalism have collaborated to create the myth of a regime dominated by a local 'planter bourgeoisie'. In reality, the economic development of the Ivory Coast since independence has given rise to a widening gap between the state elite, the rural entrepreneurial elite, and the owners of modern enterprises.[59]

As noted above, nationalist politics in the Ivory Coast arose around an organization of affluent African cocoa farmers who objected to the privileged position of competing French settlers. But the French settler position was never very strong so that the agricultural issues in the decolonization process could be resolved fairly easily and without any major transformation of rural society. Once provided with access to real political power, the ruling party of the Ivory Coast shifted its main concerns from investments in agriculture to the cultivation of resources located in urban areas: education, employment, and residential real estate. The switch was not too difficult since the nationalist leadership already had a foot in both terrains, as exemplified by Houphouët-Boigny, himself an owner of large cocoa lands but also a medical graduate of the most advanced school in French West Africa and an experienced middle-level bureaucrat.

In its efforts at 'Ivorianization' of the private sector, the Ivory Coast state has not, like the Kenyan authorities, had to worry about taking over established export cultivation. Instead the main effort at promoting an indigenous bourgeoisie has concentrated upon urban manufacturing and commerce and new agrobusiness enterprises in the countryside. The statistical record of this undertaking does not indicate great success.[60] Even more revealing than the numbers of Ivorians with shareholdings or managerial positions in this modern sector is the nature of their participation. First of all, the largest Ivorian investor by a considerable margin is the state and the most significant indigenous managerial roles are in state enterprises. Ivorians with savings available from their salaries have followed a very cautious investment policy. They have tended to buy small numbers of shares in the larger and more successful expatriate firms within the country, to send a considerable amount of their capital abroad, and to establish control over local assets on a largely risk-minimizing basis: leasing forestry and urban real estate to Europeans, and buying into petty African businesses such as taxis, shops, and produce farms operated along traditional low-capital lines.[61]

It has been argued that a more autonomous and daring national bourgeoisie will eventually emerge from this situation. However, since the late 1970s the state has been forced to close or narrow down a number of its large-scale farming enterprises precisely because they offered opportunities for foreign suppliers and local elites to collaborate in unaffordably wasteful private aggrandisement. The state has given Ivorians control of certain categories of middle-range urban enterprise, such as bakeries, but it appears that these kinds of monopolies generate little real growth. The state element in Ivory Coast capitalism thus seems to act more as a broker for a dominant external economy than a base for indigenous private enterprise. It is obviously too early after independence to judge whether such a pattern of development can satisfy the ambitions of a growing middle class, to say nothing of the remainder of the population, whose relationship to the system will be dealt with below.

Kenya, for better or worse, has come to represent the one case in Africa of a national bourgeoisie able to compete with foreign entrepreneurs on something like their own terms.[62] The historical basis for this development lies in the disruptive effect of settler colonialism on the Kenya countryside where, as already noted (see Chapter 7), very marked class differentiation had taken place among the African population long before independence. The Mau Mau rebellion accompanying the nationalist struggle was powerful enough to ensure the removal of British support from the well-entrenched settlers, but too weak to impose any kind of egalitarianism on the structure of landholding or Kenyan society in general. The Kenyan political elite thus contained a large proportion of actual or would-be landowners who sought not only to protect existing holdings but also to take over European forms of agriculture and to use political connections to establish their own modern urban enterprises.

The patronage role of the Kenyan state in this process resembles that of the Ivory Coast in some important respects: there are regulations for 'Africanization' (as distinguished from supporting the established Asian entrepreneurial class) capital is made available to Kenyan businessmen at favourable rates; and positions in parastatal enterprises provide privileged access to various rewards from foreign capital. The local stock market, foreign investments, along with rentier and petty enterprise of various kinds also play a major role in the portfolios of indigenous capitalists. But in a number of large-scale areas such as major distributorships, shoe manufacturing, and industrial tea production, Kenyan African entrepreneurs have created independent firms and managed to win over significant market shares from established multinationals.

In Kenya the state has provided resources for influential and skilled Africans to establish an autonomous position within their own national economy. Some observers have criticized this new entrepreneurial bourgeoisie as a 'transnational class' which has won a place for itself in the world economy without necessarily changing the pattern of Kenyan development. But to test this proposition, as well as the less dynamic accommodation by Ivory Coast capitalists, it is necessary to look beyond the elite.

As might be expected from the general pattern of African economic development, if not from Western experience, capitalist regimes have established better relationships with organized labour in the formal sector than have socialists. In the case of Ivory Coast, the state again has a very dominant role, as the local labour movement before independence had been relatively weak and limited mainly to white-collar employees linked with guild-like associations of petty entrepreneurs, particularly *transporteurs* (taxi and truck drivers or owners).[63] Since coming to power the Ivory Coast regime has attempted both to placate and to control labour. Placation consists of minimum-wage laws guaranteeing an actual rise in the living standards of urban workers (the rural labour force, mainly immigrant, is paid considerably less) and recognition of union leaders as members of the semi-formal 'national council' convoked by President Houphouët-Boigny at irregular intervals to discuss major policy issues. Control is exercised by a single, party-based organization embracing all trade unions and limitations upon the right to strike (not always maintained). It is sustained by a general absence of opposition to the government except (during the early years of independence) on the rates of Ivorianization of middle-range positions. The austerity of recent years has brought strikes by such groups as schoolteachers, reflecting the consciously middle-class character of the labour movement in the Ivory Coast but also its potential for leading dissent should the regime cease delivering its economic rewards to those within the establishment.

Kenyan labour organizations cherish a history of stronger and more autonomous action within the independence movement, based in part, as already noted above, on the earlier and less orderly industrialization of the country.[64] When the leading trade union figure in the nationalist movement, Tom Mboya, moved into government, the unions themselves were placed under a centralized organization headed by party loyalists. However, in apparent contrast to the Ivory Coast (and again the unevenness of data must be taken into account here) the individual Kenyan unions seem to have maintained considerable autonomy in selecting their immediate leaders, making wage demands, and even going out on illegal strikes. Workers within the formal sector in Kenya have essentially accepted the existing economic system and are more representative of the broader population than those elements which have been most militant in the Ivory Coast union movement. At the same time, they stand in close relation to a far more volatile informal urban sector.

Both Ivory Coast and Kenya were urged during the 1970s by generally friendly international agencies to give more positive attention to the promotion of indigenous capitalism through the support of informal-sector enterprise.[65] Both capitalist systems do, in fact, provide optimal conditions for the legitimate growth of such activities in linkage with the growing and relatively unrestricted formal sector. Neither Ivory Coast nor Kenya, however, has done much more than tolerate informal-sector undertakings whose promise as a source of autonomous African development, rather than as a means of low-level survival in the urban environment, remains questionable.

As might be expected, we have relatively little information on the informal sector in the Ivory Coast.[66] Its broad base, however, seems to consist of poorly capitalized, mainly immigrant-operated enterprises with little possibility for advancement. A 'transitional' sector has a greater native Ivorian component, is better financed and able to take some advantage of state support, but not linked in any dynamic way either to major modern industries, or to such potentially expansive autonomous activities as low-cost residential construction (restricted by government housing policies). If we are to believe the analysts of the Ivory Coast regime, the state has shown success in maintaining the informal sector as a combination of classic low-level equilibrium for the majority and a monopolistic upward mobility for a minority (the classic example being licensed bakeries). Possibly the key to this success is the acceptance by the poorest element in the capital and primate city, Abidjan, of its status as immigrants from outside the national borders who are satisfied with the accumulation of small surpluses for eventual repatriation to their impoverished home countries (mainly Burkina Faso and Niger).

The informal sector plays a much larger role in Kenya. It is a function and also a measure of a capitalist system far less effectively under central control.[67] At the official level, the Kenyan government has never followed up on various promises to support informal-sector artisans or seriously implement site-and-service housing schemes. Nairobi urban authorities have frequently harassed and even destroyed large sectors of the city's unauthorized work and living quarters. However, the victims of these policies have also had their own representatives on the City Council as well as other political and business connections with influential public figures, so that most of their economic activities have been able to continue and even grow. Studies of the Kenya informal sector in the early 1970s provided classic evidence of its immobility, but the more recent survey by William J. House indicates that artisans here have been able to move beyond recycling scrap from the formal sector to taking on sub-contracts for services *to* the formal sector.[68] Success of this kind could be one of the greatest achievements of Kenyan capitalism. By the same token, failure of informal-sector development could have disastrous consequences, since the population of Nairobi has grown at a rate vastly beyond the capacity of formal-sector absorption. Its potentially explosive capacities were demonstrated in the riots which accompanied the abortive air-force coup of 1982.

In their rural policies, both Ivory Coast and Kenya are distinguished from socialist regimes by their support for the continuation and even expansion of smallholder commercial farming, both in its established form and as the basis for the formation of a rural bourgeoisie. However in practice the differences between the two capitalist cases here are almost as striking as their joint contrast with socialist experiences.

Despite various efforts at diversifying commercial agriculture, Ivory Coast has continued to depend for the bulk of its foreign exchange earnings on the two staples of colonial export production, cocoa and coffee.[69] The expansion of this sector since independence has continued to produce, as it did earlier, considerable differentiation between farmers in the size of their landholdings and the degree to which they make use of hired labour. However, just as in the classic colonial peasant syndrome (see Chapter 6), this disparity of access to resources has not produced full capitalist relations within the agricultural economy. Richer farmers work with their hired labourers in the fields, and the latter, even when immigrants, can generally look forward to acquiring land of their own. Investment by cocoa and coffee farmers in agricultural technology (even at the level of insecticide sprayers) has remained minimal. Instead accumulations of surplus wealth continue to flow out of agriculture into enterprises such as transport and marketing (including advancement of loans to poorer farmers), education for children seeking urban careers, and more recently the construction of modern housing in provincial towns for rental to locally posted state bureaucrats.

Despite its rhetoric of support for peasants and planters, the Ivory Coast state in practice provides few incentive for the reinvestment of cash-crop profits in private agriculture. Indeed, the difference between producer prices and export prices maintained by the *caisse de stabilisation* is so great that the largest part of these profits is directly appropriated by the state and invested by it either in urban sectors or new, large-scale agricultural enterprises. State-financed farming projects do provide some basis for the emergence of new rural classes in the form either of managers, or outgrowers (on varying scales of ownership) using more capital-intensive cultivation systems. But up to now these ambitious schemes have succeeded at best only in occupying a minor proportion of national agricultural output. Essentially Ivory Coast capitalism has maintained peace with its rural constituency in much the same way as the colonial regimes did: by leaving peasants relatively undisturbed and providing opportunities for steady, if limited, gains in agricultural income and small, but not overly risky, investments in the off-farm sectors of the economy.

Rural class relations in Kenya likewise followed the inherited colonial pattern but the result here has been both a more marked expansion of peasant cash-cropping and a greater penetration of capitalist relations into agriculture.[70] The major colonial trading commodities – coffee for export and maize and dairy products for both domestic and foreign marketing – continue to hold their position in post-independence Kenyan agriculture and are still produced on a mixture of smallholder and large-scale farms.

The peasant sector has expanded most dramatically (although in continuity with late-colonial policies). Infrastructure and direct government support were extended to previously neglected areas outside the settler regions and portions of the former European reserves were redistributed to African smallholders. The 'estate' sector of agriculture also grew, as more-successful peasants no longer met legal obstacles to the formal consolidation of their holdings and the use of ploughs drawn by oxen or tractors, fertilizer, and other modern technologies. Many of the former European estates were also retained on their former scale when transferred to indigenous ownership or cut up into relatively large portions which could only be purchased by wealthy Africans. Finally, the one crop to gain a major share of export production, tea, was increasingly grown by outgrower smallholders, integrated into modern factory processing systems.

Despite the existence of parastatal marketing boards to control marketing, the Kenya government has generally maintained pricing policies which favour producers who, like urban workers, squatters, and entrepreneurs, are able to exert some political pressure on those in authority. Major losses to farmers have occurred through corruption within the marketing organizations but these (especially the co-operatives controlling coffee and dairy and meat products) are even closer to the realm of producers and susceptible to periodic purges if not ultimate correction.

Although Kenyan peasants are thus subjected to relatively low taxation, government policy has still favoured the larger landholders. This rural capitalist class parallels urban entrepreneurs in its confident ability to take over European roles and is directly linked to major industrial enterprises through such undertakings as the tea industry. But economic observers have raised the same questions about the efficiency of the new African landed elite as were asked about their European predecessors or the indigenous estate farmers of another East African capitalist economy, Malawi: is privileged access to public support justified by their contribution to national wealth?[71] In terms of strict output per hectare cultivated, it appears that peasant smallholders are more efficient, although not in ratios comparable to such examples of true misallocation as, for instance, the Ghana State Farms Corporation.

But the ultimate justification of an African landowner class lies not in its performance in one particular activity, but rather its role in creating a more locally linked base of intensive development than would be possible under either the egalitarian programme of rural socialism or the peripheral stability of the countryside under the Ivory Coast version of capitalism. In Kenya this is again a very critical issue because the contributions of rural capitalism to the creation of a national bourgeoisie are impressive, but the shortages of land and very manifest inequalities of class income have created great resentment against the new economic elite.

Conclusion

While there has been an effort throughout this chapter to avoid drawing firm conclusions from the very tentative data available to us on post-colonial African economic development, certain patterns clearly suggest themselves. One is that the more ambitious state-directed development programmes have not been successful. The second is the persistence of peasant agriculture as a mainstay of African economies, more often in opposition to development plans than as their basis. Finally, despite the call among recent revisionist critics for a 'bourgeois revolution' to counteract the abortive étatism of the last decades, the positive historical evidence in favour of a capitalist path, or even stage, is still very weak.[72]

Thus the changes referred to in the opening section of this chapter make for a more dramatic narrative of initiative and conflict than the events of the classic colonial era between the two world wars, but no happy ending of economic transformation is in sight. Given the weakened international position of Africa, one lesson to be learned from historical contemplation might be that the continent should return to the less pretentious development modes which prevailed before the unsettling events of the Great Depression, the Second World War, and decolonization. The case of the Ivory Coast demonstrates the degree to which such a strategy is still viable but also its limitations. Even without the departure from cautious planning which brought about the current debt load of Houphouët-Boigny's regime, such factors as demography and the need for a modern sector dynamic enough to absorb the expectations of rural producers would inevitably undermine the old étatist-peasant formula.[73] South Africa represents another form of colonial continuity, in this case based upon nearly total transformation to modern, industrial forms of production but, for that very reason, unable to assimilate economically the majority population which it has subjected to such severe political and social repression.

It is obvious which forms of economic development have failed but not at all apparent what constitutes meaningful success. The easiest solution for outsiders, as articulated in numerous journalistic writings of the mid-1980s, is to dismiss sub-Saharan Africa as a massive catastrophe, the 'sick person' of the modern world economy.[74] But such a view prophesies on the basis of short-term conditions which – despite recent reports of high death rates from malnutrition – have not yet gained anything like an irreversible momentum. On the basis of material in this chapter, it is impossible to provide a serious alternative vision of the future. But it may be worthwhile to conclude this entire book with a review of the more extended past and the broader picture of African economic change which it suggests.

Notes

1. Hopkins (1973) p. 254f.
2. Callaghy (1984) pp. 5–68, 111–37 for a recent review of this literature and a neo-absolutist (using Louis XIV as a model) argument.
3. Wasserman (1976) p. 133.
4. Friedland and Rosberg (1964) especially pp. 4–9.
5. Southall (1978); Rosberg and Nottingham (1966) p. 83f.; Zolberg (1964) pp. 66–71.
6. Amin (1969) p. 26f. 142–8; Kennedy (1980) pp. 57–9; Kilby (1965) pp. 6–16, 88f.; Nafziger (1977) p. 126f.
7. Gbagbo (1982) p. 98f.; Sorrenson (1967) pp. 117–18f.
8. Morgenthau (1964) p. 174f.; Joseph (1977) pp. 103–67; Rathbone (1973); Schatz (1977) p. 84f.; Sklar (1963) pp. 446–60.
9 The orthodox radical position is defended in Sandbrook and Cohen (1975); the major statement of the labour aristocracy thesis is Arrighi (1973).
10. Stichter (1978); Amsden (1971), for European efforts, also in Kenya, to create harmless labour unions.
11. Berg and Butler (1964); Henderson (1973).
12. Peace (1979) p. 49f.; see Bates (1981) for the general 'urban bias' in African economic policies.
13. Hanna and Lynne (1971) pp. 27–41; Sabot (1979); Vennettier (1976) pp. 32–48.
14. Bromley and Gerry (1979); Hart (1970); Sethuraman (1981).
15. Austin (1964) pp. 66–77.
16. Lonsdale (1968).
17. Austen and Headrick (1983) p. 86f.; Frechou (1955).
18. Austin (1964) pp. 59–66; Maguire (1969); Wallerstein (1964); Zolberg (1964) pp. 62–5, 70–4.
19. For recent typologies see Rosberg and Jackson (1982); Sandbrook (1982); Young (1982).
20. For an overview see Rosberg and Callaghy (1979); Young (1982) pp. 22–182; case studies; Johnson (1978); Jones (1976); Ottaway and Ottaway (1981) (on the second generation socialist regimes).
21. But see Schatz (1977); Joseph (1978); Williams (1976); Zartman (1983).
22. Young (1982) is probably the best of the recent surveys of African approaches to development but can be criticized for too literal an interpretation of ideology.
23. Collier (1982); Shaw (1982).
24. For the following sections, see separate bibliographies on each country. For general points which are not footnoted, the main sources are: Killick (1978); Roemer (1984) (Ghana); Fauré and Médard (1982) (Ivory Coast); Fransman (1982) pp. 142–231 and Hazlewood (1979) (Kenya); Barkan and Okumu (1984) (Kenya and Tanzania); Coulson (1982); Lele (1984) (Tanzania).

25. Miracle and Seidman (1968) on Ghana state farms; Coulson, 1982, pp. 237–62 for a summary of the very extensive literature on ujamaa; on specific issues, see below.
26. Dozon (1979); France (1982); Pillet-Schwartz (1978, 1980) (Ivory Coast); Buch-Hansen and Marcussen (1982) (Kenya).
27. Monson and Pursell (1979); Mytelka (1984); Valette (1980) (Ivory Coast); Leys (1980) (Kenya).
28. Frank (1971); Wilson (1982).
29. Le Vine (1976); Hyden, Goran (1979), 'Administration and Public Policy', in Joel P. Barkan and John J. Okumu, *Politics and Public Policy in Kenya and Tanzania* (New York: Praeger), pp. 93–113.
30. Killick (1978) pp. 11–26; Clark (1978) especially pp. 74–9, argues that ujamaa was theoretically a reaction against 'big push' policies, but in practice continued to attempt rapid, centrally directed transformations of both industry and agriculture.
31. Woronoff (1972).
32. Biersteker (1978); Curry and Rothchild (1974); Hymer (1972); Rood (1975); Vernon (1977); Widstrand (1973).
33. Kitchen (1983) p. 45; Lipson (1985) pp. 108–11.
34. Cohen and Tribe (1972); Schatz (1969).
35. Payer (1974); Stryker (1979).
36. Oertly (1971); Thompson (1969) p. 258f. (Ghana); Clark (1978) p. 188f.; Coulson (1977); Kim (1978); Kunya (1976) (Tanzania).
37. Killick (1978) pp. 249–51; Graham (1982) especially pp. 224–31.
38. Coulson (1982) pp. 231–4.
39. Mittelman (1981) pp. 202–28; Stryker (1979).
40 Watts and Lubeck (1983).
41. Masini *et al.* (1979); Mytelka (1984); Tuinder (1978) pp. 86–94 (Ivory Coast); Kaplinsky (1979); Langdon (1981a); Swainson (1980) (Kenya).
42. Campbell (1975); Langdon (1981b); Mytelka (1981).
43. France (1982); Killick (1981b).
44. Nyerere (1977) p. 1.
45. e.g. Fitch and Oppenheimer (1966) especially pp. 19–25; Shivji (1976).
46. Esseks (1971); Garlick (1971); Kennedy (1977, 1980); Rathbone (1973).
47. Beckman (1976).
48. Chazan (1983).
49. Lele (1984); Resnick (1976).
50. Jeffries (1978); Kraus (1979); Silver (1978); Nkrumah (1963) p. 100.
51. Bienefeld (1975); Bolton (1978); Friedland (1967); Mapolu (1976).
52. Nkrumah (1963) p. 100.
53. Jones (1976) pp. 221f., 246–53; Killick (1978) passim; Cliffe and Cunningham (1973).
54. Hart (1970); Harris (1983).
55. Stren (1982).
56. Killick (1978) pp. 118–20.
57. Freyhold (1979) p. 54f. and Van Velzen (1973) (for the kulak-staff argument); Coulson (1982) pp. 235–71; Hyden (1980) (for the peasant vs. state position).
58. Lofchie (1978); but see counter-arguments and qualifications by Raikes (1979); Ellis (1982).
59. Gastellu and Yapi (1982); Groff (1980); Hecht (1983).
60. Tuinder (1978) pp. 151–5.
61. Miras (1982); Mytelka (1984).
62. The debate on the nature of the Kenyan bourgeoisie can be followed in Fransman (1982) pp. 142–231; Godfrey and Langdon (1976); Martin (1978); Swainson (1980).
63. Cohen (1974) pp. 65–8, 107–9, 296, 296–305; Zolberg (1964) pp. 205–7.
64. Clayton and Savage (1974); Sandbrook (1975); Stichter (1982).
65. Tuinder (1978) pp. 297–8; Burrows (1975) pp. 326–7.
66. Cohen (1974) pp. 208–11; Miras (1982); Joshi *et al.* (1976) pp. 49–60.

67. Bujra (1978/79); Chege (1981); Hake (1977); King (1971); Nelson (1979); House (1981); Werlin (1974), p. 228f.
68. House (1981).
69. See note 59 above; also Gbetibouo and Delgado (1984): Lee (1980); for the decline of the earlier staple, timber, see Arnaud and Sournia (1979).
70. Leo (1984); Oketh-Ogendo (1981).
71. Kydd and Christiansen (1982); Edinburgh (1984) (this collection became available too late to be taken into full account here; however both it and Leo (1984) suggest that in the 1980s Malawi and Kenya have made important concessions to the interests of smallholders at the expense of large-estate agriculture).
72. Hyden (1983) p. 200 (it is noteworthy that the author, who knows Kenya well, does not view it as an exemplary case of the African capitalism that he has in mind); for an 'official' statement of the current liberal position see World Bank (1981).
73. The prediction by Amin (1967) that Ivory Coast's late start as a major export producer was all that explained its post-colonial success, has proved premature; but for a more insightful comparison with Ghana see Gastellu (1981/82); for a restatement of Amin's argument, see Campbell (1978).
74. Anon. (1984).

Bibliography

1. *General*

Amin, Samir (1969), *Le Monde des affaires sénégalaises* (Paris: Editions de Minuit)

Anon. (1984), ' "Dark Continent" image revived', *Africa News*, vol. 22, no. 10, p. 1f.

Arrighi, Giovanni (1973), 'International capital, labour aristocracies, and economic development in tropical Africa', in Giovanni Arrighi and John S. Saul (eds), *Essays on the Political Economy of Africa* (New York: Monthly Review Press), pp. 105–51

Austen, Ralph A. and Rita Headrick (1983), 'Equatorial Africa under colonial rule', in David Birmingham and Phyllis M. Martin (eds), *History of Central Africa*, Vol. 2 (London: Longman), pp. 27–94

Bates, Robert H. (1981), *Market and State in Tropical Africa* (Berkeley: University of California Press)

Berg, Elliot J. and Jeffrey Butler (1964), 'Trade unions', in Coleman and Rosberg (eds), pp. 340–81

Biersteker, Thomas J. (1978), *Destitution or Development? Contending Perspectives on the Multinational Corporation* (Cambridge: MIT Press)

Bromley, Ray and Chris Gerry (eds) (1979), *Casual Work and Poverty in Third World Countries* (Chichester: Wiley)

Callaghy, Thomas M. (1984), *The State–Society Struggle: Zaire in Comparative Perspective* (New York: Columbia University Press)

Coleman, James S. and Carl G. Rosberg (eds) (1964), *Political Parties and National Integration in Tropical Africa* (Berkeley: University of California Press)

Collier, Ruth (1982), *Regimes in Tropical Africa* (Berkeley: University of California Press)

Curry, Robert L. and Donald Rothchild (1974), 'On economic bargaining between African governments and multinational corporations', *Journal of Modern African Studies*, vol. 12, no. 2, pp. 173–89

Dunn, John (ed.) (1978), *West African States: Failure and Promise* (Cambridge: Cambridge University Press)

Edinburgh (1984), *Malawi: An Alternative Pattern of Development* (Seminar Proceedings, Centre of African Studies: University of Edinburgh)

Frank, Jr, Charles R. (1971), 'Public and private enterprise in Africa', in Gustav Ranis (ed.),

Government and Economic Development (New Haven: Yale University Press), pp. 88–125

Friedland, W.H. and C.G. Rosberg (1964), *African Socialism* (Stanford: Hoover Institution Press)

Gutkind, Peter C.W., Robin Cohen, and Jean Copans (eds) (1978), *African Labour History* (Beverley Hills: Sage)

Hanna, William John and Judith Lynne (1971), *Urban Dynamics in Black Africa* (Chicago: Aldine)

Harberger, Arnold C. (ed.) (1984), *World Economic Growth* (San Francisco: ICS)

Henderson, Ian (1973), 'Wage-earners and political protest in colonial Africa: the case of the copperbelt', *African Affairs*, vol. 72, no. 288, pp. 288–99

Hopkins, A.G. (1973), *An Economic History of West Africa* (New York: Columbia University Press)

Hyden, Goran (1983), *No Shortcut to Progress: African Development Management in Perspective* (Berkeley: University of California Press)

Hymer, Stephen (1972), 'The multinational corporation and the law of uneven development', in Jagdish N. Bhagwati (ed.), *Economics and World Order from the 1970s to the 1990s* (New York: Macmillan), pp. 113–40

Johnson, R.W. (1978), 'Guinea', in Dunn (ed.), pp. 36–55

Jones, William I. (1976), *Planning Economic Policy: Socialist Mali and her Neighbours* (Washington: Three Continents Press)

Joseph, Richard (1977), *Radical Nationalism in Cameroun: Social Origins of the UPC Rebellion* (Oxford: Clarendon Press)

Joseph, Richard (1978), 'Affluence and underdevelopment: the Nigerian experience', *Journal of Modern African Studies*, vol. 16, no. 2, pp. 221–39

Kilby, Peter (1965), *African Enterprise: the Nigerian Bread Industry* (Stanford: Hoover Institution Press)

Kitchen, Helen (1983), *United States Interests and Africa* (New York: Praeger)

Kydd, Jonathan and Robert Christiansen (1982), 'Structural change in Malawi since independence: consequences of a development strategy based on large-scale agriculture', *World Development*, vol. 10, no. 5, pp. 355–75

Lipson, Charles (1985), *Standing Guard: Protecting Foreign Capital in the Nineteenth and Twentieth Centuries* (Berkeley: University of California Press)

Lonsdale, John M. (1968), 'Some origins of nationalism in East Africa', *Journal of African History*, vol. 9, no. 1, pp. 119–46

Morgenthau, Ruth Schachter (1964), *Political Parties in French-Speaking West Africa* (Oxford: Clarendon Press)

Nafziger, E. Wayne (1977), *African Capitalism: A Case Study of Nigerian Entrepreneurship* (Stanford: Hoover Institution Press)

OEEC/OECD (Organization for European Economic Cooperation/Organization for Economic Cooperation and Development) (1961–84), *The Flow of Financial Resources to Countries in the Course of Economic Development* (Paris: OEEC/OECD)

Ottaway, David and Marina Ottaway (1981), *Afrocommunism* (New York: Africana Press)

Payer, Cheryl (1974), *The Debt Trap: The IMF and the Third World* (New York: Monthly Review Press)

Peace, Adrian J. (1979), *Choice, Class and Conflict. A Study of Southern Nigerian Factory Workers* (Brighton: Harvester Press)

Rood, Leslie L. (1975), 'Foreign investment in African manufacturing', *Journal of Modern African Studies*, vol. 13, no. 1, pp. 19–34

Rosberg, Carl G. and Thomas M. Callaghy (1979), *Socialism in Sub-Saharan Africa: A New Assessment* (Berkeley: University of California Press)

Rosberg, Carl G. and Robert H. Jackson (1982), *Personal Rule in Black Africa: Prince, Autocrat, Prophet, Tyrant* (Berkeley: University of California Press)

Sandbrook, Richard and Robin Cohen (eds) (1975), *The Development of an African Working Class* (Toronto: University of Toronto Press)

Sandbrook, Richard (1982), *The Poliltics of Basic Needs: Urban Aspects of Assaulting Poverty in Africa* (Toronto: University of Toronto Press)

Schatz, Sayre P. (1969), 'Crude private neo-imperialism: a new pattern in Africa', *Journal of Modern African Studies*, vol. 7, no. 4, pp. 75–92

Schatz, Sayre P. (1977), *Nigerian Capitalism* (Berkeley: University of California Press)

Sethuraman, J.V. (ed.) (1981), *The Urban Informal Sector in Developing Countries: Employment, Poverty, and Environment* (Geneva: ILO)

Shaw, Timothy (1982), 'Beyond neo-colonialism: varieties of corporatism in Africa', *Journal of Modern African Studies*, vol. 20, no. 2, pp. 239–61

Sklar, Richard (1963), *Nigerian Political Parties* (Princeton: Princeton University Press)

Stryker, Richard S. (1979), 'The World Bank and African development: food production and rural poverty', *World Development* vol. 7, pp. 325–36

U.N. (United Nations), Statistical Office (1961-80), *Yearbook of International Trade Statistics*

UNCTAD (United Nations Conference on Trade and Development) (1972-85), *Handbook of International Trade and Development Statistics* (New York: United Nations)

Vennettier, Pierre (1976), *Les villes de l'Afrique tropicale* (Paris: Masson)

Vernon, Raymond (1977), *Storm Over the Multinationals: The Real Issues* (Cambridge: Harvard University Press)

Wallerstein, Immanuel (1964), 'Voluntary associations', in Coleman and Rosberg (eds), pp. 318–39

Watts, Michael and Paul Lubeck (1983), 'The political classes and the oil boom: a political economy of rural and urban poverty', in Zartman (ed.), pp. 105–44

Widstrand, Carl (ed.) (1973), *Multinational Firms in Africa* (Uppsala: Scandinavian Institute of African Studies)

Williams, Gavin (ed.) (1976), *Nigeria: Economy and Society* (London: Collings)

Wilson, III, Ernst J. (1982), 'Contested terrain: a comparative and theoretical assessment of state-owned enterprises in Africa' (African Studies Association Meetings, Papers)

World Bank [Elliot J. Berg] (1981), *Accelerated Development in Tropical Africa* (Washington, DC: World Bank)

Young, Crawford (1982), *Ideology and Development in Africa* (New Haven: Yale University Press)

Zartman, I. William (ed.) (1983), *The Political Economy of Nigeria* (New York: Praeger)

2. *Ghana*

Austin, Dennis (1964), *Politics in Ghana 1946-1960* (Oxford: Clarendon Press)

Beckman, Björn (1976), *Organising the Farmers: Cocoa Politics and National Development in Ghana* (Uppsala: Scandinavian Institute of African Studies)

Chazan, Naomi (1983), *An Anatomy of Ghanaian Politics: Managing Political Recession, 1969-1982* (Boulder, Col.: Westview Press)

Cohen, D.L. and M.A. Tribe (1972), 'Suppliers' credits in Ghana and Uganda: an aspect of the imperialist system', *Journal of Modern African Studies*, vol. 10, no. 4, pp. 525–41

Esseks, John D. (1971), 'Government and indigenous private enterprise in Ghana', *Journal of Modern African Studies*, vol. 9, no. 1, pp. 11–29

Fitch, Bob and Mary Oppenheimer (1966), *Ghana: End of an Illusion* (New York: Monthly Review Press)

Garlick, Peter C. (1971), *African Traders and Economic Development in Ghana* (Oxford: Clarendon Press)

Gastellu, Jean-Marc (1981/82), 'Les plantations de cacao au Ghana', *Cahiers d'ORSTOM*, vol. 18, no. 2, pp. 225–54

Ghana, Central Bureau of Statistics (1961-9), *Quarterly Digest of Statistics* (Accra)

Graham, Ronald (1982), *The Aluminium Industry and the Third World: Multinational Corporations and Underdevelopment* (London: Zed)

Hart, Keith (1970), 'Informal income opportunities and urban employment in Ghana', *Journal of Modern African Studies*, vol. 11, no. 3, pp. 61–89

Jeffries, Richard (1978), *Class, Power and Ideology in Ghana: The Railwaymen of Sekondi* (Cambridge: Cambridge University Press)

Jones, Trevor (1976), *Ghana's First Republic* (London: Methuen)

Kennedy, Paul (1977), 'Indigenous capitalism in Ghana', *Review of African Political Economy*, no. 8, pp. 21–38

Kennedy, Paul T. (1980), *Ghanaian Businessmen: From Artisan to Capitalist Entrepreneur in a Dependent Economy* (Munich: Weltforum)

Killick, Tony (1978), *Development Economics in Action: A Study of Economic Policies in Ghana* (New York: St Martin's Press)

Kraus, Jon (1979), 'The political economy of industrial relations in Ghana', in U.G. Damachi et al. (eds), *Industrial Relations in Africa* (New York: St Martin's Press), pp. 106–68

Le Vine, Victor T. (1976), *Political Corruption: The Ghana Case* (Stanford: Hoover Institution Press)

Miracle, Marvin P. and Ann Seidman (1968), *State Farms in Ghana* (Madison: Land Tenure Center)

Nkrumah, Kwame (1963), *Africa Must Unite* (London: Heinemann)

Oertly, Walter Victor (1971), *Wirtschaftliche Zentralprobleme Ghanas seit der Unabhängigkeit: Entwicklung der Primärproduktion und aussenwirtschaftliche Verschuldung* (Bern: H. Lang)

Rathbone, Richard (1973), 'Businessmen in politics: party struggle in Ghana, 1949–1957' *Journal of Development Studies*, vol. 9, no. 3, pp. 391–401

Roemer, Michael (1984), 'Ghana, 1950–1980: missed opportunities', in Arnold C. Harberger (ed.), *World Economic Growth* (San Francisco: ICS), pp. 197–230

Silver, Jim (1978), 'Class struggle in Ghana's mining industry', *Review of African Political Economy*, no. 12, pp. 67–86

Southall, Roger J. (1978), 'Farmers, traders, and brokers in the Gold Coast economy' *Canadian Journal of African Studies*, vol. 12, no. 2, pp. 185–211

Thompson, W. Scott (1969), *Ghana's Foreign Policy, 1957–1966* (Princeton: Princeton University Press)

3. Ivory Coast

Amin, Samir (1967), *Le développement du capitalisme en Côte d'Ivoire* (Paris: Editions de Minuit)

Arnaud, Jean-Claude and Gerard Sournia (1979), 'Les forêts de Côte d'Ivoire: une richesse en voie de disparaître', *Cahiers d'Outremer*, vol. 32, no. 127, pp. 281–301

Campbell, Bonnie (1975), 'Neo-colonialism, economic dependence and political change cotton textile production in the Ivory Coast', *Review of African Political Economy* no. 2, pp. 36–53

Campbell, Bonnie (1978), 'The Ivory Coast', in John Dunn (ed.) *West African States Failure and Promise* (Cambridge: Cambridge University Press), pp. 66–116

Cohen, Michael (1974), *Urban Policy and Political Conflict in Africa: A Study of the Ivory Coast* (Chicago: University of Chicago Press)

Dozon, Jean Pierre (1979), 'Impasse et contradiction d'un secteur de développement l'exemple de l'option "riziculture irriguée" en Côte d'Ivoire', *Cahiers d'ORSTOM* vol. 16, nos. 1/2, pp. 37–58

Fauré, Y.A. and J.F. Médard (eds) (1982), *Etat et bourgeoisie en Côte d'Ivoire* (Paris Karthala)

Fréchou, Hubert (1955), 'Les plantations européennes en Côte d'Ivoire', *Cahier d'Outremer*, vol. 8, no. 1, pp. 56–83

France, Ministère de la Coopération et du Développement (1982), *Entreprises publiques et Côte d'Ivoire* (Paris: Ministère de Relations Extérieures

Gastellu, J.M. and S. Affou Yapi (1982), 'Un mythe à décomposer: la "bourgeoisie de planteurs" ', in Fauré and Médard (eds), pp. 149–79

Gbagbo, Laurent (1982), *La Côte d'Ivoire: économie et société à la veille de l'indépendance* (Paris: L'Harmattan)

Gbetibouo, Mathurin and Christopher L. Delgado (1984), 'Lessons and contributions of export crop-led growth: cocoa in the Ivory Coast', in Zartman and Delgado (eds), pp. 115–47

Groff, David Euston (1980), 'The development of capitalism in the Ivory Coast: the case of Assi-Kasso, 1880–1940' (Unpublished PhD dissertation, Stanford University)

Hecht, Robert M. (1983), 'The Ivory Coast economic "miracle": what benefits for Africans?', *Journal of Modern African Studies*, vol. 21, no. 1, pp. 125–53

Joshi, Heather, et al. (1976), *Abidjan: Urban Development and Employment in the Ivory Coast* (Geneva: ILO)

Lee, Eddy (1980), 'Export-led rural development: the Ivory Coast', *Development and Change*, vol. 11, pp. 607–42

Masini, Jean et al. (1979), *Multinationals and Development in Black Africa: A Case Study in the Ivory Coast* (Farnborough: Saxon House)

Miras, C. de (1982), 'L'entrepreneur ivoirien ou une bourgeoisie privée de son état', in Fauré and Médard (eds), pp. 181–229

Monson, Terry D. and Garry C. Pursell (1979), 'The use of ORC's [Overseas Resource Costs] to evaluate indigenization programs; the case of the Ivory Coast', *Journal of Development Economics*, vol. 6, pp. 119–39

Mytelka, Lynn Krieger (1981), 'Direct foreign investment and technological choice in the Ivoirian textile and wood industries', *Vierteljahresberichte: Probleme der Entwicklungsländer*, vol. 83, pp. 61–80

Mytelka, Lynn Krieger (1984), 'European business and economic development', in Zartman and Delgado (eds), pp. 149–73

Pillet-Schwartz, Anne-Marie (1978), 'Les grandes entreprises de cultures et la production des paysans en Côte d'Ivoire', *Études Rurales*, vol. 70, pp. 65–79

Pillet-Schwartz, Anne-Marie (1980), 'Une tentative de vulgarisation avortée: l'hévéaculture en Côte d'Ivoire', *Cahiers d'Études Africaines*, vol. 20, nos. 1/2, pp. 63–82

Tuinder, Bastiaan A. den (1978), *Ivory Coast: The Challenge of Success* [World Bank Report] (Baltimore: Johns Hopkins University Press)

Valette, Alain (1980), 'Résultats et réflexions sur une étude empirique de l'industrialisation de la Côte d'Ivoire', *Cahiers d'ORSTOM*, vol. 17, pp. 45–83

Woronoff, Jon (1972), *West African Wager: Houphouet Versus Nkrumah* (Metuchen, N.J.: Scarecrow)

Zartman, I. William and Christopher Delgado (eds) (1984), *The Political Economy of Ivory Coast* (New York: Praeger)

Zolberg, Aristide R. (1964), *One-Party Government in the Ivory Coast* (Princeton: Princeton University Press)

4. Kenya

Amsden Alice (1971), *International Firms and Labour in Kenya, 1945–1960* (London: Cass)

Barkan, Joel D. and John Okumu (eds) (1984), *Politics and Public Policy in Kenya and Tanzania* (New York: Praeger)

Buch-Hansen, Mogens and Henrick Secher Marcussen (1982), 'Contract farming and the peasantry: cases from western Kenya', *Review of African Political Economy*, no. 23, pp. 9–36

Bujra, Janet M. (1978/79), 'Proletarianization and the informal economy: a case study from Nairobi', *African Urban Studies*, no. 3, pp. 47–66

Burrows, John R. (1975), *Kenya: Into the Second Decade* [World Bank Report] (Baltimore: Johns Hopkins University Press)

Chege, Michael (1981), 'A tale of two slums: electoral politics in Mathare and Dagoretti', *Review of African Political Economy*, no. 20, pp. 74–88

Clayton, Anthony and Donald C. Savage (1974), *Government and Labour in Kenya, 1895–1963* (London: Cass)

Fransman, Martin (ed.) (1982), *Industry and Accumulation in Africa* (London: Heinemann)

Furedi, Frank (1974), 'The social compositon of the Mau-Mau movement in the White Highlands', *Journal of Peasant Studies*, vol. 1, no. 4, pp. 486–505

Godfrey, M. and S. Langdon (1976), 'Partners in underdevelopment: the transnational thesis in a Kenyan context', *Journal of Commonwealth Political Studies*, vol. 14, pp. 42–63

Hake, Andrew (1977), *African Metropolis: Nairobi's Self-Help City* (New York: St Martins Press)

Hazlewood, Arthur (1979), *The Economy of Kenya: The Post-Kenyatta Experience* (Oxford: Oxford University Press)

House, William J. (1981), 'Nairobi's informal sector: an exploratory study', in Killick (ed.) (1981a), pp. 357–68

Kaplinsky, Raphael (1979), 'Export-oriented growth: a large international firm in a small developing country', *World Development*, vol. 7, pp. 825–34

Kenya, Ministry of Economic Planning and Development/Finance and Planning (1965–85), *Economic Survey* (Nairobi)

Killick, Tony (ed.) (1981a), *Papers on the Kenyan Economy* (Nairobi: Heinemann)

Killick, Tony (1981b), *The IMF and Economic Management in Kenya* (London: Overseas Development Institute, Working Paper No. 4)

King, Kenneth (1971), *The African Artisan* (London: Heinemann)

Langdon, Steven W. (1981a), *Multinational Corporations in the Political Economy of Kenya* (New York: St Martins Press)

Langdon, Steven W. (1981b), 'North/South, West and East: industrial restructuring in the world economy', *International Journal*, vol. 36, pp. 766–92

Leo, Christopher (1984), *Land and Class in Kenya* (Toronto: Toronto University Press)

Leys, Colin (1980), 'State capital in Kenya: a research note', *Canadian Journal of African Studies*, vol. 14, no. 2, pp. 307–17

Martin, D. (1978), 'Dépendance et luttes politiques au Kenya, 1975–1977', *Canadian Journal of African Studies*, vol. 12, no. 2, pp. 233–56

Nelson, Nici (1979), 'How women and men get by: the sexual division of labour in the informal sector of a Nairobi squatter settlement', in Ray Bromley and Chris Gerry (eds), *Casual Work and Poverty in Third World Countries* (Chichester: Wiley), pp. 283–302

Oketh-Ogendo, H.M.V. (1981), 'Land ownership and land distribution in Kenya's larger-farm areas', in Killick (ed.) (1981a), pp. 329–38

Rosberg, Carl G. and John Nottingham (1966), *The Myth of 'Mau Mau': Nationalism in Kenya* (New York: Praeger)

Sandbrook, Richard (1975), *Proletarians and Capitalism: The Kenyan Case, 1960–1972* (Cambridge: Cambridge University Press)

Sorrenson, Keith (1967), *Land Reform in the Kikuyu Country* (Nairobi: Oxford University Press)

Stichter, Sharon (1978), 'Trade unionism in Kenya: the militant phase, 1947-1952', in Peter C.W. Gutkind, Robin Cohen and Jean Copans (eds), *African Labour History* (Beverly Hills: Sage), pp. 155–74

Stichter, Sharon (1982), *Migrant Labour in Kenya: Capitalism and African Response, 1895–1975* (London: Longman)

Swainson, Nicola (1980), *The Rise of Corporate Capitalism in Kenya, 1918–1977* (Berkeley: University of California Press)

Wasserman, Gary (1976), *The Politics of Decolonization: Kenya Europeans and the Land Issue, 1960–1965* (Cambridge: Cambridge University Press)

Werlin, Herbert H. (1974), *Governing an African City: A Study of Nairobi* (New York: Africana Press)

5. *Tanzania*

Bienefeld, M.A. (1975), 'Socialist development and the workers in Tanzania', in Richard Sandbrook and Robin Cohen (eds), *The Development of an African Working Class* (Toronto: Toronto University Press), pp. 239–60

Bolton, Dianne (1978), 'Unionization and employer strategy: the Tanganyikan sisal industry, 1958–1964,' in Peter C.W. Gutkind, Robin Cohen and Jean Copans (eds), *African Labor History* (Beverly Hills: Sage), pp. 175–204

Clark, W. Edmund (1978), *Socialist Development and Public Investment in Tanzania, 1964–1973* (Toronto: University of Toronto Press)

Cliffe, Lionel and John Saul (eds) (1973), *Socialism in Tanzania*, Vol. 2 (Nairobi: EAPH)

Cliffe, Lionel and Griffiths L. Cunningham (1973), 'Ideology, organisation and the settlement experience in Tanzania', in Cliffe and Saul (eds), pp. 131–40

Coulson, Andrew C. (1977), 'Tanzania's fertiliser factory', *Journal of Modern African Studies*, vol. 15, no. 1, pp. 119–25

Coulson, Andrew C. (1982), *Tanzania: A Political Economy* (Oxford: Clarendon Press)

Ellis, Frank (1982), 'Price and the transformation of peasant agriculture: the Tanzanian case', *Bulletin of the Institute of Development Studies, University of Sussex*, vol. 13, no. 4, pp. 66–72

Freyhold, Michaela von (1979), *Ujamaa Villages in Tanzania: Analysis of a Social Experiment* (New York: Monthly Review Press)

Friedland, William H. (1967), 'Co-operation, conflict, and conscription: TANU–TFL relations, 1955–1964', in Jeffrey Butler and A.A. Castagno (eds), *Boston University Papers on Africa: Transition in African Politics* (New York: Praeger), pp. 67–103

Harris John (1983), *Tanzania's Performance in Meeting Basic Needs: The International Context* (Boston: Boston University Press)

Hyden, Goran (1980), *Beyond Ujamaa in Tanzania: Underdevelopment and an Uncaptured Peasantry* (Berkeley: University of California Press)

Kim, Kwan S. (1978), 'Industrialization strategies in a developing socialist economy – an evaluation of the Tanzanian case', *The Developing Economies* (Tokyo), vol. 16, no. 3, pp. 254–68

Kunya, Musette (1976), 'Import substitution as an industrial strategy: the Tanzanian case' (Dar es Salaam: Economic Research Bureau Papers)

Lele, Uma (1984), 'Tanzania: Phoenix or Icarus?', in Arnold C. Harberger (ed.), *World Economic Growth* (San Francisco: ICS), pp. 159–95

Lofchie, Michael F. (1978), 'Agrarian crisis and economic liberalization in Tanzania', *Journal of Modern African Studies*, vol. 16, no. 3, pp. 451–71

Maguire, G. Andrew (1969), *Toward 'Uhuru' in Tanzania: The Politics of Participation* (Cambridge: Cambridge University Press)

Mapolu, Henry (ed.) (1976), *Workers and Management* (Dar es Salaam: Tanzania Publishing House)

Mittelman, James H. (1981), *Underdevelopment and the Transition to Socialism: Mozambique and Tanzania* (New York: Academic Press)

Nyerere, Julius K. (1977), *The Arusha Declaration Ten Years After* (Dar es Salaam: Government Printer)

Raikes, Philip (1979), 'Agrarian crisis and economic liberalization in Tanzania: a comment', *Journal of Modern African Studies*, vol. 17, no. 2, pp. 309–16

Resnick, I.N. (1976), 'The State Trading Corporation: a casualty of contradictions', in Mapolu (ed.), pp. 71–89

Sabot, R.H. (1979), *Economic Development and Urban Migration: Tanzania, 1900–1971* (Oxford: Oxford University Press)

Shivji, Issa G. (1976), *Class Struggles in Tanzania* (New York: Monthly Review Press)

Stren, Richard (1982), 'Underdevelopment, urban squatting, and the state bureaucracy: a case study of Tanzania', *Canadian Journal of African Studies*, vol. 16, no. 1, pp. 67–91

Van Velzen, H.U.E. Thoden (1973), 'Staff, kulaks and peasants: a study of a political field', in Cliffe and Saul (eds), pp. 153–79

10

Growth and Dependency, Autonomy and Marginalization
A Retrospective

The argument in the previous chapters has, it is hoped, been sufficiently clear to preclude the need for extensive summary of their contents. But at this point it is relevant to ask whether a view of African economic development reaching back to the beginnings of domesticated food production offers a less gloomy picture than the record of the middle and late twentieth century.

The terms in which such a retrospective will be framed are those of the subtitle and introduction to this book: 'growth' as the indicator of increases in African economic activity in the course of the centuries which have been covered; 'dependency' as an expression of the ever closer and more asymmetrical relationship between Africa and its partners in the world economy. The link between these two themes can also be articulated as an opposition of autonomy – the capacity for sustaining growth, however limited, from indigenous resources – and marginalization – the containment and self-definition of all growth, however extensive, within the context of external domination.

The basis for autonomous growth in the African economy resides in the domestic sector, as defined in Chapter 2. Here there was an early and sometimes quite rapid adoption of food-source domestication and metallurgy which owed little to external influences. However the scale, technology, and social organization of domestic production was limited by a combination of ecological and cultural factors. African societies did exchange surplus goods with one another, did develop some sophisticated tools and techniques, and did divide labour along specialized lines. But compared to other parts of the world, especially those ultimately in closest contact with Africa, the quantities and geographical scope of trade, the range of techniques (especially those employing rotary motion and non-human power), and the degree of separation between units of consumption and units of production remained constricted.

The opening up of frontiers of commercial contact between Africa and societies on the other side of the Sahara Desert, the Indian Ocean, and the Atlantic stimulated increases in surplus production and accumulation, new food sources, and new social formations dedicated to various types of market exchange, production, and management. However, it is difficult to see in any of these growth centres a fundamental transcendence of the limitations of the domestic economy.

The most thorough integration of external exchange with internal activities occurred in the West and Central Sudanic zones of West Africa as a result of both Saharan and Atlantic contacts. But the West African Sudan is a region of Africa particularly vulnerable to ecological stress. Moreover the success of its external articulation depended in good part upon the weakness of its earliest trading partner, the Islamic Mediterranean economy, and the natural protection of desert and forest against effective penetration from outside. The Sudan is thus a model of autonomy within limitations which does not fit other areas of the continent, where growth and dependency were both more evident.

East Africa, exposed along its Indian Ocean coast to another aspect of the same Middle Eastern and Asian world as the West African Sudan, never developed a comparable system of wide-ranging commercial networks, commercialized mining and agriculture, and urban centres of artisanry and cosmopolitan life styles. For brief moments in the late medieval period, Kilwa on the southern Tanzanian coast and Great Zimbabwe in the Zambezi Valley interior achieved impressive levels of urban arts and industry, but they declined just as the Sudanic cities of West Africa were reaching new peaks of economic integration. The entry of Europeans into the Indian Ocean trade brought greater levels of East African growth as Zanzibar, under Omani Arab rule, managed to concentrate coastal trade, send its merchants into the distant interior, and organize major plantation agriculture. But direct exposure to world oceanic trade, even when confined to a single point on the coast, provided little incentive for intensification of productive technology and organization in the interior and even accounted, throughout East Africa, for a decline in artisanal activity as well as an increase in destructive violence.

Atlantic Africa, with the fullest exposure to European commerce, experienced the most impressive economic growth of any pre-colonial region on the continent, but did so with the least transformation of its domestic economic base. Commerce here, when not controlled by previously established Sudanic merchants, tended to integrate small, mutually competitive regions. Artisanal activity grew at the finished product level because of easier access to intermediate textile and metal goods, but the techniques of processing raw materials stagnated or even declined. Urban centres and political organizations for controlling trade were numerous and varied, but none could concentrate the kinds of integrated economic economies found in a Kano or medieval Kilwa, to say nothing of the proto-industrial and fully industrialized sources of imported goods on the northern and western shores of the Atlantic.

Political domination of Africa by representatives of these modern metropoles did not transform the continent's economy in the European image. New forms of infrastructure, particularly a more powerful state and mechanized transport, vastly increased market opportunities but did little to alter the systems of production. Over most of colonial Africa, the characteristic source of commercial goods remained the peasant holding, providing expanded or entirely new crops on the basis of traditional tools and social relationships. In Southern Africa and some settler regions of East and Central Africa, the combination of intrusion by competing European farmers and an ecological situation more conducive to change engendered intensified African agriculture, including animal traction and capitalistic class relations. However, the larger pattern of racial/class antagonisms in South Africa and the limited scope of post-colonial development in Kenya, Malawi, and Zimbabwe make it difficult to measure the positive impact of these transformations on the indigenous African economy.

The post-colonial economy of most of tropical Africa has been characterized by explicit failure; massive attempts at agricultural and industrial development which have produced few constructive results and much malaise, including extensive starvation. The outlines of these dilemmas need not be rehearsed so immediately after an entire chapter which was devoted to them. But here again we are left with the question of whether those elements in the contemporary African economy which display some degree of autonomy – the 'uncaptured peasantry' and the informal urban sectors – represent an historical dynamic which can sustain Africa through its modern travails or are instead the expression of a pathological marginalization.

The motif of autonomy can easily be traced throughout the major stages of African economic history. The early emergence of agriculture and metallurgy was a remarkably independent process. Throughout almost a millennium-and-a-half of extensive commercial contact with more developed external societies, Africa retained its political independence and a capacity to withdraw from or switch markets when existing arrangements no longer provided satisfactory levels of profit. Even in the colonial period, the initiation of peasant cash-cropping and the appropriation of modern agricultural methods from settlers frequently occurred outside the framework of European control. In the post-colonial economies, the expansion of the informal urban sector again testifies to African abilities to confront needs and opportunities with material resources and social forms of their own choice and design.

Viewed in these terms the 'failure' of Africa to develop economic structures similar to those of the capitalist West seems irrelevant. Even those institutions within Africa which represent the West can be by-passed through withdrawal into still extant rural and urban autonomous sectors.[1] At the same time it becomes increasingly difficult to celebrate African autonomy when an increasing proportion of a dangerously growing population is drawn into cities where informal enterprises ultimately depend upon resources from the modern sector and the continent appears less and less able to feed itself.

It is just as easy to see the roots of the present dilemma in an economic history interpreted as a continuous process of marginalization. The shift to domesticated food production put African populations into a universal demographic pattern which has always been harder to sustain in risk-laden tropical environments. As Africa's market integration into the world economy increased, its relative importance to external consumers declined. However much such a trend might have induced individual African producers to withdraw from the export market, the expansion of Western capacities for penetrating the continent, both preceding and following the more obvious situation of colonial rule, has made it difficult to define African economic roles collectively without reference to external centres.

The pathological dimensions of this relationship are expressed in the increasing recourse to idioms of deviance both among African thinkers, who equate capitalism with witchcraft,[2] and devotees of modernization, who imply, even with such positive terms as 'economy of affection' and 'informal sector', that autonomous African undertakings represent some form of resistance or crime.[3] However, the fact that these accusations come from both sides at least indicates a continuing vitality on the part of the autonomous/marginalized African economy.

How, then, do we strike a balance between these contrasting perceptions of African economic history? Certainly it is impossible to return to the optimism of those Europeans and Africans who, at various points in their mutual history 'discovered' within the vast spatial scale of the continent resources which would create a new centre of the world economy. At the same time, despite the record of slave trading, colonial conquest, white-settler exploitation, and recent hunger, it is difficult to define Africa simply as a victim of the world economy. In the past, at least, Africans have always managed to recover from various demographic and political disasters and assert some degree of control over their own universe.

The root dilemma of Africa's economic development has been the asymmetry between the role of the continent in the world and the degree to which that world – or at least its dominant Western sector – has penetrated Africa. Previous chapters have noted the contradiction between limited immediate Western market concerns with Africa and the intensity of such penetrative efforts as the anti-slavery and exploration campaigns, the colonial partition of the late nineteenth century, the neo-mercantilist binge of the period immediately after the Second World War, and the competitive aid programmes of the post-colonial era. These efforts imposed upon Africa an infrastructure out of harmony with its basic productive systems. In their latest forms, such contradictions account for the over-ambitious étatism of the stronger African economies discussed in Chapter 9 and the starvation and violence in the poorer regions of the continent whose post-colonial history has hardly been touched upon here.

If Africa is unlikely to transform itself in the image of the most advanced sectors of the world economy, possibly the external world is now beginning to change in a direction more compatible with enduring African conditions. We can see this trend in the hesitantly increasing awareness among leading industrial powers that even for them the intensive exploitation of natural resources brings risks of environmental crises and the exhaustion of energy sources.[4]

At the same time, the newest 'high technology' of the West, as represented by the electronic computer, can be diffused in a region like Africa without the costs of external dependency which accompanied the importation of earlier industrial goods. Africa is certainly not likely to take a leadership role in an enterprise so dependent upon an alien cultural tradition. However, distribution and operation of both the finished products of electronic technology and its intermediate production processes is far easier than in the case of 'lumpy' smokestack industries. Moreover, the effects of such a diffusion, as with earlier electronics communications media, allow remote regions to become culturally integrated into the mainstream of world development on a basis never previously possible.[5]

Futuristic speculations cannot be pursued at too great a length in an historical study, however broad. But the kind of solution which has to be imagined for Africa at some later date reveals something about the patterns which emerge from the past. Africa has shown a remarkable capacity for economic growth and survival at the same time as it has moved into a closer relationship with an international economy operating on completely different terms. Autonomy has been an important achievement of this history, but in the long run becomes an increasingly negative option, a response to marginalization rather than an alternative to it. The great accomplishments of Africa's economic past represent an adjustment to domestic and external circumstances over which neither Africans nor outsiders could exercise direct control. The conditions of the 1980s show this conjuncture in its most threatening form. However the demonstrated energy and resiliency of Africans and the changing contours of the world economy make it conceivable that even the present crises will eventually be overcome.

Notes

1. Chazan (1983) pp. 197–201 provides a particularly optimistic account of this process.
2. Ngugi (1982).
3. Hyden (1980) p. 18f. For the complex, but largely unheroic relationship between the concept of criminality and African marginalization, see Austen (1986) and other essays in the same collection.
4. Phillips et al. (1980) predicts that an African-type ploughless agriculture will dominate American farming in the near future.
5. Servan-Schreiber (1981) p. 214f.

Bibliography

Austen, Ralph A. (1986), 'Social bandits and other heroic criminals: a European concept and its relevance to Africa', in Donald Crummey (ed.), *Banditry, Rebellion and Social Protest in Africa* (London: Currey), pp. 89–108

Chazan, Naomi (1983), *An Anatomy of Ghanaian Politics: Managing Political Recession, 1969–1982* (Boulder, Colo.: Westview Press)

Hyden, Goran (1980), *Beyond Ujamaa in Tanzania: Underdevelopment and an Uncaptured Peasantry* (Berkeley: University of California Press)

Ngugi wa Thiong'o (1982), *Devil on the Cross* (London: Heinemann)

Phillips, Ronald E. et al. (1980), 'Non-tillage agriculture', *Science*, vol. 208, no. 6, pp. 1108–13

Servan-Schreiber, Jean Jacques (1981), *The World Challenge* (New York: Simon & Schuster)

Appendix

The tables and graphs that follow are mainly designed to illustrate various points in the preceding chapters, where references to them may be found. However they also provide an independent version of an argument which has pervaded this entire book: the simultaneiety of Africa's growing involvement with the world economy and its marginalization for that economy. This process is particularly evident in Table A4, which contains a sub-plot about South Africa's very strong (if somewhat unstable) role in international trade.

It is unfortunate that statistical material of this kind is easily and reliably available only for the external dimensions of African economic history. Students who wish to get some idea of the data which can be used for measuring internal development, at least in recent times, should consult Mitchell (1982); the UNCTAD *Handbook*; and the World Bank, *World Tables*.

Table A1 *Comparative efficiency of transport systems linking Africa and outside trading partners*

	Sahara camel caravans	Indian Ocean shipping	Atlantic Ocean shipping
Tons per voyage	60–300[1]	100–500[4]	75–225[8]
Tons per man	0.5–0.6[2]	5–7[5]	9–14[9]
Travel time	30–45 km per day = 70–90 days (North Africa to Sudanic Sahel)	130 km per day = 25–30 days (Zanzibar to eastern Gulf, India)[6]	70 km per day = 79 days Europe–West Africa[10]
Technology changes			
AD 1–800	shoulder saddle[3]	lateen sail	not applicable
800–1500	astral navigation, oral knowledge of route	astrolabe, compass, rudder, written navigation manuals	caravel vessels, Atlantic routes discovered
1500–1900	nothing	nails, etc., rudders, sextant, size increase[7]	navigational knowledge, instruments; steering; copper sheathing; vessel size, etc.[11]

[1]Boahen (1964) p. 120. This figure is based on an average camel load of 120–150 kg and caravans ranging from 500 to 2,000 camels. The estimates of 6,000 to 12,000 camels per

caravan found in Godhino (1969) p. 119 and Mauny (1961) pp. 290, 401 seem to refer to salt carriage across only a portion of the Sahara.
[2]Méniaud (1912) pp. 118–19. Based on one man per four camels carrying 120–150 kg each.
[3]Bulliet (1975) pp. 111f. (the shoulder saddle is a North African variant of the North Arabian saddle).
[4]Lewis (1973); Moreland (1939); Nicholls (1971) pp. 75–6 (this last source is excellent on the inexactitude of European measurements of indigenous Indian shipping capacities before the twentieth century).
[5]Prins (1965/66); Villiers (1948). These are both calculations based on twentieth-century observations, but since Indian Ocean sailing craft were probably smaller at this time than in the period predating steam navigation, we can assume that the ratios are, if anything, underestimates of efficiency.
[6]Nicholls (1971) p. 74; Villiers (1948). These are rates possible only when the monsoon winds blow in the appropriate direction.
[7]Hourani (1951) pp. 93ff.; Johnston and Muir (1962); Tibbets (1971). The construction influences of the European contact, other than the use of iron nails, are rather complicated; there is some controversy about how advanced steering and navigation devices were before 1500.
[8]Gemery and Hogendorn (1978). The data in this article and the entire Atlantic column of the above table refer to wooden sailing ships, mainly engaged in the slave trade, up to the late eighteenth or early nineteenth centuries. The efficiency advantages of later European iron ships using steam power are too obvious to require demonstration here and, in any case, made most of their impact on Africa in the colonial period.
[9]Gemery and Hogendorn (1978).
[10]Anstey (1975) p. 17n; North (1968). Given the amount of data available on the Atlantic slave trade, it would be possible to calculate a more comprehensive and reliable figure, but this effort has not yet been undertaken.
[11]Gemery and Hogendorn (1978) provide very extensive information on technological innovation in Atlantic slave trade shipping.

Figure A1   *Slave prices, 1638–1775*[1]

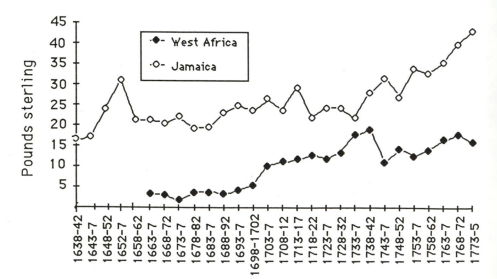

[1]Bean (1975) pp. 72–7.

Table A2   *Slave trades out of Africa*

Route	Period (AD)	Size (millions)	Annual rate (thousands)
Red Sea	650–1920	4.1	3.2[1]
Swahili Coast	650–1920	3.9	3.1[2]
Trans-Saharan	650–1910	9.0	7.1[3]
Islamic total		17.0	13.1
Atlantic	1450–1900	11.7	26.0[4]
Global total		28.7	39.05

[1]Austen (1979).   [2]Austen (1977).   [3]Austen (1979).   [4]Lovejoy (1982).

Figure A2   *Palm oil prices, 1831–1939*[1]

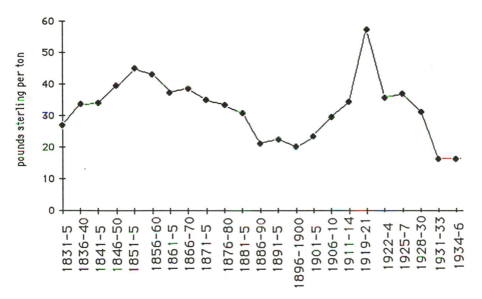

[1]Dike (1956) pp. 50–1, 99; Mulhall (1892) pp. 475–8; Mulhall (1903) pp. 792–3; Webb (1911) p. 492; *The Economist*, 1909–14; Hancock (1942) p. 340.

Table A3   *Gold Exports*

---

1. Pre-colonial South-east Africa

Dominant power	Period	Annual average (metric tons)
Islamic	1100–1450	1.5[1]
Portuguese	1500–1600	0.5[2]
Portuguese	1600–1750	0.5–1.0[3]
Portuguese	1750–1900	0.1–0.5[4]

---

2. Pre-colonial West Africa

Period	Routes	Annual average (metric tons)	
800–1480	Trans-Saharan		0.5–1.5[5]
1480–1720	Trans-Saharan	0.1–0.2[6]	
	Guinea Coast	0.7–1.7[7]	= 0.8–2.0
1720s–1820s	all		'smaller'[8]
1825–1900	Trans-Saharan	0.1–0.2[9]	
	Guinea Coast	0.8[10]	= 0.9–1.0

---

3. Major twentieth-century producers[11]

	Gold Coast/ Ghana	Rhodesia/ Zimbabwe Annual averages (metric tons)	South Africa
1900–1925	7.1	17.3	244.8[12]
1926–1950	15.3	20.0	363.7
1951–1975	23.4	16.5	756.2

---

[1]The available estimates for this period are difficult to work with. Figures given to the Portuguese from Muslim sources in the first decade of the sixteenth century range from 7.6 to 8.5 tons and are correctly dismissed by historians as grossly exaggerated. See Godhino (1969) pp. 270–1; Duncan (n.d.). The archaeological work of Summers (1969) as revised by Phimister (1976) gives a sense that production was higher in this period than in the subsequent centuries, but even Phimister's downward estimate of 1.5 million ounces (46.7 tons) for local gold *production* (he does not indicate what portion of this was exported) seems unrealistically high.

[2]Duncan (n.d). This figure is based upon estimates of total *Portuguese* official and illicit trade. There is no way of knowing the amounts of continued Islamic trade, although this may have been considerably reduced, leading to a net lower regional level, by the Portuguese efforts at monopoly.

[3]Duncan (n.d); see also Curtin (1983) pp. 236–7. The sources for this period vary considerably in reliability and comprehensiveness, but Duncan provides the best (although even less precise than indicated here) general estimate.

[4]Isaacman (1972) pp. 71, 88; Phimister (1976).

[5]Curtin (1983) pp. 238–41 (based on twentieth-century productivity estimates and sixteenth-century European exports).

[6]Based on later nineteenth-century North African import figures in Miège (1961–3) Vol. 3, pp. 361–2; Newbury (1966); Soetbeer (1879) p. 47.

[7]Curtin, 1983, pp. 241–50.

[8]There are no statistical records from which the exports for most of this period can be estimated. However, evidence of various kinds, e.g. the import of Brazilian gold indicates that West African gold exports had diminished considerably during the eighteenth century, probably due to the competing commercial and manpower demands of the expanded slave trade, see Bean (1974). British Gold Coast (Ghana) customs records for the early nineteenth

century, although clearly not indicative for the region or even the Gold Coast as a whole, suggest a rather small trade for this period. See Soetbeer (1879) p. 46; Metcalfe (1964) p. 110.
[9]See note 2 above.
[10]Curtin (1983) pp. 239, 250–2; Metcalfe (1964) pp. 110, 115, 168; Soetbeer (1979) pp. 46–7.
[11]See Mitchell (1982).
[12]This average is based on only twenty-two years, since the South African gold mines did not return to their pre-South African War level of production before 1904.

Figure A3   *Terms of trade: Senegambia, 1823–50*[1]

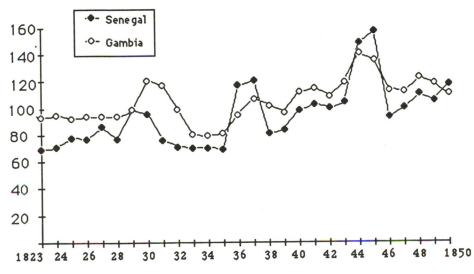

[1]Curtin (1975) p. 111.

Table A4   *Sub-Saharan African participation in world trade, 1710–1980*

1.	Africa's role in British trade, 1710–1980 (selected years)[1] (millions of £ sterling)			
Year	British imports from Africa	As percentage of total British imports	British exports to Africa[2]	As percentage of total British exports
1710	0.014	0.3[3]	0.069	1.0
1725	0.068	1.0	0.284	3.3
1740	0.063	0.9	0.111	1.4
1754	0.022	0.3	0.235	0.2
1772–3	0.080	0.6	0.177	4.5
1780–1	0.029	0.3	0.255	2.2
1789–90	0.087	0.5	0.799	4.0
1797–8	0.062	0.3	1.085	3.6
1815	0.325	0.5	0.393	0.6
1830			0.334	0.8
1845			1.896	2.7
1860[4]	5.9	2.8	4.7	2.9

Table A4   *continued*

		(minus South Africa)		(minus South Africa)
1875	10.1[5]	2.6 (1.2)	8.3	2.9 (1.0)
1890	16.2	3.5 (0.8)	14.2	4.3 (1.3)
1906	46.8	6.9 (1.1)	38.6	8.3 (4.7)
1920	132.0	6.6 (3.2)	104.5	6.7 (4.3)
1925	93.9	6.9 (3.4)	67.9	7.3 (5.8)
1931	85.4	8.8 (2.1)	42.5	9.4 (4.3)
1938	118.4	10.0 (3.9)	65.8	12.4 (4.8)
1948	491.8	19.6 (4.3)	242.2	14.7 (7.3)
1952	527.3[6]	14.3 (7.3)	406.7	14.9 (9.5)
1960	721.5	14.5 (7.4)	449.9	14.0 (5.9)
1970	1 202.2	12.6 (5.7)	736.1	9.1 (5.0)
1980[7]	5 836.2	10.4 (2.1)	3 409.9	6.9 (4.9)

2.   Africa's role in French trade, 1875–1910 (selected years)[8]
(in millions of francs)

Year	French imports from Africa	As percentage of total French imports	French exports to Africa	As percentage of total French exports
1875	43.8	1.2	59.4	1.5
1890	61.6	1.4	28.2	0.8
1905	41.4	0.8	27.5	0.5
1920	1 634.3	3.4	539.2	2.0
1925	1 877.5	4.5	1 531.5	3.3
1931	1 295.2	4.5	2 379.5	3.5
1938	3 804.2	8.3	1 581.2	5.2
1948[9]	64 580.0	9.3	42 010.0	9.7
1952	1 592 000.0	13.4	163 040.0	11.5
1960	2 262 080.0[10]	7.3	2 281 610.0	6.7
1970	8 320 720.0	7.9	6 302 070.0	6.3
1980	31 693 000.0	5.6	31 508 000.0	6.7

3.   Africa's role in Portuguese trade, 1861–1970 (selected years)[11]
(as percentage of annual Portuguese total)

Year	Imports	Exports	Year	Imports	Exports
1861	3.0	4.0	1931	8.0	12.5
1875	2.5	5.0	1938	10.0	13.0
1890	2.5	6.0	1948	8.0	25.0
1905	3.5	15.0	1952	13.0	25.0
1920	4.0	13.0	1960	14.0	25.0
1925	7.0	12.0	1970	15.0	23.0

4.   Africa's role in North Atlantic trade, 1938–79 (selected years)[12]
(in millions of $US)

	Total African Trade	(without South Africa)	As percentage of US–West European trade[13]	(without South Africa)
1938	1 803	(903)	6.5	(3.5)
1948	6 246	(3 290)	9.6	(5.1)
1952	7 645	(5 230)	8.7	(5.9)
1960	10 772	(7 183)	7.4	(4.9)
1970	21 991	(14 731)	5.8	(3.9)
1979[14]	102 558	(73 179)	5.5	(3.9)

[1]Main sources: Mitchell (1962) (to 1938); Great Britain, Department of Customs (1875–1970); up until 1845 these figures include trade from North Africa, but not Egypt; the intervals between years are based on consistency, relationship to major historical changes, and availability, particularly when, as in Mitchell's series for 1772–98, both general British and African trade figures are cited from the same original source.

[2]Includes both domestic-goods exports and re-exports of imported goods.

[3]As suggested by the disparity with exports, import percentages for the eighteenth century do not accurately indicate Africa's significance for the British economy as a whole, since they do not include the value of Africa's most valuable export of this period, slaves, which went to the New World rather than Britain. The British share of this trade, measured on the basis of delivery prices in the West Indies, was worth about £60–70,000 per annum from 1701 to 1800; see Bean (1975); Lovejoy (1982). However, to calculate its relevance to British trade as a whole it would be necessary to divide it by a figure representing the total international commerce of both Britain and the receiving colonial areas (not all of them within the British Empire). More relevant would be the role of slaves and slave-produced sugar in the British economy, a subject which has been studied, and debated, at considerable length by economic historians (see above Chapter 5, note 3).

[4]From this point on African trade figures exclude North Africa.

[5]Because gold and (for most years) diamonds are not included in general British import figures, starting with 1875 (the first reporting year following the South African mineral revolution) these very important African commodities have had to be calculated separately from tables of bullion imports included in Great Britain, Customs and reports of the diamond-exporting countries (unless otherwise stated, the last are also taken from Great Britain, Customs).

[6]For 1952 and 1960 the data on diamond imports are taken from the following sources: Angola, Reparticao Tecnica de Estatistica Geral; Belgian Congo, Secretariat General; East Africa, High Commissioner; Saylor (1967); South Africa, Department of Customs and Excises.

[7]Source for this year, Great Britain, Department of Trade (1980); the absolute numbers from this source are probably too high since they consistently exceed those in Great Britain, Central Statistical Office (1983), which is presumably corrected; unfortunately, the Board of Trade does not provide retrospective figures in its annual publications but because the breakdown for Africa vs. 'other developing countries' is far more complete than in the CSO statistics and the proportions of over-estimation seem to be consistent, I have used these figures. No source for 1980 indicates the origins of British gold imports, and very likely most of South Africa's exports for that year did not go directly to London. However, since this was the record year to date for the value of South African exports and a very low year for its main rival on the world market, the Soviet Union (see Kaser, 1983) it has to be assumed that the bulk of Britain's listed total gold imports for 1980 came ultimately from South Africa.

[8]Main source: France, *Annuaire Statistique*. The figures here differ considerably from those in Fieldhouse (1971) pp. 642–5; the latter includes Algeria, always one of France's major trading partners, in the African statistics while the present table solely concerns sub-Saharan Africa.

[9]Figures for this year are taken from France, Ministère des Finances; unfortunately this source gives annual trade figures by complete country breakdown only in provisional form for the year of publication; comparison of the 1948 provisional figures with a more definitive (but insufficiently detailed) account for the same year published in a later volume suggest that the proportions are roughly accurate.

[10]French import figures for 1960 and 1970 omit gold; however, both the statistics on gold production in French Africa (United Nations), the limited French data on sources of gold imports, and general accounts of the world gold market (Green, 1983; Weston, 1983) suggest that virtually all French imports of African gold came by way of London and have thus been accounted for in British–African trade statistics.

[11]Source: Clarence-Smith (1985), pp. 230–1. The material is presented by the author as a graph showing the percentage of Portugal's trade with her entire African and Asian colonial empire. Unfortunately, the published trade statistics in Portugal, Instituto Nacional de Estatistica are neither complete nor uniform enough to substitute for Clarence-Smith's

280   *Appendix*

compilation. However, since the African territories of Angola, Cabinda, Guinea-Bissau, and Mozambique made up the overwhelming bulk of this empire, the data seem to be a fair index of Portuguese African trade. Moreover, the published data which are available suggest that the small trade with the tiny Asian territories of Goa, Macao, and Timor, which should be subtracted from this table, roughly equals the annual Portuguese trade with South Africa, which should be added.

[12]Main source: United Nations (1962, 1983). This publication does not, however, include gold transactions in any of its trade tables; these are particularly difficult to recover on a world basis since no sources other than Great Britain, Customs Dept indicate the origins of gold imports and much international gold trading obviously involves the recycling of imports from primary producers with no effective value added by the secondary exporter. The UN trade figures have thus been supplemented with the following: international gold *production* statistics (UN; these exclude the Soviet Union); Soviet exports to Western markets (Great Britain, Customs Dept; Kaser, 1983); South African *export* statistics (International Monetary Fund; Mitchell, 1982; these are substituted for the UN South African production statistics because South African gold exports vary significantly, in both directions, from production figures in any given year). For general information on the international gold movements, prices, etc. used here, see Green (1983); Weston (1983).

[13]This is obviously a somewhat arbitrary base for calculating Africa's share of world trade. However it does include the major trading partners of Africa while biasing its rather low percentages in Africa's favour by excluding Asian countries (especially China, India and Japan) which have carried on significant trade with some African countries (see Mitchell, 1982, for these figures). The important issue here is to measure Africa's participation in all world trade against that of the countries which have had the most influence over African economic development.

[14]This year has been chosen because both 1980 and 1981 (the last years for which full data is presently available) were periods of uniquely high prices for gold and petroleum, resulting in African proportions of world trade slightly higher than in 1970; because the prices of both these commodities have gone down considerably since that time (see Nigeria and South Africa in Figure A5 below), 1979 more accurately represents the trends of Africa's role in world trade during the 1980s.

Figure A4   *Colonial era terms of trade, 1900–60*[1]

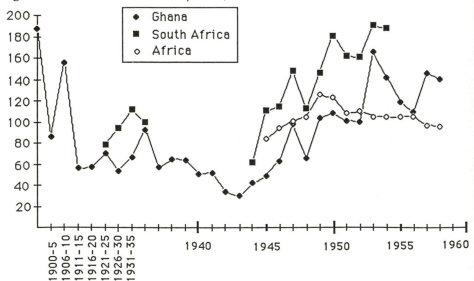

[1]Hymer (1971), pp. 136–7 (for Ghana); South Africa, Department of Statistics, p. 16.5 (for S. Africa); UN (1961), p. 429 (for Africa).

Figure A5 *Post-colonial terms of trade, 1960–83*[1]

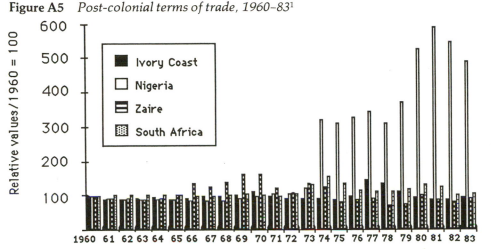

[1]UNCTAD (1977, 1980, 1985) Table 7.2; South Africa, Department of Statistics, p. 16.5; Villiers et al. (1985) p. 157; the four countries shown here represent, respectively, an agricultural exporter (Ivory Coast); a petroleum exporter (Nigeria); a mineral exporter (Zaire); and (South Africa) an exporter mainly of gold and diamonds, but also of industrial goods. The declines indicated for petroleum and gold by the last two years on the graph were even more accentuated in the mid-1980s.

Bibliography

Angola, Reparticao Tecnica de Estatistico Geral, *Anuario Estatistico*

Anstey, Roger (1975), *The Atlantic Slave Trade and British Abolition* (London: Macmillan)

Austen, Ralph A. (1977), 'The Islamic slave trade out of Africa (Red Sea and Indian Ocean): an effort at quantification' (Unpublished paper, Conference on Islamic Africa: Slavery and Related Topics. Princeton University)

Austen, Ralph A. (1979), 'The trans-Saharan slave trade: a tentative census', in Henry A. Gemery and Jan Hogendorn (eds), *The Uncommon Market: Essays in the Economic History of the Atlantic Slave Trade* (New York: Academic Press)

Bean, Richard (1974), 'A note on the relative importance of slaves and gold in West African exports', *Journal of African History*, vol. 15, no. 3, pp. 351–6

Bean, Richard (1975), *The British Trans-Atlantic Slave Trade, 1650–1775* (New York: Arno)

Belgian Congo, Secrétariat Général, *Statistique du commerce extérieur de l'Union Douanière de la Congo belge et du Ruanda-Urundi*

Boahen, A. Adu (1964), *Britain, the Sahara, and the Western Sudan, 1788–1861* (Oxford: Clarendon Press)

Bulliet, Richard (1975), *The Camel and the Wheel* (Cambridge, Mass.: Harvard University Press)

Clarence-Smith, Gervase (1985), *The Third Portuguese Empire, 1815–1975* (Manchester: Manchester University Press)

Curtin, Philip D. (1975), *Economic Change in Precolonial Africa: Senegambia in the Era of the Slave Trade*, Vol. 2 (Madison: University of Wisconsin Press)

Curtin, Philip D. (1983), 'Africa and the wider monetary world, 1250–1850', in J.F. Richards (ed.), *Precious Metals in the Later Medieval and Early Modern Worlds* (Durham: Carolina Academic Press), pp. 231–68

Dike, K. Onwuka (1956), *Trade and Politics in the Niger Delta, 1830–1885* (Oxford: Clarendon Press)

Duncan, T. Bentley (n.d), Unpublished ms. on Indian Ocean trade (University of Chicago)

East Africa, High Commissioner, East African Statistical Department, *Quarterly Economic and Statistical Bulletin*

Fieldhouse, David K. (1971), 'The economic exploitation of Africa: some British and French comparisons', in Prosser Gifford and Wm Roger Louis (eds), *France and Britain in Africa: Imperial Rivalry and Colonial Rule* (New Haven: Yale University Press), pp. 593–662

France, *Annuaire Statistique* [published by various government bureaus in various years]

France, Ministère des Finances et des Affaires Économiques, Direction Générale des Douanes et Droits Indirects, *Statistique mensuelle du commerce extérieur de la France*

Gemery, Henry A. and Jan S. Hogendorn (1978), 'Technological change, slavery and the slave trade', in Clive Dewey and A.G. Hopkins (eds), *The Imperial Impact: Studies in the Economic History of Africa and India* (London: Athlone Press), pp. 243–58

Godhino, Vitorino Magalhaes (1969), *L'économie de l'empire portugaise au XVe–XVIe siècles* (Paris: Mouton)

Great Britain, Central Statistical Office, *Abstract of Annual Statistics*

Great Britain, Department of Customs, *Annual Statement of the Trade of the United Kingdom with Foreign Countries and British Possessions* (before 1920 these reports are published as part of the Parliamentary Papers; the series ends in 1976)

Great Britain, Department of Trade, *Overseas Trade Statistics of the United Kingdom*

Green, Timothy (1983), *The New World of Gold* (New York: Walker)

Hancock, W. Keith (1942), *Survey of British Commonwealth Affairs*. Vol. 2, *Problems of Economic Policy, 1918–1939*, Part 2 (London: Oxford University Press)

Hourani, George Fodio (1951), *Arab Seafaring in the Indian Ocean in Ancient and Medieval Times* (Beirut: Khayats)

Hymer, Stephen (1971), 'The political economy of the Gold Coast and Ghana', in Gustav Ranis (ed.), *Government and Economic Development* (New Haven: Yale University Press), pp. 129–80

International Monetary Fund, *Balance of Trade Yearbook*

Isaacman, Alan F. (1972), *Mozambique: The Africanization of a European Institution: the Zambezi Prazos, 1750–1902* (Madison: University of Wisconsin Press)

Johnston, T.M. and J. Muir (1962), 'Portuguese influences on shipbuilding in the Indian Ocean', *Mariners' Mirror*, vol. 48, pp. 58–63

Kaser, Michael (1983), 'The Soviet gold-mining industry', in Robert G. Jensen et al. (eds), *Soviet Resources in the World Economy* (Chicago: University of Chicago Press), pp. 556–96

Lewis, Archibald (1973), 'Maritime skills in the Indian Ocean, 1368–1500', *Journal of the Economic and Social History of the Orient*, vol. 16, pp. 238–64

Lovejoy, Paul E. (1982), 'The volume of the Atlantic slave trade: a synthesis', *Journal of African History*, vol. 23, no. 4, pp. 473–501

Mauny, Raymond (1961), *Tableau geógraphique de l'Ouest Africaine au Moyen Age* (Dakar: IFAN)

Metcalfe, G.E. (1964), *Great Britain and Ghana: Documents of Colonial History, 1805–1957* (London: Nelson)

Méniaud, Jacques (1912), *Haut-Sénégal-Niger (Soudan Français): géographie économique* (Paris: E. Larose)

Miège, Jean Louis (1961–3), *Le Maroc et l'Europe (1830–1894)* (Paris: PUF)

Mitchell, B.R. (with Phyllis Deane) (1962), *Abstract of British Historical Statistics* (Cambridge: Cambridge University Press)

Mitchell, B.R. (1982), *International Historical Statistics: Africa and Asia* (New York: New York University Press)

Moreland, W.H. (1939), 'The ships of the Arabian Sea about AD 1500', *Journal of the Royal Anthropological Society*, vol. 69, pp. 63–74, 173–192

Mulhall, Michael George (1892), *The Dictionary of Statistics* (London: Routledge)

Mulhall, Michael George (1903), *The Dictionary of Statistics* (4th, revised edn, London: Routledge)

Newbury, C.W. (1966), 'North Africa and Western Sudan trade in the nineteenth century: a re-evaluation', *Journal of African History*, vol. 7, no. 2, pp. 233–246

Nicholls, C.S. (1971), *The Swahili Coast: Politics, Diplomacy and Trade on the East African Littoral, 1798–1856* (London: Allen & Unwin)

Phimister, Ian (1976), 'Pre-colonial goldmining in southern Zambezia: a re-assessment', *African Social Research*, vol. 21, no. 1, pp. 1–31

Poquin, Jean-Jacques (1957), *Les relations économiques extérieures des pays d'Afrique Noire de l'Union Française, 1925–1955* (Paris: A. Colin)

Portugal, Instituto Nacional de Estatistica, *Anuario Estatistica*

Prins, A.H.J. (1965/66), 'The Persian Gulf dhows: two variants in maritime enterprise', *Persica*, vol. 2, pp. 1–18

Saylor, Ralph Gerald (1967), *The Economic System of Sierra Leone* (Durham: Duke University Press)

Soetbeer, Alfred (1879), *Edelmetall-Produktion* (Gotha: J. Perthes)

South Africa, Department of Customs and Excises, *Foreign Trade Statistics*

South Africa, Department of Statistics (1980), *South African Statistics*

Summers, Roger (1969), *Ancient Mining in Rhodesia and Adjacent Areas* (Salisbury: National Museum of Rhodesia)

Tibbets, G.R. (1971), *Arab Navigation in the Indian Ocean Before the Coming of the Portuguese* (London: Royal Asiatic Society)

UN (United Nations), Statistical Office, *Statistical Yearbooks*

UNCTAD (United Nations Conference on Trade and Development) (1972–85), *Handbook of International Trade and Development Statistics* (New York: United Nations)

Villiers, Alan (1948), 'Some aspects of the Arab dhow trade', *Middle East Journal*, vol. 2, pp. 399–416

Villiers, Les de et al. (1985), *Doing Business with South Africa* (New Canaan, Conn.: Business International)

Webb, Augustus, D. (1911), *The New Dictionary of Statistics* (New York: E.P. Dutton)

Weston, Rae (1983), *Gold: A World Survey* (London: Croom Helm)

World Bank (1983), *World Tables: the Third Edition. Volume I. Economic Data* (Baltimore: Johns Hopkins University Press)

Index

233–59 *passim*; summary, 235
Sofala, 59
Sokoto Caliphate, 47, 123, 141
Somalia, 59, 62, 71, 211, 234
Somalis, 132
Songhai 37, 42
Soninke, 42
Sonrai language, 42
sorghum, 13, 15, 170
Sotho, 160
South Africa, 114, 122–3, 155–87
  passim, 198, 214–15, 224, 258,
  269 South African (Boer) War,
  164, 166, 175, 185
South African Labour Party, 185
South Asia, 15, 34, 36, 59ff., 204
South Asians, *see* manufacturing,
  industrial; merchants;
  plantations
South Sea Bubble, 110
South West Africa, 162
Southeast Asia, 60, 171, 204, 210
Southern Africa, 123, 155–87
  passim, 214–15
Southern Rhodesia, *see* Zimbabwe
Soviet bloc, 217
Soviet Union, 204–5, 245
spices, 36, 81
sprayers, 145
squatters, 170, 175, 177, 257
stagnation, 100–2
Stallardism, 166
Stanley Pool, 90
starvation, 16, 160, 271, 272
state capitalism, 235
State Farms Corporation (Ghana),
  237, 251, 252, 258
State Trading Corporation
  (Tanzania), 250
state
  and agricultural production,
  225, 232, 237–9, 252–3; and
  European settlers, 158–87
  passim; and factors of
  agricultural production, 47,
  172–7; and industrialization,
  182–7, 216, 237–8; as corporate
  shareholder, 238, 254; as
  economic investor, 126–8,
  172–7, 185; control of currency,
  134–6; control of food prices,
  183, 230, 253; domination of
  economy, 180, 224–8, 233, 249,
  258; international debts, 198,
  243–8; intervention in market,
  61, 62, 65, 83, 93–4, 110, 117,
  129, 134, 136–7, 143f., 198–211
  passim, 212, 225, 230, 232, 250,
  257; post-colonial economic
  performance, 236–40; public
  finance, 203; regulation of
  wages, 255; *see also* elites, state
states, development of, 22–3
statistics, 36, 37, 38, 42, 59, 61,
  86–7, 100
steam power, 111
  see also shipping
steel, 14, 46, 128

stock market, 254
Stone Bowl peoples, 12
strategic vs. economic concerns,
  126–7, 164, 217
strategy, 115, 168, 215
sub-contracting, 256
subsistence, 5, 9–26, 72, 94, 122,
  136, 138–46 *passim*, 156, 158,
  159, 165–7, 172, 176, 216, 255
Sudan
  Central, 34, 36, 39, 42, 45;
  Nilotic, 1, 32, 67; Western, 34,
  36, 44; Western and Central,
  31–51, 72–3, 74, 81, 83–6, 92,
  99, 102, 115, 127, 132, 269;
  modern state, 203
Suez Canal, 128
sugar, 46, 71, 86, 109–12, 115, 158,
  160, 171, 237–8
sulphur, 182
Sumbwa, 66, 70
supermarkets, 212
supplier credit, 242
surprix, 206
Sutton, J.E.G., 11
Swahili, 56, 64, 72, 141
Swaziland, 169
sword handles, 39, 45, 46
swords, 14
  see also blades
Syndicat Agricole Africain, 227

Tabora, 63, 73
Tanga, 63
Tanganyika Concessions Ltd., 163
Tanganyika, *see* East African
  (Tanganyika) Groundnut
  Scheme; Tanzania
Tanganyika, L., 63
TANU (Tanganyika African
  Union), 250–1
Tanzania, 12, 20, 58–74 *passim*,
  96, 124, 127, 128, 142, 156, 168,
  169, 171, 172, 178, 180, 269
  as case study of post-colonial
  socialism, 234–59
Tardieu, Andre, 199
tariffs, 110, 116, 136, 182–6, 246
taro, 15
taxation and tribute, 48, 61, 62,
  65, 94, 98, 126, 135, 136, 141,
  143–4, 172–7, 180, 181–6, 203,
  209, 232, 242, 246, 252, 257
  see also tariffs
taxicabs, 231, 254, 255
Tazara, *see* Great Uhuru railway
tea, 171, 238, 243, 245, 246, 254,
  257
technology, 2, 4
  advanced, 1; African domestic,
  10ff., 268; agricultural, 10ff.,
  47–8, 73, 97, 138–46 *passim*,
  157, 178–80, 208, 257–8, 268–9;
  commerical, 242; European, 20,
  109; high, 271; manufacturing,
  47–8, 99f., 216, 242, 248;
  military, 113–14, 157; mining,
  162–8 *passim*; Muslim, 46;

transport, 58, 88, 113–14, 126–9,
  179
  see also metallurgy; transport
Tedmekka, 34
Tegdaoust, 33
Teghaza, 34
Tekedda, 34
tenant-farmers, 172, 175, 179
terminology, 5
terms of trade, 92, 112, 130, 140,
  204, 209, 216, 225, 230, 232
Tete, 61
textiles, *see* cotton
theft, 165
theory, 1–5, 9–10, 16, 18
  dependency, 2–5, 63, 101–2;
  market, 2–5, 19, 100–1, 111,
  138, 143f., 187, 235, Marxist,
  2–5, 11, 18–19, 101, 116, 117,
  132, 138, 143f., 187, 214, 215,
  235; modernization, 235; on
  peasants, 137–8, 143–5;
  perspectives compared, 178, 187,
  197, 229, 235; radical, *see*
  Marxist; structuralist, 2–5,
  137–8, 143–5, 197, 235
  substantivist, 2–5, 19, 20–1,
  44, 93
Tichett, 12, 33
tick-borne relapsing fever, 68
tie ridging, 232
Timbuktu, 35, 38, 39, 45
tinplating, 140
Tippu Tip, 66
tires, 87, 237
tobacco, 39, 46, 87, 160, 170, 176,
  243
  American dark-leaf, 172;
  Turkish-leaf, 172; Virginia-leaf,
  172
tourists, 133
tractors, 145, 214
trade
  relays, 81–2, 91–5; stoppages,
  102, treaties, 62; *see also*
  commerical organization;
  merchants
trading posts, *see* factories,
tradition, 231
traditional rulers, *see* chiefs
transfer pricing, 242, 247
transitional sector, 256
Transkei, 160, 177, 179
transnational class, 255
transport, 20, 32f., 58, 64–5, 81–3,
  97, 122–9, 142, 145, 155, 170,
  175, 180, 199, 207, 230, 232,
  257, 269
  see also caravans; horses; motor;
  shipping; technology
transporteurs, 255
Transvaal, 157, 161, 162, 164, 185
Treaty of Rome, 1957, 210
trekboers, 159, 161–2, 169, 175
  see also Great Trek
tribalism, *see* ethnicity,
tse-tse flies, 13, 68
Tuareg, 43

c, 1

Professor Austen provides the first comprehensive study of Africa's economic history. The analysis in this book draws on over two thousand years; it begins with the origins of domesticated food production and concludes in the third decade after the attainment of political independence from colonial rule. The study deals with all of black Africa, but emphasizes the regions south of the Sahara and west of the Nile Valley.

The author applies various theoretical perspectives to the two themes of internal development and external dependency. In particular, the blend of market and structural analysis constitutes a major contribution to the ongoing debate over the understanding of economic change not only in Africa but in the Third World generally.

Ralph Austen's central narrative theme is the continuous growth of domestic African economic capacities accompanied by an ever-increasing engagement with the international economy. His analysis demonstrates that the differential rates of change in the African and the European-centred world economy have simultaneously made Africa less significant to the world economy and more dependent upon it for sustaining its own development patterns.

This argument is developed through discussions of the classic domestic African economy throughout the continent, the engagement of various regions with pre-colonial international trade across desert and oceanic frontiers, the differing impact of peasant- and settler-based colonial regimes, the changing role of Africa in the modern world economy, and the experiences of representative African states in meeting the dilemmas of post-colonial development.

This book will be required reading for serious undergraduate and graduate students of African history and political economy as well as scholars, policy-makers and people concerned with economic aspects of African and Third World affairs.

'The author writes with verve and flair, and the reader is carried through the ideas and arguments with great clarity and ease . . . The coverage, which is both chronologically and geographically extensive, distinguishes it from comparable works. . . . In its comprehensive treatment of African economic history from the earliest domestication of plants to contemporary policy issues, therefore, this manuscript has no competitor.' – J. Forbes Munro Reader in Economic History, University of Glasgow.

'Among the book's many strengths are the author's ability to present contending theoretical and ideological propositions on economic "development" in a nuanced and intelligible way, h emphasis on the role of technology (a subject often overlooked) and the linkages which he makes between exchange and production.' – Allen Isaacman, Professor of History, University of Minnesota.

RALPH A. AUSTEN is Professor of African History at the University of Chicago. He was previously Tutorial Fellow at Harvard, Fellow at the Hebrew University, Jerusalem and Assistant Professor at New York University. He has been Visiting Lecturer at the University of Ibadan and Visiting Professor at the University of Yaoundé.

JAMES CURREY / HEINEMANN

ISBN 0-435-08017-2